Global Economy, Global Justice

Theoretical objections and policy alternatives to neoliberalism

George DeMartino

London and New York

First published 2000 by Routledge
11 New Fetter Lane, London EC4P 4EE

Simultaneously published in the USA and Canada by Routledge
29 West 35th Street, New York, NY 10001

Routledge is an imprint of the Taylor & Francis Group

© 2000 George F. DeMartino

Typeset in Baskerville by Bookcraft Ltd, Stroud
Printed and bound in Great Britain by
Biddles Ltd, Guildford and King's Lynn.

British Library Cataloguing in Publication Data
A catalogue record for this book is available from the British Library

Library of Congress Cataloguing in Publication Data
CIP data have been applied for

ISBN 0-415-12427-1 (hbk)
ISBN 0-415-22401-2 (pbk)

For Ilene

Contents

Tables

Figures

Preface

Before reading this book I ask the reader to indulge me in a simple exercise. In your mind or even on a piece of paper, please conclude the following statement: "A good economic policy measure or outcome is one that …". In providing your conclusion, I ask that you consider the criterion (or set of criteria) that you think ought to be brought to bear when assessing economic policies and the economic outcomes they generate. What purposes should economic policy serve, and/or what outcomes should it promote? Do not be deterred if you have not formally studied economics or have not thought about this question before. I am sure that you already have at least tentative views about this matter. What are they?

Now please conclude a second statement: "When *economists* claim that an economic policy or outcome is good, they mean that it…". You may know that most economists support free trade. You may also know that these same economists also support the market economy over government planning regimes. But what I'm asking you to write down is the criterion or set of criteria they use in reaching these conclusions. *Why* do these economists support free trade and the market economy over alternative arrangements? What kinds of outcomes do they hope these policies and institutions will generate?

One final statement: "A good *theory* is one that …". In concluding this statement, consider what a good theory is to do, what features it should have, and/or what form it should take. All our lives each of us has had to make choices between contending theories. I'm asking you to reflect for a moment on the criterion of theory choice that you bring to bear (or think should be brought to bear) when confronting alternative theories.

This book is intended in part to speak to the questions raised here. My suspicion is that most people know far more about *which* policies and outcomes economists support than just *why* they hold these views. I further suspect that most people (especially students of economics) know far more about the basic principles of the theory that these economists employ – called "neoclassical theory" – than they do about just why this theory is taken to be more appropriate than the many alternative economic theories. And there are good reasons for this unevenness in economic literacy. While economists spend a good bit of time adjudicating among policy options, they rarely discuss openly the foundations of their judgements. They rarely preface their statements on trade or market economy with a clear, explicit statement about (*let alone a defense of*) the normative criterion they bring to bear in reaching their conclusions. Instead, they act as if this criterion is already well known and in little need of explication, that it is universally accepted and in little need of defense, or that normative commitments are entirely absent from the exercise of policy evaluation – that their conclusions are founded entirely on rigorous scientific logic. They also spend little time justifying their use of neoclassical theory rather than any of the alternatives to adjudicate policy matters. The inference to be taken from this silence is that this is obviously the uniquely right theory – whatever that may mean.

But none of these propositions is true. The policy conclusions neoclassical economists defend depend entirely on a normative commitment to what is called "welfarism." Without this criterion, neoclassical economists would have little basis for defending free trade or the market economy. This commitment is not universally shared – not within and certainly not beyond the confines of economic theory. Indeed, beyond economics, most specialists in the field of normative theory have little use for it. And though it is deeply biased in the policy conclusions it generates, there seems to be something of a professional agreement not to discuss it in policy debate. Listening to an economist addressing a public audience on the matter of trade, for instance, one would be hard pressed to glean just what the criterion of welfarism entails, let alone why we should adopt it.

In the same vein, the choice of neoclassical theory over alternative theories is also not obviously right. This is not to say that it is obviously wrong. It is to say that theory choice is a most complicated and contentious matter. It depends on a set of conceptions about what makes for a good theory, what a good theory is to do, what it is to look like, what form it is to take, and many other factors besides. None of these is obvious or simple. And, as I will endeavor to show in this book, each depends on normative commitments. That these commitments may be unexpressed (or even actively suppressed) in theoretical or policy debate does not make them inconsequential. But it can make them dangerous.

This book attempts to make sense of the normative foundations of contemporary economic policy debate, beginning in the abstract and moving gradually to an examination of concrete contemporary debates over global policy regimes. It is unfortunately true that most neoclassical economic textbooks, which are intended precisely to introduce students to the field, gloss over the normative commitments of the theory they teach. And this is true of much of the work of the critics of neoclassical theory as well. This book seeks to repair this theoretical omission. It seeks to clarify the chief normative commitments that neoclassical and heterodox economists bring to the policy arena, and to demonstrate that these different normative commitments have powerful effects. These commitments influence the judgements that economists make about what makes for a good economic outcome. As we will see, different kinds of economists provide different answers to this question, and this disagreement ensures disagreement about the policy options they debate. Less obvious but no less consequential, normative commitments also guide economists' judgements about what the field of economics is to be about, and the purposes it is to serve. They also influence economists' decisions about the very structure of economic theory. Indeed, economists (just like the rest of us) are guided in their choice among contending theoretical paradigms by a set of prior normative commitments – commitments of which they may not be entirely aware.

I hope in what follows to demonstrate these claims, so as to promote better critical understanding among students and others about economic policy debate. My hope is that readers will come away from this book with a deepened capacity to look beneath the surface of economic policy debate, to be able to understand and interrogate the normative commitments upon which policy claims are founded.

But the book seeks more. It seeks to elucidate just why the normative commitment of neoclassical economics to welfarism is objectionable. I draw upon and extend criticisms that are well known to political theorists and philosophers, but are unknown to most students of economics and even many economists. And it offers a deeply egalitarian, internationalist normative position, derived from the work of Nobel Laureate Amartya Sen, as a far better ethical basis for constructing new global economic policy regimes in a world of egregious and crushing inequalities. Rather than simply defend this normative position in the abstract, I attempt to test its value by investigating new policy regimes that might be consistent with it. This follows from my own view that the evaluation and critique of normative principles must focus extensively on their practical consequences. At a minimum, I hope to demonstrate that internationalist egalitarian policy alternatives are both desirable and available – and that, as a consequence, the persisting and egregious inequalities in life chances across the globe today are deeply indictable.

My purposes, then, are twofold. If I have achieved only the first – demonstrating that normative commitments lie beneath contemporary economic policy debate, that they matter, and that they must always be interrogated for their legitimacy and effects – then I will be satisfied. If I have also even partly achieved the second – encouraging others to join the lively campaign for a normative overhaul within economics away from welfarism and toward international egalitarianism – then I will have reason to hope for a better future for those who are today deprived of the most basic human freedoms and capacities. For those of us who believe that welfarism provides normative cover for the formation of policy regimes such as global neoliberalism that perpetuate gross inequality across the globe today, its displacement from economics has become a vital theoretical and even moral challenge.

Two terminological points here may prevent confusion and even distraction. First, rather than employ the awkward s/he and her/his as de-gendered pronouns, I have simply shifted from the masculine to the feminine randomly throughout the text. Second, I have largely employed the terms "North" and "South" to refer to the wealthier and poorer regions of the world. These terms strike me as less problematic than "First World"/"Third World," or "developed"/"undeveloped." But these terms are also far from ideal. Not least, they do violence to the multifaceted diversities within and similarities across these two categories. I use them merely as shorthand rather than as theoretically meaningful terms.

Acknowledgements

The idea for this book grew out of conversations with Stephen Cullenberg some years ago about the various proposals on offer by progressive political economists to restore prosperity for US workers by promoting the competitiveness of US firms in global markets. Though driven by what seemed to us to be laudable aspirations, there was something troubling about the competitiveness prescription. Our conversations led to an extended collaboration that generated several articles in which we argued that the normative foundation of this policy approach is deeply deficient. Some of the material that appears in chapters six through eight grew out of this joint work, and I thank Steve for allowing me to draw on it here.

At various points throughout the text I have cited the work of Stephen Resnick and Richard Wolff, but those citations hardly convey the level of my intellectual debt to these scholars. Though I am certain that they will find much in these pages with which to disagree, I have found their writings and teaching invaluable as I have wrestled with the matters examined in this book.

I have benefited enormously over the years from my participation in the Association for Economic and Social Analysis (AESA). AESA has provided me with friendships, intellectual stimulation and support that are hard to describe but impossible to overstate. It is a kind of community that is all too rare within the solitary and individualist world of academia. I want to express a heartfelt thanks to its members.

I have received research support from several of the wonderful graduate students of the Graduate School of International Studies of the University of Denver, where I teach. I owe special thanks to Brian Halma, Gail Kasun, Teri Martinez, Minu Palani, Signe Poulsen, Kerry Riccono, Ritu Sharma and Scott Solomon.

Thanks to Susan Sterett, who provided critical reactions to early drafts of several chapters. Ilene Grabel read and offered suggestions on several entire drafts, and I am deeply indebted to her for her vital contributions. Angela Wigmore, my editor at Bookcraft Ltd, improved the manuscript substantially through her careful editing. And thanks, finally, to the anonymous referees for Routledge who read the draft and provided the most constructive, detailed and careful commentary that I have ever encountered in my career. Their criticisms and suggestions were exceedingly helpful, and I have tried to validate their efforts by taking special care to address their concerns in the final revisions.

Introduction

The promises and perils of global neoliberalism

INTRODUCTION

Thinking and writing about "the global economy" is a perilous business. There is a temptation, overpowering for many economists, to try to reduce the unfathomable complexity of such an intractable topic to a set of simple propositions or governing laws that are comprehensible to the mortal intellect. We want to reduce the complexity, so that we can feel secure in our utterances about, say, the appropriate course of government policy, or the future trend of GDP. We want to believe that we understand this thing so that we can control or, minimally, survive it. It is in this context that we might appreciate the significance of theoretical concepts like "the market", or "free trade", or "supply and demand". These are abstractions which economists try to link together in rather mechanical theoretical narrative in an attempt to make sense of and impose order upon the chaos around us.

There are other temptations associated with this project. One is to fall prey to the "Hegelian conceit", taking on the perspective of "the last economist" who gazes out on her own world and sees in it the culmination of historical progress.[1] Standing shoulder to shoulder with Francis Fukuyama at "The End of History",[2] the last economist is positioned to deduce the general principles of how the world is and how it must be – not just for her contemporaries, but for all people for all time. Owing to the good fortune of being so situated, the last economist can see what her predecessors could not, and so can correct the theoretical errors they committed.

This latter temptation is in evidence in the most ordinary of times (if there is such a thing) but as we approach the new millennium it seems to be particularly strong. We find ourselves showered with ambitious claims by preeminent economists and other scholars that the kind of global economy that is emerging today is not just the latest experiment in economic organization, it is, indeed, the highest possible form of economy. *Global neoliberalism,* the extension of market-based economic integration across all local, regional and national borders, will provide humankind with the optimal means to achieve prosperity from now until eternity. With the perfection of the global capitalist market economy – and the consequent eradication of communism, socialism and all forms of state planning – economic history as the contest among alternative forms of economic systems will come to an end.

GLOBAL NEOLIBERALISM TRIUMPHANT

Although it has become fashionable today to claim that we live in an era of economic "globalization", this term is largely inaccurate and is, in any event, empty. On the one hand, the term is often used to refer to a state of international economic integration or interdependence – yet the world's nations and regions have been integrated in important ways for many centuries. By the beginning of the eighteenth century, for example, much of what is now called the "third world" had been parceled out among European colonial empires. France and Belgium had asserted political, military and economic control over much of Africa; England had claimed a vast colonial empire on which "the sun never set"; Spain and Portugal had laid claim to South America. Most regions of the world were integrated into a "global" economy, or at least into several large transcontinental economies. Within this arrangement, the economic fate of nations bound in an empire were substantially linked – not in ways we would be apt to support, of course, but linked nevertheless. Consider, for instance, the linkages between India and England during the heyday of the British Empire.

On the other hand, the term "globalization" is often used today to express the recent trend toward increasing international flows of goods, factors of production (such as labor, technology and raw materials) and finance. This sense of the term is more useful. These flows have indeed increased dramatically in recent years. Even in this regard, however, we must exercise caution. Our judgements about just how much the present era diverges from the past depend largely upon the particular indicators of integration and the historical period we choose for comparison. For example, while the degree of international financial integration is much greater today than it has been during most of the postwar period, it is only slightly greater than that of the early twentieth century. The same is true of trade integration (see Zevin 1992; Hirst and Thompson 1996; Dicken 1998).

If it is not meaningful to speak of globalization *per se* as a new development, then what is new about the present historical period? Far more important than increasing interdependence and the increasing magnitude of international economic flows is the changing qualitative nature of economic integration. Our era is unprecedented in the degree to which international economic intercourse is *market-based*. The actions of disconnected economic actors, such as investors, firms and consumers, are rapidly displacing explicit government direction in determining the flow of goods, services and finance within and across national borders. We may therefore say that we live in an era where global neoliberalism has apparently arrived. This shift is registered in the breakup of colonial empires, a process that was substantially completed by the middle of this century. In place of the explicitly exploitative relationships that bound colony to empire – and which facilitated the coerced flow of resources, finance and even people to the benefit of the colonizers – we see today voluntary flows in nominally free markets. In place of the command economies of Eastern Europe, in which central planning dictated employment patterns, compensation policies, and the allocation of resources across industries, decentralized economies are emerging in which all these decisions are taken by private actors joined in nascent markets. In place of powerful states making international trade, investment and aid decisions by reference to the imperatives of state security in the context of the Cold War, we see a gradual demilitarization of economic flows amongst erstwhile friends and foes alike. In place of alternative economic processes, we find the emergence of capitalist production predicated upon the establishment of private property rights over productive resources and enterprises.

The shift to neoliberalism is taking myriad forms. Under the direction of the World Bank and International Monetary Fund (IMF), developing countries throughout the world have restructured their economies to reduce the scope of government intervention and to expand the significance of the domestic market. Governments have privatized publicly owned firms, established stock markets to facilitate the flow of private finance, deregulated banking, and dismantled programs which had provided public support for domestic industries. Governments have also substantially reduced international trade and investment barriers over the postwar period, with the effect of promoting and deepening global markets. These processes of economic liberalization have been codified in new trade pacts like the North American Free Trade Agreement (NAFTA) and the World Trade Organization (WTO). If successful, the current negotiations among member nations of the Organization for Economic Co-operation and Development (OECD) over the proposed Multilateral Agreement on Investment (MAI) will deepen the global neoliberal regime. Reaching beyond explicit barriers such as tariffs, the new agreements seek to reduce government involvement in the world's economies by prohibiting what are called "technical barriers to trade". These are domestic laws (like environmental regulations) which are seen to distort trade patterns. These agreements also require governments to afford foreign firms and investors "national treatment". This requirement largely prohibits governments from promoting indigenous development by favoring domestic firms and investors over their foreign counterparts.[3]

All of these trends can be, and often are, overstated; but this, indeed, is the point. The very real shift toward market integration at the domestic and international levels has come to be understood as an inexorable process, so that the reversals that might occur are treated as temporary but grave policy errors. Proponents of this view might concede that history does not unfold in a linear pattern but, they assure us, it does have a determinate direction and ultimate endpoint. Hence, the actuality and presumed inevitability of neoliberalism are strongly self-reinforcing.

The promises of global neoliberalism

Just what is so attractive about global neoliberalism, and the principle of the market economy upon which it builds? The following chapters will explore this matter systematically, but we can begin to survey here the grand claims made on its behalf. Insofar as global neoliberalism represents the universal extension of the market, we need to understand first the virtues associated with this institution.

The market

The most forceful and coherent defense of neoliberalism appears in mainstream economic theory, or "neoclassical theory". In the view of neoclassical economics, the market is an extraordinary mechanism that allows a society – any society, no matter how small or large, simple or complex – to organize the production and distribution of goods and services *efficiently*. By virtue of the competition it establishes among firms, the market ensures that society's scarce resources are allocated across alternative uses in just that measure that benefits society most. In a competitive market economy, firms will employ the most efficient means of production; otherwise, they will be punished in the marketplace by more efficient firms that can charge a lower price. Moreover, firms will be forced to allocate resources toward the production of the goods that society most desires. A firm that produces manual typewriters when society prefers computers will simply be squeezed out of the market by the firms that meet consumer demand. Hence, although it may seem that corporations decide just what to produce and what price to charge, the ultimate authority in these matters lies with the consumer.

The market allows each individual the freedom to pursue her life plans free of unwarranted interference by others: to aspire to be a doctor, pianist, or gardener as she sees fit, and to compete fairly with others who have chosen the same path for the rewards which that occupation affords. While no one is guaranteed success – indeed, such a guarantee would subvert the incentive system that the market entails – each is provided the opportunity to strive to reach the goal that she has fashioned for herself. The market also provides each individual with the opportunity to secure those goods and services that she most desires through voluntary exchange, within the limits set by her budget. And each individual is free to increase her budget by dint of self-improvement (such as the acquisition of new skills) and saving. These generate the rewards of rising wages and interest income, respectively.

In the neoclassical view, the market also fundamentally improves upon alternative means and patterns of distribution of shares of the social output. In place of government allocation of shares across constituents, the market ensures that the distribution of rewards across economic actors is tied to their respective contributions to output. Although many advocates of neoliberalism are hesitant to call market-dictated distributions "just" (for reasons we will pursue in subsequent chapters), there is a strong presumption that by rewarding contribution in this way the market advances the collective interest of society as a whole. This is because the desire for more income will drive economic actors to acquire the skills and capacities that make the greatest social contribution. In seeking to serve themselves, they unwittingly serve the community at large.

This last result is emblematic of the more general neoclassical view of the power of the market. Neoclassical theory holds a rather unattractive view of human nature. In this view, human nature is marked with an indelible egoistic, self-oriented impulse that drives the human actor to seek *her own betterment* rather than the broader social good. Being "rational", each actor always makes those choices which leave her best off. In the words of one prominent neoclassical economist, "we live in a world of reasonably well-informed people acting intelligently in pursuit of their self-interests" (Stigler 1981, cited in Sen 1987, 17); elsewhere he adds, "self-interest dominates the majority of men" (Stigler 1975, cited in Sen 1987, 22). Even apparently "altruistic" behavior yields to this assessment: I help others if and to the degree that I somehow benefit myself.

This view of human nature is taken from the pioneering work of the classical economist Adam Smith. In a celebrated passage, Smith put it this way:

> It is not from the benevolence of the butcher, the brewer, or the baker that we expect our dinner, but from their regard to their own interests. We address ourselves, not to their humanity but to their self-love, and never talk to them of our own necessities but their advantages.
>
> (Smith 1982, 119, first published 1776)

In the contemporary neoclassical view, this egoistic impulse determines human behavior in the marketplace, where the consumer is seen to allocate her budget across available goods and services so as to acquire just that combination which will yield her maximum benefit. This impulse also drives her non-market behavior, such as whether to marry or divorce, to have children (and if so, how many), or to break the law. We are, in this view, entirely driven by this rational desire to maximize our own personal benefit, as we define it for ourselves. Or *almost* entirely: as another economist puts it, "the average human being is about 95 per cent selfish in the narrow sense of the term" (Tullock 1976, cited in Mansbridge 1990, 12).

The market is such an extraordinary institution because it manages to harness this rational, self-oriented behavior in service of the collective good. The market generates growth and prosperity for all, not because any individual actor intends or seeks this outcome, but as an unintended consequence of each agent's determined efforts to secure his own happiness. The "invisible hand" of the marketplace co-ordinates the activities of innumerable self-oriented economic actors, who may not care one whit for each other's welfare, in such a way that the social good is assured.

Under a neoliberal regime, the government is to play an important, but clearly subordinate, role in facilitating economic activity. The government is to establish those laws and institutions which allow the market to function well – such as the enforcement of transferable property rights and the protection of other legal guarantees. The government is also called upon to correct certain market failures, such as the costs imposed on society by a polluting firm, and to provide those "public goods" that are inadequately generated by the market (such as national defense). But the heavy lifting of co-ordinating production and distribution is left to the market. The state's role is to support and assist the market, not to contravene it.

The global market

Global neoliberalism would extend market organization to the international arena. Global neoliberalism entails the removal of political obstacles to the free flow of goods, services and capital across national borders. Just as an investor in New York is largely free to move his funds to Chicago in pursuit of better returns, global neoliberalism would allow a corporation in Germany to invest its funds freely in Malaysia or Ireland. Just as New Yorkers import orange juice without restriction from Florida, so would Floridians be free to import clothing from Mexico. Under a global neoliberal regime, the market forces which operate domestically would determine the international flow of all goods and resources.

The achievement of global neoliberalism therefore entails the emergence of a one-world economy, tightly integrated through a one-world market. In this ideal, national borders are largely divested of their economic significance. Individual economic actors from London to Bangkok drive global economic outcomes through their mutually beneficial interactions in impersonal markets. In place of heavy-handed state directives, the world's consumers, workers, firms and investors resolve the daunting economic dilemmas of what goods will be produced, where each good will be produced, and how these goods will be distributed.

In the view of its proponents global neoliberalism extends the efficiency benefits of market organization across national borders. If clothing can be produced more cheaply in Mexico (by virtue of its cheaper labor) than in the US, the clothing industry will migrate to Mexico in search of the higher profits that production there affords. In consequence, consumers worldwide will benefit from falling clothing prices and hence come to enjoy a rising standard of living. At the same time, this flow of investment to poor countries where labor costs are low promises rising wages for those with the lowest living standards. Global neoliberalism therefore promises rising prosperity for all the world's inhabitants.

Individuals benefit from global neoliberalism in other ways that some advocates take to be even more fundamental. The deepening of market integration within and across national borders promises to provide the vast majority of humankind the liberty to formulate and pursue life plans free from tyrannical rule for the first time in modern history. Responding to market signals and driven by one's own preferences, each world citizen is to be free to seek that opportunity which yields her maximum benefit. Rather than have one's output appropriated without fair compensation by the colonial administrator, one can choose to sell it to the highest bidder at home or abroad. Rather than be forcibly shipped to the New World as a slave to work on a plantation, one can book a flight there in pursuit of a better career – or not, *as one chooses*.

There is still more. Under a global neoliberal regime, state economic policy loses its nationalist character. Rather than obstruct market outcomes in pursuit of gains for its own citizens, nation states co-operate in furtherance of the mutual interests of the world's inhabitants. Rather than pursue naked self-interest, nation states submit to the wiser course of enlightened self-interest. Hence, global neoliberalism provides the economic foundation for harmony among national governments and their people. Global neoliberalism promises us prosperity, and it also promises us peace (cf. Fukuyama 1989, 18).

Advocates claim that global neoliberalism also protects the cultural autonomy of distinct nations and communities. This is because it leaves to each nation the authority to determine for itself the kinds and extent of social policies it may pursue, such as the strength of its worker safety and health regulations, or the manner in which (or even whether) it fights employment discrimination. Under a neoliberal regime, for example, trade and investment agreements are largely to be silent with respect to such matters. One government's insistence that its worker rights or environmental standards be incorporated into trade agreements is read as an illegitimate infringement of the national sovereignty of other nations, and an unwarranted imposition of its own cultural mores on other countries with different, but equally valid, notions of the social good.

The emergence of the market economy across the globe represents, finally, the conquest of outdated and ultimately harmful political *ideologies* by the singularly true economic *science*. From the collapse of command economies in Eastern Europe and Asia, to the shift away from state-directed "*dirigiste*" economic organization across Latin America, the trend toward market integration is seen to validate the claims of neoclassical economic theory against those of Marxian and other outdated pseudo-scientific perspectives. While for much of this century neoclassical theory was challenged in the economics profession across the globe by various heterodox doctrines, the closing of this century seems to coincide with and symbolize the closing of economic disputation. In the new millennium, all right-minded economists will surely be neoclassical!

The Asian crisis and neoliberalism

We might be forgiven for asking whether the Asian financial crisis – which erupted in the summer of 1997 and has since spread beyond the region – has shaken the confidence of the advocates of global neoliberalism. After all, the crisis would seem to demonstrate that unfettered international capital flows in global markets can and do disrupt well-functioning economies, inducing severe economic, social and political dislocation. Official reports of the United Nations Conference on Trade and Development (UNCTAD) provide evidence of severe economic and social dislocation in those countries at the epicenter of the crisis. In South Korea, long taken to be a rising economic powerhouse, the number of unemployed increased fourfold from 1996 to the middle of 1998. Those suffering most from this dislocation are the unorganized workers in small and medium-sized enterprises, and especially female workers who have been the first to lose their jobs. Thailand's unemployment increased from five hundred thousand to two million, while Indonesia's unemployment grew from just under four and a half million to between ten and fifteen million during the same period (UNCTAD 1998a, ch. 3).

The crisis has thrown millions of people into poverty. UNCTAD estimated that the poverty rate in Thailand had risen by a third by the end of 1998; in Indonesia, the estimated increase is 50 per cent. These figures portend long-term economic losses as well as immediate hardship. As poverty increases, struggling families are withdrawing their children from school so that they can contribute immediately to their household's survival. Thailand's drop-out rate has tripled since the onset of the crisis. As a consequence of this loss of skills and training, the effects of the crisis may extend through the working life of the next generation. Making matters worse, the duration of the immediate crisis (originally predicted to be sharp but short) is now projected to extend into the year 2002 (UNCTAD 1998a). Finally, the crisis has undermined the economic performance of countries well beyond Asia, such as Brazil, and has weakened economic growth across Europe. Surely the crisis has given pause to neoliberal advocates about the costs and benefits of this regime. Or has it?

The crisis has prompted some neoclassical economists to pay more attention to the unintended consequences of economic liberalization, to be sure. Throughout the crisis, concerns have been raised about the unpreparedness of some developing countries as they reduce the barriers separating their domestic economies from global markets. World Bank chief economist Joseph Stiglitz has argued that developing countries might need to retain capital controls (which restrict short-term capital flows) over the short run while they strive to establish both sufficient domestic banking regulations to ensure financial stability and the state capacity necessary to oversee this vital sector (*Wall Street Journal* 9/4/98). Noted monetary economist Ronald McKinnon (1991; *New York Times* 9/20/98) has emphasized the need for developing countries to adopt the appropriate sequence of liberalization stages so that they reap the benefits that liberalization affords. Other influential economists (like Paul Krugman) have concluded that the countries in crisis may need to re-institute temporary capital controls to secure breathing space to shore up their domestic economies, before reintegrating into global financial markets (*Wall Street Journal* 9/4/98 and 9/25/98). It bears emphasis, however, that these proposals target only the appropriate means by which developing countries can fully integrate into the global neoliberal regime. They speak to the timing and stages of the shift toward global neoliberalism, but they do not call into question the inevitability and desirability of that regime.

Despite this new concern over the timing and steps toward liberalization, what is most striking about the crisis is that it has been taken by most defenders of neoliberalism as evidence of the need to deepen and extend the neoliberal regime. In the mainstream neoclassical view, the crisis resulted primarily from undue government involvement in economic affairs coupled with the immaturity and underdevelopment of market mechanisms – not from the play of international market forces *per se*.[4] In this view, East Asian economies are deeply flawed by the extensive protections that these governments have traditionally provided to powerful business interests and investors. Under these "crony capitalist" regimes, economic élites recognize that they are insulated from severe economic losses through government intervention. They can therefore take excessive risks in the full knowledge that they themselves will not suffer the consequences of failed ventures. Under such circumstances, for instance, investors are apt to overborrow to engage in speculative activities – confident that they will not be foreclosed in the event that they cannot repay their debts. Hence, crony capitalism entails an environment in which market signals that would otherwise suffice to prevent crisis are overwhelmed by artificial incentives that induce irresponsible economic practices. From this perspective, the obvious solution to the crisis is for the affected countries to adopt pure market-based economics systems in which the laws of supply and demand drive economic behavior and outcomes. Once these countries have adopted true market economies, they can and must fully reintegrate into the global neoliberal regime.[5]

This response to the Asian crisis encapsulates the contemporary neoclassical view of twentieth-century economic evolution and theoretical progress. While we have much to learn about the dynamics of free-market economies, and while the emerging global neoliberalism stands to serve up many new empirical anomalies that will require ever new theoretical elaboration, the basic tenets of economic theory are now well established and are certainly beyond disproof. Among these, the central doctrine is that until humankind evolves into some other form of creature than it is today, the free market economy is now and forever shall be best. As we overcome the remaining (formidable) obstacles to the perfection of the one-world economy, we will establish the conditions for a rising wave of prosperity and liberty the likes of which the majority of humanity has never before enjoyed. We will bequeath to our children the basis for untold wealth, enduring peace, freedom and happiness. All they will need to do is complete the project we have pioneered. We will go to the grave having done far more than our fair share on behalf of those who will follow. We will have delivered humankind to the end of economic history.

Reasonable doubts?

Under these circumstances, it is not altogether surprising that critics of global neoliberalism are wont to feel a bit like uninvited party-crashers wherever economists gather to exchange ideas. Having backed the wrong intellectual horse, be it Marxism, post-Keynesianism, institutionalism or some other disproved paradigm, critics can now be found sulking in the corridors at the annual professional meetings griping about the horrors of the global economy and pining for the next global crisis that will validate their critiques. For their part, neoclassical economists just don't understand these critics. After all, if neoliberalism stands to deliver all that it promises, then the dissenters would have to be ideologically driven, professionally embittered or simply inept not to share in the celebration. *Why are these people not happy?*

The short of it is that many dissenters, within the economics profession and without, in the wealthier North and in the poorer South, bear many grievances against global neoliberalism. First and perhaps foremost, the dissenters largely share a normative commitment to substantive equality in economic outcomes rather than to the personal liberty that neoliberalism promises. As domestic and global neoliberalism has deepened over the past several decades, inequality of income and wealth has increased dramatically – both within and across national borders. Aggregate world data are particularly notable. According to the United Nations Development Programme (UNDP), in 1960 the countries with the richest 20 per cent of the world's population had aggregate income thirty times that of those countries with the poorest 20 per cent. By 1980, that ratio had risen to forty-five to one; by 1989, it stood at fifty-nine to one (UNDP 1992, 34). In this thirty-year period of neoliberal ascendance, then, *inequality between rich and poor countries doubled.* The comparison between rich and poor people, taking into account inequality within each country, gives even more dramatic results. The UNDP estimates that by 1989 the ratio of the average income of the world's richest 20 per cent of individuals to that of the poorest 20 per cent had reached 150:1 (UNDP 1992, 34).

Of course, the correlation between deepening neoliberalism with rising inequality could be spurious. Critics point out, however, that *domestic* income inequality has grown most significantly in those countries that have pursued domestic neoliberal reform most aggressively, such as the US and the UK. For instance, data provided by the International Labour Organization (ILO) indicate that the share of the US population earning less than 50 per cent of the median US income rose from 14.8 per cent in 1974 to 19.2 per cent in 1994. At the same time, those earning over 200 per cent of the median income rose from 7.7 per cent of the total population to 11.9 per cent. For the UK, the share below 50 per cent of the median grew from 5.7 to 13.1 per cent, and those above 200 per cent of the median rose from 6.8 to 8.1 per cent from 1969 to 1986. Compare these records with the experience of Sweden, a country that retained a good measure of social democratic economic governance during this period. From 1967 to 1992, the share earning less than 50 per cent of the median *fell* dramatically, from 10.4 per cent to 5.8 per cent; at the same time, the share above 200 per cent of the median declined from 3.1 per cent to 2.5 per cent (ILO 1996).

For the critics, these data provide *prima facie* evidence that neoliberalism induces inequality – domestically, and globally. Growing inequality validates the suspicion that global neoliberalism rewards those who are already best off and best able to exploit the opportunities that the global economy provides, while punishing those with less means. Despite whatever formal liberties the neoliberal economy might provide, dissenters stress the real substantive inequality of life chances that economic inequality induces. In the face of growing inequalities, the economic growth that neoliberalism promises may fail to deliver the improvement in economic welfare with which it is typically associated, and may interfere with the achievement of important political and economic rights and opportunities. Not least among these is democratic governance in the form of genuine political equality.

Three faces of global neoliberalism

Critics allege that the shift toward global neoliberalism introduces substantial threats to the economic security of working people and their communities across the globe. To appreciate their arguments, we need to consider separately three distinct faces of global neoliberalism.

The global market

The first entails the formation of what may be called the "global market". In place of isolated national or regional markets, we find today thoroughly integrated world markets for many goods and services. The global market has resulted from two primary forces, technological change and government policy reform. Advances in telecommunications and information processing provide producers and merchants with rapid information about market conditions all around the globe; advances in transportation systems allow them to ship goods far more cheaply and quickly than in the past, enabling them to take advantage of marketing opportunities wherever these appear. Augmenting these technological changes, governments have chosen to reduce substantially the policy barriers that have historically separated national markets. In 1940, the average world tariff on manufactured goods was about 40 per cent; by the mid-1990s, it had fallen to about 4 per cent. Together, these factors have had impressive effects. Since the Second World War, the growth in trade has far exceeded the growth in economic output. For example, between 1950 and 1994, while world manufacturing production rose by a factor of five, total world manufacturing exports grew fourteenfold (Dicken 1998, 24; 92–3). According to UNCTAD (1998b, 5), the divergence between the growth rates of output and trade has widened even further in the mid- to late 1990s.

The global workshop

The second face of global neoliberalism is the "global workshop" under the auspices of the multinational corporation (MNC). MNCs have existed in one form or another since the creation of the chartered European trading companies of the fifteenth century (Dicken 1998, 20). But the postwar period has been marked by dramatic increases in their relative number and size, and by significant changes in their character.

The increase in MNC activity is reflected in part in aggregate data on foreign direct investment (FDI). FDI entails the construction of or acquisition of a controlling interest by a firm in an enterprise abroad. FDI has increased particularly rapidly since the mid-1980s. Total world FDI flows averaged $77 billion from 1983 to 1987, but had increased to $318 billion by 1995. From 1970 to the late 1980s, FDI flows from the North to the South remained stagnant, averaging only $18 billion from 1983 to 1987 (just over 23 per cent of the world total). Since the late 1980s North–South FDI flows have accelerated dramatically. Indeed, by 1995, net FDI flows to the South accounted for over 31 per cent of the world total, reaching about $100 billion (International Finance Corporation 1997).

Throughout the nineteenth century and the first half of the twentieth century, FDI was concentrated in resource extraction, agricultural production and infrastructural investment, especially (but by no means exclusively) in the South. Large European and US corporations undertook extensive mining operations, ran large plantations and contracted with governments in the South to build railways, canals and other infrastructure. In contrast, from the 1960s to the present, MNCs have increasingly concentrated on manufacturing (and, more recently, services). MNCs now control vast manufacturing enterprises that span national borders. Today, about 50 per cent of all FDI in the South is in manufacturing and services (Todaro 1997, 537).

A striking indicator of the rise of the global workshop is the trend in "intra-firm" trade. This refers to the cross-border flow of components and final products between subsidiaries and branches of the same corporation. Today this is the fastest-growing share of trade, having risen from about one-fifth of world trade in the early 1970s to about one-third of world trade by the early

1990s. For the US, intra-firm trade has risen particularly dramatically: "US intra-firm exports increased by nearly two-thirds between 1977 and 1982 and by over 70 per cent between 1982 and 1989" (UNCTAD 1994, 143).

The changing composition of intra-firm trade provides further evidence of the changing character of MNC activity. The trend in intra-firm trade has been away from natural resource-based commodities toward manufactured goods (UNCTAD 1994). This changing character reflects the shift toward "outsourcing" associated with the global workshop, in which firms seek the lowest-cost site for each stage of production. To take just one example, by the late 1980s, the Ford Escort combined inputs produced in fifteen different countries (Dicken 1992).

Although the data on FDI and intra-firm trade provide a compelling portrait of the size and significance of the MNC, they actually underestimate the extent of the global workshop. This is because the global web through which MNCs control production often entails various inter-firm relationships, such as subcontracting, licensing, the creation of spin-offs, consultancies, etc. These relationships vary from temporary, market-mediated (or "arms-length") transactions at one extreme, to deep and enduring, extra-market linkages on the other. Insofar as many of these arrangements join nominally distinct corporations through inter-firm contracting, they do not qualify as FDI; moreover, flows between them do not qualify as intra-firm trade. Hence, as Dicken (1998) contends, we may be certain that the influence of MNCs in the global economy is substantially greater than these numbers suggest. Indeed, recent estimates indicate that MNCs account for over 70 per cent of total world trade in goods and services. Many of the largest corporations today command more resources than most countries:

> [The] largest MNC in 1993, General Motors, had sales revenues in excess of the GDP of Thailand. In fact, its gross sales exceeded the GDP of all but seven developing countries (China, India, Brazil, Indonesia, Mexico, Argentina, and South Korea). The five largest MNCs had combined revenues in excess of the GDP of many developed countries including Switzerland, Australia, Spain, Sweden, Canada, and Belgium. Were we to examine the 150 largest economic entities (both companies and countries), we would find that more than half (86) were MNCs.
>
> (Todaro 1997, 535)

The same factors that promoted the global market have also facilitated these transformations in the MNC. The co-ordination of research, planning, production, shipping and marketing across national borders requires the dependable and fast transmission of information, the inexpensive shipment of components, goods and people, and the rapid processing of vast amounts of information. It is no coincidence, Dicken (1998) reminds us, that MNC activity accelerated dramatically with the introduction of commercial jet airliners in the 1950s. But technology alone would have been insufficient to generate the expansion in MNC activity over this period. Just as with trade, government policy choices have been a decisive factor. The shift to global neoliberalism has been associated with important government initiatives to liberate firms from domestic restrictions on their international operations. Since the early 1980s in particular, nations across the globe have reduced or entirely rescinded all sorts of performance standards and other restrictions on foreign corporations in hopes of attracting investment, employment and income (Edelman Spero 1990, ch. 8). The substantial decline in official aid from the North to the South over the past two decades (an additional feature of the shift to global neoliberalism) has left poorer countries with little choice but to reduce these restrictions in order to attract badly needed capital. New multilateral agreements have contributed to this new corporate freedom. NAFTA, which joins the economies of Canada, the US and Mexico into a single, unified free trade and investment zone, requires each signatory to grant national treatment to all firms from across the continent – essentially granting them continental citizenship rights. Armed with this protection, US firms in particular have substantially expanded their operations in Mexico since the treaty took effect in January 1994.

The global casino

The third face of global neoliberalism is the emergence of the "global casino" (Strange 1986). Today finance travels across national borders nearly instantaneously, as large institutional investors anticipate and respond to currency and equity price fluctuations. In the past, investors and firms entered foreign exchange markets largely to facilitate international trade and lending. Today, speculators swamp other participants in these markets. Unhinged from real sector economic activity, trading in this market has grown astronomically in recent years. In 1977 foreign exchange trading amounted to $10 billion per day. By the mid-1990s, this trading had risen to $1.3 *trillion* per day, or over $400 trillion per year (*Denver Post*, 10/4/97). This increase by a factor of one hundred and thirty compares with just over a doubling in the volume of world trade during this period (Council of Economic Advisors 1997, 244). The globalization of finance also allows large investors to engage in international portfolio investment, playing stock and bond markets across the globe from an office in London, Bonn or Mexico City.

As with the global market and the global workshop, we find technological change and government policy reform as the pivotal factors encouraging the emergence of the global casino. Telecommunications and information processing technologies allow the largest institutional traders to move into and out of national markets nearly instantaneously, as opportunities and sentiments change. This would not be possible if governments had chosen to retain the various forms of capital control which existed during much of the postwar period. Instead, first the US and Britain, and then most other developed countries abandoned their controls on most short-term international capital flows during the 1980s (Helleiner 1995). Developing countries, pressed for financing especially in the context of the debt crisis, soon followed. By the end of the 1980s, many developing economies had privatized their banking systems, established stock markets and otherwise deregulated short-term capital flows so as to encourage foreigners to purchase domestic equities and bonds.

Indicting neoliberalism

Critics find each face of global neoliberalism to be potentially damaging. The expansion of trade decreases the insulation from competition afforded to a local manufacturer by physical proximity to a market. So long as tariffs and transaction costs (and other political factors) prohibited extensive trade, the existence of a manufacturer abroad with a competitive advantage had little impact at home. But in the global market, a community's economic security depends upon the competitive success of local firms *vis-à-vis* firms across the globe. Workers unlucky enough to serve a corporation that fails the global competitive test may find themselves without work, income or security.[6]

Critics are particularly concerned about the effects of the global workshop. They contend that the geographic flexibility that MNCs enjoy today leaves communities that are dependent on the firm for employment increasingly vulnerable. Indeed, communities around the world may find themselves today placed into rather direct competition with one another for jobs and income. Firms can and do confront their workers with the demand that they accept lower wages and benefits as a condition for retaining their jobs. Those workers who resist may take small solace in their principles as the firm on which they depend relocates to a more hospitable environment, where workers are less militant. A recent study of labor relations and union organizing efforts in the US in the aftermath of NAFTA yielded startling findings in this regard. According to the report's Executive Summary:

- Where employers can credibly threaten to shut down and/or move their operation in response to union activity, they do so in large numbers. Overall, over 50 per cent of all employers made threats to close all or part of the plant during [a union] organizing drive ...
- In the 40 per cent of the campaigns where the union won the election, 18 per cent of employers threatened to close the plant rather than bargain a first contract with the union, and 12 per cent of the employers followed through on threats made during the organizing campaign and actually shutdown (*sic*) all or part of the plant before a first contract was reached. Another 4 per cent of employers closed down the plant before a second agreement was reached. This 15 per cent shutdown rate within two years of the certification election victory is triple the rate found by

researchers who examined post-election plant closing rates in the late 1980s, before NAFTA went into effect.

(Bronfenbrenner 1996, Executive Summary 2)

Most importantly, the study found that threats of plant closing were not correlated with the competitive position of the firm. Financial conditions seem to have played virtually no part in firms' decisions to close or to threaten to do so. Threats were, however, strongly correlated with the mobility of the industry (e.g., the threats were much more frequent in manufacturing than in health care), lending credence to the view that enhanced mobility enhances a firm's leverage in dealing with its workforce. On the basis of this study, the researcher concluded that "NAFTA has created a climate that has emboldened employers to more aggressively threaten to close, or actually close their plants to avoid unionization" (Bronfenbrenner 1996, Executive Summary 3).

In short, a firm's geographic mobility shifts the balance of power from workers on the one hand to multinational corporations and large investors on the other. Governments are also affected by corporate mobility. Like workers, local governments may find it difficult to ensure appropriate corporate behavior. Government efforts to protect worker health and safety or the environment through legislation might induce the firm to seek other sites at home or abroad that promise weaker standards and lower costs. Those firms that do not relocate may find it difficult to survive market competition from those firms that enjoy lower costs elsewhere. These same factors might undermine the effect even of national legislation in these areas to a degree that impairs the ability of domestic firms to compete in global markets.

Advocates of global neoliberalism claim that unfettered FDI flows promote global economic efficiency and hence generate rising prosperity for all, as we have seen. As corporations seek out lower costs by relocating to lower-waged countries, they ensure an improvement in the living standards of those who are worst off. In this case, an increasing degree of insecurity (especially for wealthier workers in the North) might be a price well worth paying, especially if we are concerned about global inequality.

Unfortunately, the critics reply, FDI flows are very unevenly distributed. First, the majority of FDI is destined for countries in the North, and so does not improve the lot of workers in the South. Moreover, those flows that do reach the South are extremely concentrated. In the mid-1990s, for example, China received about 38 per cent of all North–South FDI, while the top ten destination countries together received close to three-quarters of the total (World Bank 1997). Of these, only China was classified by the World Bank as a "low-income" country. By contrast, the far poorer countries of sub-Saharan Africa, where the need is unarguably greatest, received only 2.2 per cent of total North–South FDI. All told, Hirst and Thompson (1996, 67–8) estimate that 91.5 per cent of all FDI flowed to only 43 per cent of the world's population in 1996 – and this 43 per cent was by no means the neediest.[7] Against the neoclassical claim that neoliberalism will generate universal improvements in living standards, the critics charge that it perpetuates and deepens economic unevenness.

The global casino presents problems that are somewhat different but equally troubling. The race among investors to anticipate and take advantage of the next hot market leads to massive inflows and outflows of funds, causing successive speculative booms and busts as sentiments run from optimistic to pessimistic and back again. Insofar as the availability of portfolio investment influences investment in plant and equipment, and thereby economic growth, these flows have come to play an increasingly powerful role in shaping the economic circumstances of communities across the globe. These effects are greatest by far in capital-poor developing economies, where the changing perceptions of foreign investors can induce an immediate and deep financial crisis. Especially when investor sentiment about a developing country's prospects turns bearish, the economy may be badly bruised by capital flight, a collapse in the value of the domestic currency, and by the harsh policies (such as high interest rates) deemed necessary to stanch the crisis (Grabel 1996, 1999a). In the view of the critics, then, the Asian financial crisis (and the 1994 Mexican crisis before it) represents an entirely predictable and inevitable consequence of the headlong rush since the 1980s toward liberalized international capital markets.

These last two examples raise the broader issue of the effects of global neoliberalism on national policy autonomy and sovereignty. Critics argue that global neoliberalism undermines the ability of even the most powerful nation states to pursue policies that serve the majority of their inhabitants if and when those policies run counter to the interests of wealthy investors and large firms. For example, a nation that pursues expansive monetary policy to stimulate economic growth may find its efforts sabotaged by flight from assets denominated in the domestic currency as investors pursue the higher rates of return that are available abroad. This may depress the value of the nation's currency, raise inflation and (in the short run) lead to a deterioration in its balance of trade – so that the policy effectively subsidizes the country's trading partners at the expense of its own citizens. In an integrated neoliberal world economy, the critics conclude, powerful investors in global financial markets routinely hijack monetary policy.[8]

The critics level other charges. Many claim that competition under neoliberal conditions systematically punishes disadvantaged economic actors who lack the political power to secure compensation from the winners for their losses. For example, a government that attempts to increase corporate or personal income taxes on the wealthy so as to provide funds for retraining or income supports for displaced workers may confront all manner of tax evasion strategies, including the shifting of assets abroad. Rather than generate increasing prosperity for all, global competition might therefore come to deepen and cement existing inequalities by reducing the political power of those who are worst off. Hence, despite the nominal liberty that the market affords, the market might act as an arena of powerful coercion that undermines fundamental political freedoms and rights (Tilly 1995).

Two related points will suffice to conclude this preliminary litany of grievances. Critics reject the neoclassical presumption that human nature is inherently egoistic or selfish (involving the pursuit of maximum individual pleasure). Indeed, the dissenters tend to be skeptical about the purported usefulness of the concept of human nature at all. Most reject the presumption that there are some essential, ineradicable human drives or aspirations that are locked into our genetic makeup and that exist independent of time and place – especially when this presumption is invoked in policy debates. In contrast, the dissenters argue that the behavioral orientation that neoclassical theory presents as the universal essence of human nature is instead historically contingent (see Chapter 2). Indeed, the personality structure that the proponents of neoliberalism invoke in defense of the market is, if anything, *endogenous* to the neoliberal economy itself – the produced result of the incentives and pressures that the free market induces! In a world lacking sufficient social provision for schooling, health care, and even basic material well-being – and in which social station, privilege and even basic political rights depend on our economic prowess – we may have little choice but to orient much of our behavior around furthering our own interests. If egoism is endogenous to neoliberalism, then the defense of this form of economic organization by reference to this form of human agency is at best circular. The critics might agree that the neoliberal economy would be optimal, were all humans to be indelibly stamped with the kind of nature that neoclassicals presume. But they insist that if human nature is instead malleable, the product in part of the specific world that humans inhabit, then we are entitled to question whether we want to live under an economic system that produces this kind of human nature. Perhaps alternative economic systems might support the flourishing of alternative human subjectivities that together generate better economic, political and social outcomes. A central challenge facing neoliberalism's critics, then, is to envision and work to create such alternative systems.

This insight leads to a final critique that reaches beyond the effects of global neoliberalism *per se*, and which focuses instead on the theoretical edifice that defends it. Critics contend that in their drive to formulate a timeless, universal, objective account of how the economy must be structured, the proponents of neoliberalism have generated the most powerful economic *ideology* of the past several centuries. In this account, the success of neoclassical theory stems not from its purported scientific principles, objectivity or verisimilitude. It results instead from the attractiveness of the vision of science to which it aspires, and from the power of the interests which are best served by the type of economic system that it celebrates. The persuasiveness of the neoclassical defense of neoliberalism is therefore grounded in its rhetorical attributes and political consequences, not its epistemological properties. Moreover, in this case, any claim that global neoliberalism represents the culmination of economic history should induce a discomfiting chill among those who prize open intellectual engagement and political pluralism (cf. Grabel 1999b). This claim, too, might be a rhetorical device that suppresses alternative theories and visions of how societies might better organize their economic institutions. In this case, it is incumbent on the dissenters to couple theoretical critique with compelling and engaging accounts of alternative economic systems.

Adjudicating the debate

This book is principally intended to contribute to the latter project. The book is driven in part by a conviction that the dissenters have it more right than wrong. Global neoliberalism is apt to lead to many of the effects recounted above and is, on this basis, ethically indefensible. The book is also driven by a conviction that the closing of economic debate that is sought by the defenders of global neoliberalism stands to be as deleterious to human emancipation as is this economic system itself. The loss of the many traditions of dissent within economics is apt to lead to a single-minded pursuit of damaging policies, and to an intolerable intellectual hubris among theorists and policymakers.

There are, of course, multiple ways to adjudicate a debate of this sort. The most common within the social sciences is to seek empirical confirmation of one perspective or disconfirmation of another. This book will not undertake such an examination. Even a cursory review of the empirical evidence gathered to date demonstrates that all sides in these debates can and have documented their respective claims. This isn't to say that the various positions are equally "right". It is to say that severe methodological difficulties attend the empirical adjudication of any debate of this sort. To believe that one can adjudicate the debate on empirical grounds, one must be prepared to commit to rather strong and dubious assumptions about the nature of the world we seek to know, the cognitive ability of the researcher to grasp this world through theoretical construction, the exogeneity of "facts" and "data" to the conceptual framework that the researcher employs, the unbiasedness of the processes of fact identification and selection, etc. These matters (which are addressed below) are now and have been for some time the subject of much heated debate in the philosophy of science. Without claiming that anything like a consensus has emerged, it is more than fair to say that the discussions have yielded ample grounds to be skeptical at least about claims that one theory or another has been proven by reference to the empirical record. It is therefore not surprising that empirical evidence to date has had precious little effect on the debate over neoliberalism. One is hard pressed to find in the literature a convert to the other side in the debate based on empirical revelation.

Our treatment will sidestep rather than resolve this matter by approaching the debate from another direction – by reference to a normative rather than an empirical standard. The jump to normative matters is hardly less fraught with difficulties than the engagement with empirical issues, to be sure. The debate over global neoliberalism to date has, however, largely ignored normative matters. This oversight has undermined the critique of neoliberalism on the one hand, and the ability of the dissenters to generate alternative visions of global economic integration on the other. Hence, the goal here will be to take each side at its empirical word, if you will, while accessing the debate by foregrounding the seemingly simple normative question: what makes for a good economic outcome? What criterion or set of criteria should we engage when we want to assess economic policy and/or economic outcomes? We will see that much of the disagreement over global neoliberalism stems from normative rather than empirical controversy. We will begin, then, by interrogating the normative criteria employed by the neoclassical defenders of global neoliberalism. We can then explore whether alternative normative criteria would better serve the goal of achieving good policy and good outcomes.

It should be clear that this debate is not just of academic interest. The outcome of the contest among academic economists shapes actual, on-the-ground economic policy in rather powerful ways. The quickening pace of neoliberal economic reform at the level of the nation state and in the arena of international relations reflects (and indeed, has influenced) the ascendance of neoclassical thought throughout the economic profession and in other academic disciplines (such as political science) over the past twenty-five years. Powerful domestic institutions such as national central banks, but also multilateral financial institutions (such as the IMF) and development banks (such as the World Bank) have come to embrace the neoliberal agenda in the belief that this regime is uniquely capable of generating economic prosperity. In short, the debate over global neoliberalism is of the utmost consequence to those who inhabit the earth today, and to those who will follow.

OUTLINE OF THE BOOK

This book is organized into three principal sections. Part 1 comprises three chapters which explore the normative debate over neoliberalism in the abstract. The presentation there and throughout the book is non-technical but precise enough to illuminate what is at stake in this regard. Chapter 1 presents the "welfarist" normative standard of neoclassical theory. It explains what welfarism entails, and demonstrates that it is the natural outcome of the rather severe inter-personal relativism and reductionism upon which neoclassical theory is constructed. The central features of this approach are rather straightforward. Indeed, the persuasive power of neoclassical thought stems in part from the elegance with which it builds from its rather simple initial assumptions to its dramatic policy conclusions. With an understanding of welfarism in hand, we turn in the following chapter to a demonstration of the manner in which neoclassical theory generates its strong defense of neoliberalism. No prior economic training is presumed here, as the exposition is illustrative rather than technical. Nevertheless, the chapter relies on the formal analytical tools of supply and demand to demonstrate the neoclassical view of the market, and it presents these concepts graphically. Though the formalism of neoclassical theory can be distracting, these concepts are too important to omit from an exposition of its defense of neoliberalism. Some formalism must therefore be risked here. Those who have taken a basic economics course will find all this straightforward; it is my hope that others will also find it accessible.

The final section of Chapter 2 presents a critical examination of welfarism. As we will see, welfarism is vulnerable to a host of damaging criticisms and has, for this reason, been largely rejected by many economists and most normative theorists outside of economics. Following from this critique, Chapter 3 then investigates a family of alternative, egalitarian normative perspectives that have been advanced by prominent political theorists, philosophers and others. This discussion includes a brief treatment of the egalitarian normative perspectives associated with two heterodox economic schools of thought, institutionalism and Marxism. The chapter then explicates and defends a normative position that captures the egalitarian spirit of these accounts, one that draws directly on the path-breaking work of philosopher-economist and Nobel Laureate Amartya Sen. Sen advocates the normative principle of "capabilities equality". The chapter examines just what this concept entails and presents some of its virtues as a normative principle for assessing economic outcomes.

While Part 1 investigates neoliberalism in the abstract, absent considerations of context, Part 2 turns explicitly to the matter of the normative status of *global* neoliberalism. Chapter 4 extends the normative discussion of Part 1 to the international context; the following two chapters turn to two contemporary economic policy debates in which the case for global neoliberalism is contested.

An important and troubling complication arises whenever we try to think about assessing economic (or, for that matter, political, social or cultural) policy or outcomes in the global context. This complication is the result of the existence of cross-cultural differences. Different communities have historically developed distinct beliefs, religious doctrines, philosophical systems, and normative frameworks. For example, different communities theorize the significance of gender, or the relationship between humanity and the non-human environment, in different ways. For many scholars, this diversity renders problematic the task of generating norms for assessing international policy regimes – regimes that necessarily span distinct communities. Where different societies have produced distinct beliefs, they ask, what basis is there for cross-cultural assessment and critique? Indeed, is there any basis at all for making such judgements? Are we warranted in using *our own* notions of the right and the good to assess the practices of others, when they do not share our notions? If not, what alternative basis might there be for undertaking such assessments? Lastly, how are we to construct and/or evaluate global policy regimes in the face of cross-cultural diversity? Whose values should prevail, and whose rules should govern, in the formation of policy regimes that cut across distinct cultures?

Insofar as our focus here is on global policy, this issue must be confronted directly. This is the task of Chapter 4. We will see that two principal theoretical positions have emerged in discussions over cross-cultural critique. The first perspective is moral objectivism, which claims that there is but one uniquely true normative code; once apprehended, this code can and must guide assessment of policies and outcomes in all societies – even those that do not subscribe to it. The second perspective is cultural relativism. It holds that no such objective code does or can exist and, hence, that each separate community does and should devise its own ethical code for guiding and assessing its own behavior. While the first position has the virtue of providing a firm basis for identifying and resisting oppression, wherever it may occur, critics charge that it is inherently prone to cultural imperialism, as members of more powerful societies try to impose their own ethical code on others. By contrast, the second position promises the virtue of cross-cultural respect. Objectivists charge, however, that it provides no basis for distinguishing between tolerable and oppressive cultural practices. Hence, this perspective may lead to acquiescence and resignation in the face of obvious and severe injustices.

Both of these criticisms have merit. In devising an alternative norm, we must therefore investigate the degree to which it provides the basis for opposing oppression on the one hand, while respecting defensible differences on the other. But how can one normative framework possibly do both? Is it not the case that any single, universal normative position that we are likely to imagine will necessarily be guilty of imperialist aspirations? Chapter 4 will argue that while the tension between cross-cultural critique and respect cannot in principle be "solved", the Senian perspective of capabilities equality can at least provide a framework for managing it in a reasonable way. To make this case, the chapter presents and defends an internationalist ethic founded upon the concept of capabilities equality which is designed to chart this middle course – an ethic that cuts deep enough to root out oppression, while remaining tolerant of defensible diversity.

The following two chapters examine carefully two policy issues that stand at the center of the debate over global economic integration – national competitiveness and international trade. In each of these debates, three distinct perspectives have emerged. These are distinguishable by their respective claims over the inevitability and desirability of global neoliberalism. The first is the "neoclassical vision". It combines a deep suspicion about any policy initiative that seeks greater national competitiveness with a resolute defense of free trade. Both policy stances are based upon a commitment to internationalism which takes the form of a conviction that global neoliberalism provides the best opportunities for universal improvements in human welfare.

We will find that the neoclassical defense of global neoliberalism (particularly free trade) is tied to a rather strong form of cultural relativism, which in turn follows from the interpersonal relativism described in Chapter 1. Neoclassicals argue that members of one society must accept the legitimacy of the different social mores that exist in other societies, and the different production, employment and environmental practices with which they are associated. Hence, they object to the demands often articulated by labor and environmental activists that trade policy should be used to encourage other countries to adopt a certain set of practices. On first encounter, this agnosticism might seem to insulate neoclassical theory from the temptations of cultural imperialism; indeed, many defenders of the paradigm make just this claim. We will see, however, that this relativism is, in fact, indefensible. The neoclassical vision manages to fall into the traps associated with *both* moral objectivism and cultural imperialism – no small feat, indeed. It does this by relying on cultural relativism to provide the basis for universal and absolute claims about how the economies of *all* societies must be structured, regardless of whatever diversity they otherwise exhibit.

The second position is less elegant and internally coherent but has, nevertheless, achieved good standing among many economists and especially among policy analysts. I will refer to it herein as "progressive nationalism" to signal both its chief pillars and the rather stark contradiction upon which it is founded. In the competitiveness debate, advocates call for progressive "competitiveness-enhancing" strategies and policies to ensure that a nation survives the intensifying battles in global markets. In the trade debate, its proponents call for "strategic trade" as a means of promoting the prosperity of a nation's citizens. These two groups of progressive nationalists do not necessarily agree with each other – some competitiveness enhancers are also free traders, for instance. Yet I treat them here as a unified position because of strong affinities among them. Like partisans of the neoclassical vision, proponents of both competitiveness policy and strategic trade believe that global neoliberalism is largely inevitable, but they refuse the neoclassical notion that all of humanity necessarily stands to benefit under this new global regime. Instead, they believe that a neoliberal regime can devastate the inhabitants of those countries that do not perform well relative to their rivals. Their policy prescriptions are intended to provide a blueprint for national policymakers, to ensure economic success in this new, dangerous environment. Those who advocate national competitiveness have presented several alternative policy regimes for achieving this objective. Chapter 5 will therefore survey various distinct contributions to the competitiveness literature. The three chosen – the human capital, corporate governance and flexible specialization approaches – have proven to be the most influential over the past two decades.

The advocates of national competitiveness and strategic trade surveyed here fall broadly within the liberal-left tradition. Taking root during the 1980s, at a time of economic dislocation and a conservative resurgence in the US and across Europe, these theorists sought to discover a policy mix that could restore the basis for prosperity for working people. It is not surprising, then, that we will find a common normative commitment to economic equality animating their rejection of neoclassical policy prescriptions. What is surprising is that we will find this egalitarianism to be rather tightly bounded – circumscribed by national borders. Yet no normative defense of this nationalism appears in this literature. Having theorized global neoliberalism and international market competition as natural and yet dangerous, the competitiveness enhancers seem to have little choice but to compromise their egalitarianism by seeking prosperity for one country's inhabitants at the expense of others.

The third position is "egalitarian internationalism". Its proponents also conclude that global neoliberalism is potentially damaging but they resist the view that it is inevitable. Instead, they argue that global policy regimes are largely open-ended and contingent rather than rooted in any determinant historical trajectory. Given the normative deficiencies of global neoliberalism, they claim that we can and must devise an alternative global policy regime that embodies a different vision of global economic intercourse. To the degree possible, this alternative must insulate communities from the devastating effects of market-based integration, while promoting the benefits that international economic intercourse can induce. In addition it must accord with a form of egalitarianism that is appropriate to the international context. In the national competitiveness debate, proponents of egalitarian internationalism call for "competition-reducing" policies that remove fundamental aspects of social life from the orbit of inter-firm and international competition. In the trade debate, they call for "fair trade".

This perspective is founded on a model of the economy that is markedly different from that embraced by neoclassical proponents of neoliberalism, and by the progressive nationalists. We will therefore take some time to elucidate this alternative model. In particular, we will take account of the way in which this model breaks with the severe "reductionism" of neoclassical thought – a reductionism that will emerge clearly in the exposition of the neoclassical vision in Chapters 1 and 2. I will show how and why the neoclassical reductionism provides its adherents with a clear and rigid policy blueprint. This determinacy can be comforting for those who want and need the apparent security of unambiguous policy guidance. I will argue, however, that we stand to gain much greater space for creative thinking about policy matters by forgoing the security that reductionism affords.[9]

For their part, the egalitarian internationalists have proposed various means for insulating critical aspects of social life from the ravaging effects of global competition. For example, they seek to remove vital conditions of work (such as workers' rights) from competition through the universal

Table 1 Summary of policy prescriptions

	National competitiveness	*Trade*
The neoclassical vision	Against rompetitiveness policy	Free trade
Progressive nationalism	Competitiveness-enhancing policies/strategies	Strategic trade
International egalitarianism	Competition-reducing policies	Fair trade

application of harmonized labor standards. These proposals are motivated by internationalist concerns, and in this sense, they share something with their neoclassical antagonists. Like neoclassicals, the egalitarian internationalists reject strategic trade and competitiveness-enhancing strategies to promote national prosperity. Hence, we must be sure to take stock of just why they refuse to endorse global neoliberalism. The specific topic of international trade will provide the means to clarify the dispute between the two camps. We will see that the disagreement between them over trade is largely the result of the different normative commitments that the parties bring to the policy arena, and to the distinct models of the economy and society that each embraces. Table 1 summarizes the respective positions of these three perspectives.

The final section of the book turns to more speculative matters. Chapter 7 investigates just what kinds of policy might become imaginable once we embrace international egalitarianism and the associated normative standard of capabilities equality. This is a rather radical normative position, as we will see. The proposals that it yields are therefore far beyond the pale of contemporary policy discourse. The proposals of Chapter 7 are to be taken seriously, if not literally. They are framed as proposals for the year 2025 in the hope that thinking in this way might allow us to silence temporarily the inhibiting voices that always arise within us whenever we try to think about a radically different world from the one we inhabit. These are the skeptical voices that counter every novel proposal with the charge of impracticality. Social progress, when it comes, often entails the pursuit of institutions, policies and norms that, not too long before, had seemed anything but practical. If we refuse to allow ourselves to imagine a world very different from our own, we have slim chance of realizing significant social and economic reform.

Chapter 7 also considers the contribution that the principle of capabilities equality can make to the establishment of a politics that might succeed in securing the policy reforms advocated here. Over the past decade or so, myriad new social movements have emerged across the globe that in one way or another are resisting what they see to be the dangers of global neoliberalism. Though often national in membership and participation, these movements have begun to reach across national and regional borders to share information and even to co-ordinate their activities in pursuit of their mutual goals. But these movements often come to loggerheads over particular policy reforms. Unfortunately, the fissures separating social movements in the North from those in the South often run particularly deep, owing to the very different economic, political and cultural conditions that they face.

I will argue that a commitment to the principle of capabilities equality might help these movements to discover new forms of internationalism and new avenues of reform that fulfill their respective social aspirations. This discussion will return to and draw out the implications of the question posed in Chapter 4 about the relationship between cross-cultural critique and respect. I will argue that capabilities equality provides advocates of justice the world over with the right to judge practices and institutions in their own and others' cultures. It also demands of them the willingness to submit their own societies and ways of life to the judgement of others. Capabilities equality provides the basis for a fully dialogical politics of negotiation and compromise, and for a gradualist politics that can seek small improvements in the here and now even as it demands rather pronounced and radical adjustments over time. In short, it can provide practical guidance for concrete politics in the world as we know it, while it demands of us that we keep an eye on the kind of radically different world we seek by the year 2025.

Part 1

Normative matters

What makes for a good economic outcome?

It is sometimes good to begin at the beginning. Confusion in policy debates often arises from what is left unsaid or what is taken for granted. This is particularly true in debates over global economic integration. Observers of the debate over free trade, for instance, might come to conclude that the debaters are talking past each other and, indeed, they are. A cacophony of competing monologues often arises in the place where reasoned dialogue should prevail because of partisanship to distinct normative frameworks – partisanship that generally remains implicit and unspoken. In part, this section is intended to begin to cut through the confusion by teasing out the normative positions that inform contemporary economic policy debates.

A reasonable starting point might be to ask the question, "*what makes for a good economic outcome?*" At the most basic level, what overriding purposes do we hope that economic policy will serve? This is obviously a fundamental question, and yet it is rarely posed in economic policy debate. Policy analysts presumably have notions in their heads of what makes for good economic outcomes; otherwise, it is difficult to imagine just why they would be partisan to one policy option over another. What are we to infer, then, from the absence of sustained discussion of this question? Is it that we all share the same answer, so that posing the question would waste time and energy that ought to be applied instead to an examination of the empirical effects of the policy options under review?

We know that this answer cannot be correct. When we listen to popular political discourse, we can easily discern contending, often antagonistic perspectives about what makes for good outcomes lurking beneath the surface of policy debate. When we turn for guidance to the fields of political theory and philosophy, where questions of this sort are constantly under review, we find substantial disagreement of the most fundamental sort surviving through the millennia. What we find is that this very simple question refuses to submit to simple answers. We disagree amongst ourselves about what makes for good outcomes (often quite passionately) because our views on this matter relate to our most basic visions about what is right, good or fair. If the question "*what makes for a good economic outcome?*" is missing from most economic policy debate, we should conclude that it is actively suppressed, not simply overlooked.

This suppression is consequential. It undermines the quality of public discourse by contributing to confusion about just what is at stake in important policy matters. It invites the conclusion that policy debate primarily or even solely entails disagreement about predictions or estimates of the concrete effects of a policy initiative. But this view is dangerously incorrect.

Consider a debate over a pressing public policy matter, such as tax or welfare reform, free trade or, in the case of the United States, affirmative action. Adjudicating any of these matters entails two distinct (but as we will see, interrelated) moments which, for lack of careful attention, tend to be mishandled in much policy discussion. One might be thought of as discerning the actual, on-the-ground effects of the policy initiative. This assessment may be straightforward in principle, but it is anything but simple in practice. Debate over a policy often precedes its enactment, and so we are forced to make best guesses about its future impact. Forecasting in the social sciences is, however, notoriously difficult. Predictions of how a certain policy will affect a particular population must take account of all the direct and indirect effects, while taking account of all the other relevant changes that will simultaneously occur independent of the policy change. This is generally regarded to be impossible, so modeling the future impact of a policy is generally undertaken assuming *ceteris paribus* – that all else remains the same while the direct or immediate effects of the policy unfold. This convention allows the analyst to make guesses, to be sure. We ought to have no trouble, however, understanding why different researchers can reach dramatically different predictions about the same policy, or why what appears to be the most carefully specified, scientific predictions can easily turn out to be most off the mark. As John Maynard Keynes (1936) remarked long ago, the future is simply unknowable.

The problem of assessing a policy's impact is equally contentious when we attempt to interpret the past rather than predict the future. The reason is similar: the pathways of interaction between causal variables are exceedingly complex. This complexity of the social and natural world defeats the efforts of the most gifted researchers to map the full and ultimate effects of any policy or event. Ideally, an assessment of this sort should compare what did happen following a policy initiative to what would have happened had the policy not been pursued. Yet we do not know (nor can we ever know) just what would have happened without the policy's impact, precisely because that historical path was foreclosed when the policy initiative was enacted. So we compare what did happen with *what we think might have happened* – and assessing *that* is hardly easier than predicting the future.[10]

It ought not to be surprising, then, that a good bit of policy debate entails disagreements about a policy's actual impact. Will a new free trade agreement generate higher or lower unemployment in a particular industry or region, and how long will this effect endure? Will welfare reform increase or decrease the poverty rate? Will reducing the government's budget deficit promote growth or stagnation? Will ending affirmative action yield a race-blind meritocracy or cement a race-based structure of privilege and privation?[11]

This moment of policy adjudication, the empirical moment, is by no means trivial, but it is by no means the only moment, either. To see this, let us assume that in a particular case, all parties to a debate agree on the likely concrete effects of a policy initiative (that they might all very well be wrong is beside the point). In this case, can we presume that a consensus will be readily forthcoming? Absent bad faith, partisan politics or misguided ideological commitments, can we presume that all fair-minded, reasonable people will agree on the merits of the initiative?

Well, we could, perhaps, if all reasonable people subscribed to the same notion of what makes for a good outcome. In this case, we could rightly claim that those who do not agree with us were motivated by some special interest. All reasonable people do not, however, subscribe to the same notion of what makes for a good outcome. Different people hold contending normative accounts of the good, and they bring these differing accounts to matters of policy adjudication, as they should. Policy dispute is often reduced to largely unarticulated disputes about normative visions. We would do well, then, to foreground this terrain – to make explicit the normative visions that influence partisanship in policy debates – prior to an assessment of the debates themselves.

Two quick examples will help clarify what is at stake. What if a consensus were to exist that a new free trade pact would generate economic growth, but would also exacerbate a nation's income inequality? Whether we support it in this case might then depend on our particular account of the good. Are the virtues of economic growth more important than the evils of rising inequality? Is growth itself even to be taken as a virtue; or inequality, an evil? Or what if a consensus were to exist that economic growth would exacerbate ecological degradation? Whether we support it in this case might turn on whether we view the "human-made capital" (e.g. the new theme park) that we are gaining to be a sufficient substitute for the "natural capital" (e.g. the forest) that we are sacrificing – a judgement which would again depend largely on our normative perspectives (cf. Daly 1991). One might take the view of many neoclassical economists, who argue that such matters might be adjudicated scientifically (and absent normative judgements) via some form of cost–benefit analysis, in which we determine whether the gains from free trade (or growth) more than offset the losses from rising inequality (or environmental degradation). But the objection can and has been raised that the act of comparing costs and benefits of this sort entails all manner of normative commitments which are suppressed in the name of science (Sagoff 1988). After all, the comparison of benefits and costs requires that we reduce these to some sort of common denominator, such as money. If we take a moment to think about this, we will realize that translating social benefits and costs into any common denominator is a value-laden exercise. How, after all, do we compute the dollar value of the benefit of preserving a forest or a species, or even a single human life, so that we might compare this bene-fit to the cost of preservation? Economists have generated myriad clever techniques to facilitate such measurement and comparisons, of course (see Dorfman 1993). For example, it is not uncommon to infer the value of a per-son's life from his earnings, since earnings are taken to be a measure of his contribution to society. Hence, the World Bank chief economist Lawrence Summers could argue without embarrassment that pollution (which might lead to a loss of life) causes less damage in poor societies where wages are lowest![12] This ingenuity should not distract us, however, from attending to the antecedent value judgements upon which these exercises are predicated.

In short, abstracting from empirical disputes about policy is as likely to sharpen the normative dispute as to yield consensus about a policy initia-tive. But this is useful: normative matters are at the heart of most policy dis-putes in economics (and beyond), not least the contest between those who accept and those who refuse the claims made on behalf of global neoliberalism. Attention to normative matters may also encourage us to do what economists generally avoid doing – to articulate explicitly and defend a vision of the good so as to persuade others of its merits, while opening it up to their interrogation. And we may find that an engagement with the question "*what makes for a good economic outcome?*" provides the basis for envi-sioning new policy initiatives that we have heretofore been unable to imagine.

THE INTERPENETRATION OF EMPIRICAL AND NORMATIVE ASSESSMENT

So far this discussion has treated the empirical and normative moments of policy adjudication as strictly separable. In so doing, it echoes a longstanding tradition in the social sciences, one that licenses economists to focus on empirical matters while (apparently) leaving normative matters to others. This has allowed us to consider the importance of normative questions. We must now take one further step, and recognize that the idea that normative and empirical matters are independent is at best naïve. In fact, the normative and empirical moments of policy adjudication are thoroughly and necessar-ily intertwined, inconvenient though this may be.

To see this, let us consider first the matter of *fact selection*. Which facts are to be taken into account in adjudicating policy disputes? This question arises because any policy is likely to induce an infinity of effects. Yet policy debate generally focuses on only a handful. We might then ask, how do we or should we select those few facts that will be determinative in our assessment of policy? To return to the above example of the merits of a trade agreement, why should we select economic growth or income inequality as relevant to the process of policy adjudication? Why measure them at all? Why are these data more germane to the matter of policy adjudication than, say, the color of the hair of the policy's principal beneficiaries? This, too, is a fact pertaining to the policy, but we ignore it as unimportant or irrelevant (though we might not so quickly dismiss the color of the skin of the principal beneficiaries). This fact is rendered irrelevant by the normative commitments we carry that attach value (negative or positive) elsewhere, such as to growth and equality but not to the beneficiaries' hair color. Our normative commitments, then, drive our fact selection, upon which our policy adjudication will turn. Indeed, without normative commitments, fact selection in the domain of policy adjudication would be nonsensical and arbitrary if not entirely impossible.

The fact–value connection is still more complicated. The particular data that one economic paradigm recognizes as such may not achieve standing in other paradigms. This is because facts themselves are "concept-dependent". In addition to providing other services, concepts provide the foundational work of facilitating *fact identification*. This suggests that if we disagree about concepts, then we are also very likely to disagree about facts. For example, consider the question "Has NAFTA led to an increase in the rate of exploitation of labor in North America?". This is a straightforward empirical question. This question does not, however, make sense to neoclassical economists, as they do not recognize the concept of "exploitation" in the sense in which it is used here. The concept of labor exploitation arises within Marxian economic theory and is, indeed, fundamental to that theoretical enterprise. Some Marxists spend a good deal of time measuring it, in the way that other economists measure GDP growth; but unlike the latter economists, those who measure exploitation cannot avail themselves of the latest official government data, because the theories that drive the government's data collection and reporting do not include the concept of exploitation. Hence, from the perspectives of neoclassical economics and government statistical accounts, the fact of exploitation does not exist as such.

In short, the entirely empirical fact of a change in the rate of exploitation following NAFTA can only be recognized once we embrace a theoretical narrative within which this concept has meaning. This is also true, however, for all other questions of fact. Even the simple physical fact that water changes from solid to liquid form at zero degrees centigrade depends on the concepts of heat, matter, measurement and others too numerous to list. Without these concepts, the fact *as such* does not exist. Different theoretical paradigms construct their own, unique sets of concepts, including those responsible for fact identification. One theory's fact will fail to appear at all in another that refuses the concept which gives rise to it. So, while neoclassical theory will rely on data concerning levels of social welfare (as we will see in Chapter 1), alternative theories ignore these data because they refuse the validity of the concept of social welfare.

The last point to be made in this regard concerns *theory choice*. The fore-going discussion points to the impossibility of choosing one theory over another based strictly on empirical evidence because what we take to be "the evidence" is itself theory-dependent. This implies that theory choice is also at least partly a normative matter. One theory promises analytical elegance and parsimony in conceptual foundations; another, though less elegant, promises greater verisimilitude. Which do we choose? Which is the *right* kind of theory? Which are the correct criteria for guiding the choice? This decision would seem to require a universally valid, objective standard of theory selection – a guiding epistemology, perhaps – but how then do we choose *that*?

As much as we may desire it, we must conclude that an unimpeachable, objective foundation for making the choice of which theory to embrace, which will bring in its train so many other judgements that we will make (such as which economic data to recognize and select), simply does not exist. All the way down, our choices will reflect our values as much as our "objective" judgements. Discomforting though this recognition may be, it cannot be otherwise. Hence, when a researcher gives reasons why it is uniquely right for all of us to endorse a theory that promises one sort of virtue over another, she sheds far more light on her own normative commitments (on what it is *she* values) than on the science of theory choice.[13]

REDUCTIONIST VERSUS ANTI-REDUCTIONIST THEORY

As this discussion suggests, contending theories differ not only in terms of the concepts that they embrace. Equally important, theories differ in terms of the logic or analytical structures that they employ to link these concepts into compelling accounts of their subject matter. Today, one of the chief fissures dividing contending theories across the social sciences entails a profound disagreement about what is called "reductionism" or "essentialism". Reductionist accounts have predominated in economics (and throughout the social sciences) for most of this century. Reductionist science proceeds in three steps. Step one entails the identification of those causal factors that are taken to be fundamental in driving historical events; these are the "essences" of the theory. This identification requires a practice of discrimination in which the theorist must distinguish between the causal essences on the one hand and other factors that are subordinate or marginal. These we might refer to as "contingencies". The second step involves linking the privileged essences through simple analytical structures into explanatory models. This is the province of "pure theory". Once the model is constructed, the final step of reductionist explanation can commence. For any event to be explained, we suppress all the factors that have been identified *ex ante* as marginal or contingent, and attempt to "reduce" the event to the effect of the model's essences (DeMartino 1993).

This is not to say that reductionist accounts fully ignore all causal variables not embraced by the model as essences. Instead, non-essential forces are indeed understood to play a part in the unfolding of historical events. The role assigned to these non-essential factors is, however, subordinate in the sense that, unlike the essences, their impact is fleeting, contingent, and often unpredictable. For instance, non-essential factors may color the landscape against which the primary, essential factors exert their effects; or they may influence the timing of the events induced by the essences. In neither case do they determine the direction or course of human history. And because they are fleeting, contingent and variable, they are not amenable to determinative theoretical accounting. They influence events from beyond the terrain of the theoretical, if you will, rather than commanding a central place in reductionist discourse.

We will find that neoclassical theory is an exceedingly sharp exemplar of reductionist social science. In this account, economic events are largely reducible to a very small set of powerful essences, not the least of which is "human rationality". We will see that neoclassical theorists presume rationality to be *the* fundamental, universal determinant of human behavior and affairs. Yet many theorists today reject reductionism as misleading and even harmful.[14] In its place, these theorists offer what may be called anti-reductionist or anti-essentialist social analysis.[15] This kind of theory commences with a rejection of the bifurcation of causal variables into the two classes of essences and contingencies. In this view, events are not reducible to some small set of privileged factors. Instead, events result from what is called the "overdetermination" (or the complex interplay) of the infinite factors that constitute the social totality. While, like reductionist theory, anti-reductionist theory also must choose some manageable set of concepts with which to commence social analysis, the concepts are treated as simple entry points into analysis – as convenient and hopefully fruitful places to begin – not as essences of human affairs (Resnick and Wolff 1987a).

I raise all of this here because the contest over global neoliberalism (like many other policy debates in the social sciences today) entails in part a contest between reductionist and anti-reductionist theoretical approaches. This controversy often causes impatience (even annoyance) among those encountering these debates. Can't we simply terminate this methodological debate scientifically, a student might be forgiven for asking, so that we can get on to what really matters in the field of global political economy? Can't we just submit this methodological controversy to empirical testing, and then choose that kind of theory which best accords with the world out there?

As I hope is by now apparent, this cannot be done. There is no objective (or empirical) way to resolve a controversy of this sort. The choice between reductionist and anti-reductionist theoretical protocols represents, if I may dare say it, a *normative* commitment on the part of the theorist. Some theorists simply cannot face the possibility that the world, in its deepest structures, is not profoundly compatible with reductionist premises. The thought of a world in which all variables play a part, and in which no subset stands as fundamental essences, is too frightening or otherwise discomforting and offensive. These theorists argue that anti-essentialist theory gives rise to sloppy thinking, to a carefree, "anything goes" sort of mentality that may have a place in fiction or poetry, but certainly not in the social sciences. In this view, anti-essentialist theory provides no basis at all for policy guidance. It is the coward's path that detours around the difficult task of taking a stand, making predictions, and being partisan in the world.

In contrast, other theorists find anti-reductionist theory to be liberating. Freed from the constraints placed on us by reductionist analytical structures, they argue, we are encouraged to develop far more nuanced historical accounts of the past, and understand the myriad possibilities for policy action in the present and in the future. These theorists view reductionist accounts as efforts to constrain social experimentation through arrogant claims about the way the world really is. Reductionism provides its adherents with an illusion of understanding and control which may comfort them as they face a chaotic world, but this illusion is a poor foundation for sustaining the kinds of grand social engineering to which they are prone. Though anti-reductionist accounts provide "messy" narratives and open-ended (perhaps even uncertain) policy guidance, this induces humility on the part of the policymaker that just might prevent egregious and costly mistakes. In any event, such messiness is a worthwhile price to pay for the creativity that this approach imparts.

Which is the right kind of theory to choose? The answer we give will depend in part on whether we value the certainty, precision and closure of reductionist theory or the flexibility, experimentation and perpetual aperture of anti-reductionist theory. The chapters which follow will provide an opportunity to consider the relative virtues of these two kinds of theoretical structure. We will explore the reductionist structure of neoclassical theory, before turning to an alternative economic model that is explicitly anti-reductionist. I confess that my partisanship to the latter will be made explicit in what follows. It is my hope, nevertheless, that this presentation will allow the reader to reach her own judgements on this important matter.

If different economists bring different data to policy adjudication, or embrace different kinds of theoretical structures, then this might ultimately be the consequence of distinct normative commitments. The separation of fact and value that is so commonly presumed in the social sciences today – that is taken to license the pursuit of positive science as a thoroughly objective exercise[16] – must be displaced by a mode of investigation that recognizes their deeply embedded connections. Making sense of empirical policy disputes therefore requires careful attention to normative foundations, even though (perhaps especially when) those involved in the disputes may view themselves to be engaged in a thoroughly objective enterprise.

We turn now to an extensive normative investigation of the contest over economic policy regimes.

1 Neoclassical theory and welfarism

INTRODUCTION

Although those who have struggled through the obligatory Economics 101 training in college may choose to differ on this point, the persuasiveness of neoclassical theory stems in part from its simplicity. Beginning with a straightforward set of assumptions about human capacities and the natural world, it quickly generates a powerful set of theoretical conclusions about how the economy should be structured. This elegance is often lost in the pursuit of mastery of the details, to be sure, so that many economics students have scant sense of just what all the details they study are for. In the following exposition I purposely exclude all unnecessary details, so as to reveal the analytical power of neoclassical theory and particularly, its chief policy implications.

Neoclassical theory and the neoclassical "vision"

As will become apparent in the following discussion, adherents of neoclassical theory view it to be a thoroughly scientific enterprise, patterned on the natural sciences. We will see momentarily just what this self-conception implies – suffice it to say for now that it is extraordinarily consequential and deeply problematic. When neoclassical economists and others who embrace this tradition enter policy debates, however, they routinely reach beyond what the science of neoclassical theory proper permits them to say, invoking instead what I will refer to throughout this book as the "neoclassical vision". While the neoclassical theory that appears in advanced microeconomic textbooks licenses only carefully proscribed policy prescriptions, recognizing that real-world conditions complicate greatly a policy's effects, neoclassical visionaries generally hazard grand policy claims irrespective of the constraints imposed by political, economic and social context. These grand claims are authorized by the broader neoclassical vision; and it is in this far more charismatic (one might even say imperial) form that neoclassical theory generally reaches the ears of policymakers and the public. Often we find prominent neoclassical theorists indulging in the neoclassical vision in order to gain advantage in public policy debates.

The term "vision" signals something more or other than a scientific model. Those who consider themselves scientists adamantly eschew visions. They commit to particular propositions, test them, revise them when necessary and expand upon them when possible. This enterprise is surely enabled by some overarching theoretical framework that provides the concepts and methods for the science to occur. But the term "vision" suggests something beyond these attachments. It suggests that its advocates are in the grasp of and/or exploit a set of ideological rather than strictly scientific commitments.

This sense of the term is intentional. When we encounter neoclassical claims in contemporary policy debates, we confront not simply an articulation of neoclassical science, narrowly construed. We confront a broad complex of complementary economic, political and cultural arguments, the wisdom of which is generally taken as given and even self-evident.

Today the neoclassical vision is quickly ascending to the status of the official, secular worldview across the globe, despite whatever claims we might make about democratic or pluralist societies neither needing nor tolerating an official worldview (this, we might think, is the monopoly of authoritarian regimes). It is employed by non-academics as much as it is by economics professors; it is in the air we breathe, so much so that we find students entering their first economics classes to be already initiates to the neoclassical way of thinking. Though they might bridle at having to master the concept of cross-price elasticities, they need little schooling in the chief analytical and policy conclusions of the theory. They enter their first economics class as potential neoclassicals awaiting activation.

The question of why a particular social theory achieves the status of official worldview in a particular social and cultural context is a difficult one, far beyond the scope of this book. In part, the internal logic and structure of a theory contribute to its ascension. So also do the rhetorical devices that are deployed in its defense. In this respect, the success of its advocates in portraying neoclassical theory as an objective science (as against, say, the "dogma" of Marxian theory) has surely enhanced its stature within and beyond the economics profession. But it bears emphasis that circumstances and conditions external to the theory play a critical role. Theories are embraced and achieve standing in part by virtue of the salience of the problems they purport to solve. But a theory's success is also influenced by the political and economic interests it serves (and threatens). Indeed, academics often recognize this – they make this very argument regularly when dismissing the popularity of a theory that they themselves oppose.[17] They typically apply the pejorative "ideology" to those theories that they believe take root in the soil of political and economic interests rather than in practices of objective science. What they generally fail to accept is that the social theories they themselves endorse also serve some interests over others, and that this service conditions the theory's status. For instance, prominent neoclassical Paul Krugman (1992; 1994b) never tires of defending neoclassical science against the ideologies that oppose neoclassical policy prescriptions. While his opponents (mere "policy entrepreneurs") are captured by powerful extra-theoretical interests, he and his neoclassical colleagues remain entirely impervious to the forces that benefit from the policy conclusions they prescribe.

This chapter and the next elucidate the central principles of neoclassical theory as they typically appear in microeconomics textbooks. In the policy discussion that begins in Chapter 2 I will liberally substitute the term "neoclassical *vision*" for "neoclassical *theory*" because it is the former that is at the heart of contemporary economic policy debate. While neoclassical theory proper recognizes all sorts of complications that arise in a market economy, the neoclassical vision dismisses these complications as largely insignificant and in any event, beyond effective redress through government intervention.

A caveat is in order. The policy prescriptions associated with the neoclassical vision are not endorsed by all "mainstream" economists. Two classes of economist come to mind. The first are what I will call the "pragmatists". These economists do not consider themselves to be "neoclassical". Instead, they view themselves simply as economists, using the grab bag of techniques (such as cost–benefit analysis) provided by economic theory to explore the pressing social problems they confront. They are the mechanics of the profession, solving problems using concepts and tools the origin and status of which they happily ignore. While these pragmatic economists tend toward consensus over a wide range of policy matters – most such economists are free traders, for instance – we also find important areas of disagreement, reflecting their own personal normative commitments, the degree to which they think that reality matches up with the assumptions of theory, and so forth. Some vote for conservative political parties that promise smaller government and greater reliance on the market; others cast their votes for liberals whom they hope will enact policies to redistribute income to achieve greater equality.[18]

The second group comprises the "pure theorists". These economists very much think of themselves as neoclassical. Indeed, their labors are designed to expand and improve the neoclassical model in order to resolve the kinds of lingering theoretical anomalies that plague every theoretical exercise. They do not much concern themselves with the relationship between these investigations and the world beyond – indeed, they may know (or care) very little about what we call "the economy". Their work is entirely inaccessible to non-specialists, and they would never consider writing editorials on pressing policy issues for the *Op-Ed* section of the *New York Times*.

These two groups of economists are unlikely to endorse all of the policy prescriptions of the neoclassical vision. The pragmatists might argue that the economic tools they use do not sustain grand policy claims; the pure theorists might argue that neoclassical science does not authorize them. Though it is beyond the scope of this book, it can be said that both complaints have merit. The neoclassical vision entails far more than the selective and careful application of neoclassical techniques or pure theory to narrowly proscribed policy questions. It entails the use of a severely reductionist logic (described above in Part 1) in which all economic outcomes are theorized as the ultimate effect of the theory's essences. It entails the presumption that all alternative economic theories that embrace alternative concepts and explanatory logics are necessarily deficient. It also entails the presumption that neoclassical theory is not just useful in some times and places to make sense of and respond to some pressing social problems, but is uniquely correct and uniformly applicable in all contexts for all time. We will see that the founding assumptions and internal logic of neoclassical theory encourage these universalist claims. They do not, however, necessitate them. Those pragmatic and neoclassical economists who refuse such claims might therefore consider undertaking a careful critique of the neoclassical vision, to demonstrate how precisely it reaches beyond and violates the theory which it claims as its source of legitimacy.

In Chapter 2 we will turn to policy debates in the global economy and investigate the policy correlates of the neoclassical vision. For now, our immediate goal is to attend to the matter of the normative commitments of this vision. To do that, we must begin with the initial assumptions of neoclassical theory, upon which this vision stands.

INITIAL ASSUMPTIONS: THE ESSENCES OF NEOCLASSICAL THEORY[19]

The neoclassical vision is founded upon three fundamental assumptions that give rise to neoclassical theory; the first two relate to the inherent capacities of human beings (or human nature); the third relates to properties of physical nature.

The consumption proposition

The first assumption we may call the "consumption proposition". This assumption holds that *individuals are endowed with the ability to choose rationally from among the sets of opportunities they confront.* The operative concept in this proposition is "rationality". In simplest terms, this entails the idea that whenever faced with a choice, an individual will make that decision which yields greatest personal satisfaction, or what economists often call "utility". Implicitly, this assumes that individuals are by nature egoistic and self-oriented. They are driven to serve their own needs – not the needs of society. As we will see in Chapter 2, one of the most notable achievements of the neoclassical vision is its discovery of an economic governance structure that marshals this egoistic, selfish orientation into socially benevolent behaviors and outcomes.

The concept of rationality is elaborated substantially in the neoclassical vision. Most important for present purposes, the ability to choose rationally is predicated on the existence of what is called a "preference ordering" in the mind of the chooser. A preference ordering is simply a set of likes and dislikes, or tastes. Confronting a choice, the rational actor checks his preference ordering and makes that selection which yields maximum personal utility. For any two options, a preference ordering will provide a ranking: the first option might be preferred to the second, the second to the first, or the two might be equally valued. Absent a preference ordering, the act of choosing might become arbitrary and capricious – in a word, non-rational.

To understand the full import of rationality in this context we need to draw a distinction between the *structure* of a preference ordering (*how* things are ranked) and the *content* of preference orderings (just *what* is preferred). Rationality circumscribes quite narrowly the structure that any preference ordering can take. For example, in considering any two bundles of goods, a rational preference ordering must exhibit the feature of consistency. If I prefer bundle A to bundle B, then I cannot simultaneously prefer bundle B to bundle A. Rationality is also taken to ensure what is called "the law of diminishing marginal utility". This means that as I consume more of a particular good, I receive less additional (or "marginal") satisfaction from each additional unit consumed. After a long hike, for instance, the third glass of water gives me less additional (marginal) pleasure than did the second. Finally, we must take note of the critical assumption of "insatiability", or the view that *we always prefer more rather than less*. More of any good will yield greater total utility than will less, and this drive to have more is without limit. Simply put, the rational actor can never have enough (Little 1957).

What does rationality imply about the content of preference orderings? What can we say about what a rational person will prefer – such as when she confronts a choice between bananas and oranges, or Metallica and Mozart? Or when she confronts a choice between the preservation of a wetland and the building of an additional shopping mall in the space that the wetland occupies? The answer is nothing whatsoever.[20] Neoclassical theory holds tightly to a rather severe form of *interpersonal relativism*. Each individual, being rational, is taken to know best what she desires and needs. *This point is fundamental*: there is simply no warrant within neoclassical theory for the economist to interrogate the propriety of a rational agent's choices. It is altogether nonsensical to ask whether the preference for this over that is correct (or rational). The science of neoclassical economics provides no basis for making such evaluations.

One last point about preference orderings must be made here, although the significance of this assumption will remain somewhat obscure for the moment. Neoclassical theory assumes that preference orderings are "exogenous" to our economic activity. This means that we develop our respective preference orderings prior to and independent of our participation in society's economic institutions, like the market. Our preference orderings are well established before we go to the store to buy some combination of goods – the act of shopping does not alter or transform our preferences, but merely allows us to act upon them in pursuit of maximum satisfaction. Moreover, our preference ordering is in no way affected by the level of income we receive, or the type of labor we perform. We may therefore think of a person's preference ordering as reflecting her deepest personality structure and true desires, as constituting her unique individuality.

The production proposition

The second proposition is somewhat simpler to describe: *humans are endowed with the ability to transform elements of nature (through work or labor) so as to produce goods that meet human needs, and they do so rationally.* Note again the qualifier of rationality. In this context, rationality implies that when humans undertake through labor to produce goods that meet their needs, they do so efficiently or without waste. If two techniques for growing wheat are available to a community, and these two are equal in all respects save that one yields more wheat than the other per unit of labor expended in wheat farming, then rational producers will choose to employ the more efficient technique. It would be irrational for them to do otherwise. Further, when a new technique is discovered that is more efficient in this sense, rational producers will switch to the new technique. We call this chosen technique "technology" – it is the best available means for producing any particular good under existing conditions.

The scarcity proposition

The third proposition is an assumption about physical nature, and may be summed up simply: *all output (in the form of goods and services) requires inputs from nature, and since nature's bounty is finite, output must also be finite.* The first part of this proposition merely states that we cannot get something from nothing: absent raw materials and the labor necessary to transform them into useful goods, and we have no output. The second part implies that for any particular society at any particular point in time, only so much can be produced. The attainable level of production will be determined by its existing technologies and by the supply and quality of its labor and other raw material inputs (called its "endowments").

This proposition is extraordinarily consequential. First, when coupled with the assumption of insatiability, it implies that output will always be *scarce*. Human society will always desire more than can be provided. By virtue of these two propositions, the concept of sufficiency does not and cannot appear within the neoclassical vision. Instead, we find a ceaseless competition by each for more. The human condition is therefore marked by an ineradicable tension between infinite wants and finite supply.

Second, the scarcity proposition implies that all actions entail what economists call an "opportunity cost". This means that undertaking any action requires that we forego something else. In the economic realm, for instance, the labor and steel applied to automobile production are not available for building bicycles; hence, we can measure the opportunity cost of producing a car by the number of bicycles society must forego to produce it. Formally, the opportunity cost of any activity is the value of the next most preferred activity that must be foregone to pursue it. The opportunity cost of reading this book might be the pleasure that otherwise would be available from watching a film, or the knowledge that could be gained from reading the next best available book.

Third, this proposition entails the idea that humanity confronts a perpetual stream of choices. Every action we take requires that we forego an innumerable array of other actions. This is equally true of our economic and non-economic activities. By virtue of being human, we are condemned to a life of difficult trade-offs and choices.

In neoclassical theory (and the broader neoclassical vision), however, we have no reason to fear this fate. By virtue of the first proposition, we know that humans are uniquely endowed with the ability to choose *rationally*. Hence, the innumerable choices we face ought not to be taken as overwhelming or daunting, but as the means for maximizing human satisfaction. Indeed, the more choices available to a society, the better off it will be, given the uniqueness of each member's preference orderings. A society with more choices stands to provide a surer basis for yielding more satisfaction to more individuals. Ideally, then, we would want to construct some kind of economy that yields maximum space for individual decision making about what to do, what to buy, where to live, how to work. Evidently, the superior economy must privilege individual choice as the best road to enhance personal satisfaction.

These three propositions are rather simple and intuitive. But, we might reasonably ask, what is their origin? For instance, how do we know that each of us is rational in the particular way specified by the theory? What is the basis for this capacity? The answer to this question is taken to be non-economic in nature. Neoclassical theory does not explore the origins of rational choice – this would be the province of psychologists, anthropologists, biologists or perhaps sociologists. For the economist, the existence of this capacity is taken as given. This is what makes it an assumption. Every theory, in every discipline, must make such initial assumptions; otherwise, it would be impossible for them to proceed (Resnick and Wolff 1987b). There is nothing illicit, then, about the fact that neoclassical theory does not provide concrete proof that preference orderings of the sort it specifies actually exist. Nevertheless, we may have other reasons to object to them, as we will see.

What is economics?

We should take note, finally, of the combined theoretical import of these three entry point concepts. If we accept them as reasonable places to begin, then we are led to an understanding of the field of economics as *the science of choice under conditions of scarcity*. This is indeed the definition of economics that appears in virtually all introductory texts. Unfortunately, it is generally presented as the obvious and only possible definition; as the natural domain of economics. We should see, however, that this particular definition of economics is derived directly from neoclassical theory's initial assumptions. Absent any of these three propositions, this definition of economics would make little sense. For example, if either human desires were satiable, or nature's bounty infinite, output would not necessarily be scarce. Absent insatiability and/or finitude, we might find ourselves inhabitants of Eden, with more than enough to go around. Absent scarcity, the neoclassical definition of economics loses its purchase. In a non-scarce world, what we now call economics would appear at most as a narrow field of inquiry for addressing a delimited field of policy questions – constituting but one branch of a wider (and differently defined) field of economics, rather than the entire field.

The important point to note here is that the particular object of analysis deemed appropriate by neoclassical theory (choice under conditions of scarcity) is internally constructed within theory. It does not (and cannot) exist prior to the theory it commends. Indeed, within the broad field of economics we find various contending theoretical perspectives, each with its own set of initial assumptions and, as a consequence, its own specification of what is economics. For John Maynard Keynes and his disciples, economics is hardly the science of choice under conditions of scarcity – it is instead the study of how to achieve full employment and macroeconomic stability. For Karl Marx and contemporary Marxists, economics is the study of class, which concerns who produces the social surplus, who claims it, and how this surplus is distributed throughout society.[21] This is not to say that the neoclassical vision is somehow suspect for generating its own specification of what is economics; it is rather to emphasize that this is but one specification, one that depends on its own initial assumptions. Equally important, a theory's definition of economics (and the selection of initial assumptions from which it follows) always reflects an important *normative* decision – one that must bear up under careful normative critique. And as we will see, critics of neoclassical theory argue that neoclassical theory's assumptions and definition of economics are normatively deficient.

One further preliminary matter remains. Notice that in this discussion of initial assumptions we have heard little about the role of values in economic theory. This omission was by no means accidental: neoclassical theory is self-consciously silent with respect to value judgements. We have already observed one instance of this in the severe interpersonal relativism of the theory concerning the content of preference orderings – in the economist's refusal to judge peoples' likes and dislikes. Neoclassical theory is portrayed as a value-free science of economic matters (as "positive science") in the same way that physics is taken to be a value-free science of the natural world. It is referred to as the "queen of the social sciences" precisely by virtue of the degree to which it models economic behavior and outcomes in abstract mathematical formulations that exclude disputations over values. In short, many of its adherents take neoclassical theory to more closely approximate "science" than does any other economic or social theory.

NORMATIVE MATTERS

Later we will extend this discussion of the neoclassical vision by examining just what kind of economy is deemed best – although even this cursory examination of initial assumptions leads us rather narrowly toward the free market as the ultimate form of economic organization. More immediately, we must grapple with the question of the normative criterion that these assumptions yield. The criterion is called "welfarism", and it arises in what is called "social choice" theory. As with the broader neoclassical theory, social choice theory is a complex body of theoretical propositions, technical theorems, and the like. For our purposes we can safely sidestep these details so as to uncover the rather powerful intuition underlying this technical edifice.

We first need to take account of one further definition. In the neoclassical vernacular we say an outcome (economic or otherwise) is "efficient" if no one can be made better off without making at least one other person worse off. Taking a familiar example, assume that I walk into my classroom with $100 and distribute this money equally among my students. Once this distribution is completed, the situation that obtains is efficient in the neoclassical sense. This is because any one student can be made better off at this point only if at least one other student is made worse off (e.g., if I take money away from the second to give to the first). On the other hand, if I accidentally drop $5 on the floor while making this distribution, then the situation is not efficient; in this case, one student could be made better off at no one else's expense, simply by picking up the $5 note from the floor.

Now let us consider an alternative scenario. What if, instead of distributing the money equally, I were to give all $100 to one student, leaving nothing for the others. Would this situation be efficient? Indeed it is, because the only way that one of the unfortunates could be made better off after the initial distribution is made is for me to take away some money from the lucky recipient, making her worse off. This thought experiment serves to convey a striking feature of efficiency; to say that an outcome is efficient is to say nothing at all about equity or fairness. The former is taken to be a value-free concept; the latter is deeply value-laden.

Whenever we have an efficient outcome of this sort, we say that we have achieved "Pareto optimality", or maximum social welfare. We have now entered the realm of normative matters: in the neoclassical vision, an outcome is best that achieves maximum social welfare. But what does this mean? And how can we get from the seemingly innocuous, value-free concept of efficiency to this important normative conclusion?

Welfarism and utilitarianism

Simply put, welfarism is an approach to assessing economic outcomes that is derived exclusively from the subjective states of those affected by the outcomes. Each individual is taken to be able to evaluate her own condition under alternative economic outcomes. On this basis, each individual is able to express preference among alternative social states, just as we have seen that she can express preference among alternative bundles of goods. In the case of my students just described, the one student who would receive the full $100 would surely choose that distribution (provided she is "rational") over the alternative distribution in which each student shares equally. Being rational, the individual will express preference for that social state that yields to her the greatest amount of utility or happiness.

It is easy to see how an individual ranks alternative economic outcomes. What if, however, we want to devise a ranking of economic outcomes from the perspective of society as a whole? If utility could be measured in units that were standardized across individuals, the way that income can be measured in a nation's currency, then we might proceed by adding up the utility level of each individual under each of the two outcomes. In this case, we might then designate that outcome best which yields the highest sum total of utility across all of society's members. Indeed, in the formulations of "utilitarianism" by Jeremy Bentham (1977, originally published 1776) and his successors, this was precisely the approach taken for assessing alternative states.[22] Through the early part of this century, neoclassical theory embraced this normative framework.

This approach has since been abandoned within neoclassical theory. Objectors contended that no suitable metric exists for comparing individuals' respective utility levels, insofar as levels of desire are entirely subjective and interpersonally unique. While in principle we could observe a consumer in the marketplace and, by virtue of his actual spending pattern, infer the general contours of his preference ordering, we could not in principle observe how much more or less utility he would derive from a good than would another consumer. While an individual's preference ordering could be revealed, there is no reliable mechanism for revealing *interpersonal utility comparisons* (Robbins 1938). Complicating matters further, critics of utilitarianism argue that there is no appropriate metric for comparing precise differences in utility even for one individual. Unlike in the case of measuring length, where it makes sense to say that one object is ten units (e.g. meters) longer than another, comparable comparisons of utility make no intuitive sense. The statements "I get five more units of utility from an apple than an orange" and "I like apples twice as much as oranges" are simply not taken to be useful, informative or trustworthy. As a consequence, economists came to question and ultimately abandon the kind of scale used to measure length or volume that allows for the precise measurement of differences in magnitude

– called the "cardinal" scale – for one that only allows for determination of distinctions of more or less – called the "ordinal" scale.[23]

If there exists no standardized metric for measuring each of our levels of utility, then there is no objective way to add up the utility that would accrue to society from any particular economic outcome. In this case, how can we begin to assess which of two alternative economic outcomes is best for society as a whole?

The modern neoclassical approach to the assessment of social states is called "welfarism". Welfarism is deeply rooted in the utilitarian tradition. It carries forward the utilitarian commitment to consequentialism, and its focus on peoples' subjective states as the exclusive basis for valuing outcomes. It breaks with utilitarianism only by rejecting the notion that utility can be measured in standardized units and then summed across individuals. As a result, it rejects maximum total utility as its normative desideratum.

In welfarism, the summation of utility is replaced by what is called the "Pareto criterion". We say that some outcome A is Pareto superior to some other outcome B if at least one individual in a society prefers A to B, while no one prefers B to A. In this case, only outcome A could be efficient, in the sense defined above. To return again to our earlier example, outcome B might be the case in which, while distributing the $100 to my students, I accidentally drop $5 on the floor. Outcome A would be the situation in which one student picks up the $5. In the latter outcome, no other student has been made worse off (and so none of them would have reason to prefer situation B to A), while the one quick-footed student surely favors situation A to B. In short, whenever we have an inefficient outcome – say, where unexploited opportunities for gain remain, such as when the $5 lies on the floor – there will exist at least one efficient outcome (one student picking it up) that satisfies this criterion for Pareto superiority. An outcome for which no other outcome is deemed Pareto superior is called a "Pareto optimum".

This approach is wonderfully elegant. Unfortunately, it is also largely irrelevant in actual concrete policy adjudication. Were we to survey members of a society about most non-trivial economic policies or outcomes, we would likely find that their preferences do not line up so neatly. Unlike this first scenario, we might normally expect to find that some people prefer one outcome to another, while others have the opposite preference. To return to an earlier example, some individuals might prefer to pave a wetland to build a shopping mall, while others might prefer to preserve the wetland. In such cases of preference conflict, we confront the problem that both options are efficient in the sense given to the term by neoclassical theory. Under the Pareto criterion just described, it would seem that we could say nothing in this type of case about which makes for the better economic outcome. If this is the typical kind of case, then how are we to proceed in adjudicating economic outcomes, policies and so forth?

The simplest and most commonly adopted solution to this problem has come to be known as the Kaldor–Hicks criterion, after the economists who introduced it (see Kaldor 1939 and Hicks 1939). Under this approach, outcome A is deemed Pareto superior to outcome B if those who are better off under A (the "winners") can fully compensate those who are better off under B (the "losers"), and still enjoy net benefit. In Hicks' words, there is:

> a perfectly *objective* test which enables us to discriminate between those reorganizations which improve productive efficiency and those which do not. If A is made so much better off by the change that he could compensate B for his loss, and still have something left over, then the reorganization is an unequivocal improvement.
>
> (cited in Little 1957, 92, emphasis added)

On this basis, Hicks maintains that the compensation principle substantially broadens the range of cases in which the Pareto criterion can guide policy assessment. Now, the economist can adjudicate even those policy debates over which society's members are themselves divided. Moreover, it achieves this extension without the introduction of value judgements: Hicks defends the compensation test as entirely "objective".

This latter welfarist approach, which embraces the compensation principle, plays a central role in modern policy debates over trade. For now, the general example of economic growth might serve well to illustrate the implications of this approach. Let us consider two economic outcomes facing a society, one in which there is less total output (outcome B), and one in which there is more (outcome A). Assume further that under this second outcome, although society as a whole is richer, some of society's members receive less than they did under the first. Others, obviously, have more, given that the total to be distributed has increased. Which of these outcomes (A or B) is Pareto superior, if either?

Under the first approach of welfarism, neither of these outcomes is Pareto superior, because some individuals will prefer outcome A, while others will prefer outcome B. But under the Kaldor–Hicks compensation approach we can conclude that outcome A, in which the size of the economic pie is larger, is unambiguously Pareto superior: because there is more to distribute, the winners can fully compensate the losers while still enjoying a net increase in their own income. Given the assumption of insatiability, the winners therefore enjoy a net increase in utility – a net benefit. Extending this example, we find embedded within the neoclassical vision – in the combined effect of its entry point concepts and its embrace of welfarism – a deep-seated bias in favor of efficiency and economic growth. Just as at the level of the individual more is always preferred to less, for society as a whole an economic outcome that entails more is deemed superior to one that entails less. At any given moment, then, it is imperative that the economy produces as much output as possible given the supply of available inputs, while over time, it must generate increasing output.[24]

Note that the Kaldor–Hicks criterion emphasizes *potential* as opposed to *actual* compensation in assessing rival economic outcomes. As the Hicks quote indicates, the test is not that the winner actually does fully compensate the loser, only that he can do so while still enjoying net benefit. Kaldor and Hicks justify potential as opposed to actual compensation by focusing on the cumulative impact of a series of policy choices over time. They suggest that while any given individual might suffer from any particular Pareto superior policy choice, she is likely to be a winner "on average over all [Pareto superior] policy moves" (Zajac 1995).[25]

Seemingly less problematic is the case in which full compensation actually occurs, of course.[26] After full compensation, the initial losers under A become indifferent between the two outcomes, while the winners prefer A due to the existence of the net benefit. In this case, then, we are returned to the first welfarist approach, in which conflict among society's members is absent.

Welfarism and the neoclassical vision

As the example of growth indicates, welfarism fits neatly with the entry point concepts founding the neoclassical vision. First, welfarism appears to free economists from the burden of making value judgements. The welfarist assesses economic states exclusively by reference to the values of the individuals affected by those states, "without even asking what those values are" (Sugden 1993, 1951). This carries forward the agnosticism of neoclassical vision with respect to the content of people's preference orderings – it is deemed to be none of the economist's business what it is that brings people satisfaction. The economist passes no normative judgement on what it is that people desire. That something is desired is reason enough to give it value in the economist's ledger. Whether a desire is valid and whether it should be validated by the economy are matters for others to decide – not for the economic scientist. *Having constructed economic actors as rational, the economist has no grounds for judging their judgements* (cf. Tool 1979).

Second, this form of welfarism does not permit interpersonal utility comparisons, as we have seen. We cannot say whether redistribution of a fixed sum that benefits some but harms others would be Pareto superior, because we have no metric for assessing whether the increased welfare of those who would gain thereby more than offsets the lost welfare of those who would lose. Together with the choice of peoples' subjective states (utility levels) as the sole basis for assessing outcomes, this ban on interpersonal utility comparisons has a profound consequence. Neoclassical theory (and the broader neoclassical vision) is ambivalent about the vexing matter of inequality. If an extreme example might be permitted: "Would society be better off if the government were to redistribute $100,000 of a billionaire's fortune to a program that inoculates poor children, thereby improving their health and maybe even saving lives?" The liberal's affirmative response comes quickly, of course. Let us pursue this question, however, within the framework of neoclassical theory. Assuming that our billionaire prefers to have this money rather than not, we must conclude that he would suffer harm were he to be deprived of this $100,000. How would this loss of utility compare with the increased utility of those who would be inoculated? Well, the absence of any metric for making such comparisons forces the conclusion that we simply cannot say. While there may be good ethical or other reasons for undertaking this redistribution – something that the community at large might consider when debating such matters – from the strict welfarist standpoint, we cannot conclude that society's social welfare has increased thereby. It may be that the billionaire has such a massive fortune precisely because he gains tremendous satisfaction from each and every last dollar earned, so that the deprivation of even this relatively small sum would cause him tremendous despair![27]

These commitments and their consequences are treated as commonsensical in the neoclassical tradition, so that they need no defending. For instance, concerned about the state of economic knowledge in the US today, the Federal Reserve Bank of Minneapolis (1998) contracted with an independent research organization to conduct an "Economic Literacy Survey". The bank reported the results in its December 1998 issue of *The Region*. It found the mean score of 45 per cent on this multiple-choice exam to be telling. But far more instructive are the questions and "correct" answers it provided. For present purposes, we should consider question two: "What is the most important task of all economies?" The four possible answers provided by the bank are:

(a) To balance imports and exports.
(b) To balance the government's budget.
(c) To make the best use of scarce resources.
(d) To save money to reduce the national debt.

Driven by the logic of neoclassical theory, the bank has no difficulty identifying "c" as the correct answer. It defends the answer with the following explanation:

> The economic wants of people in any society are virtually limitless. Resources are scarce; thus, every economic system must choose how to make the most efficient use of its scarce resources to produce those goods and services it desires or needs most.

This answer and explanation are dictated by the welfarist commitments of neoclassical theory. What is particularly notable is that the question of equality is not even raised in any of the possible answers provided. As we will see, many non-neoclassical economists, political theorists and others would argue that the most important task facing at least some economies is to ensure that all of society's members receive a fair share of the total social output, or to overcome poverty. Evidently, they would not only be mistaken, but their holding such views would signify their economic illiteracy! These kinds of answers are entirely suppressed in neoclassical theory by its attachment to value-free science, and the initial assumptions that operationalize this attachment.[28]

This is not to say that neoclassical economists are callous in the face of inequality and privation. It is to claim that neoclassical theory provides little guidance for addressing such matters, and indeed represents an obstacle to egalitarian projects. Given the goal of achieving value-free science, this consequence ought not to be surprising: the matter of inequality, and of what kind of distribution is inherently just, is by necessity value-laden.

The neoclassical vision and distribution

What, then, if anything, does the neoclassical vision have to say about distribution – about how the social product of an enterprise, community, nation, or even the world as a whole should be divided among various claimants? The simplest answer might be that this is taken largely to be a non-economic question, as the above discussion suggests. This is, however, only part of the story. For there exists in the neoclassical vision an implicit commitment to a particular structure of distribution. This commitment might be summed up as *"in the first instance, to each according to her contribution"*.

"According to her contribution"

When we go to work, we contribute not only to our own welfare, but also to the welfare of all of society. After all, by dint of our labor and other non-labor contributions, we increase total output, so that there is more for all of us to share. We do not all make equal contributions, however. By virtue of our particular skills, work disposition and habits, and our accumulated non-labor endowments, such as savings, land, and other resources, each of us makes a unique net contribution to society's total output. Those of us who have invested the time, sweat and energy to build our knowledge and skills (our "human capital"), and those who have sacrificed consumption opportunities to amass savings for investment, make larger contributions to total output. In contrast, those of us who have resisted opportunities for self-improvement, and/or who have accumulated little land or savings, hardly make a contribution at all.

The implicit distributional commitment of the neoclassical vision is that each of us should be compensated in direct measure to our net contribution. Those with higher "productivity" should receive higher reward. There are two principal claims involved here, an intrinsic and an instrumental claim. The intrinsic claim is that it is right that those who contribute more should receive higher rewards, as just compensation for their beneficial behaviors. This is a strong normative claim, and it is not one that all neoclassical economists would be comfortable making. It is associated especially with those economists who are most influenced by the philosophy of John Locke and by libertarianism, such as the Austrian school of economics (e.g. Ludwig von Mises and Frederick Hayek), but also many Chicago school neoclassicals (e.g. Milton Friedman).

Locke (1690) argues that a person has an inherent right to own that which she creates – both directly through her own labor, and indirectly through the capital she employs to hire the labor of others. Locke reaches this important normative conclusion on the basis of a simple intuitive argument. First, Locke contends that "every Man has a *Property* in his own *Person*. This no Body has any Right to but himself" (cited in MacPherson 1962, 200). This is a natural right that cannot be legitimately abridged by society or government. Second, man has a right to attempt to survive, and this can only be accomplished by appropriating for himself elements of nature. He achieves this by "mixing" his labor with nature, thereby transforming it into necessary goods. Hence, though nature is provided to mankind in common, the act of individual labor provides the normative foundation for individual appropriation. Each person acquires the exclusive right to possess and consume that which his own labor has created. In Locke's words, "The *Labour* of his Body, and the *Work* of his Hands, we may say, are properly his" (cited in MacPherson 1962, 200).

Locke extends this right of property to include that output produced by the labor of others whom one has hired. He reaches this conclusion by emphasizing that the right of property in one's own person and labor must entail the right to alienate it to others through voluntary exchange. In this respect, one's labor is no different from other property. As MacPherson argues:

> To Locke a man's labour is so unquestionably his own property that he may freely sell it for wages. A freeman may sell to another "for a certain time, the Service he undertakes to do, in exchange for Wages he is to receive." The labour thus sold becomes the property of the buyer, who is then entitled to appropriate the produce of that labour. Hence, the income that flows to the owner of capital is also taken to be inherently just.
> (MacPherson 1962, 215)

The modern libertarian view of distribution is consistent with these Lockean propositions. In this view, any distribution of a society's output is just provided only that it arises from legitimate processes. As prominent libertarian Robert Nozick argues, "The complete principle of distributive justice would say simply that a distribution is just if it arises from another (just) distribution by legitimate means" (Nozick 1974, 151). Presuming a just, prior distribution – that is, one that did not arise via the infringement of peoples' rights – the outcome of a series of voluntary exchanges between free individuals must also be deemed just, regardless of the patterns of distribution that follow therefrom. If those who make the greatest contribution are able to secure through voluntary exchange a greater reward, then the inequality that results therefrom is entirely just. Indeed, from this perspective, government initiatives to redistribute income in pursuit of greater equality are read as unjust, insofar as they "violate persons' rights not to be forced to do certain things" (Nozick 1974, ix, quoted in Zajac 1995) such as sacrifice their rightfully acquired property.

Those neoclassical economists who refrain from the intrinsic argument summarized here nevertheless endorse the instrumental (or efficiency) argument for tying reward to contribution. By rewarding most those who make the largest contribution, we provide a powerful incentive for each of us to undertake behaviors that are ultimately in the interests of all of society. A low-waged janitor with the appropriate mental capacities has an incentive to seek an engineering degree; if successful, she will earn a higher private reward in the form of a higher salary, but will also make a much higher net contribution to total output. Society as a whole benefits from her pursuit of greater private reward.

"In the first instance"

Of course, many in society produce nothing at all, either during portions of their lives (when they are infants or elderly, or when they are infirmed), or during their entire lives (if they are in some way incapacitated in ways that prevent "productive" work). Few neoclassicals (if any) would argue for their complete exclusion from a share of total social output. Presumably, all of us share a commitment to taking care of those who cannot provide for themselves; beneficence toward the "deserving poor" is widely accepted today among advocates of most theoretical perspectives.[29]

What degree of provisioning should society make for the unproductive? To what rewards are they entitled? Here, the neoclassical vision provides little guidance, for this question is seen to lie squarely in the domain of value judgements. Instrumental (efficiency) arguments still apply, of course: in cases where the unproductive can be made productive, the argument can be advanced that a sufficient distribution should be made to effect this (re)habilitation. In this case, value-neutrality might be (apparently) preserved via the recommendation of the use of cost–benefit analysis as the appropriate, scientific means for making this judgement. But this then would be seen as the non-normative matter of determining just what distribution to the unproductive will generate an efficient, Pareto optimal outcome. Beyond this, neoclassical theory has little to say.

CONCLUSION

In this chapter we have seen how neoclassical theory builds from a simple set of entry-point concepts to its chief normative criterion of welfarism.

Welfarism is seen to provide a basis for adjudicating among alternative economic outcomes by relying exclusively on the subjective states of the economic actors who are affected by those outcomes. Taken to be rational choosers, with well-defined, exogenously given preference orderings, these agents are deemed to know best what is in their interest. Hence, the economist has no warrant for assessing their judgements.

Welfarism is therefore understood by its adherents to be a normative criterion that is largely value-free. This virtue makes it ideally suited to the project of neoclassical theory, which strives to achieve the status of science largely by eschewing value judgements. To say that an outcome is Pareto optimal, for instance, is only to say that it is efficient – it is not to say anything at all about whether it is also fair.

We turn now to the matter of what kind of economic system best accords with the opening assumptions, logic and welfarist normative framework of the neoclassical vision. We will find that this apparatus generates an analytically elegant and compelling defense of the free market as the optimal economic arrangement. Following this demonstration, we will undertake a critical examination of welfarism. We will see why most normative theorists find its failings to be fatal.

2   Welfarism and the market

INTRODUCTION

In Chapter 1 we explored the initial assumptions of neoclassical theory. Here we will see how those initial assumptions are worked up into a rather rigid set of conclusions about how the economy – any and every economy – should be structured. For the moment, we will consider an individual, isolated economy – one that is not integrated with others – so that we can concentrate on the logic of the theory in its simplest form. In Part 2 we will see that the arguments presented here regarding any individual economy apply with equal force to the global economy. This is not surprising: what is particularly striking and, for many, attractive about the neoclassical vision is the elegance with which it moves from this simple collection of initial assumptions to its powerful, universal policy conclusions. Yet for its detractors, this elegance reflects its severe reductionism, which they reject.

This chapter concludes with a presentation of a wide-ranging normative critique of welfarism and the idealized free market. The critique interrogates the purported objectivity of neoclassical theory. As we will see, critics contend that social science cannot be value-free, and that the pursuit of this kind of science is bound to lead neoclassical visionaries to commit basic normative errors. The critique then turns to the reductionism of neoclassical theory, as it plays a substantial part in debates over the nature of global economic integration.

Let us recall briefly the initial assumptions we encountered above. The first two pertain to human nature and capacities. Humans are endowed with the ability to choose rationally from among the sets of opportunities that they face. The qualifier of rationality is the key proposition here, as we have seen. It implies that human nature is marked by an egoistic orientation reflected in the pursuit of maximum personal satisfaction or utility. Unpacking this concept, we found the further assumptions of the existence of a well-ordered, exogenous preference ordering, reflecting a person's individuality; a boundless rapaciousness; and the law of diminishing marginal utility. While neoclassical theory has a good bit to say about the structure of preference orderings, it has nothing at all to say about their content. The latter is taken to be an entirely private affair, one that lies beyond the reach of normative judgement by the economist.

Humans are also endowed with the ability to transform nature through labor so as to produce goods that meet human needs, and they do so rationally. Rationality implies that humans will adopt the best available means for production, which we call technology.

The third assumption concerns the attributes of physical nature: we only receive output from the investment of inputs, and since nature's bounty is finite, output (over any given period of time) must also be finite. Combined with the assumption of insatiable desires, we see that the finitude of nature ensures that output will also always be scarce. All human actions therefore entail an opportunity cost, and choosing in the face of such costs is taken to be a defining, ineradicable feature of the human condition. It follows that economics is to be understood as the science of choice under conditions of scarcity.

We took note of one further building block of neoclassical theory – not so much an initial assumption as a self-understanding which, as such, shapes the theory's conclusions every bit as much as do these assumptions. Neoclassical theory strives to the status of "science", as that term is commonly understood. Following Friedman (1953), neoclassical theory is taken by its practitioners to be value-free in the way that physics and chemistry are taken to be value-free. Neoclassicals emphasize the legitimacy of the positive–normative distinction, holding, that is, that one can explain the object of analysis (a molecule or an economy) simply as it is, free from any judgements about what it should be. Targeting the first rather than the second of these enterprises – the positive as opposed to the normative – neoclassical theory believes itself to avoid difficult value judgements. We took note of the key strategies by which this avoidance is secured, including its studied agnosticism regarding the content of preference orderings, its ban on interpersonal utility comparisons, and its related selection of welfarism as its chief principle of normative assessment.

INSTITUTIONAL COMMITMENTS: CELEBRATING THE MARKET

We can now proceed to the chief question of this chapter, namely, what kind of economic system (if any) is deemed best within the neoclassical vision, and how is this institutional endorsement secured? How do we move from this simple set of initial assumptions to this kind of policy conclusion?

We must begin, of course, by assuming an economy populated by the kind of rational actors specified in the initial assumptions of neoclassical theory. Each is a bundle of unfulfilled desires upon which she is prepared to act in making rational choices. The respective preferences of each actor are also unique. In the aggregate, society's members want a good many *different* things. Ideally, it would seem, we would then want an economy that provides each actor with maximum opportunity to make those choices that will provide her with personal satisfaction. By necessity, this must be an economy where a very large number of choices are available. These choices must range over what it is that we want to consume (an orange or an apple), and what it is we want to be (a doctor or a secretary). It must, however, also be an economy that protects our relative autonomy; to the degree possible, my decision must be independent of yours. That I prefer apples to oranges should not preclude your choosing oranges instead. It would then seem that we would want a thoroughly decentralized economy, where the preference ordering of each consumer is determinative of her own choices.

Even at this preliminary point, we can see that we are moving away from the pole of central planning, or any other sort of government direction of economic affairs, toward some sort of market economy. A market economy certainly seems to provide agents with a high degree of relative autonomy in their economic behavior: you are free to choose oranges without obstructing my pursuit of apples. Nevertheless we face a potential problem with the market that must be overcome before we can crown it the optimal form of economic organization. Recall that each of us is posited in the neoclassical vision to be essentially egoistic, driven to pursue his own personal welfare rather than the good of society. We are essentially rather unattractive, Hobbesian sorts of creature, capable of rather malevolent social behaviors. Unless constrained to do otherwise, the kinds of agents described in the opening assumptions of neoclassical theory might be expected to do more harm than good in pursuit of their own maximal pleasure. A market economy that provides economic actors with a high degree of relative autonomy in pursuit of maximum utility might therefore also unintentionally provide maximal space for social harm.

The ideal economic institution must be one that can somehow cope with this drive toward self-oriented behavior, so as to generate socially benevolent outcomes. *What kind of institution could possibly do that?* Organized religions try, of course, by re-shaping peoples' preferences so that they seek the right ends (God's grace, compassion, benevolence, etc.). This mission entails firm value judgements about what are appropriate preferences and is, for that reason, foreclosed to neoclassical economists who refuse this kind of normative assessment. Neoclassicals must search instead for some sort of economic system that secures the social good by exploiting rather than resisting our deepest personal motivations.

We can readily see that a market economy allows for maximum individual choice and personal autonomy, but can it also do *this*? Can it also marshal our individual pursuits into socially benevolent outcomes? That neoclassical theory can answer this question affirmatively is perhaps its greatest theoretical achievement, one with tremendous political and ideological import. To see how it generates this answer, we need to take a moment to investigate its view of this magnificent institution, the market.

The market brings together two kinds of economic actor: consumers and firms. Consumers come to the market with some medium of exchange, or what we call money.[30] They also come with their preferences, in pursuit of maximum satisfaction given the constraint imposed by their incomes. In the market consumers confront firms, which come ready to supply the goods and services that they desire. When firms supply these goods, they are not enacting some moral obligation to meet social needs, or even some government mandate to provision society. Instead, they seek maximum return on their investments – maximum profit. A market exists whenever and wherever these two actors transact – be it in the town square, shopping mall, or over the Internet.

Based on the initial assumptions of the theory, what can we say about the behavior of these two kinds of actor? Well, it turns out that we can say quite a bit. The first dozen or so chapters of every introductory textbook in microeconomics undertake to answer this question; for our purposes, we can summarize the conclusions simply. Before we do, however, we need to make two further assumptions. The first concerns technology; the second, market structure.

Ancillary assumptions

Neoclassical theory assumes what is called the "law of diminishing marginal returns". This law states that as production of a good is increased (using available technology) over a short run period, the cost of each additional (marginal) unit produced will be higher than that of the previous units. For instance, consider an automobile manufacturing firm that has been producing the same number of automobiles per week for an extended period of time. Being a rational profit maximizer, we know that the firm has been using the optimal mix of machinery and labor, or that mix which minimizes the firm's per unit cost of production. Now assume that a decision is reached on a particular Monday that the firm should increase production for that week, perhaps because of an unanticipated increase in consumer demand. Under these circumstances, the firm will not have sufficient time to install new machinery, or to build a bigger factory; nor will it want to. All it can do is to try to run its existing machinery longer, and this will entail an increasing use of labor. As the firm was previously operating at the optimal input mix, the increase in the labor–capital ratio will reduce efficiency. The net effect will be that each additional unit of labor allocated to production will yield less net contribution to output. Hence, each extra car produced that week will cost more. The technical way of saying this is that in the short run the "marginal cost" (the extra cost of each unit) rises as production increases. This relation between marginal cost and output does not hold in the long run, because the firm can decide to change its scale of operations (e.g. adding more machinery) to adjust to the change in production quantity.

Markets come in many forms, from what are called "perfectly competitive" to "concentrated". The former requires a large number of relatively small sellers and buyers – so many, in fact, that none of them alone can influence the broader market. Instead, each takes the existing market price as given. Perfect competition also requires that firms are free to enter and leave the market without restriction, such as would exist in the presence of patent or licensing requirements. Each supplier produces and sells a homogenous product, leaving consumers indifferent among the output of different firms (there are no brand names). Finally, perfect competition entails the assumption of "perfect information". This means that all market actors have complete information about not only prices but also the best available production techniques. If any one firm discovers a new technology, the new technical knowledge is instantaneously transmitted to all other firms (which, in the absence of patents, immediately exploit it). Where these conditions are not met – where for instance one firm is so large relative to the market that it exerts effective market power – we say that there exists a "market imperfection".

Market imperfections are often problematic, for reasons that will become clear in what follows. Hence, just as with most textbooks, we will examine the functioning of the perfectly competitive market first, to discover the general virtues that the neoclassical vision associates with the market generally. Subsequently we can return to the matter of market imperfections, to see how they complicate the general picture, and what (in the neoclassical view) can and should be done about them.

The market and social welfare

In the market, consumers allocate their budgets so that they receive the maximum utility that their money can buy, given existing market prices. As the price of any one good rises, all else being equal, they will generally buy less of that good while increasing their purchase of other goods. This is because the good whose price has risen now provides less utility per dollar. Hence we find an inverse relationship between a good's price (P) and the quantity demanded (Q). This important relationship is captured in the downward sloping "demand curve" (D), a curve that shows the quantity of a good that consumers will purchase at any given price (see Figure 2.1). Firms respond to price changes in the opposite way. If the price of a good rises, all else being equal, firms will supply more. The simplest intuition behind this proposition is that firms earn a higher profit as the price rises. There is a more precise reason, however, which is not intuitively obvious: the firm's marginal cost curve is its supply curve (S).

We know that the firm's marginal costs increase with production in the short run, due to the law of diminishing marginal returns. If we graph the relationship between the quantity produced and the marginal cost, we generate an upward sloping curve. Being rational, the firm will produce that level of output which maximizes its profits. What is that quantity? The firm

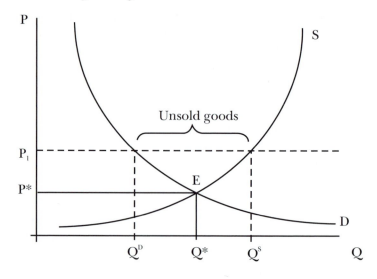

Figure 2.1 Market demand and supply

increases its profit whenever it produces a unit with a marginal cost that is lower than the market price. In contrast, it loses profit on each unit for which the marginal cost is greater than the market price. It follows that the firm should increase production until the marginal cost of the last unit produced just equals the market price (where MC = P). This implies, however, that the firm's marginal cost curve is its supply curve, as it gives us the quantity that the rational firm will choose to supply at any given market price. Hence the supply curve is upward sloping (see Figure 2.1).

Taken together, the behavior of these two kinds of actors yields a startling conclusion. *Left to its own devices, without any government involvement, the perfectly competitive market will gravitate to that level of output and price that is socially optimal.* This extraordinary finding is often unappreciated by the audiences of undergraduates to whom it is delivered, partly because of confusion surrounding the technical proof, but also because the conclusion is so widely taken for granted even by the economically uninitiated. But we can safely say this: *this is the most important and powerful conclusion of any social science, in the history of the modern social sciences.* There has never been another conclusion that has been so widely taken as true, or has so dramatically shaped social institutions. This conclusion underlies economic and social policies across the globe today and is thereby shaping the life chances for the billions of people who inhabit it. Hence it bears careful consideration.

In a given market, we call the price charged by suppliers for a particular good the "market" price. We need not concern ourselves with how this price came about; we must concentrate instead on what happens next. Let us assume that, at this market price, the demand for this good emanating from consumers is less than the quantity that the firms have supplied. This will occur at any price above P* in the graph, such as P_1. At P_1, we can see moving along the dashed horizontal line that the quantity that consumers are prepared to purchase (Q_D), given by the demand curve, is less than the quantity that firms are prepared to produce (Q_S), which is given by the supply curve. As members of market societies, we know very well what then transpires: facing crammed shelves of unsold goods, firms reduce the price in order to move the goods. We call this a "sale". Consumers find advertisements in the local papers, and as the price falls, more utility-maximizing consumers decide to include more of this good in their purchasing decisions. As a consequence, the firms' surpluses fall as the market price falls.

There is no science to pricing, however – suppliers can't check consumer demand data in the local papers – and so it is likely that the price reduction is not exactly right. Either the price decrease is too small, leaving firms with a lingering surplus, or it is too large, so that firms cannot keep up with the increased consumer demand. In the first case, firms will then lower the price again so as to clear out the oversupply (while planning reduced production runs). In the latter case, firms will raise the price to increase profits.[31]

A market may be thought of as a mechanism of price and quantity adjustment, then, where price falls whenever supply is greater than demand, and where it rises under the opposite condition. If this process works properly, a price should eventually be discovered at which a notable event occurs: the quantity that consumers are prepared to buy at that price exactly matches the quantity that firms are prepared to sell. This is the famous point of "market equilibrium", represented graphically by the intersection of the supply and demand curves in Figure 2.1 (marked "E"). In Figure 2.1, the equilibrium price and quantity are designated P* and Q*, respectively. There is much to be said for this equilibrium.

Notice first that at P* there is no unmet need emanating from consumers: all those who want to buy *at this price* can do so. Similarly, there is no unintended, unsold inventory: firms have sold all that they produced. There is neither shortage (requiring consumers to queue for a scarce good) nor surplus (requiring firms to reduce supply). This means, however, that there is no incentive for firms or consumers to change their behaviors; absent surplus or shortage, the market is at rest (hence the designation "equilibrium"). Over the next period (be it a day, week or month), the price of this good and the quantity sold will remain the same. Only outside "shocks" to this market, such as a change in the costs of production of this good (which will shift the supply curve) or the introduction into the market of a competing good (which will shift the demand curve), will force an adjustment in this market.

Our immediate concern is not with the neoclassical treatment of the technical aspects of the market, but with the more important social functions that it is performing. When a consumer considers whether and how much of a good to buy at a particular price, he is actually conducting a *cost–benefit analysis*. "Will the pleasure I receive from buying a unit of this good", he must ask, "be greater than the pleasure I would receive were I instead to buy any other good of the same cost in the market?" The consumer therefore always considers the opportunity cost of making this purchase. If he does make the purchase, it is because (being rational) he has determined that the benefit of so doing outweighs the cost he incurs in the form of foregone pleasure from the next best available good. If he buys more than one unit of a particular good, then we can infer that despite the law of diminishing marginal utility, the last unit purchased brings him greater pleasure than would the purchase of another good (or collection of goods) of the same cost. For the sake of comparison, we might take the price he is willing to pay for each unit of a good to be a monetary measure of the benefit he receives from each unit of this good. If he would be willing to pay $2 for the first apple and $1.50 for the second, then we can infer that he will receive $2 worth of satisfaction from the first, and $1.50 from the second.[32] Given that "marginal" means extra, the amount a consumer is willing to pay for each unit can be taken as the "marginal personal benefit" he will receive from that unit.

Just as each individual does this, so will society as a whole. When we observe that consumers as a group are willing to buy one more unit of a good at a certain price, we may infer that they are receiving that much "marginal social benefit" (MSB) from that unit.[33] Hence, we may take the market price of any good to reflect the MSB that society will receive from the last unit purchased of that good. If society is willing to buy 5,000 apples at a price of $1.50, then the MSB of the last apple purchased is $1.50. Insofar as the demand curve tells us how much society is willing to purchase at any particular price, we can think of this curve as the MSB curve (see Figure 2.2).

But we can say more. The price of the good also represents the opportunity cost of producing it. When a firm undertakes to build a bicycle for sale, it must pay for labor, raw materials, energy, and other inputs. As each of these resources is limited (we know that nature is finite by the third assumption of neoclassical theory), society faces an opportunity cost when the bicycle is produced. The opportunity cost of building a bicycle is equal to the MSB that would have been attained from the other goods that could have been produced with these same resources. When the bicycle is built, the firm must charge a price that incorporates all these resource costs; otherwise it would lose money in selling the bicycle. Assuming sufficient competition in the bicycle market, such as would exist under the assumptions of perfect competition, the market price will just cover these costs. A firm that tries to charge a price higher than this will be competed out of business by other firms. Taken together, these two conditions suggest that we can think of the market supply curve as the good's marginal social cost (MSC) curve – it shows us the opportunity cost to society of producing each additional unit of the good. Hence, the supply curve is marked MSC (see Figure 2.2).

Let us consider carefully just what all this means. For any particular unit of a good, the associated point on the demand curve indicates its value to society, its MSB, while the associated point on the supply curve indicates the

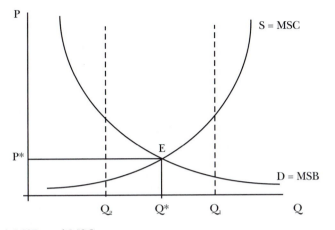

Figure 2.2 MSB and MSC

opportunity cost of producing it, its "marginal social cost" (MSC). The market may therefore be thought of as an institution for comparing (marginal) costs and benefits. If the price of a good is higher than what people are willing to pay for the last unit produced, this indicates that the opportunity cost of producing that last unit is greater than its social benefit. Less of this good should be produced, given society's preferences, and under the operation of the market, *less will be.* The market, acting on its own without need or benefit of government direction or dictate, will reduce production of any good that is using up too much of society's scarce resources. Conversely, a good for which a shortage exists at the market price is one that is being undersupplied from a cost–benefit perspective, because the shortage signals that the MSB of the last unit purchased is greater than the MSC of producing it. In a market economy, however, there is no need for us to worry: by itself, the market will ensure that more is produced to rectify this misallocation of resources.

What can we say of equilibrium? *At the equilibrium quantity, the value that society places on the last unit produced is exactly equal to the opportunity cost of producing it.* This is indicated by the intersection of the MSB and MSC curves. And this, it turns out, is *precisely the optimal level of output* from the perspective of society as a whole, given the preferences of its consumers. To see this, let us assume that from an initial position of equilibrium in the market for bread, the government decides to try to enhance social welfare by mandating that more bread be produced. Let us assume that the government directs bakers to produce the quantity of bread indicated in Figure 2.2 by Q_1, which is to the right of the market equilibrium, Q^*. We know, however, that society will receive less extra benefit from each unit produced because of the law of diminishing marginal utility. At the same time, by the law of diminishing marginal returns, we know that it will face a rising opportunity cost for each additional unit. If the MSB and MSC of bread were equal at the equilibrium quantity, they surely will diverge at quantities above equilibrium. Above this quantity, the MSC of producing each additional unit will exceed the MSB derived from it, measured in terms of what society is willing to pay (to see this, compare the MSB and MSC along the dashed vertical line at Q_1). Hence, despite its noble intent, the government initiative has led to a diminution in social welfare. The resources that were exhausted to produce all the bread beyond Q^* could have been better used in the production of other goods.

What of the reverse situation? What if the government decides that too many cigarettes are being produced and it issues a production limit at a lower quantity than that associated with the market equilibrium? In this case, at the lower level of production the MSB of the last cigarette produced exceeds the MSC of producing it (see Q_2 in Figure 2.2). In this case, social welfare could be enhanced by increasing cigarette production back toward the equilibrium quantity.[34] Once again, the government intervention has reduced rather than increased social welfare.

The government might also seek to improve upon the market equilibrium by legislating the price of a good rather than quantity. For example, concerned about price inflation in housing, a municipality might implement rent control to prevent low-income people from being forced out of their homes. In this case, the government simply imposes a "price ceiling", below the market equilibrium price, above which rents are not allowed to rise. This is indicated by P_1 in Figure 2.3. What does our neoclassical model of the market suggest will come of this initiative? Given the new, artificially low price, suppliers of apartments (such as developers and building owners) will supply fewer housing units to the market than they would at equilibrium, while consumers will demand more. We see this by tracing along the horizontal line from P_1 to the supply and demand curves, respectively. The gap between these two curves at P_1 indicates the existence of a housing shortage at the new, artificially low price. Hence, rent control creates the problem of involuntary homelessness where no such problem had previously existed.

Now let us consider a market not for output, but for labor, an input. In this case, workers represent the supply side of the market, selling their labor power, while firms represent the demand side of the market. A law to impose a "price floor" in the labor market, a minimum wage, might be motivated by a desire to increase the wages of the working poor above that associated with the market equilibrium. The effect of this misguided measure, however, will be to generate unemployment: at the higher, imposed wage, more people are willing to work (given that the reward for doing so is now higher), but firms will reduce employment in order to reduce their labor costs.[35] To see this, assume that Figure 2.3 reflects the labor market, and consider any imposed price above P^* (such as P_2).

These examples reveal that any government-induced movement away from the market equilibrium will reduce social welfare. The free market, entirely on its own, finds that quantity at which the MSB equals the MSC of the last unit

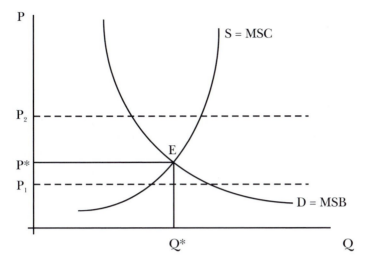

Figure 2.3 Price ceiling and price floor

produced. As we've now seen, this is the quantity that generates maximum social welfare. The market is thus an extraordinarily efficient cost–benefit mechanism, one that requires no government research, no extensive consumer or producer surveys – indeed, a mechanism that is essentially free. Once market prices have been established, each individual consumer is free to conduct her own cost–benefit analysis, to determine how much of each good to buy at the market price. Being rational, as we have seen, she will choose just that mix of goods that maximizes her own utility, subject to the constraint imposed by her budget. Once each consumer has made her choices, it can be shown that the outcome is Pareto optimal – that no one can be made better off without making at least one other person worse off.[36] The market has generated the sort of efficiency so highly prized by neoclassical welfarism, *all by itself*.

One additional point remains to be made. In the market economy, though the firm is the *proximate* agent of production, consumers *ultimately* determine all production decisions. Unlike planned economies, production in a market economy will occur only if it is validated in the market, by virtue of the autonomous, private decisions that consumers make. Firms that do not produce precisely what consumers desire simply will not survive. We therefore say that the consumers are "sovereign", casting their dollar ballots in the marketplace just as they cast their political ballots in the voting booth. Indeed, people exert more effective control over the economy in their role as consumers than they do over the government in their role as citizens. This is because in the marketplace they can vote directly for what they want, without reliance on an undependable intermediary (a politician); they can register the strength of their desires by concentrating their purchases (voting many times rather than once); and they can disaggregate their votes so as to buy just that mix of goods that will yield maximum satisfaction, rather than being forced to buy a mix of goods (policies) all at once by voting for one candidate who best approximates (always imperfectly) their bundle of political preferences (Seneca and Taussig 1984).

I stated above that the claim that the market on its own will find that level of price and output that is socially optimal, is the most powerful proposition in the history of the modern social sciences. I should now add that the simple market diagram used here is the most powerful analytical device in all of the social sciences. Extraordinarily elegant, it almost single-handedly bears the full analytical weight of sustaining the neoclassical vision. This device follows directly from the entry-point concepts of neoclassical theory, and reflects its normative commitments to welfarism. To understand this diagram, then, is to grasp in large measure the neoclassical celebration of neoliberalism.

The market and distribution

We have said nothing so far about how the market distributes total social output across economic actors. Just as there is a market for each kind of output – each good and service – so also is there a market for each particular kind of input, or resource. These include, for example, land (of various sorts and qualities), labor (of various skills), and capital. Each of these is taken to contribute to output. In a market economy, these input markets serve as the vehicle that distributes the total social product. What is it, then, that governs the relative shares that flow to the agents who supply these resources?

We noted in Chapter 1 that neoclassical theory endorses the distributive principle "in the first instance, to each according to its contribution". We saw there that this is taken to be socially beneficial, as it generates increasing social welfare. For example, earning a wage commensurate with her productivity encourages a worker to seek additional education and training. As she does so, she makes a larger social contribution. So the question that arises is whether the market brings about this outcome.[37]

The fortunate answer furnished by neoclassical theory is that it does indeed. The example of the labor market will suffice to demonstrate the logic of the theory in this regard. In this market, the equilibrium wage is determined by the interaction of supply and demand, just as in all other markets. Also, as we have just seen in our discussion of the price floor, suppliers are not firms but individuals in pursuit of income, while firms that hire labor constitute the demand side of the market.

The initial assumptions of neoclassical theory tightly constrain the behavior of these two kinds of actor. On the supply side, each hour of labor entails a foregone hour of leisure; given the law of diminishing marginal utility, each extra hour of leisure foregone entails a greater relative sacrifice. Hence, a worker will only increase his working time if the wage per hour rises. We therefore find that the labor supply curve is upward sloping: a higher wage induces a greater willingness to work.[38] On the demand side, the opposite relation holds: firms will hire less labor as the wage increases. Facing a rising wage, firms will undertake to find other substitutes for labor in order to reduce costs, perhaps by introducing labor-saving machinery.

We also know that as a firm tries to increase its output in the short run by hiring more labor, the value of the extra output (the so-called "marginal revenue product") of each additional worker will fall, given the law of diminishing marginal returns (see above). For example, while the third worker hired by a pen manufacturer might increase total output by six pens per hour, the contribution of the fourth worker might be only five pens per hour. If the firm sells each pen at a market price of $2.00, then the marginal revenue product of the third worker will be $12.00 per hour (six units times $2.00 per unit), while the marginal revenue product of the fourth worker will be only $10.00 per hour. Figure 2.4 presents a marginal revenue product of labor (MRP_L) curve, which shows the relationship between the level of employment (on the horizontal axis) and the marginal contribution of each worker, measured in dollars (on the vertical axis). The curve has a downward slope that reflects the law of diminishing marginal returns.

Facing a marginal revenue product of labor curve of this form, we can investigate how the firm will make its decision regarding the number of workers to hire. Continuing the present example, we can be sure that the firm will hire the fourth worker, with a marginal product of $10, only if the market wage is $10 per hour or less. So long as the market wage remains even

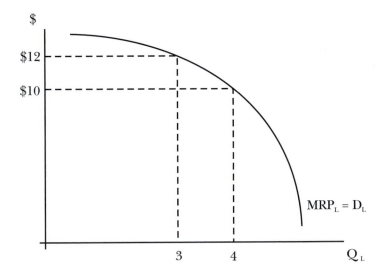

Figure 2.4 The marginal revenue product of labor and the demand curve for labor

a fraction below $10 per hour, the firm increases its profits by hiring this extra (or marginal) worker. Being rational, we can be certain that the firm will do so. This also means that the marginal revenue product of labor curve is also the firm's demand curve for labor (D_L): it shows us, after all, the quantity of labor that the rational firm will hire at any given market wage.

A terribly consequential result follows, however. By hiring workers until the last (marginal) worker taken on makes a net contribution to the firm just at (or slightly above) the market wage, the firm serves as the principal cog in a distribution system in which labor is paid in direct proportion to its (marginal) productivity. While it would be irrational for a firm to hire at the $10 market wage a worker whose contribution to the firm (whose marginal productivity) will be less than $10, so would it be irrational to stop hiring so long as the marginal worker's contribution is above $10. In short, the equilibrium market wage will equal the productivity of the last worker hired. As a group, then, all laborers earn a wage equal to their marginal productivity – not because the government dictated this outcome, but automatically as a result of market forces.

Applying the very same logic, we find that all other contributors to production also earn a reward equal to the marginal productivity of the factor they supply. The rent that flows to the landlord and the interest that flows to the lenders are equal to the marginal productivity of the last unit of the input that each supplied. *Each, then, receives a reward dictated by his particular contribution.*[39]

This conclusion provides insight into the neoclassical view of the origins of income inequality. Those with high incomes are endowed with a relatively abundant stock of productive resources, such as land, capital and/or skill and knowledge. Those who fare poorly in income are relatively lacking in these resources – they have little in the way of capital or land to commit to production, and/or are in possession of meager human capital. Contributing little to output, they secure little in return.

This line of argument, however, begs an important question. How is it that different actors come to be in possession of such different resource endowments in the first place? And is it legitimate that those with greatest endowments (however achieved) should receive greatest rewards in the market? Given what we've now learned about the struggle of neoclassical theory to remain value-free, we should not be surprised to learn that most neoclassical textbooks have precious little to say about this matter. The neoclassical essences and reductionist structure, however, provide an analytically neat vantage point from which to assess this matter. Those inequalities in resource endowments that have arisen "naturally" through the operation of the perfectly competitive market economy are entirely legitimate, just as Nozick (1974) claims (see Chapter 1). Absent theft, extortion and other illicit extra-market means of wealth transfer, the endowments that agents face today are largely the consequence of a series of past voluntary decisions. If they (or their ancestors) chose to save rather than spend all of their income on consumer goods, or if they (or their ancestors) chose to invest in their own human capital, then they will command a larger pool of endowments today than those who did not make such choices. Being rational, each agent continuously consults his own preference ordering and maximizes his own personal welfare when making these decisions. Some choose to forego consumption today in order to secure savings for investment; others choose instead to exhaust their current income to achieve more immediate pleasures. Over time, these different decisions yield unequal resource endowments. Insofar as these inequalities result from the exercise of personal liberty rather than autocratic decree, they are entirely defensible. Indeed, to challenge the inequality of the market economy on normative grounds would be to challenge the legitimacy of the market economy *in toto*. After all, a system that privileges the individual choice of rational actors must hold those agents accountable for the decisions they make.

Let us pursue the connection between contribution and reward for one additional moment, as this distributive principle will factor heavily in debates over globalization. What if we find that wages in the US are ten times those in Mexico? What are we to make of this situation, assuming the presence of perfectly competitive markets in both countries? The logic of neoclassical theory is unambiguous: on average, the productivity of US workers must be ten times that of Mexican workers. This is so, presumably, because US workers are supplied with a much greater stock of capital equipment with which to work, and are in possession of far greater education and skills than are their Mexican counterparts. Both groups therefore receive what they deserve, measured in terms of their respective contributions to output. If we are troubled by this disparity in wages, the solution is not to impose a higher minimum wage in the Mexican labor market, for we know that such a policy initiative will generate unemployment, economic inefficiency and misery. The solution is to enhance the human capital of Mexican workers, and especially to increase the stock of capital with which they work. As the human and physical capital rises in Mexico, so will its wage level, reflecting the rising productivity of its workforce.

The market and economic progress

This last example raises an important question: if we accept the normative framework of welfarism, then how are we to best facilitate an improvement in the well-being of Mexican workers whose productivity and earnings are miserably low? How can this productivity level be raised, so as to provide for a rising standard of living?

So far we have found only that the perfectly competitive market will generate what is called "static efficiency", the efficient allocation of given resources across industries at any particular moment in time. When we consider the problem of improving productivity over time, however, we are no longer focusing on the distribution of *fixed* resources, given *existing* technology and preferences. We are focusing instead on how best to enhance the quantity and especially the quality of resources (such as labor skills) and how best to improve technology. Only these will promote rising productivity, which is both necessary and sufficient to ensure rising incomes and social welfare. Therefore we need to investigate whether the market, besides ensuring static efficiency, also generates "dynamic efficiency", or increases in the productive capacity of an economy over time.

As many neoclassical economists readily admit, neoclassical theory has had little to say about the determinants of technological change. Historically technological change has been treated as an exogenous event – inexplicable by reference to the perfectly competitive economic model we have explored here. In policy debates advocates for the neoclassical vision nevertheless argue that the free market does indeed generate dynamic efficiency far better than any other economic system. For many neoclassical visionaries, the purported dynamic efficiency of the market is even more notable and important than the static efficiency it yields. After all, given the assumption of insatiability, we need to discover some kind of economy that promises increasing *per capita* output. Only this will ensure increasing social welfare over time. If we had to choose between an economy that failed to maximize social welfare relative to existing resources at any given moment (that is, was statically inefficient) but that generated increasing output over time (that is, was dynamically efficient), and one that exhibited the opposite properties (was statically efficient but dynamically inefficient), we would have good reason under neoclassical premises to choose the former. Over the long run the former is apt to yield a higher level of social welfare.

Fortunately for neoclassical visionaries, we are saved from making this choice by the discovery that the free market promises both static and dynamic efficiency. To understand the link between the market and dynamic efficiency, we must focus again on the incentives provided by the free market, to which we have already alluded. In a perfectly competitive market economy those who provide resources to production face powerful incentives to increase their contributions to output. If a carpenter finds that her skills command a substantially higher wage in another city, where carpenters are scarce, she may relocate in pursuit of the higher wage but, simultaneously, she will increase her net contribution to social output (the higher wage indicates that her productivity will be higher in the new location). If an owner of capital finds that the return on his investment will be higher in Louisiana than in New York, he will shift his investment to reap the higher reward. By relocating, he will also enhance his social contribution. The reward to capital in Louisiana is high, in this account, because it is so scarce relative to labor. Each unit of capital in Louisiana will therefore yield a high marginal revenue product. The migration of capital to capital-starved Louisiana, while earning a high reward for its investor, will also increase Louisiana's capital stock, and thereby raise the productivity of Louisiana's labor. This is, as we have now seen, the only viable means for raising Louisiana's wages.

Just as the market provides resource owners with the incentive to find the highest possible reward for the resources they currently possess, it also drives them to increase the quantity and quality of the resources they have to sell. Consumers have an incentive to direct a portion of their current income into savings that they can then invest in exchange for increasing income in the future. This increases society's total capital stock, and thereby increases labor productivity. Workers also have an incentive to invest in human capital through additional training and education; as they acquire human capital, they receive a larger share of total social output commensurate with their increasing net contribution to social welfare.

Inter-firm competition also entails the kinds of incentive which induce dynamic efficiency. Unlike the firms which populate a planned economy, and which can survive for quite some time despite all manner of inefficiencies, firms in a competitive market economy must adopt the best existing technologies in order to survive. No government edict is necessary to ensure that firms adopt efficient practices – the market dictates in this regard are unforgiving. Moreover, each firm has a strong incentive to generate new technologies that reduce resource cost per unit of output. If it succeeds, it stands to gain rising profits; if it fails to do so, it faces a severe competitive threat from other firms in its industry.[40] When firms do find new technologies, the amount of total output that can be produced from given resources increases. In short, then, competition increases total output per capita and enhances social welfare.

The World Bank makes the case for the dynamic virtues of the free market. In response to the question "What causes economic growth?" the Bank argues as follows:

> The benefits enjoyed by labor in the fast-growing economies are not the result of job creation in the public sector or wage increases mandated by government. Expanding employment opportunities and rising wages are the consequences of growth and economy-wide increases in output per worker. A market-based development strategy achieves these outcomes through investment decisions by firms, households, and government. The search for more profitable activities encourages businesses – whether family farms, informal sector enterprises, or large corporations – to invest in equipment, new technology, and the training of workers. Households, seeking higher earnings from the hours they spend at work, will invest in their own human capital through improved health and nutrition and through schooling and training. Governments contribute directly by investing in public goods such as rural roads. But a market-based development strategy means that governments, above all, must enable businesses and households to invest in themselves, for example by protecting property rights and providing access to education.
> (World Bank 1995, 18–19).

To summarize this vitally important point: in the neoclassical view, the free market enhances dynamic efficiency via an incentive structure that equates reward with contribution. Each agent has an incentive to find that site in production where it can make the largest contribution. Each agent also has an incentive to improve the quality of the resources it owns, so as to improve its productivity. And each firm has the incentive to discover new technologies to reduce costs. Together, these incentives lead economic actors to take actions which expand the economy's productive potential.

MARKET IMPERFECTIONS

I alluded above to the problem of market imperfections, and it is time now to address this matter. The perfectly competitive market of which we have spoken so far is taken to be free of imperfections. In the first instance, this means that no one firm has influence over the market price (or what is called "market power"). In the presence of market power, such as when one firm monopolizes an industry, the market equilibrium will no longer be Pareto optimal. The monopoly will use its market power to restrict output below the quantity at which the MSB is equal to the MSC of the last unit produced, so as to keep prices and profits high.

A second kind of imperfection involves what are called "public goods". These are goods that, once produced and provided to some consumers, are available to all other consumers. For example, if a firm undertakes to clean up the atmosphere in a region and to then sell the commodity "clean air" to inhabitants of this region, it faces the problem that this good will become available to all inhabitants as soon as it is produced. Hence, there may be no way for the firm to charge consumers for their use of the good. This is because there is no convenient means to prevent those who do not pay for the good from gaining access to it. Hence, private profit-making firms do not have an incentive to produce public goods.

"Externalities" represent a third type of market imperfection. These are costs (or benefits) associated with economic activity that are not borne by the party imposing the costs. For example, when a firm producing steel absorbs labor, capital and other inputs, it must pay for these in the appropriate markets, and these costs will be reflected in the market price for steel. If the firm also pollutes the atmosphere when it makes steel, however, and if it is not forced to pay for the use of this resource, then this cost will be borne not by the firm but by society. Hence, the market price for steel will fail to incorporate the full opportunity cost to society of producing it. In this case, the market equilibrium in the steel industry will not be optimal. More steel will be produced than would occur were the firm to have to pay for all of its costs of production. Consequently, the MSC of the last unit produced will exceed its MSB.

A fourth market imperfection concerns the adequacy of the information that is available to agents when they undertake their economic decisions. All of the conclusions reached above about the virtues of the perfectly competitive market require the strong assumption that all market actors are fully informed about the full range of economic opportunities available to them, and about the full economic environment in which they operate. Lacking complete information, agents are apt to make all kinds of consequential errors that will distort the market outcomes that would otherwise occur. For instance, if firms have incomplete information about the viability of a new technology that can improve resource use, they may fail to invest in it. In this case, the free market fails to achieve static or dynamic efficiency.

What is to be done in the context of imperfections of this sort? The simplest, most general answer is that in such cases, the government is warranted in intervening in the market to induce the market equilibrium that would be forthcoming if no such imperfection existed. In the case of the monopoly, a regulatory commission could be established to supervise its behavior. Typically, such a commission dictates the price the monopoly can charge (allowing it some "fair" return on its investment), and ensures that it serves all consumers who might need the service it provides. For example, a telephone monopoly might be required by law to provide an affordable telephone service to all households in the region it monopolizes. The case of public goods warrants government provision, as these goods will not be sufficiently supplied by the market. This rationale justifies government expenditures on national defense, public health and education, criminal justice, environmental protection, and so forth. Ideally, the government must devise ways to ascertain just how much consumers value each of the public goods that it provides, and should produce just that amount so that the MSB of the last unit produced is exactly equal to its MSC. That is, the government should try to replicate the outcome of the perfectly competitive market. This is the domain of cost–benefit analysis. In the case of externalities, the government should implement policies that force those agents which cause externalities to "internalize" them. For example, the government might impose a tax on each unit of pollution emitted by a firm, so that it is forced to pay for the waste-absorptive capacity of the atmosphere that it uses. This will increase the marginal cost of production, and induce the firm to seek ways to reduce pollution while reducing the supply of the good it produces.

Finally, the case of imperfect information might warrant government actions to override market signals, to bring about the outcome that would arise were market actors in possession of perfect information. This argument is sometimes provided by advocates of "industrial policy" to defend the idea that the government should channel investment directly to promising sectors or projects that fail to attract sufficient financing from private investors. In a world of imperfect information, these advocates claim, the government can do a better job of "picking winners" than can the market.

In all of these cases, we find that the market on its own will fail to reach the equilibrium point that maximizes social welfare. Recognition of the existence of market imperfections of these sorts, then, might be taken to open the door within the neoclassical vision to extensive government involvement in the economy, substantially weakening the theoretical case for neoliberalism. This is especially true were these markets imperfections to be the rule rather than the exception. In this case, we would have little reason to expect that the market equilibria that actually emerge across the economy are associated with Pareto optimality. Unfortunately, even a casual survey of modern market economies indicates that these imperfections are truly ubiquitous. On this basis, many pragmatic economists and policy analysts have found in neoclassical theory sufficient grounds for substantial government intervention.

Government failure

But matters are not quite as simple as this brief treatment suggests. Problems arise as soon as we consider the efficacy of the government interventions which are necessary to correct these imperfections. Neoclassical theory brings its initial assumptions to bear in this context, examining whether there is good reason to believe that the government will act appropriately once it is licensed to intervene in the economy. The conclusion reached in this regard is rather pessimistic. After all, the same rational, egoistic actors who constitute the economy also populate government bureaucracy. When we ask what drives these actors in their role as bureaucrats, we are compelled by the initial assumption of human rationality to conclude that they seek to maximize their own individual welfare, not the welfare of society as a whole. For neoclassical visionaries, rationality is taken to be a universal assumption about human nature, not a narrow assumption about our economic natures. Hence, the rational agent occupying government office will undertake to satisfy his own needs rather than those of the constituency he serves, when and if he can.

We have seen that the market is a magnificent device for co-ordinating our economic activities precisely because it transforms our private, egoistic drives into socially benevolent outcomes. Though each agent seeks to serve his own ends, his efforts to do so produce unintended socially benevolent consequences. The question that arises, then, is whether there exists any comparable mechanism within government to ensure the same result in the political sphere. Unfortunately, the troubling answer provided by neoclassical theory is that there is not. The bureaucrat might therefore be expected to take steps to maximize his own power, influence and salary rather than serve the mission for which he was hired. We therefore confront the potential problem of "government failure" whenever we enlist the government to solve a "market failure".

In the neoclassical view there are many other potential sources of government failure. One that has attracted the most attention in recent years is known as "rent-seeking" (Krueger 1974; Buchanan, *et al.* 1980). Rent-seeking entails socially wasteful efforts to secure a share of social output that is incommensurate with one's own contribution – such as expenditures by an industry to lobby government to secure tariff protection. Once it becomes apparent to economic agents that the state is willing and able to intervene in the economy so as to ameliorate market imperfections, all agents have an incentive to convince the relevant government officials that they are the victims of an imperfection, real or imagined. The likely consequence is a political free-for-all, with constituents forming interest groups and undertaking extensive campaigning to secure some favorable government intervention in the economy, such as a subsidy for the economic activities with which they are associated. In this case, government action to correct market imperfections is likely to be driven by the relative power of the distinct groups lobbying for redress rather than by the actual extent of existing imperfections.

Unfortunately the problem of rent-seeking is particularly apt to arise in those domains of economic activity that the government has decided to regulate, such as monopolies, where market imperfections may be greatest. In these cases, neoclassicals worry, those appointed to protect the public interest are apt to become "captured" by the very industry that they regulate. Partly this is because those with sufficient knowledge and expertise to regulate an industry are themselves industry insiders. Regulators might therefore be expected to both come from and quickly return to the very industry that they are expected to regulate. As such, they may identify principally with the viewpoint and needs of the industry, rather than with the consumers whom they are appointed to protect. As this occurs, the regulatory process becomes a chief vehicle by which the monopoly extracts rents from other economic actors.

Neoclassical visionaries also reject the idea that in a world of imperfect information the government is better suited than private investors to pick winners. Following Hayek (1949), neoclassicals typically reject the idea that the government is in possession of better economic information than market actors.[41] Instead, Hayek argues that market participants possess far greater "knowledge of the particular circumstances of time and place" (Garrison and Kirzner 1987, 611), and are therefore better positioned to make critical bets about the viability of new products and technologies. In an uncertain world, the autonomous information gathering, guesses and gambles of the many separate actors constituting an economy will suffice to discover and exploit new technologies. These actors gain intimate knowledge of economic opportunities through their day-to-day activities. The market also provides them with the appropriate incentives to gather and act upon this knowledge. Some of the experiments and gambles they undertake will fail, of course; but even these failures will provide valuable information about what to try next. Others will succeed – and, as a consequence, society benefits. All of this dynamic experimentation and learning-by-doing is threatened, in the neoclassical view, once the government assumes for itself the role of picking winners and directing finance to those enterprises which *it* finds promising. Lacking appropriate experience and incentives, the government is far more apt to choose unwisely. Making matters worse, the intrusion of the government in this way distorts the behaviors of other market actors by introducing opportunities for successful rent-seeking. Firms now have an incentive to mount pressure on government officials to secure assistance in the form of subsidies, exclusive contracts, and protection from competitors (as through tariffs on imports), rather than concentrate on discovering and perfecting technological innovations.

How do we proceed, then, when we confront market failure, once we recognize the likelihood of government failure? Once again, the neoclassical vision provides an answer that is extraordinarily elegant. *We must undertake to infuse market accountability and incentives into the provision of government service, so as to minimize the space for government failure.* The first-best solution in this regard, of course, is to privatize public services outright. The trend in the US toward the placement of convicts in private, for-profit prisons exemplifies this trend. A second-best solution is to introduce market mechanisms into public services. For example, as many neoliberals now advocate, we might solve the problem of poor quality in public education by introducing the market mechanism of vouchers, so that parents can "buy" the services of those public (and even private) schools that they view as effective. In the view of its neoliberal proponents, this mechanism forces lagging schools (especially their teachers and administrators) to improve the quality of the services they provide so as to avoid closure – just as they would if they sold soap in a competitive market. When these two approaches are not possible or practical, we should undertake cost–benefit analysis to determine whether (imperfect) government involvement in the market would make a net contribution to or a net reduction in social welfare. In this case, we are essentially comparing the magnitude of the market failure with the magnitude of the government failure that would necessarily arise with government intervention. And when we do this, we may find that the inefficiency associated with the latter would more than offset any efficiency gain resulting from correcting the former. For example, political lobbying by environmentalists and firms over the magnitude of an effluent charge – or by consumers and firms over the price that a monopoly can charge – might very well yield an outcome that is more inefficient than that which would have occurred naturally in the imperfect market.

This neoclassical approach to adjudicating the merits of government intervention requires those who would advocate for it to prove not only that a market imperfection exists, but also that the government measures proposed to correct it would yield a net social benefit, taking fully into account government failures. As should be apparent, this is not an easy case to make. Hence, we may conclude this brief discussion of market and government failures by noting that there is in the neoclassical vision a rather pronounced bias in favor of small, unobtrusive government. Whenever possible, government services should be privatized. When that is not possible, the market mechanism should be brought to bear on government agents to ensure accountability. In all cases of market imperfections, the burden is to be placed on advocates of government intervention to prove their case. The default position lies squarely against intervention. The neoliberal aversion to active government is therefore preserved even in the face of evidence of extensive market failure. A market economy with imperfections is certainly inferior to one without imperfections. In the neoliberal view, however, it is apt to yield far better outcomes than one in which an expansive and active government bureaucracy is given a general mandate to correct market failures.

Initial assumptions as essences

We conclude this extended abstract discussion of the neoclassical defense of the market with an observation introduced above, which concerns the logic of neoclassical theory. We have noted on several occasions the elegance of the theory, and I have suggested that this quality accounts substantially for its appeal. This is especially true among those advocates who see in it the closest approximation to the natural sciences.

We have observed in the above discussion of the neoclassical vision the manner in which economic outcomes are traced directly to the initial assumptions of the theory. What accounts for the equilibrium between price and quantity in a market? The demand and supply behaviors of consumers and firms, respectively. What accounts for these behaviors? Consumer rationality, producer rationality, and scarcity. What accounts for the distribution of income? The very same factors, this time conditioning behaviors in input markets. How are we to explain the behavior of the government when it undertakes to intervene in the market? The same answer gets full credit.

What we see here is evidence that the initial assumptions of neoclassical theory are not just entry point concepts – not just convenient or useful places to begin. Rather, they are offered as essences: they serve as the fundamental, timeless, invariant drivers of human affairs. These assumptions are not specified as appropriate some of the time but not others, in some contexts but not others. They are taken instead to be universal and indelible attributes of human and physical nature. Further, they are taken to be *the most forceful determinants of economic (and other social) outcomes.*[42]

SUMMARY

We have before us now the heart of the neoclassical case in favor of the market as the optimal form of economic organization. The market is taken to be optimal in the specific sense that it best accords with the initial assumptions of neoclassical theory – assumptions about human and physical nature. Neoclassical theory demonstrates that the market is uniquely suited to handle a daunting challenge facing all societies. The challenge is how to orchestrate the private behaviors of egoistic, self-oriented rational economic agents so as to generate behaviors and outcomes that are socially benevolent. The market economy does not demand that the state try to shape peoples' preferences so as to make them compassionate or altruistic. Rather, the market economy accepts peoples' motivations and preferences for what they are, allows them to act on them in pursuit of their individual utilities, and nevertheless produces maximum social welfare. It bears repeating: this is a monumental theoretical accomplishment.

We have found that the initial assumptions of neoclassical theory are not taken to be just reasonable places to commence thinking about the economy, but instead are treated as explanatory essences. Though they induce changes in the world people inhabit, they themselves are impervious to change. *This means, however, that the market is not just the optimal form of economic organization for one particular community or for one historical moment, but is optimal for all human communities for all time.* As we will see again in Part 2, the market is also the optimal institution for linking distinct national economies. By now, we should be able to anticipate the defense of global neoliberalism that we will encounter there – the virtue of neoclassical elegance, after all, is that we always already know just what policy prescription it will offer in any new policy domain. Given what humans essentially are, and given the state of the natural environment in which they are condemned to live, the market stands as the single best mechanism for producing socially benevolent outcomes.

A powerful story, indeed. I have argued that this defense of the market is the most influential of all the claims appearing across the modern social sciences. Yet not all economists are persuaded by these arguments. Many critics take issue with the empirical claims made on behalf of the market. For our purposes, we will focus instead on the arguments of those who take exception to the normative claims made on behalf of market processes and outcomes, on the one hand, and to the methodological reductionism of the of neoclassical vision on the other.

CONTESTING VALUE-NEUTRALITY, WELFARISM AND REDUCTIONISM

The neoclassical attachment to welfarism stems from its pursuit of value-free science, as we have seen. Value-free economics is, however, both impossible and undesirable. In its attempt to produce objective science, neoclassical theory actually makes rather inept value judgements. These errors disqualify welfarism as a worthy normative principle.

Contra the neoclassical view, value judgements are always implicit in the choice of initial assumptions, the logic that is used to join them in theoretical narrative, the object to be analyzed and the host of other decisions that theorists must make as they develop their discipline. Not least, the decision about *what a science is to do* – what purposes it is to serve and what problems it is to solve – is deeply value-laden. Should the field of economics be directed toward achieving Pareto optimality, or eliminating poverty? Should it teach us how to secure *maximum* output given the limited resources provided by the natural world, or how to *minimize* harm to nature while we seek to secure some *sufficient* level of sustenance? When we ask these questions, we begin to see that *the notion of economics as value-free is a value-laden fiction.* After all, without an expression of normative commitments, it is entirely unclear why economics should theorize (let alone seek) efficiency, or why it should aspire to the "objectivity" of physics. The decision to banish values to intellectual regions beyond economics (such as philosophy) is itself fully normative, but its character is obscured by the presumed value-neutrality of neoclassical economics. Hence, it ought to not be surprising that the normative commitments associated with the neoclassical vision are poorly drawn and, in the view of many, ethically bankrupt.

Value neutrality and welfarism

Heterodox economists (and others) offer a multidimensional critique of the purported value-neutrality of neoclassical theory. Here we will take account of five objections that, taken together, substantially undermine the legitimacy of welfarism.

Exogeneity of preferences

Critics object to the neoclassical choice to treat preferences as exogenous. Recall that this assumption entails the idea that our desires are formed prior to and separate from our economic activity. This assumption supports the normatively laden conclusion that in making economic choices, a person is acting upon her "true" tastes – tastes that have not been distorted by her economic involvement. Her choices are rational insofar as they reflect her deepest personality structure, untainted by fleeting whims (prompted by advertising, perhaps) or deeper scars that the existing economic institutions might inflict.

This assumption is vitally important because it warrants the economist's reliance on personal preferences in assessing economic outcomes. That people prefer situation A to B is taken to be sufficient for the economist to rank A as superior to B, as we have noted. But what if, the critic asks, peoples' preferences are endogenous to their economic activity and situations (as surely they are)? What if my desires have been altered or shaped by the very institution (be it the market or the planning board) that is supposed to allow for their fulfillment? Can we still infer that the choices I make, the preferences I reveal, are indeed my "true" preferences? Indeed, we cannot.

An analogy might serve to clarify the conceptual problem that the assumption of exogeneity is designed to resolve. When we see cult members committing mass suicide at the behest of a cult leader, do we simply conclude that this act was for the best, insofar as it evidently reflected a rational choice by those who took their own lives? Do we comfortably accept that this act must have brought them maximum satisfaction, and that they chose it by reference to their exogenous preference orderings? Hardly. Most of us are much more apt to indict the charismatic cult leader for distorting the preferences of his followers. We may conclude that these were weak or desperate individuals, which made them susceptible to the charms of the cult leader. This appellation, however, conveys our normative judgement; this aspect of their character or circumstance is something we regret, not take as simply given. As a result, we are much more likely to interpret the mass suicide as a social disaster rather than an exercise in self-actualization or utility maximization. Indeed, but for the suicide of the cult leader, we might be inclined to charge him with murder. What precludes a benign interpretation of the affair is the notion that the mediator of these peoples' happiness actually transfigured them and their desires, leading them to conclude that they desired the *wrong* end.

Now, let us suppose that those economic institutions that are claimed to facilitate our satisfaction fulfillment were also seen to influence our desires. What if, for instance, our participation in markets actually shapes our preference orderings? In this case, it would be impossible to infer that the desires we are seen to satisfy through that institution were our true preferences. In this case, we could not claim that we are necessarily best off when left to fulfill such desires, any more than we could claim that the cult members were made best off by their voluntary self-annihilation. Note also that, under these circumstances, the logical foundation of welfarism collapses. The preferences consumers reveal through their purchasing patterns can no longer be taken as a guide (or at least, a sufficient guide) for policy assessment, because they can no longer be trusted as authentic or true.

This vexing problem is elegantly sidestepped by virtue of the assumption of exogeneity. If we reveal a preference in the market for pornography, handguns or luxurious, status-inscribed yachts, we can infer that these indeed are our true preferences, and that we are better off than we would have been had we not had the opportunity to act on these preferences. By extension, and provided we are prepared to be agnostic with respect to the preferences people hold, we can conclude that the preferences we reveal as a group form an appropriate basis (perhaps even the only appropriate basis) for judging economic outcomes.

The question of whether our preferences are indeed exogenous is thus truly a momentous one. Neoclassical economists do not attempt to prove that they are. Indeed, it is difficult to imagine just how such a proof might proceed. They merely accept exogeneity as a necessary implication of rationality, a presumption of the theory that serves as an essence of human affairs. By contrast, critics refuse the notion that the economic institutions which exist in a society are innocent with respect to the content of peoples' preferences. The critics view preferences as fully endogenous, shaped not only by a society's culture, religious institutions and so forth, but also by its level of wealth, degree of economic inequality, and by all the structures and practices that constitute its economy. The preferences we reveal are always worked over, always shaped in part by those very institutions that purport to allow for their satisfaction. In a market economy, the corporation is one of the chief economic agents consciously shaping preferences, of course. Political economists of diverse heritage – ranging from institutionalists such as Thorstein Veblen (1899) to Marxists such as Paul Baran and Paul Sweezy (1966) – point out that rather than serve consumers by responding to their exogenous preferences, the corporation commits vast amounts of resources to marketing in order to induce consumers to desire precisely those goods that it is uniquely positioned to supply.[43] These theorists also allege that the preferences people hold are powerfully influenced by market outcomes such as the levels of income and status they achieve, and the set of opportunities they confront. The wealthy might cultivate "lavish tastes" that they view as appropriate to their social station, while the poor manage to secure great satisfaction from the "small mercies" that come their way. As Sen, Rawls and others have argued, it may be entirely "rational" for the poor to accept that which they cannot change, so as to be able to secure some pleasure from their lot in life (cf. Crocker 1992). The different preference orderings of the wealthy and the poor are to be taken, then, as a *consequence* of the market processes that generated the inequality between them. And in this case, we can hardly treat these preferences as exogenous to economic institutions or outcomes.[44]

This should not be taken to mean that in the view of the critics the preferences we reveal are essentially "bad", nor that we are merely dupes of the market, corporations or government planners. It does imply, however, that less weight should be given to this single factor in assessing economic outcomes. That an individual prefers A to B, or that for a given society, some state A is Pareto superior to some alternative state B, is not to be taken as sufficient grounds for our normative ranking of A over B.[45]

Preferences versus values

Critics allege that among what neoclassicals call mere preferences are very different sorts of judgement which must be distinguished analytically prior to our committing to peoples' preferences as a (let alone the sole) basis for judging economic outcomes. A person's view about what color shirt to wear should be seen as something very different from his view about whether and to what degree a wetland should be degraded to make way for a mall. While the former might safely be treated as a private affair, with little normative content and social effect, the latter ought to be seen as an important value judgement – one that might have very broad social (and natural) effects (Sagoff 1988; Anderson 1990). Neoclassical theory, however, treats them as the very same kind of decision. In both cases, the neoclassical would have us rely on peoples' exogenous preferences, expressed in terms of their willingness to pay, to determine the appropriate course of action. In the matter of the choice of shirt, the consumer should be allowed to perform a private cost–benefit analysis, and then choose that color that maximizes his utility. In the matter of the wetland, a public cost–benefit analysis should be undertaken in which individuals are surveyed independently to ascertain their willingness to pay to either promote or prevent the development project.

While the neoclassical vision is right to claim that judgements about the color of one's shirt should normally be left to the personal tastes of the consumer, it commits a consequential error of conflation when it treats the latter type of judgement in this way. This decision involves not just what we *want* as independent persons, but who we *are* as a community and society. In this kind of case, the reasons we give for our desires should be given far more weight than our willingness to pay to secure them. It is not just the *strength* of our desires, but their *validity* that matters. Indeed, basing a policy decision in a case where important values are at stake upon willingness to pay represents an egregious normative failure.

Consider, for example, other cases of this sort. Should we decide the matter of whether to allow slavery based on a cost–benefit analysis, in which our willingness to pay is decisive? Should we decide the issue of freedom of speech in this way? As Mark Sagoff (1988) has argued forcefully, insofar as these decisions entail social values, we must have the right and substantive ability to participate as *full citizens* rather than as mere consumers in public fora where these decisions will be taken. For Sagoff, the citizen must have the right and substantive ability not only to venture arguments in order to persuade, but also to hear arguments, learn and thereby be persuaded by the good arguments of others. Absent these opportunities, such as when a policy decision is reached through cost–benefit surveys which merely sum up a community's willingness to pay, we are deprived of fundamental democratic rights.

Critics identify a second objectionable conflation hidden within the neoclassical notion of preference. The neoclassical treatment of preference fails to distinguish between what Herman Daly (1991) calls "absolute needs" and "relative wants". In Daly's usage, absolute needs are those which are independent of social circumstance, such as the need for basic shelter, nutrition, clothing, etc. These are largely determined by the relation between our biological attributes and the natural environments we inhabit. These kinds of need are satiable. Relative wants, on the other hand, are those that are tied to social positioning. The desire to have the fastest car, the most precious jewelry, and the largest house are instances of such wants. These may indeed be insatiable. For Daly and like-minded critics, we can and must distinguish between the normative status of these two categories of "preference". Once we do, these critics argue, we are led by any reasonable standard of justice to privilege the fulfillment of the former over the fulfillment of the latter. In Elizabeth Anderson's words, "Given that we do recognize the distinction between urgent needs and intense desires, we can see that for a community to treat these two as on a par is to trivialize and debase the concerns of those who have the needs" (Anderson 1990, 198). To return to an example introduced earlier, Daly and Anderson would have no difficulty arguing that society should undertake the redistribution from the billionaire to inoculate the impoverished. The inoculations purchased with the money transferred from the billionaire are accorded far greater normative weight than are the subjective desires he would otherwise have fulfilled with these funds. This is true despite whatever psychic damage this transfer of funds causes him.[46]

Interpersonal comparisons

A related objection concerns the normative legitimacy of the neoclassical strategy that bans interpersonal utility comparisons while nevertheless relying on utility as the exclusive criterion for assessing social states. Critics reject the normative assessment of alternative social outcomes by exclusive reference to utility or preference. When we endorse the redistribution from the billionaire to the poor, we are explicitly rejecting utility or preference as the sole desideratum for assessing social states. We can claim that a society that undertakes such redistribution is more just because we have introduced a means for discriminating between the strength of the claims of the billionaire and the impoverished to the $100,000. While utility (or subjective states more generally) may not be comparable interpersonally, the critics argue, other aspects of peoples' existence surely are – such as their capacity to avoid starvation, or to develop their talents or avoid preventable morbidity. For the critics, as we have seen, these comparable aspects are ethically far weightier and therefore warrant much greater emphasis than peoples' subjective states when evaluating social outcomes.

The exclusive use of utility (or, more broadly, subjective states) in assessing economic outcomes also fails ethical scrutiny for reasons which relate to the earlier discussion of the endogeneity of preferences. If the wealthy do indeed cultivate lavish tastes while the poor take comfort in small mercies, then the use of utility levels as our normative standard biases our judgements against the poor. Unable to fathom a substantially better life, the poor may achieve great happiness from the crumbs that fall from the country club buffet. That they do should give us small normative comfort. We might instead rightly indict the society that grounds down human expectations to such meager levels.[47]

Agnosticism regarding preferences

Critics uniformly reject the agnosticism of neoclassical theory with respect to peoples' preferences. The neoclassical vision (and the theory upon which it is based) refuses to demand that the economic agents on whose judgements its welfarist assessments exclusively depend give good reason for the legitimacy of their desires. In this vision of social choice, we do not demand of the billionaire that he submit for evaluation his reasons for amassing a huge fortune, or for refusing redistribution to the poor. That he believes he will be able to take his billions with him when he dies, or use them to buy a place in heaven, is not a matter that troubles the economist in the least. He has his reasons, we presume (he is *rational*, after all), and that is enough for us to give full weight to his desires in assessing social outcomes. The neoclassical visionary offers this agnosticism as evidence of the respect that she accords to the economic agents about which she theorizes. But the assumption of rationality not only shields the economic agent from the critical evaluation of the economist. More importantly, it shields *the economist* from the normatively laden task of this evaluation, and allows her to proceed with economic science undisturbed by such apparently non-scientific matters.

Inequality of resource endowments

Critics also take issue with the legitimacy of the unequal distribution of resource endowments that are converted in a market economy into unequal incomes. While neoclassicals treat inequalities that result from market behavior as natural and just, critics charge that inequality in the domain of resource endowments is generally convertible to inequality in other domains, such as access to decent education, housing, nutrition and so forth. Inequalities in these domains then necessarily react back on the resource endowments that agents accrue, ensuring that inequality in resource endowments is perpetuated and deepened over time. In short, the unequal rewards that agents take from the market may have far more to do with unequal substantive opportunities to secure resource endowments than with free choice (Roemer 1988). We will revisit this argument in the following chapter.

All of these deficiencies result directly from the pursuit of value-free science. Drawing analytical distinctions between what Anderson calls "primitive preferences" and social values, or between wants and needs, entails difficult value judgements that neoclassical scientists are loath to make. The initial assumptions of neoclassical theory are artfully crafted in such a manner that they can perform critical though covert normative labor. The assumption of rationality is vital to this endeavor. Comprising exogenous and equally valid preferences, insatiability, and the impossibility of interpersonal utility comparisons, it hides the vacuity of vital neoclassical normative commitments by rendering them largely invisible. It allows the neoclassical enterprise to embrace welfarism while viewing itself as an entirely objective enterprise. This dichotomy of objective, value-free science from subjective, value-laden non-science is, however, a hopeless fiction, one that allows for the studied suppression of the kinds of arguments that have been advanced here.

Anti-reductionist economics

I have argued that the neoclassical commitment to a reductionist account of the economy follows from a normatively driven choice rather than from the way the economy "really is". Some heterodox economic traditions explicitly reject this kind of reductionism. The best known of these is "institutional economics".[48] Like other anti-reductionist alternatives, this approach refuses to presume the existence of a set of timeless, universal determinants of social affairs, such as human nature, scarcity or any other essences. Instead, human subjectivity and social affairs are seen to be the complex, even contradictory outcome of the interplay (what others call the "overdetermination") of all existing social, natural, economic and political factors, where none of these is granted privileged status as the fundamental cause of social and economic outcomes.[49]

Most often, the debate raging across the social sciences and humanities about reductionism occurs at a rather high level of abstraction, so that it can be difficult for the student to see just what is at stake, and what this method-ological debate might imply about on-the-ground social analysis. To rectify this problem, let us consider concretely how these two perspectives differ-ently approach the notion of the economy and policy analysis.

In the neoclassical vision, the market is the ultimate form of economic organization because it best accords with the essences it recognizes, includ-ing human rationality and scarcity, as we have seen. It is, on this account, the uniquely "natural" form of economy. The holistic perspective of institutionalist theory refuses to view the economy in this way. The economy is understood instead to be a socially and politically instituted process rather than a natural outcome of social evolution. In this view, there is no natural economic system; nor is there any determinant path of historical evolution toward some supposed ideal economy. Instead, any existing economy stands as the overdetermined result of diverse forces operating in the present and past which together produced the particular sets of institutions, norms, behaviors and rules that govern economic behavior and outcomes. What kind of economy we inherit is therefore a fully contingent matter, reflecting the complex interplay of political interests, cultural mores, historical acci-dent and other such factors rather than some simple, irreducible set of essences.

In the institutionalist view, what we call the economic is also always political, social and cultural. For example, relationships of power overlay the capi-tal–labor nexus, conditioning not just the level of wages but also the intensity of the work effort. Hence, forms of abstraction that treat the economy as a self-contained sphere of society, amenable to examination in isolation from non-economic factors, fail in principle to convey the complexity of economic events and the scope of economic possibilities. ust as all economic activities entail social and political relations, so are seemingly non-economic activities and practices shaped by economic processes. The formation of consumer preferences, as I have noted above, can hardly be regarded as exogenous to market processes in modern market economies. Instead, the firms that neoclassicals take to be mere means for satisfying exogenously existing consumer preferences (and over which consumers are thought to be sovereign) are thoroughly implicated in the processes of preference formation.

The dispute over reductionism also has implications for the specification of human nature and subjectivity. In the view of critics, the neoclassical vision portrays the acting subject as flat and unidimensional, as little more than a pleasure zone wired to a computing mechanism (Sagoff 1988). The former dictates utility values for any particular opportunity; the latter determines choices based on a comparison of these benefits with the associated costs. Paradoxically, though the theory is predicated upon and celebrates personal liberty and choice, its specification of human rationality strips the process of choice of any meaningful content. We are, on this account, "rational fools" (Sen 1977) whose choices are pre-programmed by our exogenous preferences. Moreover, this conception portrays the human actor as the bearer of relatively stable tastes that reflect her unique individuality; in the language of contemporary social theory, this actor is seen to be "internally unified", "self-identical", a completed work of "auto-creation". In contrast, heterodox critics offer a much richer and more nuanced account of subjectivity. In keeping with the above discussion of the endogeneity of preferences, the human actor is posited as ever in conflict with and susceptible to – indeed, constituted by – all sorts of external pressures and forces (Amariglio 1988). This "de-centered", internally heterogeneous and ever-changing human subject is deeply uncertain about what will bring greatest satisfaction. Her preferences are often fleeting and insecure. Indeed, we might find that the act of choosing something actually diminishes its capacity for generating the satisfaction sought when it was chosen. The de-centered chooser is also driven by conflicting motivations in making the choice, and these competing motivations hardly submit neatly to any singular goal, such as the maximization of utility. *And a good thing, too*: a world inhabited by the kind of agent specified in the neoclassical vision would be a barren place, populated by one-dimensional creatures little removed in important regards from other species. They would not be fully human, and their society would not be a fully human society (though it might be wealthy, and even very happy).

In the institutionalist view, the individual is first and foremost a social product, rather than an autonomous agent who participates in society so as to fulfill pre-existing needs. In the words of Marc Tool, a prominent contemporary institutionalist theorist:

> The central contention here is that the particular attitudes, motivations, beliefs, and behaviors which human beings manifest are largely determined by the character of their interaction, conformist and

nonconformist, with the intellectual, cultural, social and physical environmental matrix to which they are exposed and from which they
emerge.

(Tool 1979, 54)

As this passage indicates, the notion of the social construction of human
subjectivity entails far more than the idea that society affects the processes
of preference formation. The basic orientation of human subjectivity and
behavior is also socially constructed. Whether we apprehend each other as
equal or unequal, whether we privilege our own needs and wants above
those of our communities, whether we are first and foremost rational self-
interested actors perpetually calculating personal benefits and costs or
communal actors who disdain the ethics of such calculus as a guide to personal conduct – all of these are partly the consequences of the social, political, economic and cultural milieu in which we evolve. Karl Polanyi (1944) is
particularly forceful in this regard. Polanyi demonstrates through careful
review of historical and anthropological evidence the absence of rational
"Economic Man" from most recorded history. All sorts of society, from
those with rather simple to rather complex economies, have organized the
processes of production, exchange and distribution on principles of
gifting, generosity, reciprocity, redistribution and other similar sentiments
rather than on personal gain. On the basis of this evidence Polanyi concludes that the rational behavior given as the justification of the legitimacy
of the market system is an historical anomaly, a result of this system rather
than a universal attribute in search of an appropriate type of economy in
which to express itself. In response to Adam Smith's dictum regarding
humanity's purported natural "propensity to barter, truck and exchange
one thing for another" in pursuit of personal gain, Polanyi aptly remarks
"no misreading of the past ever proved more prophetic of the future"
(Polanyi 1944, 43). Following Smith, neoclassical theorists mistake an
attribute of human subjectivity that sometimes emerges for an indelible
attribute of human nature, and they then search for that kind of economy
that best accords with this nature. [50]

The market: an anti-reductionist account

This way of thinking about human subjectivity and the economy conditions
the institutionalist view of the market. The anti-reductionist view alerts us to
the illegitimacy of positing "the market" as an ideal type against which to
judge the faithfulness of existing economies. There are in principle innumerable possible types of market economy, distinguished from each other in
extraordinarily diverse and consequential ways. These include the institutions and rules that govern price formation, distribution, property rights
(both the kinds of goods in which private and/or public property rights may
be established, and just what these rights entail), and, particularly, the scope

of the market (what can and what cannot be bought and sold).[51] Markets that differ in any of these regards generate very different kinds of economic outcome. In this account, then, the neoclassical abstraction of "the market" is thoroughly misleading, as it implies an entity with a unified, essential and invariant nature. In place of this distortion, institutionalists emphasize the diversity of market processes and market outcomes: "the market" is presented as a heterogeneous entity taking a variety of forms as it develops across time and place. Finally, no one of these alternative models is uniquely right or natural. Our judgements about their relative virtues (and their virtues relative to various kinds of non-market economy) will depend on a prior specification of a set of normative criteria, but will also be context-dependent. These judgements will evolve in line with the processes of social evolution, experimentation and transformation that open up new institutional possibilities. This means, however, that we have no reason to give normative significance to any existing market outcome. An outcome in which there is a shortage or surplus may be as defensible as (or more so than) any particular equilibrium outcome.

Important implications follow. Unlike adherents of the neoclassical vision, who see most forms of state intervention into the market as instances of interference that induce inefficiency, institutionalists recognize that the market is not *constrained* but actually *defined by* the rules, norms, and institutions that give rise to it (cf. Dugger 1989; Polanyi 1944). The market (like any other form of economy) is institutionally embedded in the broader society – it could not exist but for the sustenance with which the broader social matrix provides it. Hence, while we may have good reason to oppose some institution (like a particular monopoly) or government initiative (like a particular regulation) that affects economic outcomes, it is nonsensical in this account to describe these as market distortions. There simply is no unmediated, natural market (or economic outcome) against which to make such judgements.

We might be better able to apprehend this alternative, anti-reductionist view of the market by translating it as best we can (though the translation cannot be perfect) into the language of the neoclassical vision. To make the discussion concrete, let us return to the example of the effect of a government imposed minimum wage law that establishes a new price floor above the existing market equilibrium wage. We found earlier that in the neoclassical view, the market for all goods and resources (including labor) will generate a unique equilibrium price and quantity at which supply equals demand. The supply and demand curves are entirely reducible to the essences of neoclassical theory – to rationality (including exogenous preference orderings, the pursuit of maximum personal satisfaction, the discovery and use of technology, etc.) and scarcity. We also found that this equilibrium is associated with Pareto optimality. If the government attempts to improve the lot of workers by imposing a price floor above the market equilibrium wage, the level of social welfare will decline as firms reduce employment opportunities. In fact, by imposing a minimum wage, the government creates involuntary unemployment where no such problem had previously existed (see Figure 2.3).

Were we instead to theorize supply and demand curves in this alternative anti-reductionist account, we would have to understand that their location depends on all sorts of factors that are ignored in the neoclassical model. These curves are by no means reducible to rationality and scarcity. Instead, they are complexly overdetermined by all the forces and factors that constitute society – *including government labor policy.* This means that a new law to raise the minimum wage will actually induce a shift in these curves. For instance, workers might find in the new government policy validation for their (perhaps suppressed) belief that they deserve higher wages. As a consequence, they alter their behavior. Henceforth, they may not be willing to work as many hours at rates of pay close to the minimum. This would result in a shift in the labor supply curve to the left (as indicated by S^2 in Figure 2.5), generating a new market equilibrium (indicated by E^2). In addition, in view of the higher wages under the new law, workers might be willing to work harder to retain their jobs. This might be because the cost of job- oss has risen as a consequence of the higher wages (cf. Bowles and Gintis 1990). Labor turnover might also be reduced, as the higher wage discourages workers from seeking other employment. In either of these cases, workers' productivity rises – yielding a rightward shift in the labor demand curve and a new equilibrium, marked E^3. *If the new equilibrium lies above the imposed minimum wage (as shown in the figure at E^2 or E^3), then the new minimum wage law introduces no involuntary unemployment.* Moreover, at both the previous and new equilibria, the MSC is equal to the MSB, and so the condition necessary for Pareto optimality obtains. In this case, the neoclassical visionary now has

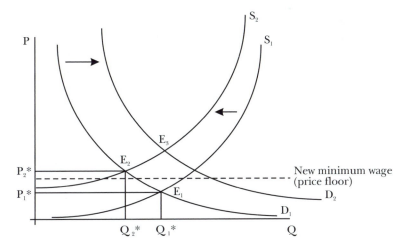

Figure 2.5 The labor market before and after the introduction of a minimum wage

a problem: with multiple distinct equilibria, we would seem to need some new criterion for choosing the right one. This would, of course, require explicit value judgements of the sort that the neoclassical vision studiously avoids.

The difference between these two accounts of the market adjustment to a political intervention is fundamental. In the neoclassical vision, a political intervention of the sort discussed here has no effect on the location of the supply and demand curves, since these are entirely reducible to the essences of the theory. Hence, the market generates but one uniquely correct equilibrium (given these essences), so that a government-induced move away from this equilibrium can be read unambiguously as a loss of social welfare. This reductionism therefore spares the neoclassical vision of a perplexing problem that it is not prepared to resolve, owing to its allergy to normative commitments. It can maintain that government intervention of this sort is necessarily socially damaging. The anti-reductionist account of the economy yields the opposing insight that any government action is as likely to generate a new equilibrium as to move the economy away from a single, unique equilibrium. Hence this latter account recognizes the need for normative criteria to choose between distinct equilibria.

As I said a moment ago, this translation of the anti-reductionist view into the analytics of the neoclassical vision is imperfect at best. This is because once we reject the reductionism of the theory, the concepts of market supply and demand curves become largely meaningless. In place of relatively stable relationships between price and quantity, we find continually shifting, even chaotic relationships. Hence the notion of equilibrium also becomes suspect. In the anti-reductionist perspective, there is no point in distinguishing those economic outcomes that are associated with equilibria from those that are not, because equilibria are never stable and, more importantly for our present purposes, they would have no necessary normative standing even if they were. While neoclassicals attempt to suppress the difficult normative judgements that attend choosing among distinct equilibria, anti-reductionists refuse the normative comfort that the concept of equilibrium provides.

If we accept this alternative account, then we begin to see that economics cannot be elegant and reductionist if it is to offer a good account of what is and what should be. We begin to see that policy prescriptions are likely to be valuable the more they are heterogeneous and context-dependent. And we might see that there is a far greater range of possible policy options than the neoclassical vision allows us to imagine.

CONCLUSION: INTERROGATING NEOLIBERALISM

The foregoing discussion allows us to see how the rejection of the essentialisms and reductionist logic of the neoclassical vision undermines its dogmatic defense of neoliberalism. Consider the essence of rationality. If all preferences are not equally valid, then we have no reason whatsoever to presume that the preferences which find fulfillment via the market are indeed those that should be fulfilled. If preferences are not exogenous, then we also have no warrant for claiming that the preferences which find fulfillment in the marketplace have any particular relationship to peoples' deepest needs and desires. It may be that the preferences expressed via the market are themselves generated by market processes. In this case, we have to admit that the market is not likely to generate maximum social welfare as this is defined in the neoclassical vision. Indeed, once we reject the equal validity and exogeneity of preferences, the concept of social welfare loses its analytical moorings. Furthermore if we refuse the centered, unidimensional notion of human subjectivity that neoclassical theory requires, then indeed we may find that the whole notion of "true" desires is suspect. In this context, though we may still decide to consider preferences in assessing economic outcomes, we should certainly refuse to accord them the status of sole normative desideratum. Taken together, these insights force the conclusion that welfarism is a deeply flawed normative framework. It therefore must fail as a defense of neoliberalism.

A rejection of reductionism also substantially weakens the neoclassical defense of the market economy and particularly its celebration of market equilibria. From the perspective of anti-reductionist economics, the neoclassical concept of equilibrium follows from a *presumption* of the market as an orderly process. Neoclassical visionaries see the market as orderly, and so they must discover a means to represent this order theoretically. The severe reductionism of the neoclassical vision provides invaluable service in this regard. It allows neoclassical visionaries to derive a market outcome exclusively from the essences of the theory – and thereby to construct the useful fiction of equilibrium – and to view market interventions that override natural market processes as welfare-reducing distortions. However, where neoclassicals see order and stability, anti-essentialists see disorder and instability. The anti-reductionist view therefore eschews the analytical device of essences. Instead, it recognizes that all market outcomes are overdetermined by innumerable factors – some stable, some fleeting, some powerful, some weak, some normatively defensible, some normatively suspect. Hence, and as we have just seen, the concept of market equilibrium itself is untenable in anti-reductionist economics. For all of these reasons, the anti-essentialist concludes that the economic outcomes generated by even a perfectly functioning free market system (absent any imperfections) is normatively naked: if it is to be sustained, it will need to find strong normative cover elsewhere.

To conclude this discussion, it bears repeating that the orthodox view of economics as value-free is at best naïve, and at worst harmful. It leads to criteria for the evaluation of policy and economic outcomes that are excessively narrow (focusing on but one aspect of social existence, peoples' subjective states) and ethically indefensible. Once we acknowledge the rightful place of

3   Distributive justice and economic heterodoxy

INTRODUCTION

Philosophers, political theorists, political economists and others have long wrestled with the matter of the normative assessment of social and economic outcomes. These scholars have generated approaches to social evaluation that differ markedly from the welfarism that has predominated within the neoclassical tradition. One important branch of thought emphasizes the concept of distributive justice, and it is this branch that has been most influential among heterodox economists.

This chapter will present several recent, influential contributions to the debate over distributive justice. Of these, the work of John Rawls is best known. Reacting to the utilitarian tradition, Rawls undertook to reorient the debate over normative assessment to encompass non-subjective criteria, and to privilege fairness over social welfare. Since the publication of his major treatise in the early 1970s, the concept of justice as fairness has gained substantial support. The following commentary will therefore commence with a consideration of his chief arguments; insofar as this work is rather well known, this summary will be brief. We will then examine the work of Michael Walzer, an influential political theorist who has undertaken to develop an account of justice that emphasizes the important differences among the social goods that communities distribute.

The chapter then turns to the normative perspectives associated with two heterodox approaches to political economy, institutionalist and Marxian theory. We will find that egalitarianism in the distribution of social wealth is among the central normative criteria within the field of political economy, if not within the neoclassical vision. Finally, we will turn to the recent contribution of economist and philosopher Amartya Sen. Deeply influenced by Rawls, Sen has offered a criterion of social evaluation that captures the normative concerns of many egalitarians, including many heterodox economists, while having several important, practical virtues. I will explicate Sen's normative criterion and then identify some of its chief virtues as a guide for assessing economic outcomes. The chapter then defends egalitarianism against the claim that it is inconsistent with human nature, as this is one of the most frequent objections raised against it. The chapter concludes by indicating how a commitment to egalitarianism invalidates the neoliberal model of economic organization.

RAWLS AND JUSTICE AS FAIRNESS

In *A Theory of Justice*, Rawls advanced a thorough critique of utilitarianism and a compelling alternative normative principle rooted in the tradition of "contractualism". The latter entails a notion of justice as fairness. Rawls' approach is complex and nuanced; yet several of his chief insights may be rendered fairly simply without extreme violence to the deeper analysis from which they flow.

Rawls sets out to discover a normative principle that would be suitable for designing the constitutional foundations of democratic society. His work explores the question:

> [What] is the most appropriate conception of justice for specifying the fair terms of social co-operation between citizens regarded as free and equal, and as fully co-operating members of a society over a complete life, from one generation to the next?
>
> (Rawls 1996, 3)

This question would not be so daunting were we to assume that all reasonable members of society shared the same conceptions of how we should live; but Rawls emphasizes the fact that in democratic society we may not make this presumption. Instead, democratic citizens are empowered to (and indeed do) develop and advocate fundamentally distinct "comprehensive doctrines" – philosophies, religious commitments and other deep conceptions about what is right. Many of these may be reasonable in the (liberal) sense of accepting the value of democratic governance.[52] But these comprehensive doctrines may be largely incompatible in the way they define the social good, appropriate personal behavior and social practices, and so forth. Where such diversity exists, Rawls asks, how might we fashion a normative principle that can provide the basis for social co-operation among society's members? What kind of normative principle is apt to secure the willing assent of those with such deep disagreements?

In response to these questions, Rawls proposes what he calls a "political conception of justice". As the term suggests, this conception is limited in terms of its field of application. Rawls seeks a conception of justice that does not compete with or displace the various comprehensive doctrines that people hold, but that instead allows them to find a way to live peacefully with each other in the same democratic space. The political conception must be one that we may reasonably expect adherents of reasonable (though distinct) comprehensive doctrines to endorse – not as a temporary strategic means of furthering their own comprehensive doctrines, but rather as the basis for an enduring, fair democratic society predicated on social co-operation.

Rawls' mission is to discover and defend a normative principle that can achieve this purpose. His novel approach entails the construction of a procedure by which rational human actors themselves discover the principles by which they can achieve social co-operation, regardless of the substantive disagreements among their respective comprehensive doctrines. Much of Rawls' argument entails specifying precisely the conditions which must be met in order for such actors to reach the right conclusions. Many of these conditions concern the nature of the individuals who undertake the exercise. Importantly in this regard, the individuals must embrace the notion of democratic citizenship, in which each person is to be regarded as free and equal. Each must be committed to reasoned discourse, in which arguments in favor of or against a particular proposition must be made in terms of what it is reasonable for others to accept.[53]

Rawls also specifies the background conditions under which individuals deliberate in their pursuit of normative principles. He asks us to presume the existence of a committee of rational deliberators, each of whom is taken to represent one of the groups of which society is composed. Each of these groups is taken to subscribe to some comprehensive doctrine or other – that is, they hold distinct religious conceptions, philosophies, etc. This committee is assigned the task of devising a political conception of justice which all (reasonable) groups in society might be reasonably expected to accept as a basis for social co-operation. Now Rawls asks us to assume, finally, that the committee's deliberations over this principle take place behind a "veil of ignorance". This means that the participants must devise the principle of justice that would apply to their society and all groups within it *prior to their knowing to which group they will themselves be assigned*. The veil of ignorance therefore separates the interests of each committee member from that of any particular group. Under these circumstances, Rawls reasons, the committee would devise the best political account of justice that would be ultimately acceptable in principle to all (reasonable) groups.

What kind of political conception would this committee devise? Rawls maintains that the committee would endorse a simple set of principles, which he captures as follows:

> (a) Each person has an equal claim to a fully adequate scheme of equal basic rights and liberties, which scheme is compatible with the same scheme for all; and in this scheme the equal political liberties, and only those liberties, are to be guaranteed their fair value.
>
> (b) Social and economic inequalities are to satisfy two conditions: first, they are to be attached to positions and offices open to all under conditions of fair equality and opportunity; and second, they are to be to the greatest benefit of the least advantaged members of society.
>
> (Rawls 1996, 5–6)

Principle *a* requires the *equal* distribution of what Rawls calls "primary goods". These are "basic rights, liberties, and opportunities, and the ... all-purpose means such as income and wealth", but also the "bases of self-respect" (1996, 180–81). "These goods," Rawls continues, "are things citizens need as free and equal persons." Justice as fairness requires that they be equally provided to all of society's members, so that each has equal *substantive* ability to pursue her conception of the good and the right (as determined by her comprehensive doctrine). Rawls contends that without sufficient means, the formal rights and opportunities that people enjoy remain empty promises. The deprived are unable to secure the "fair value" of these rights and opportunities (1996, 6).[54]

Principle *b*, called the "difference principle", modifies the first. Rawls allows for the case in which the equal distribution of primary goods may harm all of society's members. Justice as fairness permits inequality in the distribution of primary goods provided that the worst off benefit most thereby.[55]

The difference principle has strong intuitive appeal, especially in simple cases. Consider a group of people cast adrift in a lifeboat with limited food and water. Justice as fairness would warrant an unequal distribution of resources, with those who are most capable of rowing the boat receiving a disproportionate share, because this distribution would serve the interests of those least provisioned (by increasing their chances of survival) far better than would a strictly equal distribution.

This is an important qualifier, to be sure. Justice as fairness, read in full, requires equal distribution of primary goods, except to the degree that inequality will most help those worst off. It therefore incorporates into the justice principle consideration for the practical or instrumental effects of distributive patterns. This consideration plays an important part in other contemporary approaches to distributive justice, especially that of institution- alist theory. But we will see that the test required under the difference principle, though straightforward in trivial cases, can be troublesome when applied to more complex situations. At best, a determination that inequality helps those worst off is difficult to make; at worst, the difference principle invites self-serving justifications for inequality from those who gain thereby.

WALZER AND "SPHERES OF JUSTICE"

Although there is broad support for egalitarianism in some form or other among political theorists, philosophers and others, concerns have been raised about the sufficiency of strict equality of distribution. Some, like Amartya Sen, highlight the complications that result from differences across individuals that affect their respective needs and abilities (see below). Others, like Michael Walzer, emphasize the differential aspects of distinct goods as grounds for asserting a distributive principle that seeks justice through their *unequal* provision.

Like Rawls, Walzer (1983) sets out to establish a criterion for distribution of goods that is just by virtue of its inherent fairness. Also like Rawls, the domain with which he is concerned includes objects of the sort we usually classify as goods, such as food, housing and so forth, but extends beyond these to include other kinds of valuable possession. These might include political office, or a certain kind of employment or occupation, or even respect. Walzer uses the term "social goods" to include the entire range of valued, distributed entities.

Walzer's chief claim is that the particular character of each social good should determine its own criterion of distribution. An obvious example is health care: for Walzer, this vitally important social good should be distributed according to need. Simply put, those who are in poorest health (rather than those who are wealthiest) should receive the most care. Need should not, however, condition every distribution. Political office, for example, should be allocated not according to the relative personal needs of those who seek it, but according to the persuasiveness and leadership ability of the candidates. No one person deserves to be elected on these grounds, of course; we do not and should not use civil service exams to select our leaders. Rather, we should provide each with an equal ability to make her case, marshal support, excite the electorate, and earn its trust. We should then grant political office to those whom the majority of us choose. Artistic or other awards should be allocated according to merit judged against some set of criteria deemed appropriate by the relevant community and then equally applied to all those who compete. In contrast, careers should be open to talents, where those best able to serve are given the chance to do so. To be just, competition for such positions must occur in the context of a just distribution of education and training (and other vital social goods, like income), in which all are guaranteed the level of education necessary to participate as full members of society. This is not to say that education should be distributed equally, either: those with special needs must have access to sufficient assistance to develop their talents, while those with special gifts must be allowed to refine their intellects through advanced training.

Walzer offers this "complex equality", in which the character of each social good determines its distributive principle, as a corrective to univocal accounts that select but one criterion for determining the allocation of all social goods ("simple equality"). Income has served as the principal focus in many univocal accounts of justice, especially among egalitarians with socialist sensibilities. These egalitarians have objected to the means by which income has been distributed, and to the uses to which unequal income has been put. With respect to the former, Walzer argues that income should be tied to work performed, not to power, heritage, or other illicit factors that today shape the distribution of market rewards. With respect to the latter, unequal income has rightly attracted the concern of these egalitarians because it often provides the means for laying illegitimate claim to other social goods. In Walzer's terminology, money has often been a "dominant" good that corrupts the distribution of other goods, like political office. In Walzer's view, those socialists who have called for the equal distribution of income really intend that money should not hold power outside of its sphere: "what socialists want is a society in which wealth is no longer convertible into social goods with which it has no intrinsic connection" (Walzer 1973, 404). Money should not be the basis for the allocation of most other social goods, because the justice claims of complex equality demand that they be distributed according to their own inherent qualities. Instead, money should serve merely as the means of acquiring (distributing) those goods that people may desire but which are not essential for life itself, the achievement of self-respect, political efficacy, or personal flourishing. Hence money should not acquire health care, political office, careers, education, etc.

In short, complex equality entails a system in which the distribution of any one social good must not become the basis for the distribution of other social goods; that is, in which no one social good should be dominant. Each criterion of distribution must reign in its own domain, and not be allowed to spill over to others. This argument therefore undermines univocal distributive principles, because distinct social goods call forth distinct distributive criteria. The univocal egalitarian principle of need is alien to the sphere of offices; the principle of just desserts is alien to the sphere of medical care.

INSTITUTIONALISM AND REASONABLENESS

Within political economy, several important schools of thought have rejected any form of welfarism in favor of some notion of fairness. Notable among these is institutionalist theory. Institutionalist thought encompasses a range of normative perspectives. The following treatment cannot do justice to this diversity, but intends instead to explicate some of the chief normative claims that have attracted substantial support among many institutionalists.

Institutionalist theory is explicitly normative. It rejects the idea that any social science could possibly avoid value judgements, or that it should want to do so. Institutionalist theory, as we have seen, also refuses to treat human subjectivity in the manner prescribed by the neoclassical vision. In this account (as with the other perspectives to follow), human nature is malleable and largely shaped by the cultural milieu which a person enters at birth, and in which she is educated and socialized. On this account, then, preferences reveal as much about the society in which one lives as about what is truly valuable in life. Unreflective subjective states therefore provide an inappropriate guide in the formation of a value principle to drive economic research, policy formation, or social critique (see Chapter 2).

Marc Tool provides a detailed account of a normative commitment that runs through much of the institutionalist tradition. He summarizes it thus: "We now affirm that that direction is forward which provides *for the continuity of human life and the non-invidious re-creation of community through the instrumental use of knowledge*" (Tool 1979, 293; italics in original).

This is a complex principle. "The continuity of life" refers to the imperative of society to take steps to perpetuate the species but also to sustain those members of society whom it is in its capacity to save. "Re-creation of community" entails the notion that humans are, of necessity, social creatures who come to be within a particular social milieu. This milieu is alterable: indeed, it is continually in process of being recast as a consequence of human design, accidents, experiments and natural events. By extension, the "non-invidious re-creation of community" entails the pursuit of institutions, laws, customs and practices that refuse to rate or rank persons in regards to their worth. As such, this entails a proscription on stereotyping, racism, sexism, classism, or any processes which equate personal attributes or degrees of achievement (such as income) with levels of worth. Social progress requires the replacement of invidious distinctions with forms of appraisal of members' contribution, productiveness or praiseworthiness that eschew valuations of worth. The "instrumental use of knowledge", finally, captures the institutionalist assessment of theory and practical knowledge as valuable only to the degree that these serve the purposes of addressing pressing social problems. Galbraith expresses this sentiment succinctly by claiming that theory must pass the "test of anxiety" (Stanfield 1996). To serve this function, knowledge must be reliable in the sense of arising out of careful reasoning and accumulated experience rather than out of received (and unquestioned) texts or authorities. Reliable knowledge can and will change in response to the never-ending experimentation undertaken by people democratically engaged in solving the problems that they deem important and that are within their abilities to overcome (Tool 1979, 293ff). Institutionalists subscribe to what Dewey called "evolutionary positivism", or a pragmatic empirical approach to social investigation and policy application.

This multifaceted normative position is rather demanding. It entails democratic equality in the sense of the affirmation of each person's right "to be and to belong". Democracy is endorsed not on the basis of any claims to timeless, fundamental rights of man, but on the basis that it performs better than other alternative arrangements in identifying and resolving social problems, and in recognizing and correcting policy errors (Stanfield 1996).

This normative principle also demands freedom, with each member of society afforded the opportunity to experience "*an expanding area of genuine choice*" (Tool 1979, 320, italics in original). The qualifier "genuine" in this context signals the need to look beneath the mere number of options before us at any given moment in order to interrogate the range of meaningful alternatives that this number actually affords. The term "expanding" reflects again the evolutionary character of social and individual existence. At the level of society, "freedom requires the development and perfection of institutional forms to expand the spheres of discretionary involvement – genuine choice". For the individual, "freedom means the progressive enlargement of the rational, means-consequence-perceiving capacity of people and of opportunities to choose among alternative ways of organizing structural aspects of the political and economic processes" (Tool 1979, 320). This conception of individual freedom explicitly does not entail or require the relative absence of government-imposed constraints, as libertarians would have it. Instead, such constraints are vital to the protection of personal freedom itself. In common with Hegel, the institutionalist view understands that freedom follows only from the recognition of necessity.

Certainly, this is an expansive principle. For our purposes, we can focus on the more concrete question of the patterns of economic distribution that the principle implies. This principle requires justice, defined as *"the assurance to all of instrumental involvement in the social process"* (Tool 1979, 330). This notion of justice entails both intrinsic and instrumental claims in favor of distributive justice, and these are sometimes merged in institutionalist thought. Regarding the former, each member of society must be provided the means necessary to flourish as a fully human being. In this connection, Tool cites a compelling passage from Scharr:

> [The] poorest he that is in England hath a life to live as the richest he. There is the heart of the matter: each man has a *life* to live, not a role to perform; that life must be *lived*, not acted out according to some prefixed pattern; and *he* must live it, not give over the responsibility for it to someone else.
>
> (Tool 1979, 326)

Recognition of the inherent worth of each individual entails the mandate for society to provide each with at least that minimum income and support necessary to live his life fully. This requires that each must receive lifelong "education, training, skills, employment connections, and income" and the other resources necessary (in the context of his culture) to enhance his capacities (Tool 1979, 331–2).

The instrumental argument emphasizes the broader social effects of distributive patterns. Gross inequality interferes with the ability of the dispossessed to participate in the re-creation of community – to contribute to the social processes of experimentation and learning-by-doing that are so fundamental to social progress. This harms all of society's members, not just those excluded from these vital activities. Inequality also generates sub-optimal macroeconomic outcomes. William Dugger defends the attachment of "radical institutionalism" to egalitarianism on these instrumental grounds:

> More income for the poor and lower-paid workers is desirable, not only on behalf of those receiving it, but also because it keeps pecuniary

demand growing with industrial supply ... [More] income for those with low incomes will boost effective demand, boost output, and move us closer to universal affluence and full employment.

(Dugger 1989, 9–10)

This principle highlights need as the primary determinant in a just distribution but it does not explicitly require strict egalitarianism *per se*.[56] Instead, any distribution is to be judged by reference to its effects on individuals and on society. Does an unequal distribution undermine the ability of the dispossessed *to live her life*? Does it also hinder her ability to undertake "instrumental involvement" in her community? For institutionalists, these are questions that require careful empirical investigation of actual cases. As we will consider shortly when we turn to Sen, these capacities might not depend so much on absolute levels of income and wealth as on relative levels. The relatively poor may face insurmountable obstacles in living their own lives or participating effectively in the political institutions of their communities. To the degree that this can be shown, the institutionalist principle elucidated here would require rather compressed distributions of income and wealth across society's members.

Before turning to the Marxian perspective, we should take note of the view of one particularly influential institutionalist, John R. Commons, who focused extensively on the matter of labor markets and wage determination. The labor market is central to the debate over global neoliberalism, and it is an area of the debate in which institutionalists have been particularly active and influential.

John R. Commons[57]

Commons pioneered institutionalist theory of the labor market. A good bit of subsequent institutionalist work has focused on the pivotal relation between labor and capital in the market economy. Commons' career spanned the late nineteenth and early twentieth centuries. This was a time of tremendous economic upheaval in the US. Large oligopolies established control over most important industries, huge manufacturing facilities emerged which drew together hundreds of thousands of workers in industrial cities, and episodic labor strife broke out across the country. As with the institutionalist tradition more generally, Commons sought to discover and implement workable reforms which would deliver the promise of economic development to all members of society while alleviating the causes of social turmoil. His chief normative concern was to secure fairness in the capital–labor nexus. In his view, the so-called "free" labor market of the early twentieth century was neither free nor fair. Only government intervention could repair the skewed balance of power that capital wielded over labor.

Unlike neoclassical economists, Commons refuses the notion that a bargain struck by nominally free parties in a market is by definition fair. The neoclassical view stems from the simple intuition that in a free market – in which every contracting party has the formal freedom to refrain from concluding any agreement that it views as deficient – any agreement reached must be deemed beneficial in the eyes of the concerned parties. An unfair agreement will simply not be completed – or at least, must be the result of a mistake by one of the parties, and so will not be repeated. Hence, in the orthodox view, the default position in assessing market transactions must be to take them as essentially fair.

Commons' chief insight for present purposes is to see that a contract is fair only if the two parties entering into it have equal bargaining power in the formation of its terms. Commons designates the fair price achieved through contracting among genuinely equal parties "reasonable value". A contract formed under conditions of asymmetric power might be deemed mutually beneficial in the limited sense that each party gains something thereby, but could not be deemed to generate reasonable value (Ramstad 1987).

Commons focuses on the parties' "ability to wait" as the chief operational and visible component of market power. When one party in a market is more desperate to reach agreement quickly than is its counterpart, perhaps because what she has to sell is perishable or because she faces a relative absence of alternative parties with which to contract, the resulting contract reached will be unfair to that party. The greater the asymmetry in ability to wait, the greater will be the ultimate unfairness.

Through the concepts of genuine equality, the power to wait and reasonable value, Commons provides a normative basis for evaluating market outcomes. Moreover, these concepts provide direction for intervening in those markets which are marred by unfairness in order to bring about reasonable value. And in this regard, Commons identifies the labor market as a critical site in need of reform. First, he claims that the orthodox view of the labor market, in which demand and supply comprise free and equal individual actors with no market power, is an illusion. In this market, each individual worker confronts combinations of investors who are joined together in the corporation. This asymmetry is obscured by the fiction of treating the corporation as a singular entity, analogous to the single worker, even though it is itself an organization joining the resources and defending the interests of many individual investors. Second, workers and corporations do not have equal ability to wait. While the firm can refrain from reaching agreement with any particular worker (given that it represents the short side of the market), each worker needs to secure and retain employment in order to survive and to provide for her dependents. Individual workers are therefore unable to achieve reasonable value. As a consequence, the free labor market yields an inherently unjust distribution of the social product.

This asymmetry can be overcome through two chief institutional reforms: the legally sanctioned combination of workers in labor unions, and the creation of regulatory commissions to oversee and intervene in the labor market. The labor union parallels the combination represented by the e corporation, and allows workers to achieve together something they are unable to achieve individually. It enhances workers' ability to wait by pooling resources that can be distributed to union members during work stoppages, while reducing the corporation's ability to wait by removing substitutes from the market. The regulatory commission supplements the efforts of unions to ensure that genuine equality in the labor market is indeed achieved. For example, Commons argues for the imposition of "social tariffs" on imports from countries with weak labor standards as a means to prevent the weakening of the power of labor in the US (see Chapter 6).

Application of the standard of reasonable value breaks with the subjective standard of fairness implicit in the neoclassical vision. The neoclassical inference of "fairness" from "willingness" fails to give adequate attention to the possible injustice surrounding the circumstances that attend the contracting process. For Commons, a fair agreement requires fair opportunity. Just as we would hesitate to bestow the status of fairness on an agreement in which a slave "chooses" to work under onerous conditions rather than risk punishment of injury or death, so would Commons have us refuse the designation "fairness" to any agreement reached under coercive force of unequal power.

Distribution and the community

The neoclassical vision incorporates an implicit commitment to the principle of first instance distribution according to net contribution, as we have seen. In this view, the total product can be decomposed into shares contributed by each individual agent so that when added together, these respective shares sum to the total product. In contrast, institutionalists refuse this additive decomposition. Institutionalists recognize the community at large as the agent of production (Dugger 1989). The community, past and present, is a repository of the knowledges and skills, language, norms and customs that dictate a society's level of productivity and its ability to generate wealth. The schoolteacher, the health care provider, the parent and coach all leave a trace on society's ability to produce – they enter the factory in the form of the skills, temperament and aptitude of the worker whom they helped to mold. These respective net contributions cannot be parsed and added to yield total output. Consequently, distribution according to the direct net contribution of individual factor suppliers makes no sense: while those who provide the actual labor, capital and land to production are taken to be the *proximate* agents of production, the community at large is understood to be its *ultimate* source. If distribution is to reflect contribution, then it is the deeper, ultimate source of output that should count.

In the institutionalist view, then, the community at large has a rightful claim to the total social output. In the view of many institutionalists, the distribution of the total product should be largely egalitarian. For Commons, this is reflected in the notion of "reasonable value" that emerges from contracting among genuine equals, as we have seen. For institutionalists generally, an egalitarian distribution has both inherent and instrumental virtues. Egalitarianism is intrinsically right because it provides each individual fair opportunity to develop her capacities, to live a fully human life. It is also instrumentally right because it best serves the interests and needs of the broader community.

THE MARXIAN TRADITION

What is perhaps best known of the principles of the Marxian tradition is Marx's famous dictum that may be paraphrased *from each according to ability, to each according to need* (Marx 1938). For Marx, this is the distributive principle of the ideal communist society. It is a principle that is radically different from the welfarism of the neoclassical vision. But it turns out to be not all that far from the principles advanced by contemporary theorists of distributive justice, as is indicated by our brief treatment of Rawls, Walzer and institutionalism (above), and of Sen (to follow).

Marxism and class

One of the chief concepts of Marxian theory is "class". This frequently misunderstood concept follows from a rather simple presumption.[58] For any society to survive and flourish over time, those who perform the labor necessary for provisioning must produce not only enough to meet their own needs (called "necessary labor"), but also a "surplus". This is because, at any given moment, many members of society will not be able to perform the labor necessary to meet their own needs; or they (or society) will have decided that though they have this ability, they ought not apply themselves to this task. For instance, in order to survive, a society must make provision for its infants and its infirmed. A complex society will also allocate the labor of many people to tasks that contribute to the well-being of society (such as the writing of poetry), but which are not directly productive in the sense of participating in its material provisioning. If those who perform productive labor only meet their own needs, then these other members of society and these other tasks cannot survive.

   In the Marxian view, societies differ with respect to the ways in which they organize the production, appropriation and distribution of the social surplus. "Production" refers to the manner in which the social surplus comes into existence. Who performs the vitally important labor that is necessary to generate the surplus, and under what social arrangements? "Appropriation" refers to the processes and mechanisms by which initial claims are made on this surplus. Who are the initial receivers of the surplus, and by what legal rights, informal customs and other arrangements do they occupy this privileged social position? Finally, "distribution" refers to the processes by which portions of the surplus flow from the initial receivers (the appropriators) to other claimants in society. It captures the mechanisms by which the appropriators are either required or otherwise disposed to share portions of the surplus. For example, must they pay taxes to the state, or interest to lenders, or rent to landlords? Do they face pressures to reinvest a portion of the surplus? These distributions of the surplus exert powerful effects on the nature of the society in which they occur.

Marxists refer to the production, appropriation and distribution of the surplus as "class processes". In the Marxian view, these processes can be organized and structured in myriad ways. Indeed, a survey of recorded human history reveals diverse class practices and structures, comprising (for example) slavery, feudalism, capitalism, socialism and communism. Moreover, each class process may occasion diverse tensions and conflicts, or what Marxists call "class struggle". Those who produce the surplus may resist its appropriation by others, while the ultimate claimants of the surplus may mobilize to increase their respective shares. Absent here is any notion of equilibrium or social harmony.

A brief stylized account of feudalism might help to clarify the meaning and significance of class.[59] Feudalism entails a class arrangement in which those who produce the social surplus, the feudal serfs, are legally bound to the land provided to them by the appropriator, the feudal lord. Those serfs attempting to flee their bondage are liable to be hunted down and prosecuted for their transgression. Thus, although serfs are not owned by the appropriators (as are slaves under the slave class process) they are not freely contracted laborers either. Under a feudal arrangement, the surplus can take the form of "surplus labor time". This form of surplus arises when the serf is required to divide his work time between his own family's plot of land, and that of the lord. In this case, the product generated by the serf on his own land is his family's to keep; that generated on the lord's land flows to the lord without compensation to the serf. Feudal surplus can also take the form of "surplus product". In this case, the serf works the land assigned to his family full-time, but he is required to deliver to the lord some established portion of the total product at the end of the season (again, without compensation). Feudalism often entails certain extra-economic obligations between appropriator and producer; the serfs are bound to a particular lord, while the lord is often bound to provide the serf with minimally sufficient land and protection. Finally, the surplus extracted from the serf tends to be used wastefully, especially for internal and external security, and for conspicuous consumption by the appropriators. In the Marxian view, then, feudalism is a wasteful social system in the sense that it comprises no inherent mechanism to promote increasing productivity or economic growth. Instead, the social surplus generated by the serf is squandered. And as we shall see momentarily, this class process is also taken to be unjust.

The capitalist class system differs from feudalism in several important respects. First, the producers of surplus labor are nominally "free" under capitalism, rather than being bound to any one appropriator. Second, the surplus takes the form of "surplus value". This means that it ultimately flows to the capitalist in the form of money. Surplus value accrues to the capitalist because the wages paid to workers under capitalism fail to compensate them fully for the product of their labor. For example, though a worker might contribute eight hours to production each day, she might receive a wage that only entitles her to buy three hours' worth of society's total production. Each of her workdays therefore yields a surplus product that incorporates five hours of her labor that she delivers to the capitalist "gratis". This surplus product then forms the basis of the surplus value (the profit) that is realized when the output is sold. Third, the surplus generated under capitalism tends to be invested in new technologies that enhance social productivity. For many Marxists, the drive to reinvest the surplus follows from the inherent nature of capital as "self-expanding value"; for our purposes, we can interpret this tendency more simply as the result of inter-firm competition that forces each firm to seek greater productivity in order to survive and prosper. The firm that fails to reinvest the surplus may find that it suffers a competitive disadvantage in the face of innovation by its competitors. Hence, unlike feudalism, capitalism entails an inherent dynamic that generates rising levels of productivity and social wealth. Unfortunately, however, this wealth flows primarily to capitalist appropriators and to those most favorably positioned to receive distributed shares of the surplus.

Marx and "exploitation"

Marxists assess the legitimacy of class arrangements through the lens of justice. The Marxian tradition distinguishes between class arrangements that are "exploitative" and those that are "non-exploitative". The former refers to those class processes in which the producers of the surplus do not themselves lay initial claim to the surplus that they produce.[60] Instead, the surplus is taken from them without compensation. Exploitation therefore amounts to a form of social theft. Under feudalism and capitalism, the surplus flows to other claimants: to the feudal lords and capitalists, respectively. In each case, those who produce the surplus typically receive only that share of the total output that is necessary to sustain themselves. Whether they also are able to wrest some share of the surplus depends on their ability to overcome the power imbalance and other obstacles represented by the laws, institutions and customs associated with these class arrangements. Hence, societies in which these kinds of class processes predominate are marked by fundamental antagonisms between the producers and appropriators of the surplus, and by economic injustice.

In the Marxian view, capitalism represents a particularly insidious class arrangement because the form of exploitation associated with it is obscured by an appearance of equality and personal freedom in the market. Unlike slavery, the producers of the surplus under capitalism are not the property of the appropriators; unlike feudalism, the producers are not bound by law to labor their entire lives for one appropriator. Rather, the producers are legally free – free to enter the labor market and to form and terminate contracts with employers as they see fit. For Marx, they are free in an ironic sense: "freed" from ownership of the means of production – the tools and materials needed to produce – they are "free" only to be exploited by the employer of their choice, or to fall into poverty. *Formal* equality before the law therefore obscures the *substantive* inequality between producers and appropriators of the surplus, an inequality that herds workers into the ranks of the exploited (Marx 1977, ch. 6).

Capitalists typically do not rely explicitly on force to secure the surplus; indeed, the regular use of force would signal some other sort of class process.[61] Instead, workers generally (but not always, and not always happily) accept the terms of capitalist exploitation. The laws, institutions and norms of capitalist society encourage workers to seek only "a fair day's pay for a fair day's work" – a level of compensation that is commensurate with their contribution. Their claim to a share of the social output is treated as formally equivalent to the claims of those who provide other resources to production, such as capitalists, financiers and landlords. These arrangements reflect the convention that these other agents also are productive, thereby obscuring the reality that their role is merely to provide the means for workers to produce the full social surplus (and hence, to be exploited by those who appropriate it). Indeed, in the Marxian view, this obfuscation is codified and achieves scientific respectability in the form of neoclassical theory, with its marginal revenue product theory of compensation. In their pursuit of value-free economic science, Marxists conclude, neoclassical theorists contribute to the exploitation and immiseration of workers, all the while purporting to provide guidance for the maximization of social welfare!

Marxian normative commitments

The Marxian focus on class yields a normative commitment to the achievement of non-exploitative class processes. A non-exploitative class process is one in which those who produce the surplus serve also as the first claimants on the surplus; in which the producers are also the appropriators. Just as people *qua* citizens should have political rights to self-governance, so should they as workers have economic rights to appropriate the surplus that their labor generates. Marxists argue that justice requires and entails the end of institutionalized theft in the form of the right of appropriation by those who do not share in its production (Geras 1992).[62]

Now we must confront a theoretical problem. We have encountered here two distinct normative commitments in the work of Marx. On the one hand, we have a clear commitment to distribution according to need; on the other, we find a defense of the appropriation of the entire surplus by those who produce it. How are these to be reconciled, if at all? The answer is by no means clear in the Marxian tradition, and remains the subject of debate. After all, it is not difficult to imagine a society in which the producers of surplus with full and exclusive rights of appropriation live lavish lives at the expense of those who do not (or cannot) participate in its creation. Moreover, as a society experiences technological advance that reduces the need for labor, it may very well be the case that the proportion of the direct producers of surplus relative to the total population falls. In this case, restricting the right of appropriation of the surplus to those who participate in its production might very well generate a small but élite "aristocracy of labor". It is hard to imagine this sort of arrangement finding much support among adherents to Marxism, even though it would be one formally free of exploitation.[63]

We might resolve this tension between the dual Marxian normative commitments by recognizing that the end of exploitation is a necessary but insufficient condition for achieving Marx's needs-based distributive principle. Appropriators serve only as the first claimants on the surplus. What control they then have over the ultimate distribution of the surplus is entirely contingent, governed by society's laws, institutions and customs. We may not therefore infer any particular distributive outcome from a society's appropriative arrangements. Of course this is true in societies in which the slave, feudal and capitalist class processes predominate as well. One could imagine a hypothetical "capitalist" system in which the appropriators of the surplus were divested of this surplus, which is then distributed fairly equally across all of society's members. Indeed, actually existing capitalist societies do differ substantially amongst themselves in their degree of inequality of distribution. But Marxists worry that the constellation of the laws, institutions and customs that tend to arise in societies where exploitative class processes predominate generally obstruct fair distributions.[64] It is the Marxian hope, then, that a society in which the producers of surplus also serve as appropriators will be more apt to generate laws, institutions and customs that yield distributive justice. Having displaced the tyranny of rule by non-producing appropriators, a society in which non-exploitative class processes predominate might be expected to devise fairer systems of final distribution, not just of the social surplus, but of substantive opportunities and freedoms as well.

There is no guarantee, however, that this will be the case. Each of the three moments of the class process (the production, appropriation and distribution of the surplus) is a potential site of conflict among diverse social groups and a site of injustice. Hence, it would be mistaken to essentialize appropriation as the fundamental determinant of economic outcomes – as if the distribution of the surplus were a simple consequence of appropriation. The Marxian view therefore might better be thought of as coupling *three distinct spheres* of class justice: justice in the production, appropriation, and distribution of the surplus. Once we think about justice in this way, then we can recognize that the Marxian commitment to non-exploitation refers importantly but only to the second of these three spheres. In contrast, the Marxian principle *from each according to ability, to each according to need* refers importantly but only to the first and third. Taking these two principles together, we approach a multifaceted Marxian notion of justice that encompasses all three aspects of the class process.[65] This Marxian notion would entail what I will call "productive justice", "appropriative justice", and "distributive justice". The Marxian project is to establish societies that approach all three forms of justice.

SEN AND CAPABILITIES EQUALITY

The principle of distribution according to need has wide purchase among scholars of distributive justice, appearing (to varying degrees and with important qualifications) in the egalitarian visions of Rawls, Walzer, the institutionalists, and Marx. The work of Amartya Sen also falls within this tradition. Influenced by and sympathetic to the work of Rawls, Sen has undertaken to investigate how the existence of *interpersonal differences* bears upon the egalitarian project. This consideration leads him to a distributive principle that approaches that of Marx.[66]

In Sen's view, Rawls' approach to justice as fairness (which emphasizes the equal distribution of primary goods) fails to account satisfactorily for interpersonal differences, both within and across societies. Sen highlights the range of physical and mental capacities that exist across individuals, but also the variety of physical climates in which people live, the diverse institutional structures that mark their respective societies, and so forth. These important differences affect peoples' abilities to transform primary goods into the actual achievements that they have reason to value. As Sen notes, a person bound to a wheelchair will require more resources to achieve the same level of personal mobility than will others; a woman who is pregnant will require greater caloric intake to achieve the same level of nourishment. Moreover, a community that inhabits a malaria-infested region will require more medical resources than a more advantageously placed community in order to achieve the same level of health.

For Sen, these interpersonal differences are salient because primary goods are valuable only to the degree that they allow for the achievement of those states and conditions that people have reason to value. Sen refers to these as "functionings". They range from simple states, like being well nourished or avoiding preventable morbidity and premature mortality, to more complex states, like "appearing in public without shame", or achieving political efficacy. Sen designates the full set of functionings that a person can achieve, owing to her mental and physical capacities, but also to her social, economic, cultural, and other circumstances, her "capabilities". A person who faces a thicker and more extensive capability set is taken to have a higher potential quality of life than someone with a thinner, smaller capability set. Indeed, below some capability threshold level, a good human life as we know it is hardly possible at all (cf. Nussbaum 1992).[67]

Having drawn these distinctions, Sen concludes that the "focal variable" that should be equalized in an ideal society is not primary goods *per se*, but human capabilities. Owing to the existence of human diversity, an equal distribution of primary goods is apt to yield very different levels of potential achievement. If the end to which we aspire is an enhanced potential to achieve a valued life, then an egalitarian approach to justice should seek equality of that directly rather than equality of the means to live a valued life. *Contra* Rawls, then, Sen calls for the *unequal* distribution of primary goods in pursuit of equality of capabilities to achieve functionings. With Marx, this is a stance founded squarely on need.

This approach to equality has a number of virtues that we should take note of here, though their full significance for the matter at hand – theorizing justice in the context of global economic integration – will not be fully apparent until later chapters. First, like Walzer's, this is a complex account of equality. Sen rejects univocal accounts of equality on the grounds that human existence is too rich and diverse to be adequately accounted for by any one indicator. Though he chooses capabilities as a singular focal variable, capabilities comprise an extensive vector of distinct human functionings. Also like Walzer, he is troubled by the problem of domination. For Walzer, this occurs when the distribution of one social good (e.g. income) illicitly influences the distribution of another (e.g. political office). For Sen, this occurs when unequal capacities in one domain (e.g. the ability to achieve mobility) yields unequal capacities in another (e.g. the ability to secure meaningful employment). Walzer calls for barriers to prevent spillovers, so that a proper inequality in the distribution of one social good does not interfere with the distribution of another. Sen's solution is to call for the equal distribution of each and every kind of capability.[68]

Second, Sen's notion of equality privileges what may be called "substantive freedom". Sen's ideal society does not entail that each individual reach the same achievements – that is a matter for each of us to decide; only that each has the same substantive ability to do so. A person may rightly choose to refuse nutrition, or may choose to forego the degree of sheltering that is available to him. For Sen, the act of choosing is itself a valuable functioning, one that would be effaced by any distributive system that requires conformance in the lives we live.[69] We find here, then, strong affinities with the institutionalist emphasis on the obligation of society to provide each member with the means necessary to flourish and with the freedom to live his own life.

Third, the principle of capabilities equality promotes extensive (indeed, perpetual) social experimentation. It entails no necessary presumptions about the existence of one ideal set of institutional arrangements (such as neoliberalism, communism or any other). Instead, it encourages us to interrogate vigilantly the actual performance of the actually existing economic systems that arise and to press for reform to the degree that they fail to meet the demanding standard of capabilities equality. It adamantly refuses "end of history" narratives that anticipate the achievement of some final state of social organization. It takes an open-ended view of how societies might best enhance the capabilities of their inhabitants, understanding that different types of institution and practice will be necessary at different moments in time owing to changed circumstances and values of society's members. This may be discomforting to those who seek a closed, determinate model of how to organize society. It does, however, promote creative thinking about new alternatives that might better serve the egalitarian project than the restrictive models devised to date within reductionist social sciences.

Capabilities equality and the difference principle

Like Rawls, Sen is sensitive to the possibility that strict equality as he has defined it may not always be normatively defensible. Indeed, Sen has argued that there may be good reasons to append a difference principle to a system of capabilities equality. In this context, the difference principle would assert that particular functionings should be unequally distributed when those facing the smallest capabilities sets are helped thereby. In this formulation, for instance, a society may be forgiven the obligation to provide equal physical mobility to all its members if it could be shown that those with least mobility were somehow the primary beneficiaries of this inequality.

Is Sen correct in asserting a harmony between capabilities equality and the difference principle? And is the difference principle something that ought to be preserved? Taking these questions in reverse order, I will first examine a grave danger that the difference principle presents to the egalitarian project. I will then show that capabilities equality is not easily reconcilable with the difference principle, despite Sen's claims to the contrary. I will nevertheless conclude this discussion by examining how the difference principle might be operationalized within a capabilities framework in a way that minimizes the dangers it presents.

The chief problem associated with the difference principle is that it is prone to self-interested justification. Those who benefit from an unequal distribution can (and virtually always do) claim that the ultimate beneficiaries of this inequality are those who are worst off under the distribution. Consider the influence and even respectability of supply-side economics from the early 1980s up to the present. Supply-side economists (and their influential political allies, including US president Ronald Reagan and Britain's prime minister Margaret Thatcher) argued that the economic stagnation of the 1970s and 1980s was the consequence of tax policies that punished investors, and well-meaning though misguided social welfare expenditures that assisted the poor. Excessive capital gains taxes discouraged savings and investment, and so retarded advances in productivity, employment and income. Social welfare discouraged work effort and initiative by providing excessive payments to those out of work. The resulting supply-side policy mix was elegant and presented as entirely consistent with the difference principle: taxes on investment income and payments to the poor were both to be cut so as to induce greater economic dynamism. The normative problem with this policy mix, which entailed cutting taxes for the wealthy while reducing payments to the poor, was that it ensured growing inequality. But this was defended on the grounds that the chief beneficiaries would be working people and the poor, to whom the benefits of the ensuing economic vitality would ultimately "trickle down".

Supply-side analysis as such is no longer fashionable, largely because of other claims it made about the effects of tax cuts on budget deficits. The logic summarized here, however, has been fully absorbed into the neoclassical vision and its defense of global neoliberalism. Today it remains at the heart of the neoclassical attack on state direction of economic affairs. Though Rawls and other egalitarians would hardly approve, the difference principle provides normative cover for the unprecedented increases in global income inequality over the past three decades.

Rawls' approach to distributive justice relied on the device of the veil of ignorance. Those devising a just framework for distribution are to have no knowledge of the social positions or groups to which they will themselves be assigned after the distribution is undertaken. This device is intended to preclude self-serving argument of this sort. Unfortunately, disputes over distribution (and everything else) do not occur behind this veil. Those debating distribution, including when and how the difference principle is to apply, are always already embedded in their social milieu. They are already members of particular social groups, having already been assigned a particular race, gender, ancestry, degree of economic privilege, and so forth. Further, they have fairly good knowledge of these assignments prior to their participation in political contests over distribution. This is not to say that their views on distribution will be simply reducible to these assignments; were that to be so, debating justice would be a vacant exercise. It is to say that in the world in which disputes over justice actually occur, the motivation to devise self-serving defenses of inequality will be ever present.

The foregoing discussion suggests that the egalitarian will face the continual task of inspecting carefully all normative claims made on behalf of inequality. But here we encounter a second, more difficult complication. *Judgements about the ultimate effects of inequality are necessarily theory-dependent.* Judgements of this sort are never self-evident (as we examined in the introduction to Part 1 of this book), though partisans of one theory or another often treat them as such. Different theories reach distinct and often contradictory conclusions about a policy's effects. While the neoclassical vision holds that supply-side policies are apt to generate prosperity for working people, institutionalist and Marxian theories contend, as we have seen, that they are far more apt to induce widespread poverty. Hence, even if decisions about the difference principle were to be considered by a committee of representatives behind the veil of ignorance, we have no reason to presume that the committee's members will reach a consensus except in the most trivial of cases. To ensure consensus, we would have to impute to these members the *same* social theory. But this would violate the spirit of the entire exercise, which presumes at the outset the existence among reasonable people of alternative comprehensive doctrines. Rawls simply cannot have it both ways here: either he must demand that the members share the same theory so as to reach the same conclusion, or he must concede that they are apt to reach irresolvable differences amongst themselves when assessing the applicability of the difference principle. What is more, given the ceaseless ingenuity and imagination of human thinkers, we should expect that even the most egregious expansions of inequality will find support from some respectable social theory.

The framework of capabilities equality provides a strict and demanding criterion for evaluating normative claims for inequality predicated on the difference principle, one that may be particularly useful for filtering out self-serving claims. As Sen emphasizes, distinct functionings (or groups of them, for example economic, political and cultural functionings) are *interdependent*. The ability to avoid preventable morbidity, for instance, may depend on one's access to sufficient health care, shelter, nutrition, income, and many other functionings. Hence, any one "functioning failure" may interfere with many others, though the pathways among them may not always or even generally be as direct as this simple example suggests. Complicating matters further, relative inequality in any one functioning might induce relative inequality in others, and even absolute functioning failures. For example, a poor person in a market economy may not only be deprived of important goods, like adequate housing, but may also find it difficult to participate meaningfully in the political life of her community. Indeed, her relative poverty (or indeed, any functioning disadvantage) might therefore be expected to undermine her capabilities across the spectrum. Sen rightly concludes on this basis that it may be far worse to endure low income in a high-income community than in a community where everyone else is similarly poor. In the former, the poor person may suffer other functionings failures associated with being relatively poor, while in the latter context, she would not be so disadvantaged.

Taken together, these arguments suggest that it is most unlikely that inequality in any important functioning will promote the overall capabilities of those who fare worst in this one functioning. Instead, it is far more likely that one functioning failure will generate general incapacity. We should therefore conclude that real cases in which the difference principle would unambiguously apply will be the rare exception to the rule. Appreciation of the interdependence of diverse functionings should therefore lead us to examine critically any claims that relative inequality will help most those who receive least. Unfortunately, the pathways relating diverse functionings will not usually be clear (and in any event will be theoretically contested), and so a heavy burden must lie with those who would argue for inequality to demonstrate that it meets the difference principle criterion.

Nevertheless, we should not rule out the possibility that the difference principle might rightly apply in a particular circumstance. To do so would be shortsighted, perhaps generating outcomes that are harmful to the most disadvantaged, and even dogmatic. The challenge in operationalizing the difference principle is to protect against the self-interested invocation by those who would benefit from its implementation. This problem might be addressed through procedures that grant exclusive veto authority to those who would become relatively disadvantaged under its implementation. Those who would defend a policy reform that entails greater relative inequality from which they stand to benefit would be allowed to argue its merits, but they would not be empowered otherwise to participate in the decision over whether to enact the policy, for example through voting. That authority would lie exclusively with those who would be required to make do with less under the policy. But this should cause no discomfort to those excluded from the vote: if the case for the policy is well made, those voting would have every reason to give their consent, as they would stand to be the primary beneficiaries. Finally, in the event that those voting find that they made the wrong decision, they should also be uniquely empowered to reverse course so as to restore the prior degree of equality.[70]

Capabilities, freedom and liberty

We will explore other important attributes of capabilities equality in the following chapter. For now, an important distinction must be drawn to avoid confusion. Other normative systems privilege personal autonomy and freedom, of course, and some of these are explicitly anti-egalitarian. Chief among these is libertarianism, which demands the protection of *formal* rights and liberties. Libertarianism opposes what it takes to be artificial restrictions on personal liberty stemming from unwarranted government intervention into personal affairs (see Chapter 1). In this doctrine economic outcomes are just to the degree that they result from the voluntary interaction of free individuals, with each pursuing his own interests as he sees fit provided that his doing so does not infringe upon the equal rights of others (Nozick 1974). Libertarianism is therefore entirely consistent with even extraordinary inequalities in income and wealth.[71]

Despite a shared concern with personal freedom, these two doctrines are markedly different in underlying worldview and practical consequences. The libertarian view privileges the autonomous individual as primary and foundational, as the irreducible source of all capacities, preferences, rights and interests. In this view, the community emerges simply as an instrumental construction instituted by such individuals in order to protect their autonomy from encroachment as each pursues his own life plan (Nozick 1974). In contrast, Sen's view parallels that of institutionalism in treating the community and the human beings who populate it as mutually constitutive. The community shapes the life circumstances of its members, but also their personalities, ways of being, desires and capacities. In this account, it is impossible to consider the human actor outside of the social milieu he inhabits – hence, the specification of the individual as foundational is non-sensical. This does not mean, though, that social actors are merely dependent variables who absorb the social customs, norms and institutions of their communities. Rather, these socialized individuals react back upon their social and cultural inheritances, reshaping them in accord with their own judgements and interests.[72]

The fundamental difference between the libertarian and Senian conceptions of the individual and society shapes their respective accounts of personal freedom and justice. Libertarianism endorses "negative" freedom – not freedom to achieve anything concrete in particular, but freedom to devise and pursue a life plan unhindered by onerous government actions (cf. Berlin 1958). Those who fare poorly in pursuit of their goals have no right to exploit the coercive force of government to overcome their own failings. Government initiatives to reduce inequalities in social wealth are therefore deemed unjust insofar as they infringe upon the liberties of those whose rightful claims to property are thereby abridged. In contrast, Sen's commitment to equal substantive freedom reflects the view that the community has a strong obligation to each of its members, to provide her with the means she needs to flourish at a level achievable by others. Negative freedom is not enough. Indeed, to the degree that it gives rise to inequality in substantive freedoms, it is normatively indefensible. In this view, a community that refuses to take measures to promote and equalize capabilities can be indicted for preventing the full flourishing of those members whose substantive freedom it neglects.

DISTRIBUTIVE JUSTICE AND "HUMAN NATURE"

We have now explored several egalitarian distributive principles. But is any such distributive principle possible or desirable, given our common, irreducible human nature? Many have argued that any society that seeks to implement equal distributions must impose all sorts of untenable restrictions on the freedoms of its citizens, given their natural propensities to seek to accumulate wealth, compete, and achieve. Given these propensities, the restrictions will also distort economic activity. An egalitarian society, on this account, deprives itself of freedom and wealth, yielding an outcome in which all are equal, but equally impoverished (Hayek 1944). Wouldn't it be better for society to establish institutions and principles of distribution which accord with our basic drives, rather than try to suppress them in the name of fairness? And isn't this precisely the basis of the neoclassical support for neoliberalism?

In its own way, each of the heterodox approaches surveyed here rejects the essentialist notion of an inherent human nature, if that term is taken to mean some ineradicable set of drives that necessarily shape our private and social aspirations, actions and ways of being (see Chapter 2). We do have biologically inscribed needs, to be sure. In the anti-reductionist view, however, we ought not to think of human behavior as somehow reducible to these needs. If humans have a nature, a set of capacities or drives that distinguishes them from most (if not all) other species of life, it is the capacity to alter their knowledge, their understandings of themselves and their environment, and thereby to become something other than what they were. It is the capacity to strive to overcome their inherited nature (Levins and Lewontin 1985). For Marxists, this is the essential human capacity: the ability to change the physical and social environment in accord with the plans humans conjure in their minds, and thereby to change themselves.[73] Institutionalists agree, arguing only that Marxists underestimate the variety of social factors that affect human motivations and behavior (cf. Tool 1979). This view of human nature implies that when we encounter in ourselves or our societies particular attributes or ways of being that we take to be malevolent or otherwise illegitimate, we need not accept them as immutable. Rather, we are encouraged to recognize them as contingent, as fundamentally alterable through the labor we perform on our environments, and thereby on ourselves.

Much confusion and controversy has surrounded the claim of the inherent plasticity of human nature. Natural and social scientists (ranging from biologists and geneticists to anthropologists and sociologists) have attempted to distinguish that part of human behavior that is due to biology ("nature") from that due to social circumstance ("nurture"). Some have argued, for instance, that human intelligence and drives are locked into and largely governed by our genetic makeup (cf. Herrnstein and Murray 1994). For some of those who occupy the biological pole of the debate, the claim that human nature is malleable is misinterpreted to mean that humans face no biological constraints whatsoever. But the anti-reductionist argument is not that no such constraints exist; it is, rather, the more nuanced and far more tenable point that *these constraints are not ultimately determinative when it comes to the matter of how we live.* Rather than fully determine social behavior, they participate along with innumerable other factors in overdetermining our social existence (Resnick and Wolff 1987a). This means that while their effects should not be ignored, neither should they be privileged as the unmediated, fundamental cause of human behavior or social institutions.

The claim that human nature is fluid and overdetermined by both biological and social factors does not mean that anything is always possible. Indeed, the point is rather the reverse – that at any historical moment, given what "human nature" and society's institutions and norms have become, certain paths of change are possible, and many others are not. Social change, on this account, is *path-dependent.* Certain kinds of human actors, operating in a certain kind of social environment at a particular moment in time can work to alter both their own and their environment's natures, but the possibilities that exist for them at that moment are largely shaped by these existent natures. Paraphrasing Marx, we may conclude that humanity makes its own history, but not under circumstances of its own choosing. The anti-essentialist claims only that these natures can be changed, allowing society to evolve into new forms comprising new kinds of people.

All of this is by way of saying that when we encounter disputes over the nature of policy regimes and especially claims for radical reform, we ought to be wary of those who would automatically invoke what I will call the "human nature constraint". This is the refuge of those who cannot or will not risk envisioning alternative ways of being. The claim that "human nature won't allow it" is to be read, not as an irrefutable scientific proposition, but as a protest against being forced to consider that the way we have lived and taken to be right to live is, indeed, not the best (or worse, *not even an appropriate*) way to live. It is a defense against the self-repudiation that engaging alternatives often entails. And as a criterion of policy choice, it is deeply biased. The human nature constraint almost always serves to solidify the status quo against demands for social reform – be it by abolitionists, feminists or egalitarians. After all, it is far easier to legitimize what already exists by reference to it than it is to defend that which exists only in the imagination of the reformer.

Market rewards and incentives

The dispute over human nature bears directly on the matter of the role of market incentives in inducing socially benevolent behavior. Those advocating for substantive equality, whether before a gathering of professional economists or a class of first-year students, inevitably face the argument that an economy lacking monetary incentives will lack dynamism and innovation. Why should rational individuals work hard and take the substantial risks associated with innovation if they don't stand to reap substantial compensation? For example, workers will hardly strain to provide good service to their employers, or accept dangerous or onerous but vitally necessary assignments, if their compensation is not commensurate with their contribution. Moreover, the discovery of new life-saving drugs often entails the expenditure of millions of dollars on research over many years, during which there is no guarantee of success. Without the promise of substantial financial reward, there is no reason why a medical researcher will invest the time, energy and funds to the project.

The anti-reductionist reply to these claims entails, first, as we have seen, a rejection of the notion that human subjectivity is reducible to the egoistic pursuit of individual satisfaction. In place of the presumption of a universal human nature such as that specified by neoclassical theory, anti-reductionists view the human actor as a social product with heterogeneous and even conflicting needs, aspirations and sentiments. Even in a fully marketized economy, in which the egoistic orientation posited by neoclassical theory is most likely to prevail, the individual is driven by far more than sticks and carrots.

It is important to add a further argument, also fully consistent with this perspective. Even if material or financial incentives are sometimes necessary to induce certain important social behaviors, the magnitude of the necessary incentive is entirely socially determined and therefore variable. Consider the following: in 1965, the ratio of the average salary of the chief executive officers of the 365 largest corporations in the US to the average salary of US factory workers was about 44 to 1. By the 1980s, that ratio had grown to over 200 to 1; by 1997, it had reached 326 to 1 (*New York Times* 2/7/99). This startling trend begs the simple question of those who sing the virtues of market incentives: *just how much inequality in market rewards is sufficient to induce economic actors to pursue socially beneficial behaviors?* Was the ratio of 44:1 insufficient to encourage honest effort by our CEOs? Is 326:1 just enough? Can we infer from the more than sevenfold increase in the inequality in market rewards a commensurate increase in the level of socially benevolent behavior over this period? Are today's CEOs contributing more to social welfare than their counterparts ten, twenty and thirty years ago? Would a smaller increase have reduced the supply of beneficial behavior? *Where is the proof of that?* Meanwhile, the level of salaries of CEOs in other industrialized countries has been and remains far below the US level. For instance, British CEOs today earn about 60 per cent of their counterparts in the US, while Japanese and German CEOs earn only about 39 and 37 per cent, respectively (*New York Times* 1/17/99). Insofar as wages for factory workers in these countries are close to US levels (and are in some cases higher), we find much lower levels of inequality in compensation in these countries. But Japan and Germany have exhibited levels of productivity growth that exceed those of the US for most of the postwar period (even after they had approached US levels). Might we infer, then, that the CEO compensation levels (and the resulting ratios of CEO to factory worker pay) in these countries are high enough? If not, just what is the "right" level of inequality? Unfortunately, the neoclassical vision provides no answer, and in its silence on this matter it implicitly takes whatever level of inequality arises through the market as essentially correct. On this basis, it concludes that any reduction in inequality would undermine the market's incentive structure, and thereby reduce social welfare.[74]

Putting before us the question of how much inequality is enough should suffice to demonstrate the anti-reductionist view that the incentive effect of any particular level of inequality of market reward will depend fully on the context in which it occurs. Where people have come to expect small differentials in income as adequate reward for their labors, small differentials may very well suffice to induce honest effort, saving, innovation and sacrifice. Where people instead have come to expect huge differentials, it may be the case that only huge differentials may induce these behaviors. Neoclassicals might argue that this difference simply reflects differences in peoples' exogenous preferences – preferences that are therefore impervious to alteration via policy reform. But the anti-reductionist counters that this difference is fully endogenous to the institutions, norms, and existing patterns of distribution that permeate society. As such, they are malleable and susceptible to change through explicit policy interventions.

In the neoclassical vision, one's level of satisfaction derives exclusively from the level of one's own consumption, independent of the consumption level of others. Due to human insatiability, a higher income necessarily generates increasing satisfaction. But critics contend that in a society marked by substantial inequality, where one's worth as a person is tied to one's material acquisitions and income, people may gain satisfaction not primarily from their *absolute* level of income, but from their standing *relative* to other community members. Indeed, many social researchers have validated these hypotheses (Daly 1991). Related to this, a person's satisfaction might result from the acquisition of "positional goods" – such as the highest house on the hill, or the largest salary in the country club. In this case, only relative increases in income, and/or the acquisition of additional positional goods, might induce greater personal satisfaction. As soon as one executive secures a raise, his peers may feel terribly aggrieved by their relative loss. They will likely demand a higher salary in exchange for their best work. Last year's bonus of $200,000, which seemed so princely at the time, might now look paltry and grossly inadequate as just compensation for a man of one's abilities. Unconstrained by law, norms or conventions, we might therefore expect income escalation among those most favorably placed as they vie for increasing relative reward – and a consequent deepening chasm between rich and poor. As this occurs, the neoclassical visionary has no choice but to legitimize the resulting inequality as a necessary incentive to induce productive behaviors.

Recognition of the importance of relative reward for personal satisfaction in a stratified society actually may be taken to have egalitarian implications. First, it provides us with a further basis for rejecting the normative legitimacy of personal desires as the basis of social choice. As with lavish tastes (see Chapter 2), we have good grounds for discounting the preference to achieve greater income and status than others. When people desire the wrong ends, these ends ought to be disqualified as normative criteria. But the concept of relative reward also implies that even a market economy predicated upon the inducements of financial rewards can get by with far less inequality than often arises. If satisfaction is tied to one's relative standing, then we might conclude that the absolute gap in incomes and wealth experienced today is entirely unnecessary. It might very well be the case that individuals are willing to work every bit as hard when the differential rewards to which their labors give rise are a mere fraction of current levels. The satisfaction of owning the highest house on the hill may not be diminished in the least when its purchase price is, say, $300,000 as opposed to $3 million; the pleasure of commanding the greatest salary in the club may be just as great at $200,000 as it is at $20 million. The competition for relative rewards and positional goods can carry on just as aggressively when the differentials at stake are denominated in pennies rather than dollars. If indeed it is the subjective importance that gets attached to a differential rather than its absolute size that matters, then there is simply no good reason to presume that the differential needed to induce appropriate behavior be at all substantial. Hence, even were we to decide that differential rewards are sometimes necessary to induce certain beneficial behaviors (and this would have to be shown, not presumed), we are warranted in seeking to diminish these differentials to the minimum necessary to do the job.

To sum up: once we take account of the fundamental human capacity to change human nature and human society, then we can recognize that the invocation of the human nature constraint entails an important error. This is the error of elevating the merely contingent to the status of indelible essence. This constraint solidifies the status quo by strangling the imagination and staving off social experimentation in pursuit of a more just society. Moreover, even when financial incentives are desirable, we have no reason to accept the legitimacy or desirability of whatever arbitrary level of inequality emerges from market processes. Just what level of inequality will suffice to induce particular attitudes and behaviors is socially determined and variable.

Nevertheless, when pursuing radical reform, we must attend not only to what we believe is desirable, but also to what might be possible, given where we presently stand. We must be prepared to join any policy reform agenda (not least, an egalitarian agenda) to a practical, available politics that seems likely to achieve this agenda, where both the policy ends and the political means are normatively defensible. While the presumption that all radical reform is impossible is defeatist, the presumption that any reform we might imagine is always possible is utopian. The egalitarian project is poorly served by either presumption.

EGALITARIANISM AGAINST NEOLIBERALISM

I concluded the previous chapter by arguing that welfarism is a deeply flawed normative perspective, and so fails to provide a compelling normative defense of neoliberal market outcomes. The question we now need to address is whether the egalitarian perspective devised here does so. Indeed, it does not. To see this, let us consider the neoclassical ideal of the perfectly functioning competitive market system, absent all imperfections, as the basis for our evaluation. We will consider here the neoclassical view of the legitimacy of market-based rewards.

Rewarding contribution: the instrumental argument

Recall that in the neoclassical vision, distribution is to be tied entirely to contribution, not to need. Distribution based on contribution is taken to be instrumentally right. As we found, the market is taken to be an ideal mechanism of distribution in the neoclassical vision precisely because it does ensure equality between (marginal) contribution and reward. The owner of each factor of production, from labor to land and capital, receives payment commensurate with the net contribution of the factor she provides – its marginal revenue product. Chasing higher rewards, she will undertake to improve the quality of the factor she contributes to production – and thereby will yield a higher contribution to social output. Were rewards not tied to contribution, rational economic agents would have no incentive to enhance their contributions. Were rewards instead tied to need, for instance, they would have an incentive to appear more needy, so as to garner a larger share of that which they did not themselves produce.

Viewed from the perspective of Sen's capabilities framework this instrumental view of market reward fails. In the Senian perspective, the level of one's productivity is a function of one's complete set of capabilities as well as one's effort (and other choices). Inequality in physical mobility, or access to education or health care, will necessarily translate into inequality in productivity, regardless of the choices people make. In a society that has achieved relatively equal capabilities across its citizens, we might take differences in contribution (provided this was something we could measure) to be largely the result of differences in effort. But we cannot make this judgement in a society with substantial capabilities inequality. Here the range of productivity levels available to the society's members will vary considerably, despite the individual choices that they make. In this case, it becomes illegitimate to reward effort by tying compensation to contribution. In an unequal society, this formula merely rewards the capabilities-rich for their advantages. If we believe on instrumental grounds that effort should be rewarded, then we need to find some way to measure and compensate that directly. Though convenient, it is entirely illegitimate in an unequal society to take contribution as a satisfactory proxy for effort.

In the neoclassical vision, as we found in Chapter 2, this problem is suppressed. Neoclassicals recognize, of course, that an agent's market contribution (and hence current income) depends on the resource endowments that she brings to the market. In this vision, however, each agent is taken to be responsible for the level of endowments she possesses. Here we find the combined force of the essences and reductionist logic of the vision striking with a vengeance. Present inequalities in resources are the natural consequence of the distinct patterns of past decisions made by utility-maximizing, rational actors – decisions about amassing human capital, and about managing the trade-off between consumption and savings. Those with large amounts of capital (or more likely, their ancestors) evidently chose to forego consumption in the past to amass savings. Those with few endowments chose instead immediate gratification over investment and provisioning for the future. That one agent now brings to the market a large sum of accumulated capital while another brings only her ability to perform low-productivity tasks is therefore hardly cause for normative complaint. Why, after all, should we possibly want to punish the well-endowed for their past prudence? Doing so would disrupt the very incentive structure that encouraged them to pursue the socially benevolent activity of enhancing their productivity. The default position that this way of thinking yields is that each agent faces today the endowment set that she deserves, based on past decisions. An agent who is displeased with her rewards today will have an incentive to increase her resource base. If she places sufficient importance on increasing her future income, she will take the necessary steps today to augment the supply and quality of the resources she commits to production.

The notion of capabilities equality alerts us to the likelihood that differences in income will not be overcome through incentive mechanisms of the sort provided by the perfectly functioning free market. Inequalities in resource endowments and inequalities in capabilities are self-reinforcing, and so a system that ties reward to contribution is likely to induce deepening inequality over time. Public policy interventions are therefore needed to right the wrongs of inequality across the spectrum of functionings. Hence, the neoclassical claim that tying reward to contribution is instrumentally desirable fails.

Rewarding contribution: the intrinsic argument

What of the other claim about distribution that appears in the neoclassical vision, to wit: that tying reward to contribution is intrinsically right, regardless of its instrumental effects? In this view, as we have seen, an agent who contributes more to social output is inherently entitled to receive a greater share than those who contribute less.

The principle of capabilities equality, combined with the anti-reductionist perspective advanced above, encourage three objections to this claim. The first follows directly from the immediately foregoing discussion. This formulation of entitlement requires for normative support the notion that distinct individuals possess relatively equal ability to contribute to social output. Only in this case could we infer that differences in contribution reflect different choices that warrant different rewards. But as we have just considered, the perspective of capabilities equality reminds us that people do not generally have equal abilities to contribute. Inequalities in any one functioning might yield inequality in agents' productivities. In this case, the notion that greater contribution deserves greater reward fails: why, after all, should the capabilities-enriched deserve greater reward merely for being so privileged?

Institutionalist theory provides the basis for a second, related objection. As we have seen, institutionalists reject the validity of the very concept of measuring (let alone rewarding) an individual's productivity, on the grounds that her contribution depends on a host of environmental factors over which she has little control. These factors include the amount and quality of the other available factors of production; the skills and attitudes of her co-workers; the systems of norms and conventions that she and others in the workplace depend upon in orchestrating their co-operative behavior, and so forth. These are the embedded, institutionalized product of the entire community, past and present. As such, her own productivity is a fully social outcome, the produced result of systems and ways of being for which she may have little to no direct responsibility. If this is so, it become much more difficult to make the case that she has an intrinsic right to reward based upon her own individual contribution. Rather, it would seem that the community as a whole, including those not directly involved in production, is responsible for and therefore should have say in how the total social product is to be distributed.

The third objection concerns how we theorize and measure social output, so that we can undertake to divide it according to contribution. The problem might best be approached through an example. Consider two workers who perform similar tasks in two different enterprises. Let us suppose that each runs some sort of basic machine, and though they perform somewhat different tasks, each performs the same number of operations per day, and works for the same number of hours. Now suppose that one of these works in a handgun factory, while the other works in a toyshop. Let us suppose further that their labors each result in ten units per day – ten guns for the former, and ten toys for the latter – and that the market price of each gun is twice that of each toy. Let us presume finally that the two are roughly equally skilled, and so bring approximately the same amount of human capital to the market each day. Can we infer that they will make relatively equal contributions to the social output, and that they therefore deserve equal wages?

There are important senses in which their contributions are equal. For instance, it is perfectly reasonable to theorize society's total output as the physical embodiment of the labor required to produce it. We might then measure output in terms of labor time. Were we to do this, we would conclude that the two workers have made an equal contribution, insofar as they have performed an equal number of hours of labor. Tying reward to contribution, we would then find that they deserve equal compensation. The normative content of this approach is clear (though not necessarily compelling): those who sacrifice equal numbers of hours of their personal time for the sake of social provisioning should be equally compensated.

The neoclassical perspective, however, views the matter of valuing social output and measuring relative contribution differently. In the neoclassical vision, the social product is theorized as the physical embodiment of the social welfare that it provides. As a consequence, a worker's contribution to social output depends not on the hours he labors, but on the net contribution he makes to this stock of social welfare. This is his marginal revenue product (or the number of units he produces multiplied by their price). Insofar as the market price of a product reflects its marginal social benefit (see Chapter 2), price times the quantity contributed by the worker gives us a measure of his net contribution to social welfare.

We know that the two workers are producing the same number of units per day, but that the price of each handgun is twice that of each toy. In this case, the worker lucky enough to be employed by the gun factory will have a marginal revenue product twice that of his counterpart in the toyshop. He will therefore command double the wage, rightfully reflecting his larger net contribution to social output. This inequality will no doubt induce the (rational) toyshop worker to seek work in the gun factory, of course. When he does so, his marginal revenue product and wage, and the supply of handguns relative to toys, will increase. Consequently, both our relocated worker and his society will experience rising welfare.

At the risk of further repetition, it must be emphasized that the normative weight of this formulation depends on our treating market prices as "right" in the sense of reflecting social values. Only by taking the higher price of the handgun as evidence of its greater social value can we infer that the worker who produces it enhances social welfare more than does the toyshop worker – or that the shift from toy to gun production has increased social welfare. This depends in turn on our treating all preferences as both exogenously formed and equally valid. It also depends on our committing to a reductionist view of the market, so that only the essences recognized by neoclassical theory determine market prices. We discovered earlier that unless we commit to these severe assumptions, we cannot attribute any particular importance to market prices; nor can we take any normative comfort from market outcomes. If, for example, the preferences seeking fulfillment are in any sense indictable, then the equilibrium market prices for goods will be normatively suspect, and so then will be the rewards that flow to the suppliers of resource – like wages, rents, dividends and profits. And in this event, that the worker in the handgun factory earns a higher wage than his counterpart in the toyshop tells us absolutely nothing about their respective social contributions.

Generalizing from this example, we can specify a difficult set of conceptual problems that confronts all those who would draw a normative link between reward and contribution. First, they have to theorize the social product to which individual agents contribute. Second, they then have to theorize the mathematical function that relates any one agent's behavior to the total social product. One could envision the social product as the physical embodiment of total hours of the community's labor, and then allocate shares based simply on hours worked. Alternatively, one could also envision the social product as spiritual fulfillment, or the absence of suffering, or equality of substantive freedom, and then allocate shares based on one's contribution to the achievement of this goal. Under these latter alternatives, even a mediocre nurse would likely rate a substantially higher reward than would a very clever advertisement executive. Neoclassical theory chooses instead to think of the social product as a level of social welfare which stems exclusively from peoples' subjective states, and identifies marginal product as the link between the individual's contribution and the total social product. The neoclassical vision then takes the next step of valorizing marginal product as the appropriate measure of an agent's reward.

Why should we accept this formulation, from among the countless alternatives, as intrinsically right? Neoclassical theory is spared from having to defend this choice by deriving it axiomatically from its set of initial assumptions that are treated as causal essences. Having committed to these essences, there is little basis for interrogating what follows logically therefrom. But this implies that this particular normative claim fails once we surrender either the essences or the reductionist logic of neoclassical theory. Absent these essences and logic, we recognize that though peoples' subjective states may be *a* consideration when evaluating alternative economic outcomes, they are hardly the only worthy consideration.

CONCLUSION

What we have identified here as the heterodox view actually entails a family of loosely related theories. These share an aversion to welfarism. Each asks, *what makes for a good economic outcome?* And each answers that question with a particular kind of egalitarianism. Some, like Rawls, emphasize equal distribution of the goods people need to achieve a valued life; others, like Marx and Sen, emphasize actual potential achievement, and reach the conclusion that goods must be unequally distributed according to need so that all are equally able to live valued lives. All of these egalitarians take equality of substantive opportunities to be inherently right; though some (like the institutionalists) emphasize its instrumental validity insofar as it induces better behaviors, institutions, social experimentation and problem solving.

Egalitarians reject the claim that there is some essential human nature to which social and economic institutions must correspond. Instead, they understand human subjectivity to be heterogeneous, socially constructed and variable. They therefore bristle at the claim of neoclassical visionaries that only an economy that is compatible with self-interest is feasible, just or desirable. Moreover, even where market incentives are shown to be necessary, they understand that the magnitude of the incentives necessary to cajole appropriate behaviors might be paltry compared to the levels of inequality we face today.

Egalitarianism refuses to grant normative cover to the neoliberal market ideal of the neoclassical vision. But this is hardly surprising: those who champion the neoclassical vision, after all, do not claim that neoliberalism yields equality of incomes, wealth, primary goods or other outcomes. They do claim that it provides economic agents with relatively equal chances to improve the quality of their lives by dint of hard work and sacrifice, with the rewards they deserve based on the decisions they make, and with the right kinds of incentive to induce them to undertake socially-benevolent behaviors. Essentializing rational choice, they are able to suppress the degree to which non-choice variables determine peoples' substantive life chances under a neoliberal regime.

Advocates of egalitarianism demand far more than this kind of formal equality. They recognize that formal equality even in perfectly functioning markets of the sort that the neoclassical vision celebrates is apt to yield very unequal rewards across society's members. They also recognize that inequality in market rewards and substantive freedoms is apt to be self-reinforcing over time. Insofar as they view substantive equality as the vital component of a just society, they break with the neoliberal ideal as an appropriate distributive mechanism.

We have seen that the neoclassical vision that ties an agent's reward to her marginal productivity is but one token of a broader normative type that ties reward to contribution. We have found that this principle runs up against the difficult challenges of how to theorize the total social product to which the efforts of distinct agents give rise, and to disaggregate the social product across these diverse agents. Egalitarians tend to reject all approaches that equate reward with contribution, insofar as this generally entails rewarding most those with the greatest capabilities. But they particularly object to the neoclassical formulation of this link, as it is founded on weak premises about the nature of preferences that allow them to valorize the market price as inherently right. As should by now be clear, a social science that strives so hard to avoid value judgements is prone to normative errors of the most basic sort.

Part 2

Global neoliberalism

As I have emphasized throughout, one of the most seductive aspects of the neoclassical vision is its explanatory elegance. On the basis of a simple set of initial assumptions, the neoclassical vision produces dramatic and unambiguous policy conclusions. Chief among these is the claim that the unfettered market is the optimal institution around which to organize any economic system. This claim is universal, permitting of no qualifications of time, place or context. Wherever and whenever a society populated by rational humans of the sort specified by neoclassical theory comes into existence, it will be better served by neoliberalism than by any alternative form of economic organization.

We can take note now of a second aspect of this universalist impulse. Not only is neoliberalism uniquely optimal for any individual society, so is it also the optimal regime under which to integrate the economies of distinct societies. The neoclassical vision promotes what I have referred to as global neoliberalism, which entails the replacement of state- with market-mediated economic flows and outcomes, within and across all national borders. Ideally, the international flow of resources, goods and services, and the determination of income shares should be dictated by the market forces of supply and demand, as private economic actors pursue their own individual interests in the unified global marketplace. In this sense, advocates of the neoclassical vision would divest national borders of their economic significance.

Global neoliberalism therefore entails the formation of a global policy regime that comprises free trade and the free flow of resources via market mechanisms. We will investigate some of the specific arguments made in defense of this regime below. We must, however, acknowledge provisionally here the analytical efficiency with which this extension from domestic to global neoliberalism is achieved. The case for global neoliberalism requires a minimum of *ad hoc* theoretical adjustments. By contrast, the logic and intuition informing the neoclassical vision remain essentially the same in all important respects.

Global neoliberalism extends all the virtues of the market to the international arena. First, it expands consumer choice in domestic markets.

Consumers can choose domestically produced goods, or goods produced thousands of miles away. Second, neoliberalism allows each factor of production to relocate in search of the highest possible rewards. This increases the income to the owners of the relocating factors. But as we have seen, insofar as a factor's reward is tied to its marginal contribution in a market economy, this means that the factor will also yield a higher social contribution. Hence the market incentives associated with global neoliberalism generate greater economic efficiency. Third, and as we will explore in Chapter 6, global neoliberalism allows each country to concentrate its efforts on the production of those goods for which it is best suited, while acquiring other kinds of goods from other countries through trade. This specialization increases total world output, and induces higher income for all countries. Taken together, we find that global neoliberalism enhances global social welfare.

In this section we will focus on two principal aspects of the neoclassical defense of global neoliberalism. The first is the neoclassical antipathy toward active state involvement in the economy in pursuit of national competitiveness. Since the 1970s, many economists and policy analysts have argued that a nation's prosperity depends on the competitive success of its domestic firms in global markets. This argument has intuitive appeal – when a firm fares poorly in global market competition, after all, its workers generally lose their jobs, income and economic security. Proponents of this view argue for all sorts of government strategies to promote competitive success, as we will see. Neoclassicals disagree, finding national competitiveness to be analytically suspect and normatively bankrupt. Indeed, they argue that national competitiveness has virtually no impact on a nation's level of prosperity.

The second aspect that we will consider is free trade. Over the past several centuries, economists and others have voiced diverse complaints against free trade. The nature of these complaints has changed over time, as we might expect. Today, two very different alternatives to free trade have achieved some standing among heterodox economists and others – strategic trade, and fair trade. Neoclassicals have proven to be universally unsympathetic to the critiques raised against free trade. Not surprisingly, then, they are also uniformly opposed to these two alternatives.

These two controversies have proven to be among the most heated and divisive within global political economy and economic policy circles for the past two decades. Unusual alliances have emerged in these debates. For instance, many heterodox economists join ardent neoclassicals in resisting the charms of national competitiveness, despite the fact that they disagree about the nature of global neoliberalism. The chapters in this section are intended to clarify what is at stake in these debates. In keeping with the focus of the book, we will investigate the normative rather than the empirical substance of these controversies.

Three chief positions have emerged in these two debates. I will refer to these somewhat inelegantly as the neoclassical vision; progressive nationalism; and internationalist egalitarianism. Chapter 5 will undertake to explore what each of these has to say about national competitiveness; Chapter 6 will examine their respective claims about trade.

First, we must explore a difficult question that arises in the context of global economic integration; namely, how to think about formulating normative principles to assess and construct global policy regimes in a world marked by substantive cultural differences. What are we to do, and how are we to proceed, when we find that different societies hold distinct accounts of what is good or right? What are we licensed and/or obligated to do when economic integration brings us into consequential interaction with societies which have defined for themselves ways of being that strike us as not only different but also indictable against the standard of our own normative commitments? To what degree and in what ways should we take these differences into account in formulating the rules of international economic integration?

Chapter 4 seeks to elucidate these matters in the abstract. We will examine the theoretical contest between two alternative normative frameworks that inform global economic policy debates, and that offer strikingly different answers to these questions. These frameworks are cultural relativism and moral objectivism. Though most neoclassical visionaries do not draw explicit reference to this debate, we will see in Chapter 6 that in fact their vision is predicated on a strong attachment to a rather strict form of cultural relativism. In contrast, many critics of neoliberalism draw on moral objectivism. I will argue that, despite their respective laudable aims, each of these normative frameworks is deficient. In their place I will advocate the principle of capabilities equality, and will attempt to demonstrate that the virtues of this approach become particularly salient precisely in the cross-cultural context, where we must balance the competing virtues of cross-cultural respect with a universal intolerance for injustice and oppression.

4 Whose values, whose rules?

Relativism, universalism and justice

INTRODUCTION

I have argued that disputes over economic policy and outcomes often reflect fundamental normative disagreement. Normative disagreement arises across all minimally pluralist societies, of course, but even across local communities, families, and most other social groupings. Latent normative discord always threatens to upset the most outwardly placid social arrangement and most enduring social consensus, be these inscribed in religious doctrine, tradition, common sense, or reasoned discourse. And we have every reason to expect that normative controversy will flare up for the full duration of human society – at least, we might hope that it will, if we recognize normative claims as best guesses about the way the social world should be. Final normative commitments would signal the demise of human imagining about how we might better live.

Recognition of the enduring nature of normative disagreement often induces frustration and impatience with (and even cynicism about) talk of norms. Why debate something that cannot be ultimately resolved? Why waste time and effort in inefficacious talk that could and should be directed toward acting and doing in the world? Even worse, how can we discover a normative anchor to guide policy formation once we recognize the presence of such deep normative discord?

The answer to the first two of these questions is that norms matter. So far, we have approached this matter fairly abstractly; in Part 2, we will focus more narrowly on the concrete effects of normative principles in two policy areas. We will find that different normative accounts underwrite opposing global economic policy regimes. The answer to the third question is that our instruments of governance ought to promote meaningful and fair contest over the norms that will found policies and outcomes. When normative conflict is implicitly or explicitly suppressed, in academic or in public debate, a critical aspect of democratic practice is sacrificed – perhaps even hijacked. This is because normative principles are "biased" in terms of policy and outcomes. This is as it should be: adjudicating among potential policies and outcomes is precisely what normative principles are for. Hence, if either a particular normative code is imposed upon us, or we otherwise accede uncritically to a normative code that is offered as appropriate, we forfeit a significant measure of the political rights associated with self-governance.

We should take note, finally, that those who advocate a hegemonic normative code tend to shy away from normative debate. This is certainly true of advocates of the neoclassical vision, who have little to gain but much to lose today from renewed normative debate within the field of economics. Far better, from their perspective, to let sleeping dogs lie. Consequently, the burden of sustaining normative dialogue generally falls upon the shoulders of the dissenters. They must press the debate, often in the face of substantial cultural, economic and political obstacles. Democratic governance is often most severely tested in this regard. A democratic society must be able to sustain normative dispute despite the social turmoil that normative conflict can sometimes induce.

GLOBAL POLICY REGIMES AND CROSS-CULTURAL NORMATIVE DISAGREEMENT

The foregoing discussion pertains most directly to those normative disputes that emerge within a well-defined political jurisdiction, such as a stable and enduring nation state. In this context, normative disagreement is understood to be consequential because the state is ultimately required to undertake policy decisions that will apply to all. These decisions will accord better with the normative views of some members of society than with others. Insofar as each member of the relevant jurisdiction will live under the policies so enacted, a strong case can be made that each ought to have a say in its normative debates.[75] To be shut out of a community's normative debate is to be substantially disenfranchised.

But what about the problem of assessing global policy regimes and outcomes – such as the terms of a trade agreement, or the rules governing the behavior of multinational corporations at home and abroad – which, by their nature, will apply to members of diverse societies? Whose values and norms should guide the formation of such rules that must perforce emerge in the context of economic integration? In a heterogeneous world, marked by distinct cultures, competing inter- and intra-cultural accounts of the right and the good, alternative religious and secular doctrines and so forth, how should we think about the difficult matter of the construction of institutions, rules and norms that will shape *global* economic intercourse?

To be concrete: what if two nations have adopted radically different approaches to the matter of the protection of labor, or the treatment of women in the workplace (and beyond)? Let us assume that the first country has well-established regulations that ensure the protection of workers' safety and health in the workplace, and equal protection for female and male workers in all important regards, and let us also assume heroically that these measures are adequately enforced. The second country has neither of these protections. Here, workers face dangerous work environments without legal recourse, while women face various forms of employment discrimination. In each case, the country's labor standards reflect normative commitments shared by many members of the respective society – perhaps by a majority. Let us assume finally that these two countries are considering the adoption of an agreement that would tightly bind their two economies, perhaps by reducing all legal barriers to the free flow of goods and capital between them.

The question here is direct and simple: whose rules regarding labor and women's rights should apply in each of the two countries following the implementation of the economic agreement? But this simple question immediately begs another: whose normative code should be enshrined in the new agreement, if either? Surely the existence of these different labor practices will affect the flow of goods and capital between the two countries and other economic outcomes, and these effects might be substantial. For example, the difference in standards may generate differences in wage levels, and induce capital flight as some firms relocate from the first country to the second. In this case, the presence of weaker standards in the second country may generate unemployment and associated social dislocation in the first. To what degree, then, should the implementation of the agreement be conditioned on revision in the practices of one or both countries? To what degree does either of the two countries (or particular constituencies thereof) have the right to bring pressure to bear on the other to change its practices, and what forms might this pressure rightfully take?

MORAL OBJECTIVISM

The question of what to make of cross-cultural normative assessment has generally been debated in terms of a contest between two theoretical perspectives – "moral objectivism" and "cultural relativism". Moral objectivism has a long and venerable history, extending back to ancient Greek philosophy (including the writing of Plato). In this account, there exists but one true or fully adequate normative code. Good ethical inquiry over the millennia has undertaken to discover this true code, in the same way that natural scientists seek the true account of the physical world. Although objectivists acknowledge the fallibility of the human thinker, they tend to hold out the hope that this singular code will ultimately be discovered (or minimally, approached) through appropriate ethical reasoning. This account holds a progressive view of normative theory, with each generation positioned to correct the errors and build on the discoveries of the past.

Moral objectivist accounts are noteworthy for our purposes for two reasons. First, they are generally reductionist, claiming that the true code must be founded upon some universal properties of human existence which are taken to be essences. For religious objectivists, these properties are derived from the word of a deity. For secular theorists, these properties instead generally take the form of universal attributes of human nature. All humans are seen to be endowed with particular capacities, independent of time, place and context.[76] These are then taken to entail a universal set of rights and obligations *vis-à-vis* our neighbors and communities. Second, once discovered, this objective ethical system must inform social arrangements in all societies, independent of whatever cultural diversity they might exhibit. Hampshire captures well this feature of the objectivist worldview:

> [The] traditional idea of moral distinctions as founded in the nature of things implies that there is an underlying structure of moral distinctions, partly concealed by the variety of actual moral beliefs, a structure that is defensible by rational argument and by common observation of human desires and sentiments, when a covering of local prejudices and superstitions has been removed. If the underlying structure of moral distinctions has no supernatural source, it must be recognised by rational inquiry as having its origin in nature and, specifically, in human nature: that is, in constant human needs and interests, and in canons of rational calculation ... Claims of justice have always been the preferred examples of moral claims that are to be recognised by reason, and as founded in the nature of things, as not essentially diverse, and as not contingent upon any specific type of social order.
>
> (Hampshire 1982, 147–8)

The research agenda of the objectivist follows directly. First, we must identify the essence underlying the true normative code, be it of a religious or secular order. Second, we must deduce the system of rights and obligations to which the essence gives rise. Third and finally, we must legislate economic and social behaviors that are consonant with this uniquely true code of rights and obligations. If, for instance, this code incorporates gender equality, then we are warranted in demanding enforcement of this equality across all societies irrespective of whatever "prejudices and superstitions" may authorize and codify the differential status of women. In this account, those societies that have elevated gender inequality to the status of a religious or constitutional principle are not most insulated from outside normative critique, but indeed are most indictable.

Defenders of moral objectivism are right to claim that it has much to recommend it (though they would argue that they defend it not because of its practical virtues, but because of its inherent correctness). Not least of its virtues is the fact that it provides a firm basis for its advocates to engage equally in intra- and cross-cultural critique. Indeed, for the strict objectivist, national and cultural borders are of no ethical significance whatsoever, as they provide no insulation from the critical gaze of those armed with the objective normative code. For those of its advocates who are concerned about global justice, this attribute is taken to be more than attractive – it is nothing short of essential if we are to have standing in opposing the most egregious oppressions existent in the world today. Absent an objective code, after all, what basis is there to speak out against oppressive social practices in societies other than one's own?

Nevertheless, diverse theorists have raised fundamental objections against all forms of moral objectivism. First, the effort to specify the precise nature of the objective basis (the essence) of the true normative code is predicated upon nothing but a *presumption* that it indeed must exist! Unfortunately for the objectivist project, this presumption is unproven and indeed unprovable. It is something we must be willing to commit to on faith. Yet, without it, moral objectivism loses its footing. As an unambiguous and apodictic ethical code, it requires a fully *objective* and incontrovertible foundation. But there is none. The certainty that moral objectivism promises is therefore illusory: certainty based on a presumption of an objective foundation is no kind of certainty at all.

Second, even were we to find agreement across diverse cultures – even potentially all cultures – that an objective basis for normative codes must exist, we would immediately find a second intractable problem taking the place of the first. What are we to do, after all, if we find that different cultures have reached distinct conclusions about the origins, substantive nature and practical implications of this objective basis? A cursory review of the chief contending religious and philosophical doctrines existing around the world today and through history should suffice to convince us that disagreement of this sort is the norm rather than the exception. But then, we must ask, who among us is so situated as to be able to adjudicate among these incompatible objectivist codes, not just for herself and her culture, *but for all of us?* What objective authority (text, deity or finding concerning "the nature of things") should be taken to supersede others, when different people and societies invoke different objective precepts? And what are we to make of the groups *and even entire societies* that *we* deem to have gotten it wrong?

There are other important theoretical concerns that could be raised about moral objectivism, but let me conclude this very brief treatment with a political claim. In a world marked by fundamental inequalities both within and across national borders, within which some groups have substantially greater ability to impose their normative accounts on others, moral objectivism is prone to the problem of cultural imperialism. This is because, first, moral objectivism does not lend itself to negotiation or compromise, given that it is taken by its adherents to be uniquely true. Second, and as a consequence, it is likely to be imposed by its advocates on others with alternative normative accounts on grounds that those on whom it is imposed will ultimately benefit from receiving the correct word. This is what I will call a "monological" politics of proselytization, conversion and conquest – all in the name of justice, social progress, and development.

WALZER AND CULTURAL RELATIVISM

Relativist critics of moral objectivism are often motivated explicitly by abhorrence for this kind of politics. Relativists avoid what they view as the imperialist impulse of moral objectivism by holding that the basis for establishing ethical norms does not lie beneath us, as an objective entity awaiting discovery through careful archaeological excavation, but emerges instead out of a continuing, culturally embedded and fully human enterprise to construct visions of how we should live.

Michael Walzer, whose account of distributive justice we considered earlier, is among the most influential and interesting proponents of cultural relativism. Within debates in political theory over the foundations of ethics and morality, Walzer has consistently undercut universalist and essentialist claims. Walzer flatly refuses the notion of an essential foundation for normative judgements, be it sacred or secular. Instead, he contends that a community's own cultural matrix provides *the only appropriate foundation* for adjudicating the rightness of beliefs and actions within that community. In his words, a society's "rules of behavior, then, are objectively right relative to the prevailing meanings, but the prevailing meanings are not objectively right (or wrong). They are only objectively *there* ..." (Walzer 1993, 170, italics in original).

As this statement suggests, Walzer invokes a rather relaxed notion of objectivity. Objectivity is grounded entirely in the perceptions of "normal people". Moreover, the notion of objectivity applies equally to objects with social meanings (such as moral precepts) as to physical phenomena. For example, "a table that is an altar that is holy", once generally constructed and accepted as such within a particular community, has objective value *for that community*. Even the religious rebel who would deny the religiosity of the table must appeal:

> to other features of the existing cultural system or way of life, features that give him reasons, so he says, for what he does. The system as a whole still has objective value for him; he lives within the set of social constructions. Where else can he live?
>
> (Walzer 1993, 168)

In Walzer's view, a community's moral precepts cannot be checked against some context-independent standard to ascertain their faithfulness – it is precisely this notion of objectivity that Walzer displaces. For Walzer, the pursuit of such an objective standard reflects the conceit of theorists to overcome their situated mortality – it reflects the quest to complete philosophy, answering the question of the origins and content of morality once and for all. But that effort is naïve at best. Unlike a deity, who gazes upon the world as it truly is, human observers are always necessarily biased by the particular tools (of language, convention, and so forth) provided to them by their cultural milieu, which they necessarily must employ in thought. No human thinker can rise above the determinants of time, place, and context to get an unclut-tered view of normative principles; to do so would entail joining the deities at the "rim of heaven".[77] Unlike deities, human thinkers are necessarily embed-ded in and shaped by the world they seek to know. But this anti-essentialist view implies that different societies will generate distinct cultural edifices housing distinct (and perhaps incompatible) moralities and ethical systems. When they do, social and moral criticism across cultural divides becomes normatively suspect.

Walzer recognizes that the same normative demands often emerge across cultural divides. People demand "justice" in all sorts of societies, for instance. Some objectivists take this as evidence of the universality and objectivity of such principles. Walzer disagrees. In all cultures, Walzer claims, morality has a dual meaning – a minimum (or "thin") and a maximal (or "thick") mean-ing. The former is a stripped-down, abstract aspect of the latter: "[Minimal-ist] meanings are embedded in the maximal morality ... minimalism is liberated from its embeddedness and appears independently, in varying degrees of thinness, only in the course of a personal or social crisis or a politi-cal confrontation" (Walzer 1994, 3).

The thin meaning is apt to be universally accessible across borders. Maxi-mal meanings, in contrast, are culturally and historically specific and particu-lar. Hence we can readily understand the minimal demands of those who march for "justice" or "freedom", even if we have never met them nor visited their society. We can "vicariously join their parade" even though, were we to discuss justice with them, we might find their maximal meanings to be dra-matically different from our own. The minimalist meanings allow for a degree of cross-cultural understanding and assent; the maximal meanings reflect our particularities and differences.

Against the objectivists, Walzer claims that the emergence of the same moral minima across diverse cultures signifies not their origins in something beyond lived human experiences – "there is no moral Jerusalem from which meanings go forth" – but simply their contingent "reiterated social construc-tion" (Walzer 1993, 170). "Though we have different histories," Walzer writes, "we have common experiences and, sometimes, common responses, and out of these we fashion, as needed, the moral minimum" (Walzer 1994, 17–18).

Walzer's anti-essentialism is evidenced in his reading of culture and human subjectivity as well. He views culture as crosscut by contradiction, con-tinually in process of formation and evolution and the site of perpetual con-test. This feature secures the possibility for imminent critique in the form of "common complaint". Those oppressed are apt to come to theorize their oppression by drawing on the tools of opposition that their own culture pro-vides them: "Social critics commonly start from where they stand, win or lose on their own ground" (Walzer 1994, 47).

Walzer portrays human subjectivity as thoroughly de-centered (see

Chapter 2). His imagery is useful: for Walzer, the self is a constellation of "internal critics" which generate competing standards by which it assesses its motivations and actions. The self occupies the center of a circle inhabited by these diverse critics, but also is this entire constellation. The internal critics therefore not only perform a function on the self, but also constitute it. This vision of subjectivity allows for no central authority – no privileged super-ego – and so the subject must adjudicate continuously among this cast of competing equals (Walzer 1994, ch. 5).

All told, Walzer provides what seems to be a thoroughgoing anti-essentialist account of normative claims, culture and human subjectivity. This account then allows for a direct confrontation with the moral objectivist view of cross-cultural critique. We have seen that moral objectivism discounts national (and other) borders as insulation against the critique of those in possession of the true normative code. In contrast, Walzer constructs a relativist position with respect to the process of cross-cultural criticism. Walzer's inclinations are admirable: the humility that his anti-essentialism correctly induces is reflected naturally in his resistance to what one theorist has evocatively identified as "arrogant perception" (Gunning 1992). When we see morally abhorrent practices undertaken in another society, Walzer (and other relativists) would have us attempt to understand such practices within the frame of the indigenous ethical code that establishes and legitimizes such practices. Our finding that these practices are abhorrent when judged against the standard established by our own normative beliefs provides no basis for indicting the practices in the society in which they occur. Walzer's appreciation of the internal contradictions that arise within all cultures leads him to anticipate that those oppressed by abhorrent practices in another society will eventually engineer their own resistance. If and when they do, this act cancels the appeal to legitimacy of the practices so opposed, and we may then rally around the cause of the resistors. Hence, imminent critique must precede and guide external criticism.

This brings us to a critical and difficult question: what if those in another culture whom *we* view to be oppressed *willingly accept* their oppression? To recite an example developed by Walzer, what if we encounter a society in which women are objectified and traded as goods? In such a society, Walzer asks, is trade in women objectively just? What are we to think – *and what are we licensed to do* – if those so objectified and traded actually give their consent? Walzer's response is instructive and deserves quotation at length:

> I see no morally acceptable way of denying the woman-who-is-an-object-of-exchange her own reasons and her own place in a valued way of life. That does not mean that we cannot argue with her, offering what we take to be better reasons for the repudiation of (what we take to be) her object status. It does mean that, once the argument begins, she has to choose what *she* thinks are the better reasons, without any certainty as to

which ones are objectively best. But we can say, and this seems to me all
that we should want to say, that the choice is truly hers.

(Walzer 1993, 175)

What deprives us of the right to liberate her, or indeed, do any more than
argue with her, is our occupation of a distinct culture with its own maximal
morality: we are, in this matter, cultural "outsiders" who lack the moral
authority to legislate for those within. It should be emphasized that Walzer is
not making the less ambitious claim that outside intervention often is inefficacious, leading to nationalist backlash in defense of the practices under
indictment. Instead, he is making a strong principled argument – even
where we have the capacity to cancel oppressive practices in other cultures,
we lack the right to do so by virtue of our status as "outsiders".

While relativism induces a healthy degree of cross-cultural respect and
humility about one's own worldview, it also substantially restricts the field of
action for those with internationalist sensibilities who seek to rid the world
(and not just their own societies) of debilitating oppressions. Moral objectivists rightly reject this consequence of the relativist view as too limiting in the
face of obvious oppressions. To return to the examples raised earlier in this
chapter, Walzer's relativism impels the conclusion that when a country with
strong labor standards and gender equality enters into a trade agreement
with a country lacking these protections, neither country is warranted in
seeking changes in the other's practices. Each set of practices must be taken
as equally valid in its respective domain. And as we will see in Chapter 6, this
is precisely the conclusion advocated by neoclassical theory in defense of
global neoliberalism.

There would seem to be a rather pronounced contradiction between
Walzer's relativist principles summarized here, and his commitment to the
egalitarian principles that we encountered in the previous chapter. Walzer
has elucidated rather strong claims about what makes for a just distribution
of social goods, as we have seen, and these certainly rule out the practice of
trade in human persons, even when those traded willingly sacrifice their liberty. How then could Walzer possibly countenance the enslavement of
women anywhere, at any time, irrespective of what the slave feels about her
situation? The resolution to this apparent contradiction has to do with the
domain over which Walzer claims legitimacy for his egalitarianism. Walzer
emphasizes that his distributive principles are not to be taken as universals,
but as applicable only to communities such as his own that have come to
embrace liberal democratic principles founded on deep conceptions of
political equality. Walzer explicitly makes no claims at all about how other
societies that are committed to alternative political doctrines should undertake distribution. What is just in those societies depends on *their own* normative codes, not ours (or Walzer's): "A given society is just if its substantive life
is lived in a certain way – that is, in a way faithful to the shared

understandings of the members" (Walzer 1983, 313), regardless, we might add, of whatever those shared understandings are.[78]

Where does this leave us? Are we reduced to political quietism in the face of oppression abroad once we reject the arrogant perceiving associated with moral objectivism? Or might there by some reasonable way out of this impasse that allows us to weld Walzerian anti-essentialist respect and humility with an activist critical posture toward (what we take to be) unwarranted oppression?

ANTI-ESSENTIALISM VERSUS RELATIVISM: THE INSIDER/OUTSIDER BINARY

For Walzer, cultural relativism follows automatically from a rejection of the essentialist premises (and the associated reductionist logic) that underpin moral objectivism. Earlier, I offered concerns about essentialism and reductionism in the discussion of neoclassical theory, and proposed there an anti-reductionist model of the economy. I also gave reasons why we should reject neoclassical theory's reductionism in favor of this anti-reductionist model. The question now arises as to whether we must embrace Walzer's moral relativism if we commit to anti-reductionist reasoning. The answer, we will see, is that we must not. Simply put, anti-reductionism need not and indeed should not collapse into cultural relativism. The theoretical inconsistency in Walzer arises out of his failure to grasp the diverse manner in which distinct cultures are mutually constitutive, and his incomplete integration of the de-centered conception of human subjectivity into his account of cultural constructions. In this last regard, Walzer errs in his treatment of the boundaries that separate distinct cultures.

As we have seen, Walzer claims that an individual or community lacks the right to work to undermine oppressive practices in another culture (absent opposition by those who are oppressed), other than through conversation with the willingly oppressed. This is because one is a "foreigner" to cultures other than one's own. As with contributions to the relativist tradition more generally, the binary of cultural "insider" versus cultural "outsider" figures as the fundamental theoretical construction for separating those *with* from those *without* the right to press judgement on social practices. From the anti-essentialist perspective, this may indeed seem reasonable. If both the meanings of social practices and the moral codes to judge them are given internally by the particular social context within which they emerge, then cross-cultural respect and tolerance (rather than judgement and critique) would indeed seem to be the appropriate stance for the anti-essentialist outsider to take.

Appearances, however, are misleading in this case. The problem with this line of argument lies in the manner in which Walzer takes distinct cultures and the boundaries that separate them as given, so that the designation of insider/outsider may be easily traced on to the map following national, sub-national or community borders. This strategy violates the anti-essentialist premises Walzer otherwise embraces. To see this, we will consider first the manner in which distinct cultures participate in their mutual constitution. We can then turn to the more fundamental issue of the degree to which the insider/outsider binary itself is constantly displaced (or minimally, con-tested and redefined) in and through social practices, and not least by politi-cal struggle.

The mutual constitution of distinct cultures

Let us consider first a hypothetical community that has somehow managed by virtue of geography or other means to remain entirely isolated, that is, untouched in any direct way by others. Were we to find such a community, and prior to our interaction with it, we might think of it as exclusively the product of auto-creation, in the sense that its languages, practices, meanings and so forth are in some deep sense its own. In the absence of knowledge on its part about how others live, or indeed of others' existence, it will have fash-ioned its own conceptions about how to live. Note that even here, however, its conception of the relationship of its own world to others – in this case, perhaps, that there are no others, that it is unique among species and objects of the world – will affect just how it makes sense of itself. As an analogy, we might take the sum total of *Homo sapiens* existing on earth as this community. Our conception of being the only humans in the galaxy has certainly condi-tioned how we conceptualize ourselves, the existence of and our relation to our creator, our rights and obligations in the cosmos, etc. I am suggesting, then, that the "other" participates in the constitution of a culture, even in its real or presumed absence.

Now consider the case of this community upon its first interactions with another community – such as when the first anthropologist walks into the clearing and begins jotting down notes. Even if we take the community to have been auto-created prior to this moment, from this point forward the community's identity, practices and beliefs will be shaped by its interaction with the other. In the first instance, recognition of the existence of other people who are in important respects just like themselves will force a reconceptualization of their place in the world (just as the discovery of and interaction with extra-terrestrials would do). Theologies might have to be revised to account for this new finding; racial and ethnic distinctions might have to be constructed; notions of inferiority/superiority, of relative worth, of valuation would have to be reoriented to account for the existence of these other people. Decisions about the propriety of interaction, and the terms on which this interaction will occur (if at all) must be taken. In short, from this point forward, the outside culture will play a significant part in shaping the character of the formerly secluded community.

In the context in which the question of cross-cultural judgement arises today, we certainly have not only cross-cultural knowledge but also extensive interaction. Certainly in the debates over the terms of economic integration, we are by definition speaking of cases in which separate communities not only know of each other, but are in important respects joined together (co-operatively, antagonistically, or more likely, both). In this context, members of distinct cultures construct understandings of practices and beliefs that exist elsewhere, and of necessity reinterpret their own practices in this light. In so doing, they actually import the external culture into their own in the sense that this process of theorizing and evaluating the other shapes their own culture. The cultural inheritances that a community has received from the past are amended, revised, and contested in light of the new perceptions that arise in the context of cross-cultural gazing. In the process, cultures become something other than what they were. Bimal Krishna Matilal puts it this way: "[It] is wrong to think today of a culture as completely individuated and self-contained *vis-à-vis* another comparable culture … [During] contacts and confrontation traits are borrowed freely and then integrated into the borrowing culture's worldview or cosmology" (Matilal 1989, 342, 350).[79]

This is not to say, of course, that inter-cultural interaction yields convergence, let alone a homogenous one-world culture. As Matilal notes, an element of another culture (a belief or a practice) that is taken to conflict with a community's core beliefs may be rejected as abhorrent or simply wrong-headed. Even in this case, however, the confrontation with the rejected element leaves an imprint on a society's culture. The confrontation may require the construction of new justifications for the core beliefs with which the rejected element conflicts: arguments must now be advanced as to why the abhorrent practice or belief is, indeed, abhorrent.

In short, inter-cultural contact necessarily entails a process of articulation in which each entity is altered in and through the interaction. In viewing and assessing a culture, we do not have the luxury of leaving either it or our own unchanged. We have an impact upon the other culture's values, codes of morality and systems of meaning, whether we desire or attempt to or not. The latter is an inevitable aspect of the complicated process of cross-cultural exchange.

It follows that when we encounter another culture, what we encounter is the outcome of a cross-cultural interaction, not the culture in some pure, unmediated form. As Bernard Williams argues, "social practices could never come forward with a certificate saying that they belonged to a genuinely different culture, so that they are guaranteed immunity to other judgements and reactions" (cited in Matilal 1989, 342).

If this view is correct, then we might recognize that the question of what rights and obligations we have *vis-à-vis* assessment of others' ways of life is more complicated than Walzer suggests. If we, of necessity, are shaping these ways of life, largely in unintended ways, then we might recognize that we have no reason to believe that the other culture has been made the better for it. Indeed, the interaction with our own culture may very well have harmed those most disadvantaged in another. Examples are not difficult to imagine: being exposed to our lavish consumption patterns, élites in poorer societies begin to exploit those with less power for their own aggrandizement, or attempt to enhance their own influence, power and status in the world; or, observing the "audacity" with which some privileged women of our culture dress, travel, pursue careers and flaunt their reproductive freedom, men elsewhere institute more repressive (formal and informal) measures to control the behaviors of women in their own societies. In these cases, is it really enough for us simply to converse with those who are now more oppressed – might we not have some obligation to use other means to lighten their burden, to undo the harm caused by interaction with our own culture?

We should recall in this connection the argument advanced in the critique of welfarism in Chapter 2, that peoples' desires are endogenous to their economic and social circumstances. In particular, the oppressed may exhibit what Elster (1982) calls "adaptive preferences". These are preferences that devalue those states of existence that lie beyond the reach of what a person perceives to be attainable, precisely because those states are unattainable. For instance, the poor in a wealthy society may place little value on political efficacy because they have come to accept that they will never achieve it. As Sen (1990, 126) argues, "acute inequalities often survive precisely by making allies out of the deprived. The underdog comes to accept the legitimacy of the unequal order and becomes an implicit accomplice."[80] In this case, the oppressed might be unwilling (for good reason) to allow themselves even to imagine freedom from egregious oppression, despite the outsider's most forceful arguments. In this case, having failed in our attempts to convince the oppressed about their exploitation, Walzer's admonition that "the choice is truly their own" might serve to punish the dispossessed for their lack of power and their inability to envision emancipation. *Contra* Walzer, outsiders might need to act in other ways *first*, to weaken the bonds of oppression and thereby create the realization by the oppressed of new possibilities *as a precondition* for efficacious conversation. Walzer's proscriptions on action absent resistance of the oppressed rules out this path to liberation.

This discussion serves to identify a related error on Walzer's part. Walzer's rightful fear of unwarranted intervention by outsiders leads him to draw an untenable ethical distinction between speech and other forms of behavior. While many democratic societies necessarily distinguish speech from other forms of action so as to provide special protections to the former, the distinction is hardly watertight or unambiguous (cf. Fish 1994; MacKinnon 1993; Greenawalt 1995). Even in countries with such protections, protected speech often shades into unprotected action, such as when an activist incites a mob to execute a political rival. We must therefore inquire as to whether the rigid distinction Walzer draws between the legitimate speech and the illegitimate actions of the outsider stands up. But the example Walzer himself provides suggest they do not. Isn't it likely that mere discussion with the "woman-who-is-an-object-of-exchange" about the nature of her oppression will be regarded as an incendiary *act* in her society? In the plausible case where cultural norms unambiguously prohibit speech between the objectified woman and outsiders – she is a *slave*, after all – Walzer's respect for cultural legitimacy would seem to bar the very conversation that he believes the outsider is ethically permitted. In this case, whose normative principle rightly governs the outsider's behavior – Walzer's commitment to free speech, or their commitment to protect the woman from outside contamination?

The foregoing raises a broader question of the sanctity of cultural artifacts and the purposes that they serve. Social critics in the North (such as Walzer) certainly refuse to ordain all aspects of Western culture as legitimate or authentic, as worthy of valorization simply by virtue of the fact that they exist. Instead, these critics take great pains to demonstrate the many ways in which both common and high culture perpetuate various systems of oppression – based on class, gender, race, ethnicity, appearance, power and so forth. We rightly refuse to grant validity to the cultural terms (such as stereotypes) that support these oppressions; we choose instead to evaluate them by reference to their origins, histories and especially, their effects. All manner of cultural artifacts can have the effect of legitimizing existent inequalities. When assessing other cultures, then, even before we begin to undertake to construct the standards by which this evaluation might proceed, we would do well to presume that these cultures (like our own) comprise elements that have the effect of subordinating or oppressing some members of society by constructing these oppressions as natural, just, or inevitable. In this case, we might expect to find the victims of these oppressions to be reluctant to resist. By Walzer's criterion, the more powerful and insidious are these oppressive cultural artifacts, the less empowered are outsiders to support those who suffer their effects (cf. Nussbaum 1992).

To conclude this part of the discussion, let me emphasize a point that has been made implicitly: the thesis that cultures are mutually constitutive implies that *we* have always already acted upon *them* (and vice versa). When our culture confronts another, we never have the opportunity to converse first about what we take to be their oppressions prior to making other kinds of interventions in their world. What Walzer prescribes is strictly impossible – we can't return to a state of arms-length mutual regard between cultures, in which we only affect each other through dialogue, because that state cannot possibly exist.

Contesting the insider/outsider binary

We can turn now to the insider/outsider binary directly, because this is where Walzer's argument takes its most unfortunate turn. We have already begun to break down this binary. The foregoing suggests after all that distinct cultures are hardly watertight – that transborder transgressions necessarily occur whether we intend them or not. Cultures do not just interact instrumentally, while retaining their authenticity. Rather, they are always enmeshed in *internal* relationships with each other – relationships that change what each culture *is*.

Walzer's own work provides an additional basis for dismissing the insider/outsider binary upon which his relativism depends. It derives from his useful anti-essentialist account of human subjectivity. As we have seen, Walzer portrays the human actor as a constellation of diverse internal critics, or what others have called "subject positions" (Laclau and Mouffe 1985). In contrast to the neoclassical view, which posits the human actor as entirely in command of his needs, wants and values (all mapped on to his neatly structured preference ordering), Walzer presents that human actor as decentered. The actor is pushed and pulled by diverse (and potentially conflicting) aspirations, preferences and values, and must make his way in the world without recourse to any kind of stabilizing center. For example, an individual may make sense of himself as an American citizen, but also as a wagedworker, and an artist – and these diverse conceptions may entail competing perspectives on questions of rights and moral obligations. Consider his conceptions of property rights. As an American, he might embrace the right of the US government to use its military power to protect US property rights abroad; as a worker, the right to appropriate the fruits of his own labor; as an artist, the right to express himself free of the restrictions imposed by others' rights of property. These may constitute some of the internal critics at odds in the self. The construction of notions of needs, rights and obligations are therefore complex, conflicted and changing. It follows that human existence necessarily entails struggle, both within ourselves and with others, as each of us attempts to establish social practices and institutions that reflect our own (changing) understandings of needs, rights and obligations, even though we may recognize their irreducibility to something secure and independent of us. Each of us is condemned to adjudicate among competing doctrines as a necessary aspect of being social creatures and participating in the social life of our communities.

This rich and complex depiction of the self is lost in Walzer's construction of "national" or what he sometimes calls "tribal" cultures, despite his emphasis on the internal contradictions that create space within culture for imminent critique. Given our multiple, overlapping and contradictory subject positions, we do not *belong* to culture – *and certainly not to any unitary culture* – in the traditional sense that Walzer embraces. In one's subject position as woman (or woman's rights advocate) seeking genuine gender equality, one may view oneself correctly as a part of a global community that includes all women. Such an actor might thereby rightfully foment or participate in cultural struggles over identity and practices *as an insider* (if that concept is to be retained) whenever and wherever gender-based discriminatory practices are found to exist. In one's subject position as worker (or worker advocate) seeking empowerment and distributive justice, one might rightfully demand to be recognized as a member of the global community of labor; such an actor might thereby rightfully participate as an insider whenever labor conditions or property rights are at stake. In short, recognition of the multiplicity of subject positions encourages us to see that the insider/outsider divide is not simply mapped along national or tribal borders, but is itself is contested and fluid. The border separating insider from outsider depends fundamentally on the subject positions that emerge and find collective political expression. *Like culture itself, this border also is socially constructed.* We must therefore remain skeptical of strategies by which some would define others as outsiders who lack standing in intra-cultural disputes.

Walzer's chief error can be described, then, as his having privileged norms associated with nationally (or tribally) defined subject positions over those norms associated with other subject positions. The anti-essentialist perspective informing his work should lead us instead to refuse such *a priori* judgements: nation-based subject positions (and the ethical norms with which they are associated) are to be taken as no more authentic, legitimate or hermetic than those which span or disregard national cultural boundaries. As people come to construct internationalist subject positions like "worker" or "woman" that entail alternative ethical norms, we may have good reason to privilege these alternatives, politically if not epistemologically. An anti-essentialist position would not preclude our forming such judgements and partisanship, but would bar their defense by reference to objectivist claims.

AN INTERNATIONALIST ETHIC – GLOBAL HARMONIZATION OF CAPABILITIES

Where does this leave us in the debates over the rules that should inform global economic integration? To say that the binary "insider/outsider" is contingent and is itself an appropriate site of political contest is not to say that those who are concerned about justice can be cavalier about the stands we take regarding global policy regimes. It is not to license unilateral imposition of our norms (whenever we can get away with it) on those who might not share them. It gives us certain rights, to be sure, but it carries what might be felt as burdensome obligations as well. Not the least of these might be an obligation to construct a truly "internationalist" ethic, one that might be reasonable in principle to those in the North and the South who are committed to equality. In this project, anti-essentialist presumptions place us in better stead than do claims of moral objectivism. Rather than claim and defend this position in the abstract, let us instead test it via consideration of one candidate for an internationalist ethic – one based on Sen's notion of capabilities equality.

Although Sen's chief concern is to contribute to an understanding of equality as an abstract ethical principle, the attributes of the capabilities approach highlighted in the previous chapter indicate its value in constructing an ethic that can bring clarity to the dispute over the terms of international economic integration. The approach suggests the following internationalist ethic for assessing economic policy regimes: *a regime will be deemed just if and to the degree that it promotes harmonization of capabilities to achieve functionings at a level that is sufficient, universally attainable and sustainable.*

The foregrounding of "harmonization of capabilities" signals the overriding commitment of this principle to equality of substantive freedoms. A just world is one that aspires to provide each of its members with equal ability to live a valued life. That our current world neither approaches this ideal nor usually even seeks it should be a cause of embarrassment for this world, not for this principle.

To argue for equality of capabilities is to beg the question of the level at which equality is to be achieved. Neoclassical theory's commitment to welfarism is tied to a notion of maximization – the maximum quantity of goods yields maximum satisfaction, and hence, maximum social welfare. In contrast, this principle emphasizes sufficiency, attainability and sustainability. This distinction is important. First, capabilities do not depend strictly on physical magnitudes (such as levels of consumption), but also on the nature of a society's social institutions, conventions and cultural attributes. My ability to achieve self-esteem might depend as much on whether my society tolerates racism as on my level of consumption. Moreover, the pursuit of maximum consumption (by individuals or society) might interfere with the achievement of all sorts of capabilities. A society that values capabilities equality might therefore place restrictions on consumption levels (such as limits on the number and size of dwellings that a family might own and occupy). A second and related point concerns inter-generational equity, which is signaled by the inclusion of the notion of sustainability. A just society is one that not only ensures equality among its present members, but that also conducts itself in a manner that ensures the capabilities achievements of those who will follow. Institutions must ensure that the physical environment is not ransacked in pursuit of maximum wealth or utility. Third, insofar as the capabilities approach refuses to reduce distinct functionings to a common measure of value, such as utility, the concept of maximization itself makes little sense. What would it mean to maximize self-respect, for instance? From the perspective of capabilities, having the chance to live a valued life depends on the ability to achieve certain states and conditions, most of which are not usefully thought of in quantitative terms.

This normative principle calls for equalization of capabilities at a level that can be provided to all of the world's inhabitants. This necessarily entails substantial redistribution of income, wealth and resource use from the North to the South, insofar as many functionings (not least, the state of being adequately nourished, housed and clothed) depend on access to resources. But this should not be interpreted to mean that all in the North must suffer a reduction in capabilities so as to allow for an expansion of the capabilities of those in the South. Instead, the relatively poor in the North stand to secure expanding capabilities sets under this principle, as the wealthy in their own societies are divested of their command over status, political power, authority, resources and so forth. In this context, it is again important to separate out material from non-material dimensions of capabilities. Regarding the former, the poor in the North may achieve expanding access to resources under this international normative principle. In the case of the US, for instance, where over 35 million people currently lack health insurance in a largely privatized health care system, the principle of equal capabilities would entail a substantial improvement in access to health care for the uninsured. Regarding non-material dimensions, equal capabilities would entail (for example) expanding political efficacy for the politically disenfranchised. This could be achieved in the North even in the face of redistribution in income from the North to the South. In short, the expansion in capabilities for the relatively impoverished in the North is entirely consistent with an aggregate shift in resource use from the North to the South.[81] As these examples indicate, we would be mistaken to think of capabilities as a fixed magnitude to be divvied up between the North and the South.

Harmonization of capabilities to achieve functionings at a level that is sufficient, universally attainable and sustainable. This extraordinarily simple notion has the benefit of being potentially reasonable to those of diverse cultures who are concerned about justice. The principle rules out beggar-thy-neighbor strategies for promoting the well-being of any one nation's or region's citizens. It seeks harmonization, but harmonization in the direction of *increasing* substantive opportunities for most of the world's inhabitants (including, as I have argued, the dispossessed in wealthy countries). Hence, it is in principle solidaristic: it evaluates economic outcomes by reference to a substantive standard that applies equally to all. As a consequence, it may also provide a practical basis for envisioning new forms of international co-operation among egalitarians. As discussed in the previous chapter, it also promotes perpetual experimentation in the design and reform of institutions and social practices. It provides a standard for assessing institutions and practices, not a blueprint for their design.

It is undoubtedly true that any policy regime we devise might fall short of the demands of capabilities equality. Neat principles never translate perfectly into practical policy: between the intention and execution something always goes missing. Certainly, all sorts of difficult compromises will have to be made; this principle will have to be amended to take account of other normative principles that those committed to distributive justice deem to be warranted. Moreover, the capabilities approach entails difficult political problems, such as those which arise in the context of differences of beliefs across individuals as to what should count as valuable functionings (and how competing valued functionings should be ranked). Indeed, members of a community (let alone distinct communities) may identify and place value on mutually incompatible functionings: my neighbor's ability to be well armed will conflict with my ability to live in a world free of handguns. Finally, levels of capabilities might not always be easy to compare across national borders. Unfortunately or not, commitment to capabilities equality as a general normative principle does not resolve (or even provide a formula for resolving) such controversies. With Sen, though, we should recognize that such controversies are much less salient when we focus on what he calls "basic functionings". These include the achievement of adequate nutrition, the ability to avoid preventable morbidity and premature mortality, and other conditions and states that are minimally necessary for a person to live a decent life. Policy initiatives to enhance the basic capabilities of the impoverished could be made even in the face of continuing controversy over higher-order functionings.

Consideration of basic functionings reveals a further virtue of the capabilities approach. Though the principle of capabilities equality is a radical one, demanding of us tremendous change in the way we organize our societies and distribute resources, it also allows for gradual or incremental reform. We might think of the principle as a target to be approached gradually through successive policy initiatives and reforms, as we traverse a historical path of social experimentation. The principle may serve us, then, as both a standard against which to indict society, and a catalyst for generating policy approaches not yet envisioned (see Chapter 7).

Internationalism or imperialism?

If we take seriously the concern of those like Walzer who rightly fear that any internationalist normative principle (other than inter-cultural respect, perhaps) will become a vehicle of cultural imperialism, then we must interrogate capabilities equality to see whether and to what degree it is susceptible to this charge.

Three points might be made in this regard. First, the equalization of capabilities represents an approach to substantive equality that respects the diversity of human and social aspirations. Rather than require that distinct societies actually aspire to or achieve the same specific goals, it permits them to recognize distinct sets of functionings. A broad array of cultural, social, climactic and other sorts of factor will rightly shape a community's views regarding which conditions or states should count when allocating that community's resources. The approach also recognizes and accepts the principle that different communities will devise different rankings for even those valued functionings that they share. One community might take the capacity for spiritual contentment to be more valuable than the capacity for long life, while another might rightfully reach the opposite judgement.

Second, the principle of capabilities equality is permissive with respect to the means that diverse communities and nations adopt to achieve valued functionings. It allows for cultural differences to be expressed in the formation of diverse institutional structures and practices.[82] For instance, the principle of equal ability to avoid preventable morbidity could presumably be secured through diverse health care systems, ranging from privatized to socialized medicine (though this would have to be demonstrated in practice, not just claimed *ex ante*). The principle does not dictate one institutional form of health care, but it does provide a demanding criterion for assessing whether the alternative institutional arrangements that societies construct do indeed deliver equal ability to prevent premature mortality or avoidable morbidity. When a health care system fails in this regard – when it generates and sustains inequality in these functionings – it loses its claim to legitimacy.

Last but not least, this approach is agnostic with respect to the metaphysical foundation of ethical judgements. It can make room for moral objectivists as well as for relativists who refuse an objective or universal basis for normative judgements. Some agreement over what should be regarded as valued functionings, and how these might be ranked, can be reached even in the absence of consensus over the origins of these judgements. In view of the unlikelihood that the debate over the foundations of normative judgements is likely to be settled soon, or indeed ever, this is a particularly attractive feature of the capabilities approach.

In his work on capabilities equality, Sen himself has largely refrained from pursing the question of the foundations of valued functionings, implicitly leaving these judgements to the community rather than to the philosophers. Martha Nussbaum, another chief architect of this approach, has, however, pursued this matter carefully. Consistent with the arguments advanced here, Nussbaum rejects the strong claims associated with moral objectivism on the one hand and cultural relativism on the other. In their place, Nussbaum offers and defends what she identifies as an "Aristotelian" approach to discussions of capabilities. She argues that while relativists are correct to argue that no metaphysical basis exists for establishing normative codes, we can nevertheless glean from a critical survey of recorded human history extensive (though certainly not complete) overlap among diverse societies regarding what it means to be human, and what is required to live a valued human life. In her view, these reiterated conceptions can and should provide the basis for constructing a list of valued functionings, and for broadly ranking those functionings so designated. In this way, Nussbaum generates a universal normative account on an anti-essentialist foundation. She calls the product of proceeding in this way "internal essentialism", in which the qualifier signifies that the judgements reached on these matters come from within society and emerge from reasoned dialogue and investigation, rather than from the word of God or the way the world really is. As such, they are subject to perpetual change, as societies learn, adapt and evolve. This is a "historically grounded empirical essentialism" (Nussbaum 1992, 208), in which human interpretation plays the central role.

Proceeding on the basis of this empirical investigation, Nussbaum identifies two levels or thresholds of human existence. The first threshold entails the bare minimum, comprising that which is required to live a most basic human life. It is a set of limits and capabilities "beneath which a life will be so impoverished that it will not be human at all" (Nussbaum 1992, 221). It comprises basic biological needs (though these are culturally variable), naturally, such as the needs for nutrition and shelter; but a human life depends on more than just meeting these biological needs: hence the minimum includes opportunities for humor and play, and affiliation with other human beings. Particular individuals may of course choose not to avail themselves of these opportunities (or the opportunity for nourishment and shelter as well). Nussbaum's point is that a life devoid of these opportunities can scarcely be counted as a human life at all. The second threshold indicates what is necessary for a *good* human life. It, too, combines biological with social capacities. For instance, a *good* human life, Nussbaum argues, entails the ability to "live to the end of a complete human life, as far as is possible; not dying prematurely, or before one's life is so reduced as to be not worth living". A good human life also requires "being able to form a conception of the good and to engage in critical reflection about the planning of one's own life" (Nussbaum 1992, 222).

Nussbaum's list is contestable, of course. She explicitly invites its interrogation and revision when she offers it as a "thick, *vague* theory of the good". This conception recognizes the existence of entirely reasonable differences amongst us as to what counts as a valued human life, and also the eternal fallibility of human thinkers. Lacking an objective basis in some irreducible essence, this account is apt to evolve over time as societies generate new understandings of what counts as a valued human life. In Nussbaum's view, however, this is no cause for concern. Rather, the potential for evolution in thought is to be embraced as we collectively discover better ways of being.

CONCLUSION

I have argued here that the debate over the legitimacy of cross-cultural assessment has been dominated by two theoretical positions, moral objectivism and cultural relativism. In the view of its advocates, moral objectivism has the virtue of providing an unambiguous basis for challenging oppression wherever it occurs. But we took note of several important epistemological and political problems with this perspective. Not least, in a world where different people hold to different objectivist accounts, this perspective is apt to produce a "monological" international politics of conflict rather than a dialogical politics of respect, tolerance and compromise. In a world of stark international inequality, it is also likely to yield new forms of cultural imperialism. In contrast, proponents of cultural relativism see it as possessing the virtue of promoting cross-cultural understanding and respect. Unfortunately, it also yields an uncertain basis for resisting rather obvious oppressions.

A third path may exist, however, that provides a better basis for cross-cultural assessment. Like cultural relativism, this path begins with anti-essentialist presumptions. That is, it presumes that normative codes reflect best (but variable) judgements about how we should live, rather than time-less and universal commandments delivered from a deity or "the nature of things". I have tried to show that these presumptions do not necessitate cultural relativism, but instead enable and give direction to internationalist demands for universal justice. In this connection I have argued that the con-flation of anti-essentialism with cultural relativism errs by essentializing one particular kind of subject position (such as that tied to nationhood) as the singular basis for constructing legitimate understandings of ethical norms. Against this view I have argued that distinct cultures are mutually constitutive and interactive rather than auto-created and self-contained. I have also argued that any existing social formation necessarily comprises crosscutting constituencies who move among diverse subject positions, generating multi-ple and contending conceptions of rights and moral obligations. Together these insights undermine the insider/outsider binary upon which cultural relativism depends. Just as cultures themselves are socially constituted, so are the borders separating them. These evolve and change in the process of the formation of subject positions that emerge within and across legally sanc-tioned boundaries.

I have also argued that some subject positions (for example worker, *sans* national qualifier) might provide the basis for the construction of transna-tional identities and internationalist ethical conceptions, while others might not. An internationalist egalitarian political project might therefore seek to construct such subject positions, to form conceptions of rights and moral obligations that express a commonality of interests, and to mobilize in defense of these conceptions when they are resisted or denied by opposing constructions. Feminists need not be silenced (as relativism might imply) by patriarchal conceptions that construct the identities "male" and "female", men's rights and women's obligations, regardless of geographic location or the cultural dress (be it secular or sacred, First World or Third, foreign or indigenous) in which these conceptions parade.

Capabilities equality provides the basis for one compelling internationalist normative principle. The principle of the harmonization of capabilities at a level that is sufficient, globally attainable and sustainable attempts to univer-salize a claim of justice that is somewhat tolerant of cross-cultural difference. The principle allows for diverse communities to identify and rank those functionings that they value, and to devise institutions for securing those functionings, subject to the condition that all people be provided equal sub-stantive freedoms to live valued lives.

The principle of capabilities equality as elucidated here includes much to excite the antipathy of both objectivists and relativists. What I have offered as the virtues of cross-cultural flexibility will strike moral objectivists as too elas-tic and permissive to serve the purpose of rooting out oppression and pro-moting human freedom. If each society is provided substantial latitude to define for itself the functionings that it deems valuable (and for ranking the same), then what are we to do if we find their choices reprehensible? On the other hand, the relativist will likely bristle at the idea of our holding up one standard of justice as appropriate across societies, even those who do not share its basic precepts of equality. Haven't we merely substituted one imperial decree for another, and thereby failed to appreciate the equal legitimacy of normative doctrines that are different from our own? Hearing these criticisms, a non-partisan observer to the discussion might conclude that the principle of capabilities equality swings unstably back and forth between the two poles of objectivism and relativism – and hence, that it is no kind of dependable principle at all.

The defense of capabilities equality in the face of these objections requires a humble acknowledgement that it does not and indeed cannot "resolve" the debate between objectivism and relativism. It is not even offered as a proof that either of those two perspectives is wrong. Rather, it is intended as a basis for *managing reasonably* what is no doubt an ineradicable tension between the virtues of resisting oppression and accepting difference. It incorporates elements of both traditions, though (as a consequence) neither one completely or dogmatically.

That said, I would offer the following theoretical rejoinder to these criticisms. First, as I have tried to demonstrate throughout, the rejection of the epistemological claims of moral objectivism does not necessitate an "anything goes" attitude to social practices. To admit that we are not in possession of the one true normative code is not to say that we are entirely unarmed in identifying and resisting oppression. We recognize that we are guided only by our best judgements, imperfectly forged though those implements might be in the foundry of our present context of time, place and culture. *But those implements are all that will ever be available to us,* though some choose to see them as far more durable and reliable instruments. We make all sorts of normative judgements and consequential decisions every day based on little else. We would do well to keep in mind that the foundation of our judgements are just that shaky – we might then exhibit a bit more humility in the decisions we take, recognize our errors earlier, and be more apt to learn from others. But we would make an egregious and irresponsible error indeed were we to refuse to consider, judge and act, all because we lack the certainty that objectivists seek.

For their part, relativists implicitly commit the same epistemological error as do the objectivists. They too hold to the view that an objective, transcendent normative account would be necessary before we could rightly judge others and reasonably act to change their behavior. The only difference between them is that while objectivists hold that such an account exists and is available to the human thinker, relativists claim that it is not. Absent this meta-standard against which to judge the particular normative accounts that distinct societies generate, relativists conclude, we must take these particular accounts as legitimate in their own contexts. Nussbaum makes this point forcefully and with her typical elegance:

Why, indeed, should the relativist conclude that the absence of a transcendent basis for judgement – a basis that, according to them, was never there anyway – should make us despair of doing as we have done all along, distinguishing persuasion from manipulation?

In fact, the collapse into extreme relativism or subjectivism seems to me to betray a deep attachment to metaphysical realism itself. For it is only to one who has pinned everything to that hope that its collapse will seem to entail the collapse of all evaluation – just as it is only to a deeply believing religious person, as Nietzsche saw, that the news of the death of God brings the threat of nihilism. What we see here, I think, is a reaction of *shame* – a turning away of the eyes from our poor humanity, which looks so mean and bare – by contrast to a dream of another sort. What do we have here, these critics seem to say? Only our poor old human conversation, our human bodies that interpret things so imperfectly?

(Nussbaum 1992, 213)

The anti-essentialist does not feel this shame. Not having presumed the need for a normative anchor, some sort of unimpeachable meta-standard to guide and validate our judgements, the anti-essentialist is not troubled in the least by its absence. For the anti-essentialist, the dismissal of objectivist claims does not thwart the search for an internationalist normative code (as relativists argue). But it does reorient the debate over what this code might look like in an altogether healthy and democratic direction, with non-objectivist defenses of the normative values we have reason to embrace taking center stage.

In the end, the principle of capabilities equality is intended as a useful political intervention – one that can enable a kind of politics and sustain sets of policy regimes which are appropriate to the monumental challenges of embedded global inequality we face today. We must therefore investigate just what this principle entails in the context of global policy regimes. From the anti-essentialist perspective, the value of this principle depends largely on whether it can provide reasonable policy guidance for the world in which we live, not on whether it is uniquely right. Just as we have done here for moral objectivism and cultural relativism, we would do well to inquire about the kinds of politics that this principle might induce. I will argue in the concluding chapter that this principle provides a foundation for a kind of politics that is particularly appropriate for a world (like our own) of extraordinary inequalities.

Let us turn now to the two most controversial components of the debate over global neoliberalism, competitiveness and trade policies. This is the task of the next two chapters.

5   Contesting competitiveness

INTRODUCTION

"Competitiveness" is one of those concepts that separates neoclassical economists not only from many of their heterodox colleagues, but from most
policymakers and the general public. For the latter, a nation's prosperity
depends directly on the ability of its firms to achieve competitiveness in
global markets. Global competition richly rewards the winners, but often
severely penalizes the losers.

Neoclassical economists take pride in their dissent from the prevailing
view. Not only is national competitiveness not the primary determinant of
national prosperity, it is hardly of any consequence at all. For Krugman
(1994a), the "obsession" with competitiveness reflects ignorance of basic
economic principles, and distracts attention away from the more important
and yet elusive determinants of prosperity. The concern over national competitiveness is exploited by ideologues with ulterior motives wielding dangerous rhetoric in pursuit of ruinous policies. Economists must drive the stake
of scientific reasoning through its heart before it leads us down the road of
reckless neo-mercantilist economic and geopolitical strategies.

But the seductiveness of competitiveness will not be so easily eradicated.
The competitiveness formula for prosperity is prescribed today by political
antagonists who agree on little else, from trade unionists, to left/liberal
economists, to social democrats, to conservatives, to right-wing neo-
populists. While advocates present alternative, and, in many ways, irreconcilable programs to restore competitiveness, they all identify a powerful causal
link that runs from national competitiveness to national prosperity.

This chapter seeks to untangle the threads of the competitiveness debate
by classifying the contending perspectives into three categories. These will
be referred to as the *anti-competitiveness, progressive competitiveness-enhancing*
and the *competition-reducing* approaches. These are associated respectively
with the three broader perspectives that have taken center stage in debates
over global Economy, Global Justice – the neoclassical vision, and what I will
call progressive nationalism and egalitarian internationalism. Neoclassicals
cite domestic productivity growth as the chief lever by which to secure

economic prosperity. In this view, insofar as there is little the state can do to induce higher rates of productivity, state initiatives to enhance competitiveness are misguided and likely to be self-defeating. In contrast, advocates of the competitiveness-enhancing perspective claim that a nation's prosperity is tied to its productivity performance relative to other nations. In this account, what winners gain in the global economy comes at the expense of the losers. Nations must therefore pay close attention to their relative standing *vis-à-vis* their neighbors, and to implementing policies which secure an improving position in the global competitive hierarchy.

Advocates of the competition-reducing perspective seek prosperity not through restored competitiveness, but through the establishment of an appropriate set of rules and institutions which govern economic behavior. On this account, malevolent economic outcomes can be mitigated only by removing critical aspects of social, political and economic life from the market so as to insulate them from the ravaging effects of competition. Proponents often advocate the international harmonization of labor and environmental standards so as to prevent the "social dumping" that would otherwise occur.[83] The competition reducers understand that market interventions (by the state, trade unions and other actors) do not necessarily reduce efficiency, as the neoclassical visionaries would have it, but can and often do improve upon the short- and long-term economic outcomes which would otherwise occur. This finding follows from the anti-reductionist model of the economy (examined in Chapter 2) that informs their assessments.

This chapter identifies the normative commitments which underlie the three perspectives on competitiveness. The neoclassical antipathy is defended on welfarist grounds, impartially applied across all countries. The progressive competitiveness-enhancing perspective evidences a commitment to egalitarianism;[84] strangely, however, the domain over which this egalitarianism is applied is the nation. Absent here is any concern for international equality. The competition-reducing perspective is derived explicitly from the internationalist capabilities ethic introduced above. It therefore reflects a deep commitment to intra- and international equality.

The next section of this chapter surveys briefly the economic and political landscape in the US and Europe that gave rise to the competitiveness debate. This section will situate modern competitiveness policy as an adaptation of circa 1970s "industrial policy" to the rapidly changing global economic environment. There follows the main section of the chapter: this presents a substantive discussion and critical evaluation of the three major positions in the competitiveness debate, beginning with the competitiveness-enhancing perspective, and then turning to the anti-competitiveness and competition-reducing perspectives.

ORIGINS OF COMPETITIVENESS POLICY

The contemporary concern with competitiveness emerged gradually during the early 1980s in the US and Europe and escalated quickly thereafter. Notably, the debate arrived on the heels of global economic dislocation that developed during the 1970s. To appreciate the salience of competitiveness today, it is important to understand the historical context of its emergence.

The postwar period, ranging from the late 1940s through the early 1970s, was exceptional in many respects. First, productivity rates rose rapidly in the US and particularly dramatically in much of Europe and Japan. Second, this productivity growth was coupled to rising living standards for workers throughout the North, and was paralleled by impressive economic growth throughout much of the South. In the US, for instance, labor productivity and workers' wages doubled from the late 1940s to 1970, while many OECD countries performed even better. Third, the link between rising productivity and incomes succeeded in producing global economic growth without severe recessions. Increasing demand in consumers and investment goods markets sufficed to absorb the rising output of firms in these sectors, and thereby ensured sufficient profits to warrant continuing economic expansion.

For neoclassical theorists, this period validated the vitally important mechanical relationship between contribution and reward: workers' incomes rose because of and in direct proportion to their rising productivity. The line of causation in this reductionist account runs from rising productivity to rising incomes, as we have seen. For many heterodox economists, in contrast, the outcome was far more complex and, ultimately, precarious. In Marxian interpretations, the period came to be theorized through the lens of the "regulation", "social structures of accumulation" and other long-wave theories.[85] In these accounts, the postwar period was marked by a peculiar and contingent constellation of institutions which articulated production with demand and mediated power relations between capital, workers and the state. In the US, these included what came to be known as the "capital–labor accord", with strong unions bargaining industry-wide with employers over wages and working conditions for tens of millions of workers. In the ensuing bargains, firms begrudgingly recognized the legitimacy of labor unions, and provided workers with steadily rising wages commensurate with rising productivity levels. In return, unions accepted the right of employers to manage the enterprise (including the right to introduce new technologies, terminate excess workers, etc.), and also agreed to forego the right to strike during the term of labor agreements. Hence, employers secured a measure of labor peace that allowed for predictability and continuity in production. For its part, the government committed itself to counter-cyclical Keynesian macroeconomic policies that softened economic recessions and provided displaced workers with income protection. These institutional arrangements provided a fortuitous configuration of power that generated rising incomes and increasing equality that in turn validated robust capital accumulation. They also happened to induce rising labor productivity.

In both accounts, the so-called "Golden Era" is seen to have begun to unravel by the early 1970s. The following two decades were marked by declining productivity growth and profit rates in most OECD countries, and by severe economic crisis in much of Africa and Latin America.[86] The US faced the most severe and sustained decline in productivity growth, extending from the 1970s into the 1990s. During this period sectoral shifts (especially from manufacturing to services) permanently displaced millions of workers in the US, Britain and across Europe. Particularly in the US, the majority of those workers who shifted into the burgeoning non-union service sector fared especially poorly. There and in other countries that permit it, permanent, full-time positions have been steadily replaced by temporary and/or part-time contracts that do not provide the employment security, living wages, training, pensions and other benefits that have historically been associated with full-time employment (Tilly 1996; Parker 1994).

The 1970s heralded the onset of the demise of the capital–labor accord in the US; by the 1980s European unions also confronted eroding density and influence (Freeman 1994). Employer resistance precipitated steady erosion in union bargaining power in those industries where labor had always been strongest. In the US and Britain, unemployment grew fastest in the most heavily unionized regions of the country, as manufacturing firms downsized, relocated to lower-waged areas at home and abroad, or closed entirely (Bluestone and Harrison 1982). With the elections of Thatcher and Reagan the assault on labor gathered momentum. Indeed, the 1980s was the worst decade for organized labor in the US since the 1920s; by 1990 union density among private sector workers was lower than it had been prior to the passage of the pro-union National Labor Relations Act in 1935. In Britain the 1980s witnessed particularly dramatic defeats for labor, while in Europe co-operation between labor and capital came under strain even in those countries where it had seemed most secure, such as Sweden.

Since the 1980s, Europe has faced the highest rates of unemployment since the crisis of the interwar period. The official unemployment rate for countries of the European Union over the period from 1984 to 1994 averaged 9.7 per cent; since then, it has hovered over 11 per cent (OECD 1997). For OECD countries in aggregate, the official unemployment rate jumped from just 2.9 per cent in 1969 to 7.5 per cent in 1992 (OECD 1996). This level of joblessness has harmed those out of work, of course, but has also undermined the bargaining power of those holding jobs, and substantially weakened aggregate demand.

The US has fared better than Europe in this regard. Unemployment averaged 6.5 per cent from 1984 to 1994, and has trended downward since. In contrast to Europe, this period has been marked by a dramatic reversal in the trend toward greater income equality that extended through much of the post-Depression era. The income and wealth shares of the richest quintile –

and especially the richest 1 per cent of US households – have soared to heights approaching those of the 1920s (see Introduction). Since the mid-1980s the popular press has reported with awe and some consternation the rise of the "overclass", a phenomenon which has placed into sharp relief the stagnation in real incomes for up to 80 per cent of the workforce (*Newsweek* 7/31/95). Rising inequality has been associated with an abrupt rise in the rolls of the officially poor. Although the rising poverty of the period is not unprecedented, the growth of poverty in the context of a growing economy and low official unemployment rates is indeed new. The long Reagan expansion of the 1980s was characterized by a new phenomenon – the rise of the "working poor". Growth, the historic palliative for poverty, was now failing to lift the poor into the ranks of the middle class (see *Business Week* 1991; *New York Times* 11/17/91; Rassell *et al.* 1997; Mishel *et al.* 1999). By 1990, one in five children in the US was living in poverty.

Looking on the period extending from the early 1970s to the present, many observers have been particularly troubled by what they perceive as erosion of the civic fabric, particularly across industrialized countries. Feelings of mutual interdependence that had spawned broad attachments to enlightened self-interest have given way to a pervasive sense of disharmony and to a fragmentation of spheres of obligation and mutuality. These have been replaced by a naked self-interest, and by ethnic, regional, racial and class Balkanization. In the US, critics chide the wealthy who now take refuge in "gated communities" replete with fences and guardhouses that prevent access to the uninvited. When they must leave these protected estates, they drive massive "sport utility vehicles" (and some, even converted military vehicles) with impenetrable tinted glass that protect them from the gaze and reach of the frightening world beyond their windshields. In a return to nineteenth-century practices, several US states now allow people to carry concealed handguns without restriction to ensure their protection. Rather than pay taxes to fund decent public schools and adequate social welfare programs, they instead pay exorbitant fees for private schooling, security forces, alarm systems and firearms to ensure that the social decay of poverty and inequality does not spill over into and disrupt their country club lives.

Many progressives view the rise of a resurgent conservatism across OECD countries, spearheaded by Reagan, Thatcher, Kohl and other center-right leaders, as powerful indications of this social transformation. The era has also been marred by growing hostility to immigration (and recent immigrants) and, especially in the US, a distrust of supranational entities (like the United Nations) that would usurp national sovereignty and subordinate "our" interests to those who might do us harm.

Economic integration, dislocation and competitiveness

These troubling trends emerged in the context of a global shift toward Economy, Global Justice (see Introduction). By the 1970s, neoliberal integration had begun to erase the geographical fragmentation of markets and production, leading to intensifying competition in global markets. Japanese firms in particular threatened many European and US firms, even in relatively capital-intensive industries that required technological sophistication. Japan was not only producing cars that were of higher quality than those produced in Italy, France, the UK and the US, but it was doing so at lower cost. Japanese firms proved to be world leaders in other heavy industries, too, like steel; but also in electronics. Inspired by Japan's record of modernization, other Asian countries attempted to replicate its model of development and especially its impressive export performance. By the 1980s, the "newly industrialized countries" (NICs) of South Korea, Taiwan, Singapore and Hong Kong had become export powerhouses in industries ranging from textiles to machine tools.

While the Asian NICs were entering global markets from a position of strength, other developing countries were forced to enter global markets as a consequence of economic crisis. Under the tutelage of the IMF and World Bank, debt-ridden countries have since the early 1980s adopted aggressive strategies to establish balance of trade surpluses so as to be able to meet their debt obligations. In the face of declining official aid from developed countries and multilateral agencies, they have also taken steps to attract foreign private capital. The proliferation of "export processing zones" (EPZs) in debtor nations reflects these imperatives. These provide foreign firms with low-priced labor and generous subsidies and tariff and tax treatment as inducements to establish export-oriented production and assembly facilities. Although the EPZs still represent a small proportion of total employment in most developing countries, there has been a substantial growth in production and exports emanating from these areas over the past fifteen years.

The confluence of deepening market integration and economic crisis ensured that global competition would emerge as a site of contest over the distribution of employment and income. Searching for the causes of the sudden economic malaise, many analysts surmised that declining prosperity in Europe and the US was the result of the competitive shortcomings of their firms in domestic and global markets. During the 1980s, the association between prosperity and national competitiveness became deeply ingrained in policy circles.[87] The evidence was apparent in aggregate trade, productivity and income statistics: success in global markets – notably by Japan and the NICs – was correlated with rising incomes; failure – by the US and much of Europe – induced falling real incomes, rising inequality and/or unemployment, and social dislocation. From the 1980s onward, European and US analysts generated a massive literature seeking to identify the means by which competitiveness and prosperity could be restored. Much of this literature invokes the need for government strategies to create conditions for private sector competitiveness. Proponents and opponents alike often refer to these strategies with the term "industrial policy". But this usage is at least misleading, if not entirely incorrect, and it is important for us to see why.

The political economy of industrial policy

Although the postwar Golden Era is widely eulogized today as an era of social harmony and growth, the 1940s through the 1970s were marked by rather sharp ideological conflict throughout Europe and even in the US. Communist and other radical parties emerged from the war with strong political bases among workers, students and intellectuals. What is often described in neutral terms today as the "rebuilding" of Europe and Japan under the auspices of the Marshall Plan was in fact a much more contentious process, one that comprised intense struggle between partisans of antagonistic social visions. US assistance and intervention in rebuilding postwar Europe and Japan were driven in part by a concern to save these countries from communist influence. Without overstating the point, it is safe to say that the threat of a radical assault on capitalist privilege was taken to be real and immediate throughout France, Italy, and other European countries. Even within the US, where political controversy was largely channeled into skirmishes between the Democratic and Republican parties, the influence of radical activists and ideas (especially within the labor movement) was seen to pose a significant threat to national security.

An important aspect of the political struggles of this era concerned the terms by which conflict between capital and labor was to be mediated so as to contain radicalism. In those countries where US influence was strongest, such as Germany and Japan, efforts were undertaken to construct institutions of labor representation that were "non-ideological". Radical labor organizations that had emerged prior to the war were largely suppressed (although France and Italy represent important exceptions). Centrist labor organizations that posed no threat to the capitalist system were established to replace the fragmented, ideologically contested labor movements of the interwar period. In the US, where radicalism had been weaker prior to and after the war, the government succeeded in rooting out radicals from the labor movement, often with the help of centrist labor leaders (Milton 1982).

No one institutional model for mediating class conflict emerged across postwar Europe, Japan and the US during this period (cf. Boyer 1995). Many European countries adopted "social corporatism", a system in which inclusive and centralized labor and employer confederations bargain with, and under the auspices of, the state to determine incomes policies and to define more broadly the terms of the capital–labor and capital–citizen accords. The Scandinavian countries and Germany moved furthest in this direction. Social corporatism generally emerged within broader social democratic systems of mediation, which established substantial constraints on the prerogatives of capital. In Japan, the appearance of corporatist governance masked a significant subservience of unionism to capital, so that industrial relations served the interests of capital much more directly than in Scandinavia and Germany. In Britain, the terms of the "bargain" between capital and labor were less acceptable to both parties. Although displaying real strength on the shop floor, British unions failed to wield the kind of unified political power of their Scandinavian and German counterparts. Moreover, insofar as the British model of industrial relations and bargaining remained far more fragmented than on the continent, unions lacked the cohesiveness to institute economywide bargaining in pursuit of collective goals (DeMartino 1982–3). The US, finally, exhibited the greatest opposition to legislated constraints on capital, and with the exception of Japan, the least politically efficacious labor movement among these countries. It never embraced either social corporatism or industrial policy.

Attributes of industrial policy

Abstracting from important cross-national differences, we can isolate the salient features of what came to be known as industrial policy (see Table 5.1).[88] Industrial policy was understood to provide one resolution to the daunting question of the proper role of government in organizing and directing economic affairs. For continental Europe, postwar industrial policy was connected to the need to replace infrastructure and industrial enterprises, of course. But, and equally important, it was tied to the imperative to mediate domestic class conflict. It was therefore often corporatist in structure. In Sweden, where corporatist structures and industrial policy emerged prior to the war, the connection between the adoption of these institutions and the need to manage class conflict was especially direct (Korpi and Shalev 1979).

Notably, industrial policy was promoted as a means to correct inherent failings of the free market, capitalist economy.[89] To prosper, society had to be protected *from* these market failings; otherwise, they would induce unmanageable social cleavages and political antagonisms – resulting even in the overthrow of the capitalist system. In this connection, capitalism was seen to be a site of conflict between two very unequal parties: relatively powerless workers who confronted far more powerful capitalists. This imbalance led to unjust economic outcomes, such as income inequality across classes and regions. Industrial policy sought to address these failings so as to universalize the benefits that market organization could induce.

As a concomitant to this concern for inter-class equity, industrial policy was intended to sustain full employment. This was pursued through several means, not least by substantially limiting the ability of firms to shed workers during economic downturns by requiring prior notification of plans to cease or reduce industrial production, state authorization to lay off workers, retraining of redundant workers, etc. In addition, investment dictates and incentives were also tied in part to the goal of securing full employment.

The free market was seen to induce other forms of sub-optimal macroeconomic performance. In the absence of public control over investment decisions, firms might under-invest, or mis-invest, with the effect of generating economic stagnation and instability. By constraining the authority of corporate managers, society could smooth out the otherwise inevitable cycles of investment, employment and income. Hence, while Keynesian macroregulation did not necessarily entail industrial policy (or vice versa), the two could be seen as complementary means to achieve growth and stability.

Although particular industrial policies could take the form of market incentives to bring about beneficial corporate behavior, the corporatist structures and social democratic influences generally entailed more direct intervention. As such, industrial policy could be thought of as a means to "fix" capital so as to ensure appropriate outcomes.[90] By fixing capital (geo-graphically, industrially, etc.), the state stripped the firm of the option of "exit" in pursuit of profits. While neoclassicals opposed these constraints as market imperfections, advocates of industrial policy viewed them as neces-sary parameters within which the market might operate to fulfill paramount social objectives. Mechanisms for fixing capital could range from outright nationalization of corporate enterprises to corporatist bargaining, to credit control through quasi-public investment banks. While different in impor-tant respects, these mechanisms shared a commitment to overriding market signals in the important sphere of corporate investment decision making.

Finally, insofar as the architects of industrial policy viewed labor to be at a relative disadvantage, the protection of the national interest required that the state protect labor from the predatory practices of firms. Though indus-trial policy could promote the competitiveness of domestic firms, its chief purpose was generally not competitiveness, but the creation of an industrial sector that performed well in meeting the needs of society. Hence, it was to be an industrial sector that created and sustained ample employment oppor-tunities, generated productivity increases, and sustained rising incomes for the nation's citizens.

In short, industrial policy as it emerged prior to and following the war sought to accomplish two distinct classes of objectives: to promote economic

Table 5.1 Attributes of industrial policy

Mediation of domestic class conflict – capital vs. labor
Tripartite corporatism
Protection *from* the market
Full employment (of labor)
Maintenance of stability
Mandated co-operation
Fixing capital
National interest promoted through protection of labor's interests
Equality as end

---

development (which in postwar Europe took the form of rebuilding and modernizing) and to mediate what were seen to be fundamental domestic social antagonisms. Rather than focus on competitiveness *per se*, industrial policy sought the creation of stability, opportunity, full employment and equality. For all its virtues, the free market was taken by proponents of industrial policy to fail in these latter regards. For its liberal advocates, industrial policy was seen as a chief means to repair once and for all the schisms of capitalism; for its radical proponents, it was viewed as a step toward the socialization of production and distribution on the path to socialism.

From industrial policy to competitiveness

The economic turbulence of the 1970s and 1980s had contradictory effects on industrial policy and the broader Keynesian macroregulatory and social democratic regimes in which they were embedded. Economic crisis in Britain led the Labour Party to advocate a comprehensive industrial policy (first in 1964 and then again more ambitiously in 1974) (Sawyer 1991). The left wing of the Labour Party proposed extensive nationalization of large firms in major industries as a means to ensure sufficient investment to generate employment and rising incomes. The Labour Party adopted resolutions that proposed the formation of what came to be called the National Economic Board (NEB) which would acquire substantial ownership stakes in major industries. By increasing investment in the nationalized firms, the NEB would establish a moving target to be emulated by competing firms, leading to an economywide rationalization of industry, growth and rising employment. But this initiative was largely stillborn: the Labour government failed to acquire substantial ownership stakes during the mid-1970s. Thatcher's victory in 1979 signaled the growing influence of a resurgent neoclassical orthodoxy in Europe. With Thatcher's election, industrial policy was abruptly dismantled in favor of an embrace of neoliberal policies.

On the continent, the 1980s marked a gradual two-pronged ideological transition. On the right, neoclassicals came to articulate the neoliberal critique of the interventionist state. For neoclassicals, European industrial policy was identified as inefficient and counterproductive. Growing unemployment was attributed in part to the rigidities embedded in social-democratic market interventions that prevented rapid adjustment to the changing demands of an increasingly dynamic global economy. The result was seen by neoclassicals to be "Eurosclerosis": having fought a rearguard action to insulate society from the vagaries of the market, social democratic industrial policy had undermined the ability of European capital to innovate. The pursuit of stability had stifled the entrepreneurial spirit and had brought about precisely the stagnation, insecurity and punishment by the market that it had been intended to prevent.

The social democratic left developed a more complicated relationship to industrial policy during the 1980s. Still suspicious of the effects of the free market, but now tarred by neoliberals with responsibility for growing unemployment and stagnation, some social democrats began to rethink the goals, instruments and efficacy of industrial policy. In the context of deepening economic integration, policy discussions turned increasingly toward the troubling matter of European competitiveness in global markets. This intellectual transition was reflected in a series of reports on competitiveness from the European Community and European analysts. Competitiveness became a means by which to salvage state intervention in pursuit of socially benevolent outcomes.[91] But the shift from industrial to competitiveness policy represented something more than a strategic maneuver; it marked a fundamental transition in progressive thought concerning political aspirations and, more importantly, the proper role of the market in society. It therefore reflected a change in left ontology that has brought in its train a changing set of normative commitments.[92] To appreciate these transitions, we need to take a close look at the competitiveness-enhancing perspective.

THE PROGRESSIVE COMPETITIVENESS-ENHANCING PERSPECTIVE

The competitiveness-enhancing perspective is expansive, housing management theorists, social democrats, institutionalist economists and others. The focus here will be on what will be called the "progressive" competitiveness-enhancing perspective. This term refers to heterodox theorists who share two views: *first, that promoting the prosperity of its workers ought to be a (if not the) central goal of a nation's economic policy; and second, that the achievement of this goal under the conditions obtaining in today's global economy requires the enhancement of national competitiveness.*

The most important contributions to the progressive competitiveness-enhancing perspective are the flexible specialization, corporate governance, and human capital approaches. Most recent writings on competitiveness fit within one of these categories, or embrace some mix of the three. The following discussion will first identify the salient features of each, drawing attention to their distinctiveness; this will be followed by a more general discussion of their shared premises which distinguishes competitiveness policy from industrial policy, and a normative assessment.

Flexible specialization

The most influential contribution to the competitiveness debate remains Piore and Sabel's *The Second Industrial Divide*, which appeared in 1984. The persuasiveness of this book has been such that one critic of the approach has rightly drawn attention to what he calls the "flexibility fetish" in contemporary competitiveness scholarship (Curry 1992).

Piore and Sabel advance two principal theoretical claims that are consistent with institutionalist theory. First, a nation's industrial organization (the pattern and character of its industries and firms) is *institutionally embedded*. It is always situated in a dense web of social, political and economic institutions. Second, economic development is also necessarily *path-dependent*. Once a society commits to one form of industrial organization (or what Piore and Sabel call a "technological paradigm"), alternative forms recede to the margins of the economy. For Piore and Sabel, alternatives are marginalized not because of their inherent weaknesses, but because of their failure to secure the kinds of institutional support that they require to flourish. Having committed itself to the paradigm, then, a society may lack the institutional means or vision to establish a new model that is better adapted to changed economic circumstances. Together, institutional embeddedness and path-dependence therefore breed *industrial inertia*.

For Piore and Sabel, the early nineteenth century marked a contest between two distinct paradigms. This "first industrial divide" pitted the technological paradigm of mass production against craft production. In the event, mass production came to dominate the industrial landscape in the US, Britain and parts of Europe. Contemporary observers concluded that craft production could not survive the challenge of this *superior* form of industrial organization. Where craft production did persist, government policy often sought consciously to replace it with "national champions" patterned on the US mass production model.

In Piore and Sabel's view, we are living now through a "second industrial divide". Mass production has been threatened by growing instability in global markets, increasing sophistication of consumers, and new technologies that allow manufacturing firms to innovate more quickly and to secure economies of scale at much lower levels of output. These changes have given a competitive advantage to "flexible" firms that can quickly respond to changing demand. While mass producers require stable demand conditions in order to validate high capacity, the flexible firm thrives in the context of uncertainty, rapid change and enhanced consumer sophistication that rewards attention to quality and innovation.

The two industrial paradigms differ in their use of technology and labor. Mass production requires use-specific technology that is suited to long production runs of standardized products. Flexible specialization uses generalized technologies that can be easily reoriented to different production tasks. Complementing this difference, the mass-producing firm employs large numbers of relatively unskilled workers who retain little control over the production process; in Marxian terms, they are mere appendages of the machine, in which is located the knowledge and skill, rather than vice versa. In contrast, the flexible firm employs broadly skilled workers who possess sufficient knowledge to be able to innovate on the shop floor to develop new products and production methods.

Piore and Sabel draw attention to successful examples of flexible specialization, focusing in particular on the widely studied and celebrated "Third

Italy". The industrial districts of northern Italy comprise thousands of small firms that have evolved complex webs of co-operation and competition in the textile and other artisanal industries. The regional clustering of these firms is a key determinant of their success. In the view of its proponents, clustering of this sort induces external economies by attracting and retaining a highly skilled workforce that can move from firm to firm as circumstances warrant, and various forms of inter-firm co-operation in production, marketing, research, and risk-sharing. Clustering also gives these firms sufficient political weight to ensure that local government will adopt policies that are supportive of flexible specialization, such as co-ordinating marketing and enforcing labor policies to prevent ruinous forms of competition.[93]

Piore and Sabel emphasize that the effects of both mass production and flexible specialization on workers' prosperity depend upon the broader context in which they emerge. Nevertheless, they have been interpreted fairly as advocates of flexible specialization as a viable means of restoring prosperity through the restoration of competitiveness. Provided a suitable institutional structure is established to protect workers' interests, flexible specialization might be expected to enrich workers' lives on the job while providing a basis for increased wages reflecting enhanced skills.

Given their emphasis on institutional embeddedness, Piore and Sabel understand that the achievement of competitiveness through flexible specialization requires institutional changes that reach beyond the firm. A successful transition to flexible specialization would entail a reorientation in the institutions that have historically supported the mass production paradigm, not least education and labor policies and social welfare arrangements. In this perspective, then, the concept of national competitiveness makes sense – success in global markets will depend on the policies that national governments pursue in support of one industrial paradigm or another.

The corporate governance approach

I will refer to a second approach as the "corporate governance" perspective. Like flexible specialization, this perspective highlights the ways in which firms respond to increasing competition as a key determinant of national prosperity. The distinctive feature of this approach is its emphasis on the social, economic and political environment of a firm – its "corporate culture" – as a pivotal factor affecting intra-firm co-operation and conflict.

Lazonick (1991) exemplifies this perspective. Like Piore and Sabel, Lazonick pays careful attention to the manner in which past decisions shape present-day corporate strategies and economic outcomes. Those forms of industrial organization that yielded success in the past often become obstacles to success in the present, as those actors with vested interests in the old system resist fundamental change. Indeed, Lazonick demonstrates how the forms of corporate governance that propelled British and US firms to success in the nineteenth and twentieth centuries, respectively, ultimately blocked the kinds of innovation that were required to remain competitive.

A key analytical distinction in Lazonick's work is that between the "innovative" and the "adaptive" firm. The former is willing to invest in long-term strategies that promise to enhance "value-creation" (the production of useful commodities at low cost) over the long run, even though they entail higher costs in the short run. In contrast, the latter attempts to remain competitive by intensifying production on the basis of existing technologies and social relations of production. The former entails continual reskilling of workers and the search for new products and better production processes. The latter entails the sweating of labor and other means to reduce costs within the confines of existing products and processes. The former looks ahead, and takes initiatives now to position itself for future competition; the latter looks backward, and seeks to remain competitive by living off past innovations.

For Lazonick, the choice that a nation's firms make regarding these alternatives shapes the level of prosperity that its inhabitants can expect to achieve. To be prosperous a nation needs a critical mass of innovative firms which outperform foreign rivals. The innovative strategy promises better prospects for workers, including higher standards of living, greater workplace satisfaction, etc. The innovative strategy, however, entails substantial risks. Innovation entails incurring high fixed costs in the short run, as the firm must create the factors of production (such as new skills, knowledge and tools) that will ultimately provide it with competitive advantage. Only by producing factors of production not generally available on the market can the firm hope to secure an enduring competitive advantage.

The innovative firm is therefore continuously engaged in discovery, in the identification of new problems and the successful design of novel solutions. The learning-by-doing inherent in new techniques requires the full co-operation of a firm's front-line workers, upon whom the firm must depend to see the innovation through. Insofar as the innovative strategy requires a lengthy gestation period during which costs will be high and profits low, the firm must also secure the co-operation of its suppliers and financiers. Like the firm's workers, these parties must provide the firm with "privileged access" to their services; that is, they must be willing to provide these services at less than the market rate over an extended period.

How is the firm to secure this co-operation? Lazonick argues for the incorporation of the firm's workforce, suppliers and financiers as *stakeholders* in the firm's corporate community so that they identify their interests with the long-term viability of the firm.[94] For example, the firm must make long-term commitments to its workers in the form of lifetime employment contracts and profit sharing. In contrast to the prescriptions of neoclassical theory, the firm must replace market-based (or "arms-length") relationships with its resource suppliers with what Lazonick calls "organizational co-ordination". The promise of long-term rewards that are higher than those provided through market-based relationships must induce input suppliers to grant privileged access in the short run if the firm is to realize internal economies in the future.

Lazonick demonstrates the thesis on offer via a historical comparison of the competitive successes and failures of British, US and Japanese industry. In this account, the ultimate competitive crises that emerged by the late nineteenth century in the UK and by the 1970s in the US reflected the successive failure of their firms to pursue the innovative path. An exclusion of key input providers (such as labor) from the corporate community denied firms the co-operation necessary to risk the innovative strategy. When confronted with external competitive threats, first British and later US firms responded with adaptive strategies that ultimately undermined national prosperity.[95] In contrast, Japan's postwar success derives from the organizational co-ordination that binds workers, financiers and suppliers to the goals of the corporation. Obvious strategy implications follow. A firm must make long-term commitments to its stakeholders so as to secure willing co-operation to allow it to pursue the innovative strategy. For its part, the state must take steps to encourage the innovative approach. This would entail the institution of high capital-gains tax rates on short-term financial holdings to encourage long-term investing, changes in anti-trust laws and, most importantly, the use of short-term protective tariffs to insulate innovative firms from foreign competition.[96]

The industrial relations approach

An important offshoot of the corporate governance approach focuses on industrial relations as a key determinant of competitiveness. The neoclassical resurgence coupled with the electoral successes of conservatives in the US, Britain and on the continent in the 1970s and 1980s posed severe challenges to trade unions. Especially in the US and Britain, unions were identified as key obstacles to innovation, flexibility and competitiveness. In this supply-side view, the path to restored national competitiveness and prosperity ran right through the heart of organized labor.

In reaction, institutionalist economists have come to emphasize the salutary effect of unionism on corporate performance. For example, Freeman and Medoff (1984) rely on Albert Hirschman's "exit/voice" dichotomy to theorize the effects of unionism. By empowering workers within a firm and by providing them with a vehicle to mobilize in defense of their interests, unions provide workers with a vehicle to achieve the "voice" option within the firm. Unionized workers are encouraged to seek redress of grievances rather than avail themselves of the option of "exit" by quitting. The unionized firm is therefore the beneficiary of lower labor turnover.[97] Worker longevity gives the firm an incentive to invest in worker training, thereby enhancing labor productivity. Higher wages also give the firm an incentive to seek competitiveness through improved technology and productivity improvements rather than through efforts to sweat labor. In short, Freeman and Medoff find that unionized firms achieve higher productivity than non-union firms in the same industries.

Freeman and Medoff do not focus explicitly on the connection between unionism and competitiveness, but their work inspired many contributions to the competitiveness debate. Like Lazonick, these institutionalists have emphasized the connection between workers' security and their willingness to promote the objectives of management. Mishel and Voos (1992) argue that the presence of unionism enhances the effects of shop-floor participation schemes that arose especially during the 1980s in the US in response to intensifying competition. The protections afforded by unionism are also necessary to ensure the success of the flexible specialization model described by Piore and Sabel. In Mishel and Voos' view, the workforce of the successful flexible firm "must be highly skilled, involved, and motivated – willing to be deployed and redeployed flexibly ... Unions are a positive force in that they can facilitate a key ingredient of this high-performance business system: a secure, motivated, and participative workforce" (1992, 8). In addition, "the fundamental point is that high productivity, worker rights, flexibility, unionization, and economic competitiveness are not incompatible" (1992, 10).[98]

In keeping with the tenets of institutionalist theory, these accounts emphasize the effect of the environment within which competition unfolds on corporate behavior. Absent strong labor laws and protections, firms that attempt the progressive, high-waged path may face daunting obstacles, not least the unfair competition from firms pursuing the scorched-earth, labor-sweating, low-waged path. The switch to the high-performance path may therefore require an orchestrated transformation in the behaviors of firms, unions and the state.

It bears emphasis that, contrary to neoclassical theory, these arguments are predicated on the anti-reductionist model of the economy that informs institutionalist theory. The organizational co-ordination and worker empowerment through labor unions that these theorists celebrate are rejected by neoclassical visionaries as market distortions that induce perverse incentives and thereby undermine short- and long-run allocative efficiency. In this reductionist account, as we have seen, only arms-length market mediation between distinct actors can ensure an appropriate incentive structure that will induce static and dynamic efficiency. But in the institutionalists' far more nuanced perspective, certain kinds of extra-market relationships (such as long-term commitments between a firm and its suppliers, financiers and workers) can and often do induce behaviors that are conducive to the risk-taking without which innovation cannot occur.[99]

The human capital approach

The flexible specialization and corporate governance approaches call for rather pronounced changes in social and economic organization, to be sure.

But in an important sense these analyses remain rather conventional. Both equate the prosperity of a nation's citizens with the competitive success of *its firms.*

The human capital approach, best articulated by Robert B. Reich, secretary of labor in the first Clinton administration, rejects this association as symptomatic of "vestigial thought". Reich (1991) contends that the competitiveness of a nation's firms is an increasingly meaningless determinant of national prosperity in the global economy. Corporations today are "global webs" that place each function where it can be performed most cheaply. Postwar technological advances in telecommunications and transportation allow for the efficient co-ordination of far-flung industrial operations, reducing the need for close geographic proximity among research and design, marketing, production, assembly, etc. Hence, a "British" corporation might create more high-paying jobs in the US than in Britain, rendering the nationality of the corporation relatively meaningless.

If competition between nations' firms has come to mean little, however, competition between nations' *workers* has achieved paramount importance. With firms scouring the globe in search of the best site for each corporate activity, workers now compete amongst themselves for the best jobs. The nation that produces the most skilled workforce is likely to attract the best jobs and, thereby, the highest incomes for its inhabitants (cf. Cuomo Commission 1992; Prowse 1992; Lynch 1994).

National prosperity in the new global economy depends on a nation's ability to entice corporations to locate what Reich calls their "symbolic analytic" functions within its borders. Symbolic analysts are the researchers, managers, creative problem solvers and other high-skilled professionals. These jobs require high levels of education, add high levels of value to production, and consequently command high remuneration. To achieve prosperity a nation must therefore invest heavily in education, producing the most qualified potential symbolic analysts in the world. As corporations select a nation for such functions, a virtuous cycle develops: "well-trained workers attract global corporations, which invest and give workers good jobs; the good jobs, in turn, generate additional training and experience" (Reich 1990a, 59). For the US, Reich prescribes substantial increases in investment in human capital to ensure that every reasonably talented child be given the chance to become a symbolic analyst.

INDUSTRIAL VERSUS COMPETITIVENESS POLICY

We can now tease out the ways in which contemporary competitiveness policy differs from industrial policy (see Table 5.2). Most fundamentally, competitiveness policy is intended to mediate international, *intra-class* conflict. For most contributors, policy must enhance the ability of domestic firms to outcompete foreign rivals; for Reich, policy must address competition between domestic and foreign workers. For the former, a nation's workers and their firms are seen to have largely harmonious interests, provided firms can be cajoled into pursuing mutually beneficial competitiveness strategies. For Reich, although the link between a nation's own firms and national prosperity is severed, workers' interests are nevertheless best served by preparing themselves to meet corporate needs. By serving the corporation best, a nation's workers can outcompete their primary combatants, namely foreign workers. In short, the competitiveness enhancers efface the social antagonism between capital and labor that figured so prominently in policy formation in the postwar period, replacing it with international, intra-class conflict

Important consequences follow from this reorientation. The tripartite systems of governance of industrial policy have given way in the competitiveness literature to bilateral capital–state partnerships. The role of the state is to provide a context within which corporations can pursue benevolent paths to competitive success. This is tied to a further, fundamental shift away from industrial policy: the (global) market is now taken to be the optimal form of economic integration. The liberalized market sets the context within which firms must prosper or perish. Rather than shape market outcomes by overcoming the market – as through national planning, for example – desirable outcomes are to be secured by altering the strategies that firms pursue. This is true even for the corporate governance approach of Lazonick, despite his emphasis on the advantages of organizational co-ordination over arms-

Table 5.2 Industrial *vs.* competitiveness policy

Industrial policy	Competitiveness policy
Mediation of domestic class conflict: – capital *vs.* labor	Mediation of international intra-class conflict: – domestic *vs.* foreign capital – domestic *vs.* foreign labor
Tripartite corporatism	Bilateral, capital–state partnership
Protection *from* the market	Protection *through* the market
Full employment (of labor)	Efficient employment (of capital)
Maintenance of stability	Adaptation to instability via innovation/flexibility
Mandated co-operation	Enlightened, voluntary paternalism
Fixing capital	*Romancing* capital
National interest promoted through protection of labor's interests	National interest promoted through protection of corporate interests
Equality as end	Equality as means to efficiency

length market mediation. Lazonick argues that organizational co-ordination is superior precisely by virtue of its ability to outcompete market-based co-ordination in the marketplace. In the competitiveness-enhancing approach, then, the protection of workers' livelihoods must occur *through* the market, in place of industrial policy's emphasis on protecting workers *from* the market. Writ large, "the market" is taken to be the inevitable form of economic organization, so that industrial strategies must conform to its dictates. If prosperity is to be protected, this must be achieved through market-respecting initiatives.

Respect for the market yields a further distinction between competitiveness policy and its progenitor. While industrial policy was intended to yield *full employment of labor,* competitiveness policy seeks the *efficient employment of capital.* Insofar as labor's interests are now tied to that of capital and its ability to outcompete foreign rivals, policy must promote efficiency as the chief means to protect workers' prosperity.

Advocates of industrial policy view the chaotic nature of capitalist competition to be an inherent weakness of the market economy, one that can be overcome through a combination of supply- and demand-side policies. Industrial policy combined with Keynesian macroregulation could ensure sufficient investment so as to secure macroeconomic stability. Competitiveness-enhancing policy, on the other hand, takes instability to be ineradicable. Successful strategies *accommodate* instability rather than resist it. The flexible specialization approach is explicit in this regard: the industrial district is a site of continuous reconstitution of inter-firm relationships, while workers move quickly from firm to firm in response to changing circumstance and market dictate. The corporate governance approach emphasizes enduring commitments between firms and its stakeholders, as we have seen, and so may be viewed as an exception in this regard. But this is also justified on the basis of its purported internal dynamism (the discovery of new products and processes, etc.) which allow it to meet the competition. For its part, Reich's human capital approach projects a vision of the modern corporation as a whirling dervish of spin-offs, spin-ins, subcontracting arrangements and all sorts of kaleidoscopic configurations. Indeed, what is most pronounced about the new corporate form in this account is its impermanence. Competitiveness policy seeks to harness this instability in the service of prosperity.

Respect for the market is associated as well in a shift away from state-mandated behavior to an enlightened, voluntary paternalism. The main thrust of much of the progressive competitiveness-enhancing literature is that business can do better for itself by doing better for its workers. In a complementary way, rather than developing policies that attempt to "fix" capital, nations are encouraged to pursue policies that "romance" capital. The human capital approach is most explicit in this regard: the strategy is to build a first-class workforce so as to influence firms' location decisions.

Finally, while industrial policy seeks equality as an end in itself, competitiveness-enhancing policy seeks equality as a means toward a more important end, that is, competitive success. Having accepted the dictates of the market as inexorable, the progressive competitiveness enhancers have undertaken to show how socially benevolent strategies can generate competitive success. This is not an insignificant achievement, to be sure. It does, however, substantially break with traditional progressive defenses of equality and economic opportunity and security: now, these must be defended on instrumental grounds, in terms of their effects on capital.

Adjudication of the progressive competitiveness-enhancing perspective

Despite whatever other virtues it may have, the competitiveness-enhancing perspective is explicitly nationalist. Advocates of this perspective present an inherently irreconcilable worldview that ties a nation's prosperity to its *relative* performance – that of either its firms or its workforce. This perspective presents a vision of global Economy, Global Justice in which national interest is tied to besting foreign rivals. In this account, for instance, a nation must seek a higher rate of productivity growth than that of other nations, as this enhances its relative competitiveness. A nation is better off when it faces a low absolute rate of productivity growth, provided this rate is higher than that of its competitors, than when it faces a high rate of growth that nevertheless falls below that of other nations. But consider the unspoken but unequivocal implication: a policy that sabotages the productivity of other nations is just as valuable as a policy that enhances one's own productivity. If they face a debilitating military conflict that destroys their infrastructure and industrial capacity, or widespread famine or a paralyzing epidemic that destroys their human capital, good for us! If instead they manage to perform well in global markets, then perhaps we should find some way to upset their economic apple-cart. Perhaps new tariffs on their exports might do the trick.

This nationalism presents practical difficulties for the various competitiveness-enhancing proposals surveyed above. All suffer from a fallacy of composition: what might yield rising prosperity for any one country that pursues this path alone is not likely to succeed when all countries do so. Within the interpretive frame of the competitiveness-enhancing perspective, if all enjoy rising productivity at equal rates as a result of enlightened corporate governance, for example, *no one gains.*[100]

The nationalist impulse is also evident in the national policies dictated by this approach. Again, the fallacy asserts itself. For example, Lazonick calls for protective tariffs to insulate domestic firms pursuing the costly innovative path from foreign competition. Though these firms need this tariff protection, their ultimate success will depend upon their gaining free access to other nations' markets so that they can achieve economies of scale and low per unit costs. This protectionist strategy can succeed, then, only if other countries do not mimic the policy or retaliate against it. But why should other countries react so passively? Having read the book, other nations will realize that they can and should sabotage this competitiveness strategy by protecting their own markets. Hence, rather than each country risking the expensive innovative path – which would require a degree of international co-operation that this approach makes unlikely – the scene is set for a non-co-operative low-level equilibrium wherein each protects its markets to insulate its own adaptive firms.

This likelihood is entirely predictable, but Lazonick fails to explore it. This omission can be explained only by reference to the nationalist impulse that founds the competitiveness-enhancing perspective. Lazonick's explicit focus is on promoting the competitiveness of the US – one of the few countries with the political and economic muscle to influence the trading strategies of many of its partners. Unlike Mexico, for instance, the US just might be able to pursue temporary protectionist measures without incurring the retaliation of many of its trading partners. The policy prescription is therefore predicated upon the exploitation of national power by those few countries with the wherewithal to do so, in order to achieve a competitive advantage over those countries lacking such abilities.

This example signals a broader problem with the competitiveness-enhancing perspective. Though these policies are presented as universally applicable, we should recognize that, as a rule, those countries best positioned to implement them successfully are those which are already wealthy. The human capital approach recognizes this explicitly, as it encourages wealthy countries to build upon their lead over poorer countries in higher education so as to maintain a virtual monopoly over good jobs. But to the degree that competitiveness policies favor the wealthy, it stands to exacerbate rather than ameliorate severe international inequality. Yet no normative defense of this likely consequence appears in the competitiveness literature.

When we recall that the proponents of the competitiveness-enhancing perspective surveyed here are motivated by progressive and indeed, egalitarian impulses, the nationalism of their prescriptions is rather perplexing and deeply troubling. Some of the competitiveness enhancers are indeed aware of this rather striking inconsistency, although none of those surveyed here grapples explicitly with the global consequences of their perspectives. Reich's ambivalence is particularly acute. In *The Work of Nations* he focuses entirely on how the US might successfully lure the best jobs away from other countries (rich and poor) so as to promote rising US prosperity. He predicts here that low-paid routine production jobs will migrate to the poor countries. Though this will surely cement existing inequalities between the North and the South, Reich defends this distribution of jobs on grounds that any increase in employment at all will help poor countries. But elsewhere he expresses uneasiness about this nationalist formulation. In an article published at the same time that he was completing *The Work of Nations*, he proposes "multilateral, rule-oriented negotiations designed to allocate [symbolic analyst] jobs among nations according to some set of agreed-upon criteria" (Reich 1990b, 42). This call for mutually acceptable criteria to allocate good jobs fairly is laudable. If informed by a commitment to global egalitarianism, it could provide means to ensure rapidly increasing opportunities for workers in poorer countries – opportunities that might prove difficult to come by under a neoliberal regime in which their fate is tied directly to the private profit-maximizing decisions of global corporations. But note that this approach contradicts entirely the logic and presumptions that inform *The Work of Nations*. In endorsing this multilateral approach, Reich repudiates the right of corporations to allocate these jobs as they see fit, which is taken to be the central constraint facing policymakers throughout the book. But this move also eliminates the need for the US (or any other country) to expend any additional resources on education to compete for these jobs. If the distribution of such jobs is to be determined by state intervention rather than market outcomes, then there is no need to compete for them at all. Unfortunately, this alternative regime apparently marks too great a break with global Economy, Global Justice for Reich to take seriously. Hence, he retreated from this approach in crafting the fuller arguments that inform his book.

Domestically, however, each of these proposals is egalitarian, as we have seen. In each case, greater equality of income and substantive opportunities is taken to be a critical determinant of renewed competitiveness and, thereby, prosperity. This feature has given the progressive competitiveness enhancers wide credibility among liberal and left analysts. But this credibility is undeserved. As emphasized above, the commitment to equality in these accounts is *instrumental* rather than *intrinsic*. This perspective subjects equality to a daunting and inappropriate test – not whether it is defensible in its own right, but whether it can outcompete alternative models of industrial organization in the global neoliberal marketplace. The competitiveness-enhancing perspective elevates international market competition to the status of ultimate arbiter, which decides whether society can and should sustain equality.

What grounds are there, if any, for holding that the progressive approaches will necessarily outcompete less benevolent strategies in global markets? If other countries (or firms) are able to mimic the forms of industrial organization or training promoted by the competitiveness enhancers, but are able to secure workers' acquiescence through repression, might not they be able to succeed in global markets? Critics of "Toyotism" have argued persuasively that Japanese firms secured competitive success in the postwar period precisely by denying workers independent representation on the shop floor (Dohse *et al.* 1985; Tomaney 1990; Curry 1992). The company unions established after the war served to discipline rather than protect the interests of the industrial workforce. In this context, lifetime employment coupled with the associated practice of firms' hiring only at the entry level strip workers of the ability to switch firms mid-career. Hence, these workers are deprived of Hirschman's "voice" *and* "exit" – they lack effective rights within the firm, as well as the ability to leave it in search of better opportunities elsewhere. Contrary to the claims of its apologists, this case demonstrates that in the absence of strong workers' rights, the "organizational co-ordination" and "privileged access" that Lazonick celebrates can be trans-mogrified into indentured servitude, workplace coercion and super-exploitation. Similarly, as Piore and Sabel themselves recognize, flexible specialization may acquire exploitative forms in the absence of strong worker protections. In the latter case, egalitarianism may be sacrificed in pursuit of corporate interests.

I noted above that many competitiveness enhancers were dismayed by the apparent erosion in the social fabric of advanced industrialized countries following the collapse of the Golden Era. Advocates of this perspective hoped to demonstrate the instrumental virtues of social co-operation. It is therefore particularly troubling to find that their prescriptions presume and even exacerbate cross-national intra-class conflict. This perspective constructs and seeks to mobilize political identities defined by national and/or corporate affiliation. US (or GM) workers are now seen to have interests that are entirely antithetical to those of Japan (or Toyota). As a consequence, the competitiveness-enhancing perspective threatens to reproduce international cleavages among labor organizations at a time when the effective expression of labor's interests *as labor* requires a degree of international unity scarcely achieved in the past.

The construction of political identities and the framing of economic problems in nationalist terms threaten to undermine the progressive political content of these proposals. It is a small step from the assertion that French workers have interests antithetical to those of Morocco to the demand for draconian measures to limit immigration from Morocco to France, and to punish severely those immigrants who cross the border illegally. It is but one further small step to the scapegoating of immigrants for one's own economic hardships, to the denial to them of important political and social protections, and to the demand for their repatriation. This is not to say that the progressive nationalists we have surveyed here intend to provide legitimacy for the more naked forms of nationalism that have appeared across the political landscape in the US and especially in Europe (personified by France's Jean-Marie Le Pen). Nevertheless we must recognize the important theoretical affinities across their respective worldviews – stemming from the manner in which they construct political identities and interpret economic malaise – and the political affinities to which these give rise.

These shortcomings arise out of the unwillingness of the competitiveness enhancers to interrogate the *regime* that demarcates the terrain on which competition is allowed to unfold. Consequently they pose the question, *"How can any one country win?"* rather than the question, *"How can working people the world over secure a decent and improving quality of life in the face of intensifying international capitalist competition?"* Policy discussions then degenerate into disputes about the best strategies for romancing capital (or at least its better jobs).

In summary, the progressive competitiveness-enhancing perspective lacks any sort of compelling normative foundation. Its commitment to egalitarianism depends tenuously on the service egalitarianism provides to competitiveness; and this egalitarianism is further restricted to the domain of the individual nation. It is hard to see just how this nationalism could be defended; it is therefore not at all surprising that by and large, the advocates of competitiveness have not even tried to do so. Except for some isolated and thoroughly underdeveloped remarks that indicate some normative anxiety, we find no attention to the international inequality that competitiveness policies are apt to induce.

One basic normative defense of competitiveness that might have been offered is that a society cannot be indicted for failing to attempt the impossible. This defense does seem to accord with the worldview of the competitiveness-enhancing perspective. This is because this view accepts global Economy, Global Justice as both natural (perhaps even inevitable) and inherently punishing. It is precisely the conjoining of these two conclusions that provides the rationale for competitiveness in the first place. Were global Economy, Global Justice understood to be natural but universally benevolent, we would have no reason to worry about winning the competitive battle. This, as we will now see, is the view of the neoclassical vision. Were global neoliberalism understood instead to be damaging but neither natural nor inevitable, we might then seek to replace it with an alternative regime that generates better economic outcomes. This, as we will also see, is the view of the competition-reducing perspective. But once we take global neoliberalism to be both natural and potentially harmful, we are drawn to the conclusion that taking care of one's own citizens at the expense of others is the best that even abiding egalitarians can do. Our options in this case are but two: seek victory or suffer defeat. In this case, we can hardly be condemned for failing to look after our own – or for worrying overly about the welfare of others.

To date, however, contributors to the competitiveness-enhancing perspective have not made the case that global neoliberalism is indeed inevitable. Instead, they have adopted this view as an unspoken premise, one that conditions the options available to national governments as they seek prosperity for their people. Given the historical context in which this perspective emerged, this acceptance of global neoliberalism is perhaps not entirely surprising. Since the 1970s, progressives have found themselves overwhelmed with news of the advancing of the global market, from Russia, to Brazil, to Beijing. But in taking global neoliberalism as inevitable, the competitiveness enhancers have lost sight of the principles of institutionalist theory upon which they draw so skillfully in advancing their accounts of competitiveness and prosperity. Not least, they have forgotten that the policy regimes that condition market competition (and indeed, all other economic practices and outcomes) are always fully socially constructed, entirely *unnatural*, and alterable. They have forgotten that regimes that lead to unsatisfactory economic outcomes are always amenable to substantial overhaul. They have forgotten that what is most needed in times such as these is aspiration to a better regime, not acquiescence to the one treated by others as naturally ascendant.

None of this should be taken to suggest that all the means promoted by advocates of this approach are indefensible – far from it. Greater income equality, enhanced power, status and security for workers, increased public expenditures on education – all of these are eminently commendable public policies. Precisely for that reason, they should be defended and embraced as inherently right, rather than be held hostage to national competitiveness.

ANTI-COMPETITIVENESS

The neoclassical view of competitiveness can be summarized simply and elucidated quickly. Neoclassicals argue unequivocally that *the competitiveness of a nation's firms simply does not matter for national prosperity*. National prosperity is tied most immediately to a nation's own productivity. A nation's stagnating income can therefore be traced to stagnation in its own productivity growth – not to decreasing competitiveness *vis-à-vis* other nations.

The neoclassical vision breaks with the competitiveness-enhancing perspective by focusing on absolute rather than relative productivity gains. Neoclassicals claim that a nation is far better off when its own productivity rate is high, but lower than that of its trading partners, than when its own productivity rate is low, but higher than that of its competitors (Krugman 1994a; McCloskey 1993). This conclusion follows directly from the neoclassical view of distribution in a free market economy. As we have seen, the reward that flows to a provider of a factor of production equals the marginal contribution of that factor. Rising income reflects rising productivity, not increased competitiveness of domestic firms. [101]

In the neoclassical view, the error of those who embrace the concept of national competitiveness is to draw on inter-firm competition in markets to analogize relations between nations. In a market, one corporation's relative gains necessarily come at the expense of the welfare of another corporation. But in the international realm, British citizens are not generally hurt – and indeed are likely to be helped – by increasing productivity gains in Japan. With Japanese productivity rising, British consumers can acquire Japanese goods more cheaply through trade. If some Japanese firms come to outcompete some British firms, so be it: the British workers so displaced represent productive resources that are now freed up to move to other firms and industries for which Britain is better suited (McKenzie 1981). The appropriate government policy in this context is not to undertake to restore the competitiveness of domestic firms. Rather, the state might provide the displaced workers with the assistance they need to find new employment quickly in more appropriate industries and business, where British firms do compete well.

The neoclassical antipathy to competitiveness policy follows directly (see

Krugman 1994b). A focus on declining national competitiveness as the source of economic malaise is apt to generate harmful national policy, including but not limited to neo-mercantilist trade initiatives (as we will see in Chapter 6). We are apt to come to blame our own misfortunes on the supposedly illicit practices of others, and to seek retaliation when we should be thankful for the contribution other more competitive producers are making to our own welfare. A world in which the concept of national competitiveness has respectability is therefore apt to be a world of international conflict, with each nation attempting to wrest concessions from others to cover up their own economic failures. As evidence, neoclassicals point to the bellicosity with which successive US administrations scapegoated and punished other nations (not least, Japan) during the 1980s and 1990s rather than admit frankly that the US faced an entirely domestic problem of flagging productivity growth. The competitiveness obsession also contaminates discussion of other policy initiatives that ought to be thought through on their own merits, not by reference to their supposed effect on national competitiveness.

The obsession with national competitiveness relates to another popular concern that emerged across Europe and the US from the 1970s onward. Both academics and the popular press have fretted about the "decline" of the established industrial powers relative to Japan and other newly industrialized countries. Advocates of the "declinism" thesis point to the slippage of first Britain and then the US relative to the late industrializers, and seek to uncover the sources of this malaise. For example, Frost (1992) argues that both countries carried the burdens of being the world hegemon. Britain served in this capacity through much of the nineteenth century, while the US rose to this status by the early decades of the twentieth century. As hegemon, each provided the world monetary system with the "key currency". In consequence, each country was forced to tolerate the overvaluation of its currency. Each also chose to promote free trade and pursued this policy unilaterally even while its trading partners protected their own markets, fearing that any turn from free trade on its part would spark damaging trade wars. Together, an overvalued currency and the pursuit of unilateral free trade provided firms in other countries with a competitive advantage, which they successfully exploited at the expense of the hegemon.

Neoclassicals deride these kinds of analysis as nothing short of hysterical. McCloskey (1993) contends that we ought to think of rising prosperity abroad as mutually beneficial. Just as a family benefits from a rising standard of living of others in its community, so does a nation benefit from rising prosperity abroad. As Japan's income rises it increases its demand for the goods produced by its trading partners, thereby promoting rising income abroad. Moreover, rising productivity (and hence, prosperity) in the late industrializers relative to the early industrializers reflects an altogether natural process of convergence. The late industrializers benefit from the knowledge and technologies that the early industrializers have developed; their development trajectory is therefore likely to be temporally compressed. Finally,

McCloskey complains that the unwarranted fear of relative decline distracts our attention away from the truly pressing problems in today's global economy. We debate the insignificant question of why Britain has slipped from first to twentieth in per capita income when we ought to concern ourselves with why so many countries remain so poor at a time when it would seem that there exist the means to alleviate their plight. In this view, the problem is not that some countries have managed to catch up with the wealthiest countries; it is rather that so many have not.

Celebrating competition

To say that the neoclassical vision embraces *anti-competitiveness* may generate some confusion, given the importance of market *competition* in this perspective. We might therefore take a moment to clarify the status of competition in the neoclassical view before moving on.

I argued earlier that in policy debates, proponents of the neoclassical view often reach far beyond what neoclassical theory, narrowly defined, permits them to say. This is particularly true in the competitiveness debate. Neoclassical theory indicates only that the concept of national competitiveness makes no sense, and that those policies that seek to promote it are unlikely to enhance national prosperity. This is because a nation's level of prosperity is tied to its level of productivity, not to how well its firms do relative to foreign firms. On the matter of productivity, neoclassical science has little to say. While neoclassical theory can demonstrate that the perfectly functioning free market economy will generate a Pareto optimal allocation of *given* resources across firms and industries, yielding static efficiency, it has far less say about what drives productivity growth over time. Dynamic efficiency fundamentally depends upon technological advance that generates increasing productivity. But the origins of technological change remain something of a mystery in neoclassical theory proper (Krugman 1992). Generally, neoclassical theory takes that to be an exogenous event. Like a change in people's preferences, a change in technology is taken to be monumentally important. It is, however, largely taken to be non-economic in origin; as such, it is seen to fall beyond the confines of economic science.

In policy debates, a much stronger claim is made on behalf of the market, as we saw in Chapter 2. Partisans of the neoclassical vision claim that the market also induces dynamic efficiency by generating the right kinds of incentive. In a market economy, in which reward equals contribution, each agent has an incentive to increase the quantity and improve the quality of the resources that she provides to the firm. Moreover, and more germane for present purposes, market competition also provides each firm with an incentive to discover better technologies that will allow it to best its rivals. The firm that succeeds in finding new technologies that either decrease the cost of production or increase the quality of output will stand to garner profit over and above that of its rivals, at least until they succeed in duplicating its achievement. With each firm striving to achieve this outcome, consumers can expect to face improving quality and declining costs – both of which enhance social welfare.

Market competition therefore plays a critical role in the neoclassical vision. Without market competition, firms would have little incentive to seek improvements of the sorts discussed here. But this is not to be taken to mean that the government need or should take steps explicitly to enhance firms' competitiveness. On the contrary, the market is taken to be a sufficient instrument for promoting technological innovation, enhanced resource inputs, and consequently, productivity growth. State initiatives to promote competitiveness are far more apt to distort market signals than they are to augment them. After all, those firms with potential for competitive success should not need government assistance, insofar as rational investors should be willing to provide funds for their development. By contrast, those firms which fail to attract sufficient financing must be viewed as inferior to those that do, and so do not deserve state support. In short, the market, rather than government, should choose winners.[102]

The argument that there is no justification for the government to promote one domestic firm at the expense of another might seem basically right to most people who support the view that the market is best suited to determine which firms shall win and which shall lose. The further claim that government also should not promote domestic firms at the expense of foreign rivals has proven to be less persuasive to non-neoclassicals, as we have seen. But the logic is the same in both cases: in the neoclassical vision, a nation's social welfare depends not on the competitive success of its firms, but on increases in productivity. And that is best ensured by the promotion of market *competition*, not *competitiveness*. The government's role is to create and sustain free markets, setting the context in which firms vie with each other. It is not to decide the outcome of the competitive battles that the market generates.

Capital mobility

So far, we have considered the neoclassical view of the loss of competitiveness of a nation's firms to foreign rivals. As we have seen, the neoclassical vision finds this outcome to be almost entirely benign. But as many critics argue, workers in one country are often displaced by the *decision of a domestic firm to relocate* in search of cheaper costs abroad.[103] In this kind of case, managers believe that the firm can achieve greater competitiveness and profits in another location, perhaps where wages are lower. And in this kind of case, where the shedding of workers results not from the competitive failure of a domestic firm but from an explicit corporate choice, critics (including especially advocates of industrial policy, surveyed above) argue that the state can and must intervene to prevent the inevitable social dislocation that relocation will cause. Across North America, Europe, the NICs and even throughout the South, the outrage of workers and citizens in the face of corporate relocation has become widespread. Those harmed by relocation frequently demand industrial policy in the form of legal prohibitions on capital relocation, or what has been called "plant closing laws". Proposals of this sort now often require advance notice by a firm of its plans to relocate, corporate-sponsored retraining of the displaced workers, and payments by the firm to the community to cover the negative externalities associated with its decision. What, we might ask, does the neoclassical vision have to say about this kind of case?

The matter of capital mobility has risen to the top of the policy agenda among OECD and other nations in the context of recent and current rounds of negotiations over the terms of international economic integration. Several new trade agreements include extensive provisions that promote the unencumbered flow of foreign direct investment, or FDI. NAFTA is on the cutting edge in this regard, as it liberalizes FDI across North America (see Introduction). In addition, for the past several years member nations of the OECD have been negotiating the "Multilateral Agreement on Investment" (MAI). The intent behind the MAI is to liberalize FDI flows in much the same way as does NAFTA. For example, under the provisions of the January 13, 1998 draft document, OECD firms in any contracting country would be given national treatment in all other contracting countries. "Most favored nation" rules apply; these rules require each contracting nation to treat investors from all other contracting nations equally, so that a concession given to one must be provided to all. The draft also includes provisions that rescind most restrictions on foreign ownership of firms and most corporate performance requirements. Although the MAI is intended to apply initially only to OECD countries, the unambiguous long-term goal is to induce non-member states across the South to adopt its provisions.[104]

OECD nations promote unrestricted FDI in other ways. They have actively encouraged the formation of EPZs in developing countries as a means of attracting capital. The World Bank and the IMF also promote international investment funds that subsidize corporate investment in developing countries. All of these measures are intended to reduce international obstacles to the free flow of capital, including corporate relocation.

The neoclassical vision celebrates rather than condemns corporate relocation, as we might by now expect. The reasoning is consistent with a broader view of competitiveness. From this perspective, there is no meaningful difference between a firm relocating in search of higher profits and a firm closing due to foreign competitive pressures. Where there are well-functioning markets, we should expect the firm that does not relocate to more profitable sites (perhaps because of some commitment to the community) to place itself in jeopardy. The firm that remains in a less favorable location will sacrifice its competitiveness, and will ultimately be forced to close.

The same fate awaits a firm that is forced by law to stay put. Plant closing legislation cannot override the laws of supply and demand; ultimately, this legislation will merely delay the inevitable. Even worse, by postponing the plant closing, the legislation delays the necessary and entirely beneficial adjustments that are called for by competitive pressures. The neoclassical economist reminds us of the concept of opportunity cost in this context: the capital, labor and other resources that remain tied up in the inefficient enterprise, after all, are prevented from flowing to other activities for which the community (or nation) might be better suited. In the meantime, society will also face higher prices for the firm's goods than would otherwise be the case. Far better to encourage the firm to relocate to a better site, so as to promote the entirely healthy and reinvigorating process of shifting resources to new activities (McKenzie 1981).

Neoclassical visionaries also bristle against the undue violation of property rights that plant closing legislation entails. Just as workers are free to withdraw their labor from a particular enterprise in a free market economy, so must the owners of capital be free to withdraw their funds and redirect them in pursuit of the highest available reward as they see fit. As we have seen, neoclassical theory draws no meaningful analytical distinctions between capital and labor – each merely provides a different resource to the firm. Both should therefore enjoy equal formal rights – including the right of exit. If a firm does not provide its investors with the highest available return (for a given degree of risk), investors can and will redirect their funds, causing it to close.

Neoclassical visionaries also object to the notion that the state should insulate workers (or their communities) from the social dislocation associated with plant relocation through mandated corporate payments to the community. As rational agents, workers understand that a firm might relocate in pursuit of higher profits. Each worker therefore has an incentive to save a sufficient portion of her income so as to cover future, temporary income losses that might result from its closure, and to seek new skills to ensure that she will find new employment. Were she insured by government for this loss, she would have no incentive to save contingency funds or seek new skills. Moreover, were a firm forced to pay taxes in advance of closure to support a community fund for such purposes, the firm would simply reduce its demand for labor, leading to a decline in the equilibrium market wage. Workers would consequently bear the burden of the tax in the form of lower wages. Finally, a jurisdiction that introduces restrictions on plant closings will discourage new firms from siting there in the first place. Hence, the regulation induces the problems of unemployment and stagnation that it is intended to prevent (McKenzie 1981).

So much for the effects of plant relocation on the community left behind. Much of the public outcry against corporate relocation today focuses instead on what are seen to be atrocious conditions that obtain in the new facilities the corporations establish abroad, especially in the South. Critics claim that wealthy MNCs today routinely displace well-paid workers in the North so as to be able to exploit Southern workers in what essentially amount to sweatshops characterized by low pay, dangerous and monotonous work, child labor, and the absence of even basic worker rights. Critics also contend that although these MNCs have the funds to promote decent wages and working conditions, they choose instead to use their formidable power to secure the cheapest labor costs without regard to social consequences – all in the name of achieving competitiveness in the face of intense global pressures.

Advocates of the neoclassical vision again distinguish themselves through their hard-headed, coolly detached, dispassionate view of such matters. In his provocative essay "In Praise of Cheap Labor", Krugman (1997) argues that we must recognize that workers in the South benefit from the opportunity to work in the new sweatshops that have been established as a consequence of MNC relocation from the North. After all, if the workers themselves did not find this employment to be better than the available opportunities, they presumably would not take these jobs. Far better, he argues, that they should have the opportunity to secure low-waged industrial jobs than face the less desirable work in the informal sector. When assessing the normative efficacy of corporate behavior in the South, the relevant comparison is not between wages and working conditions in the North and in the South, but between wages and working conditions in these corporate facilities and other sectors in the South. Once we recognize that this is the right comparison to make, we must see that the new sweatshops in the South are to be celebrated rather than condemned. Finally, we must recognize that lower wages abroad necessarily reflect lower levels of productivity. Initiatives to force MNCs operating in the South to raise their wages would therefore necessarily result in a reduction in employment opportunities, harming the very workers whom the critics of sweatshops hope to help.

To sum up: the neoclassical vision argues unambiguously that global inter-firm competition not only does not threaten but actually promotes rising standards of living across the globe. It does this by generating appropriate incentives for resource suppliers and firms. These incentives promote dynamic efficiency, productivity growth and, as a consequence, rising social welfare. Governments therefore should seek to protect the free market, both domestically and internationally, rather than the competitive success of domestic firms. Governments should also recognize the ultimate mutual benefits that arise from plant relocation in search of competitive advantage, even when the out-migration of capital displaces domestic workers. Global social welfare is enhanced by the unfolding of the processes of market competition which induce rising efficiency, lower costs, and increasing standards of living – at home and abroad.

Assessing anti-competitiveness

Despite the objections of many critics, especially those on the left, the orthodox neoliberal project is explicitly internationalist, and this internationalism is evidenced particularly in its anti-competitiveness. The disdain for competitiveness strategies is founded upon its commitment to welfarism, as we would expect. It must be emphasized that in assessing global economic outcomes, this commitment is *applied impartially across all jurisdictions.* Just as there is no basis in welfarism to give greater standing to the interests of one person over another, so is there no basis for placing greater weight on the claims of the citizens of one nation over those of another. Free competition in global markets is therefore defended on the grounds that it is *mutually* advantageous, promoting social welfare in all countries, from the richest to the very poorest. The defense invokes a notion of enlightened self-interest that is deepseated in orthodox thought: as a general rule, each country stands to gain from the increasing efficiency and incomes enjoyed by others. Efforts to promote one's own interests by means that penalize others (such as through competitiveness strategies) are thus ultimately self-defeating.

Anti-competitiveness therefore stands as an important normative corrective to the competitiveness-enhancing prescriptions associated with progressive nationalism. Unlike the latter, anti-competitiveness can lay some claim to normative respectability. But anti-competitiveness is also deficient. This is because the neoclassical case for anti-competitiveness has little to commend it on egalitarian grounds. Though free global market competition and capital mobility are thought to promote global social welfare, and to enhance incomes in both wealthy and poor societies, these mechanisms do not ensure income equality, either intra- or inter-nationally. To be sure, we might hope that improving resource allocation globally will improve the fate of the worst off most rapidly. For instance, in the neoclassical vision the relocation of capital from the North to the South should increase labor productivity, and thereby wages. If this largely fortuitous event is not forthcoming, however, there is no basis for embarrassment for proponents of the neoclassical vision. Their commitment to welfarist normative criteria does not require (and indeed, weighs against) demands for equality of incomes. The claim can, of course, be made that the universalization of market competition provides each agent with equal freedom to decide for herself which choice *of those that are available to her* will maximize her own utility. Within our respective opportunity sets we are equally free to choose for ourselves. But unlike the capabilities perspective, this equality is formal rather than substantive. This is because in a global neoliberal regime we are grossly unequal in the opportunity sets we confront. For neoclassicals, this is as it should be: a guarantee of equal opportunity sets would distort the incentive system so vital to the promotion of social welfare, as we have seen.

There is far more to be said about the neoclassical vision in this regard. For instance, sweatshop conditions are typically permitted and even sustained by the government, which prohibits worker organization in independent unions, and denies other important worker rights. MNCs that undertake sweatshop methods are thus often operating within the purview of the law of the host country. How then should we assess the normative status of a society's laws and norms that deny workers' rights? These questions have been raised explicitly and most directly in the debate over trade regimes. We will therefore postpone their consideration until the next chapter, where we will examine the neoclassical case in favor of free trade.

To conclude this discussion, we should note that while the neoliberal vision seeks a world of international co-operation, in which a commitment to enlightened self-interest engenders mutually beneficial policies, it does not demand (or indeed, even countenance) measures that would interfere with market signals in pursuit of egalitarian distributions of rewards. Its mechanical view of distribution (in which reward equals contribution) prevents it from grasping the degree to which its internationalism may induce greater inequality of substantive freedoms.

THE COMPETITION-REDUCING PERSPECTIVE

If we accept the view of the competitiveness enhancers that global neoliberalism can be punishing, must we also conclude that each nation is compelled to seek advantage in order to avoid the harsh penalties which inevitably accompany defeat in global markets? Or might there be some alternative path that promotes equality of substantive freedoms on a global scale?

Some economists and many social activists across the globe have come to argue that an alternative path does exist. These critics of the neoclassical vision and national competitiveness advocate new policy regimes that *reduce the scope of market competition* (see Brecher and Costello 1991). This agenda entails replacing global neoliberalism with new rules of economic integration in pursuit of two related goals: reducing the social gains and losses of competition; and constraining the terms on which competition may unfold so as to promote its socially beneficial, and to minimize its socially adverse, consequences. These purposes are served in part by steps which would insulate certain critical features of social, political, cultural and even economic life from the reach of competition. I will therefore refer to this approach as the "competition-reducing" perspective.

A precedent for this approach lies in the classical doctrine of labor organization. Wherever a market for labor has developed over the course of the past two centuries, workers have struggled to form organizations with the minimum goal of removing wages and working conditions from competition. Although some radical unions seek much more than this, all pose as the first order of business the circumscription of inter-firm competition so as to try to insulate workers' livelihoods and health and safety from its reach. The goal is to ensure that firms seek alternative bases for competitiveness, so that no one firm can win a competitive advantage by exploiting its workforce beyond some codified (albeit historically contingent) level.

Historically, the effort to remove wages from competition has been largely restricted to national borders. The current movement seeks to internationalize this effort in response to the increasing speed and ease with which capital can relocate in search of lower costs, and the intensifying competition in international markets. These trends place workers across the globe into direct competition with each other for employment, income and economic security. The current initiatives are particularly unique in that they reach beyond wages and other substantive working conditions in demanding that other aspects of social life be removed from competition.

During the 1980s labor, religious and civil rights organizations secured changes in US trade policies in pursuit of this end (Cavanagh *et al.* 1988; Charnovitz 1992; Perez-Lopez 1988 and 1990; Rothstein 1993). In 1984 the Generalized System of Preferences (GSP) was amended to require the US to rescind preferential trading privileges to "any nation which has not taken or is not taking steps to afford internationally recognized worker rights to workers in the country (including any designated zone in that country)" (quoted in Cavanagh *et al.* 1988). Similar provisions were incorporated in the Caribbean Basin Initiative (CBI) in 1983, the revised Overseas Private Investment Corporation (OPIC) rules in 1985, and the 1988 Omnibus Trade and Competitiveness Act. With respect to NAFTA, environmental and labor organizations throughout North America sought to remove differences in environmental and labor standards as a source of competition. These efforts failed. In Europe, labor and other social movements fought (also largely unsuccessfully) to include provisions that would guarantee the transnational standardization of procedural and substantive conditions of employment in the European Social Charter, including workers' rights to organize unions, strike, have representation on corporate boards of directors, etc. (Silvia, 1991).

This approach demands that social, labor and environmental protections be harmonized *upward* internationally. These protections must be universalized by conscious design to prevent corporations from exploiting regional differences. The presumption is that under the neoliberal regime competition will encourage a downward levelling in conditions of life as capital flees those regions where social regulations and costs of production are highest in search of those where conditions are more favorable. This is termed "social dumping". The Mexican *maquiladoras*, which now comprise over 3,000 foreign firms along the US border, employing over one million workers and operating with little regard for the social, economic and environmental prohibitions formally adopted in Mexico, are illustrative (Friedman 1992; Koechlin and Larudee 1992). In this view, social dumping can be prevented only through explicit international accords that harmonize upwards, conferring the rights and ultimately the substantive freedoms achieved in the wealthiest countries to those that lag behind.

Re-conceptualizing market competition

Neoclassicals have little patience for such proposals, as Krugman's praise of sweatshops attests. In the neoclassical vision, after all, these kinds of measure amount to market distortions that invite inefficiency and reduce social welfare. In contrast, proponents of the competition-reducing perspective embrace an anti-reductionist account of the economy (see Chapter 2). Recall that in this account, market outcomes are the overdetermined result of all the diverse forces constituting society rather than the direct, uncluttered effect of a simple set of essences. As such, the competition reducers are sensitive to the myriad factors that mediate the effect of a market intervention on market outcomes. Whether a particular market intervention by the government (or some other institution, like a labor union) induces a benevolent or a malevolent outcome is, on this account, entirely context-dependent. On this account, finally, there is no natural market economy – there are instead innumerable possible market (and also non-market and hybrid) forms that entail distinct patterns of contribution of inputs, output of goods and services, and distributions of rewards.

The distinction drawn here between the reductionist neoclassical and the anti-reductionist, institutionalist view of the market applies with particular force to the concept of competition. As we have seen, neoclassical visionaries celebrate competition in free markets as the uniquely appropriate vehicle by which society can efficiently allocate scarce resources to diverse ends, both statically and dynamically. The rewards that flow to the victors in market competition induce a hunt for innovation in the technological and the social organization of production. In this view, robust market competition is the primary necessary condition for such innovation (cf. Porter 1990).

A more nuanced vision of competition, implicit in the competition-reducing approach, understands that market competition *per se* is neither virtuous nor evil, progressive nor regressive. But competition *per se* never exists: like all other social processes that constitute social life, competition never emerges in some pure, unmediated or universal form. Rather, it always arises in a broader social, political, economic and cultural matrix that gives it definition and determines its character as well as its broader social effects. Whether competition will be progressive or regressive, socially benevolent or malevolent, innovative or wasteful, is a fully *contingent* matter. It depends on no less than the full set of circumstances defining the historical moment. *One important subset of these circumstances entails what I have referred to here as a regime; this comprises the political and economic rules of the game that delineate the conditions under which competition is allowed to unfold, and the set of attributes of social life that it is permitted to implicate.*

The competition reducers therefore pose for themselves a theoretical challenge that moves beyond a one-sided critique of market competition. This challenge is to explore first, which aspects of social life *together with market competition* generate harmful social effects; and second, how the rules constituting domestic and international regimes might be revised, through a combination of public policy and political mobilization, at the national and international levels, so as to reap the imputed benefits of competition and economic integration.

Taking "X" out of competition

The demands for upward harmonization of social, labor and environmental protections should be interpreted in this light. This reform project poses several difficult theoretical questions. The first and in some sense primary question is this: which aspects of social life can be taken out of competition without eroding whatever progressive (static and dynamic) effects competition is understood to induce? To put the matter more precisely: is there in principle a strict, invariant limit to the terrain of social life which can be taken out of competition without undermining its tendency to generate technological innovations? Or, alternatively, is this limit historically and conjuncturally variable, such that different aspects of social life must be in play in certain moments for competition to generate beneficial effects, but need not be at all in play for the same result under other social arrangements? Let me pose the question again in another way, because much hinges on the answer. If our goal is to take some of as yet unspecified "X" (such as environmental degradation) out of competition so as to insulate social life from its effects, is the vector of aspects of social life that can be so insulated, and which "X" designates, fixed by the essential nature of market competition (or human nature)? Or does it vary with changes in culture, technology, political arrangements, ethical norms, and the manifold other aspects of social life?

The anti-reductionist theoretical perspective concludes that there is no fixed set of conditions of social life that must remain in competition in order for socially beneficial innovation and discovery to occur. Rather, what may serve as the minimum set of necessary conditions for competition "to work" in the sense of achieving socially beneficial results is necessarily socially constructed and variable. This does not mean that they are arbitrary – within a given historical context, certain conditions may indeed be required for competition to induce good economic outcomes. But just what these necessary conditions are will be determined by the entirety of factors constituting society rather than by a simplistic set of essences.[105]

This view has direct implications. It opens up the possibility that we can militate for dramatic changes in social arrangements, short of the complete abolition of market competition, so as to reduce the set of necessary conditions. It broadens the political thrust of movements for global justice to encompass such initiatives. These political struggles would be prerequisites for the success of demands to take "X" out of competition, for unless social and political arrangements are reorganized, the impetus to remove "X" might fail because it causes unforeseen social hardships[106] and/or cancels conditions that are in fact necessary for innovation in a particular conjuncture. More simply, it may be necessary to lay some substantial political groundwork as a precondition for taking some particular aspect of social life out of competition. Hence, there is a need for an integrative theoretical and political approach that advances on two distinct fronts: exploration of what can be taken out of competition *at any particular historical moment* without inducing severe social hardships; and exploration of how existing social arrangements can be altered with the effect of diminishing the set of necessary conditions for innovation, so that other social aspects may be removed from competition *in the future.*

As we have seen, the neoclassical vision emphasizes the innovation-inducing incentives associated with market competition. Political institutions that weaken competitive pressures necessarily retard technological innovation, thereby reducing dynamic efficiency and social welfare over time. Moreover, those technological innovations that are rewarded in the market are taken on that account to be virtuous, insofar as rational agents know best what they desire. But the alternative approach embraced by the competition reducers encourages us to recognize that the rules defining an economic regime also affect decisively the *kinds* of innovation (technological, social and otherwise) that are permitted and encouraged, and hence the qualitative nature of economic development. When wages, hours and work intensity are removed from competition, the sweating of labor ceases to be a viable innovation; when consumer safety laws are effectively implemented, the adulteration of input materials becomes unavailable in pursuit of competitive advantage; when strict environmental standards are enforced, new profitable technologies that increase external social costs (e.g. pollution) while reducing private costs are eclipsed by other technologies that reduce social costs. Hence, taking "X" out of competition becomes a means to alter the fundamental character not only of competition, but of innovation as well – to exert social control over this extraordinarily powerful determinant of the quality of social life (cf. Piore 1990; Herzenberg *et al.* 1990).

Adjudication of the competition-reducing perspective

The competition-reducing perspective is explicitly internationalist. Notably, it shares the neoclassical antipathy to the nationalism that informs the progressive competitiveness-enhancing perspective. Rather than pursue success in a game that necessarily blesses winners with the sacrifices of the losers, the competition-reducing approach seeks rules that promote mutual benefits. Unlike advocates of the neoclassical vision, the competition reducers refuse the notion that global neoliberalism represents a regime of mutually beneficial rules.

This approach is also radically egalitarian. The goal is to find economic regimes that promote equal substantive freedoms, within and across national borders. Unlike neoclassical visionaries, who are satisfied with the equality of formal freedoms that free market competition ensures, the competition reducers recognize that this form of market competition tends to amplify existing substantive inequalities. The competition reducers demand far more than that each of us be equally free to choose from among the opportunities provided to us. They demand that to the degree possible, each of us be provided with the same set of opportunities.

Against this criterion, market competition under the terms of global neoliberalism fails miserably. Even its most ardent supporters do not claim that competition under this regime will induce equal substantive freedoms. After all, the entire incentive structure in this kind of regime is predicated on substantive *inequalities* – it is the hope of gaining more opportunities, relative to what we have now and to what others possess, that drives us to save, invest, work hard and compete. What is more, the greater the consequences of competitive success and failure, the greater will be our incentives to strive. On these grounds, the neoclassical vision (and global neoliberalism) imposes no limits whatsoever on domestic or international inequality. In contrast, the competition-reducing perspective sets out to discover new regimes that at a minimum compress inequality in substantive freedoms. Moreover, the competition reducers seek to inaugurate increasing equality not as a means to something else deemed more important, as in the case of the competitiveness enhancers, but as a vital end in itself.

CONCLUSION

The competition-reducing perspective breaks with the competitiveness-enhancing and anti-competitiveness perspectives in fundamental ways. Rather than treat global neoliberalism as an ideal or inevitable form of economic organization, the competition-reducing perspective perceives all forms of economy to be historically contingent, socially constructed and hence amenable to even radical reform. Rather than seek ways to accommodate what it views to be a normatively flawed regime, it develops alternatives to accommodate those normative criteria which are most highly valued. In short, rather than prove that equality can survive neoliberalism, it seeks forms of economic organization that ensure equality, both domestically and internationally.

6 The trade debate

INTRODUCTION

Of all the policy arenas in which the emergence of global neoliberalism has been contested in recent years, trade has been most visible and controversial. The attention paid to trade by economists, policy analysts, government officials and the public across the globe is not misplaced. The proportion of total world economic activity accounted for by trade has risen steadily over the postwar period, and particularly over the past several decades. Moreover, during the 1990s trade negotiators across the North and the South have forged new, expansive agreements which have substantially liberalized the international flow of goods and services and even capital. The most encompassing of these is the agreement reached during the Uruguay Round of negotiations over the General Agreement on Tariffs and Trade (GATT) that generated the new World Trade Organization (WTO). This agreement followed closely on the heels of NAFTA, which will fully liberalize trade across North America over the next decade. For its part, the European Union has continued to make substantial progress toward the formation of a tightly integrated continental economy predicated on free trade and capital flows.

Each of these integration projects generated tremendous political conflict. Though ultimately ratified by the US, Canadian and Mexican governments, NAFTA faced substantial opposition in all three countries. Despite the strong support of both Republican and Democratic administrations, it proved to be the most contentious foreign policy measure in the US since the Persian Gulf War. It is noteworthy that in 1997, just three years after the ratification of NAFTA, President Clinton failed to win congressional approval for fast-track authorization that would have allowed his administration to negotiate an extension of NAFTA's provisions to other nations across Latin America. The WTO also provoked substantial opposition, especially across the South where farmers in particular have protested its likely social and economic impact. Although Europe continues to advance toward complete economic unification, labor organizations and others across the continent have expressed grave concerns about the nature and effects of neoliberal integration.

Just as with the competitiveness controversy, three distinct positions have emerged in contemporary trade debates. Also like that controversy, these positions are associated with progressive nationalism, the neoclassical vision, and internationalist egalitarianism. Progressive nationalists argue for "strategic trade". As with international competition, they view trade as a contentious affair with national winners and losers. Consequently they advocate trade policies which ensure that a country can capture the available benefits and protect itself from avoidable losses. In contrast, neoclassical visionaries argue unequivocally for free trade on the grounds that it is mutually advantageous. They endeavor to show how trade patterns founded on countries' natural differences yield increasing efficiency and social welfare for all trading partners. Internationalist egalitarians concern themselves with the terms under which trade should be allowed to take place; they advocate what has come to be known as "fair trade" as a means to advance the project of global justice.[107]

This chapter is intended to make normative sense of the trade debate, taking the three perspectives in the order in which they are listed here. We will spend very little time on the progressive nationalist perspective, as we have already sufficiently identified its chief propositions and the normative bankruptcy thereof. By contrast, the free trade/fair trade debate warrants careful attention, for two reasons. First, most of the outcry against the new trade agreements has been couched in terms of the fair trade critique. Critics argue that governments should not be permitted to pursue (or allow corporations to pursue) illicit practices, such as the abuse of labor and the environment, in pursuit of export performance. Instead, international trade agreements should specify appropriate practices, and require that all signatories to trade agreements adopt them as a condition of market access for their exports. This critique is deeply and explicitly normative. As a result, the fair traders have forced neoclassical advocates to revisit their own normative commitments. Second, and related to the first, neoclassical theorists have deflected this normative attack with a deft but problematic theoretical modification. As I will endeavor to show, the defense of free trade has required nothing less than the reworking of the foundational concept of "comparative advantage". That this adjustment has gone largely unremarked in the debates makes it no less consequential. We will see that the reworking of this concept is founded squarely on the neoclassical normative commitments that we have already investigated – particularly the pursuit of value-free science and the consequent agnosticism concerning preferences – and on a rather severe form of cultural relativism to which these commitments give rise.

The free trade/fair trade debate has crystallized around several contentious production process issues. These involve not *what* firms produce, but *how* they produce it. One of the most contentious issues in this regard concerns gender: critics charge that many countries maintain and exploit patriarchal systems that prevent women from securing adequate wages or from organizing in defense of their interests as workers. A second concerns the use of child labor in place of adult workers. A third concerns official tolerance of damaging environmental practices by producers. Each of these serves to reduce production costs and to promote a country's export performance.

To explicate this matter, I will present the well-known traditional neoclassical argument in favor of free trade, paying particular attention to the concept of comparative advantage. We will then see just how this concept has been revised in response to the demand for the harmonization of labor and environmental practices. I will extend the normative critique of the neoclassical vision and cultural relativism developed in previous chapters to the case for free trade.

The chapter then fleshes out the fair trade perspective, arguing that the normative perspective of capabilities equality provides a standard against which to interrogate practices that condition comparative advantage. We will explore several of the particular policy initiatives put forward by fair trade advocates to date. Rejecting the normative claims made on behalf of free trade hardly authorizes us to accept uncritically the various policy prescriptions put forward in the name of fair trade. Instead, we must interrogate them critically against the normative standard of capabilities equality. I will examine the strengths and weaknesses of each of the proposals put forward, in hopes of gleaning insights into new policy avenues that better accord with this normative principle.

STRATEGIC TRADE

Strategic trade is a direct extension of the competitiveness-enhancing proposals examined in the previous chapter. In keeping with the perspective of progressive nationalism elucidated there, its advocates view trade in today's global economy as a site of international conflict. Those nations that succeed in promoting certain kinds of exports will prosper, while those that fail will lag behind. Hence, it behooves a government to use the tool of trade policy (alongside the kinds of competitiveness strategies already examined) to ensure national prosperity.

Strategic traders claim that trade was not always so conflict-ridden. For instance, Lester Thurow (1992) argues that in the past, trade between nations was largely mutually advantageous. This is because nations tended to specialize in different goods, based on their respective comparative advantages (a concept that we will examine carefully in the next section). With specialization, each nation exported those goods for which it was well suited, and received in return other goods for which it was not. Specialization prevented rivalry among nations in international markets.

Trade today is of a different character, however. As Thurow sees it, all countries now seek supremacy in the very same set of key industries, such as microelectronics, biotechnology and telecommunications. These are all technologically sophisticated, high value-added industries. Not only do these high technology industries provide high wages, they also generate technical know-how that spreads to other industries (cf. Tyson 1990). These spillovers therefore enhance the rate of productivity growth in the economy, and thereby promote the nation's income growth. It is hence of paramount importance for a country to secure a foothold in these vital industries. As a result, trade today is "head to head", to use Thurow's evocative phrase. One country's success in these industries ensures another country's failure. And in this brave new world, where trade has evolved from win–win to win–lose, governments that are concerned about the prosperity of their people cannot afford simply to pursue free trade – especially when their trading partners do not reciprocate. Instead, governments must take all sorts of steps to promote the viability of their domestic firms in these critical industries.

Much to the dismay of neoclassical visionaries, progressive nationalists find support for strategic trade in neoclassical theory itself.[108] Many industries do not exhibit the characteristics of perfect competition. For example, firms in some industries face what are called "increasing returns to scale". This means that they become more efficient as they become larger. This might be because production entails large fixed costs in machinery and plant and equipment. As production increases, these fixed costs are spread out over an increasing number of units, yielding falling per unit costs. In this situation, a larger firm will be able to outcompete small firms. Over time, we should expect to find a small number of very large firms controlling the market in this industry. Finally, because of the absence of a large number of competitors, these firms will have market power, and will be able to secure higher prices and profits (and pay higher wages) than would be possible under perfect competition.

Imperfect competition has important implications for trade flows and policy. In industries marked by increasing returns to scale, it may behove a national government to provide subsidies and trade protection to domestic firms so as to give them a leg up in competition with foreign firms. This promotes the growth, efficiency and competitiveness of the domestic firms; if successful, this strategy will ensure that the higher profits and wages that are available in this industry flow to the domestic firm (and its shareholders and workers) rather than to its foreign counterparts. Hence, progressive nationalists contend, strategic trade policy must be pursued aggressively so as to enhance domestic social welfare.

Those who view trade in this way offer various strategic policies by which a nation can defend itself from the encroachments of other nations while promoting its own national champions. Especially when its trading partners are found to be engaging in strategies that protect their own markets and promote their own export performance, a nation must restrict access to its own markets in vital industries. The logic of the strategic trade argument implies that a country should undertake such measures whenever it can manage to do so – even when its trading partners are pure free traders – as the country that acts to promote a vital industry first can then gain a lasting advantage in global markets for these industries.

Assessing strategic trade

Little need be added here to the normative evaluation of progressive nationalism advanced in the previous chapter. In the hands of progressive nationalists, strategic trade is intended to advance prosperity, just as are the progressive competitiveness-enhancing strategies we surveyed above. Indeed, the rhetoric of national competitiveness infuses the strategic trade literature; we might rightly think of it as an offshoot of the competitiveness approach.

In one important sense, however, the strategic trade position has even less to commend it than the contributions to competitiveness examined in Chapter 5. In its literature we find little concern with equality, even at the level of the nation. While many of the competitiveness advocates argued for greater equality as the means to achieve better industrial performance, we find no such parallel argument in the strategic trade literature. Instead, we find advocates invoking traditional, neoclassical welfarist principles to cement their case for strategic trade policy. Nations compete over limited welfare gains from trade; best, then, for a nation to compete well through appropriate policy choices. How these gains are divvied up is of secondary normative importance.[109]

This approach is therefore explicitly nationalist. Viewing trade as a win–lose proposition, in which the chief actors are unified states, there seems little choice but for each to seek to protect itself strategically via trade policy against the ravaging effects associated with trade failure. It is difficult to imagine a compelling normative account that could give cover to this approach. For instance, while virtually all accounts of justice entail a commitment to impartiality, so that those over whom distribution takes place are treated equally in relevant ways, this account is unabashedly biased. *We* count for more in this approach, merely by virtue of the fact that it is *us*! We therefore have no reason to apologize for whatever level of welfare we are able to wrest away from others. The fact that those countries that are already wealthiest are apt to have an advantage in the ability to wield strategic trade policy, to the detriment of their poorer neighbors, implies that in practice this approach is likely to exacerbate existing inequalities among nations. One probes the literature in vain for a normative defense of this severely anti-egalitarian outcome.

THE NEOCLASSICAL VISION AND FREE TRADE

The standard neoclassical stand on trade is perhaps its best known and most widely held proposition. Advocates of the neoclassical vision uniformly endorse free trade. Historically, free trade was taken simply to entail the absence of government-imposed restrictions on the international flow of goods and services. These include import tariffs, of course, but also export and import quotas, licenses, and other policy instruments which target trade flows. All of these measures are seen to distort the trade patterns that would otherwise *naturally* obtain, and to reduce social welfare. Today free trade has also come to imply the absence of what are called "technical barriers to trade". These are laws that while purporting to achieve some domestic purpose are nevertheless seen to be excessively trade-distorting (Bhagwati 1993a).

The basic case for free trade has changed little over the past two centuries. Countries are taken to exhibit different capacities with regard to producing different goods and services. For example, one country might be more efficient in the production of agricultural products, while another might be better suited to the production of manufactured goods. We will examine momentarily just why this difference might exist; for now we need only consider how a world marked by such diversity would be affected by trade. When countries are prevented from trading, each will have to be entirely self-sufficient. In this case of "autarky", each will be forced to commit some of its resources to activities for which it is not particularly well suited. The country that is relatively better suited to agricultural production will nevertheless have to commit at least some resources to the production of manufactured goods, and vice versa. Were these countries allowed to trade, each could then commit more resources to that industry in which it is relatively efficient, while exporting some of its output to secure that good for which it is poorly suited. With each country specializing in what it does best, we should expect that the total output of the two countries taken together increases. Indeed, neoclassical theory confirms that whenever countries are marked by different production capacities, trade induces an increase in total output and, thereby, social welfare.

In the example developed here, each country is more efficient than the other in one industry (the first in agriculture, the second in manufacturing). It is therefore not surprising that trade will lead to greater aggregate efficiency, with both countries gaining from trade. But what if one country is relatively more efficient in both industries? Won't the country with lower efficiency suffer from trade, as its markets are swamped by output from producers in the other country?

The counter-intuitive answer is that it will not. Neoclassical theory holds that even in this case, both countries are likely to benefit from trade, because each country will be expected to specialize in that industry for which it is *relatively* efficient. This means that the country with higher efficiency across all industries will specialize in that industry in which its advantage is greatest, while its trading partner will specialize in that industry in which its own disadvantage is smallest. In economic terminology, we say that each country has a *comparative advantage* in that industry for which it is relatively best suited. All countries therefore have a comparative advantage: for the less efficient country, it is in that industry in which it is least deficient. And neoclassical theory also demonstrates that when countries trade based on their comparative advantages – exporting what they produce relatively well and importing what they do not – total world production rises and all countries typically enjoy rising income, consumption and social welfare.[110]

The distributional effects of trade

To say that all countries stand to benefit from trade is not to say that all economic actors within those countries benefit equally, or at indeed at all. Neoclassical trade theorists have generated various formal models for ascertaining just how the effects of trade will be distributed across the economy. These distributional effects are by no means trivial. Estimates indicate that the distribution effects of a shift toward free trade eclipse the efficiency (growth-promoting) effects by a factor of five to one (Rodrik 1997, 30). For our purposes, we need consider but two of the central theoretical propositions that relate to distribution.

The first result that we must consider is the well-known "Stolper–Samuelson" theorem. In this model of trade, nations are marked by differences in their "factor endowments". For instance, one country might be relatively well endowed in capital, while another might be capital-poor but well endowed in unskilled labor. Prior to trade, each country must allocate resources both to the production of goods that are capital intensive, and to those that are labor-intensive. Once trade begins, each country will specialize in those industries which utilize its more abundant factor most intensively. That is, the capital-abundant country will specialize in capital-intensive production, while now importing goods that are labor-intensive, while its trading partner will do the reverse. In aggregate, both countries stand to gain from this new trade.

According to the theorem, some economic agents will lose out under trade (at least in the short run). Those agents providing the scarce factor in each country will face a decline in the demand for the factor they provide, and hence, falling income. In the case we are developing, low-skilled laborers in the capital-rich country will face a falling demand for their services as their country now imports the goods they produce from the new trading partner. In contrast, the owners of capital in the capital-poor country likewise face declining demand, and hence a reduction in compensation for the factor they supply.

The second result is the "factor price equalization" theorem (FPE). As its name suggests, this theorem holds that (under certain conditions) trade will equalize the reward that a particular factor earns across national borders. For example, in a world with no market distortions and complete free trade, the wage for labor of a particular level of skill will converge, yielding one worldwide equilibrium wage.

Neoclassicals support free trade despite these distributional results. The second creates no normative problems; indeed, as we will consider momentarily, the fact that trade moves us closer to equal reward for equal contribution across the globe is taken to be one of its virtues. The first result, on the other hand, requires that those who are injured from trade be compensated by the winners, in keeping with the tenets of welfarism. Only if the losers are fully compensated by the winners can we conclude that the shift to free trade is Pareto improving.[111]

The sources of comparative advantage

Since David Ricardo introduced the concept of comparative advantage in the early nineteenth century, the notion that free trade benefits all countries has been a central tenet of orthodox theory. Even most heterodox economists have accepted the basic logic involved in this proposition. Nevertheless the concept of comparative advantage is at the center of the contemporary controversy over free trade. To understand what is at stake in this regard, we need to explore the matter of the origins of comparative advantage.

Why might two countries have distinct comparative advantages? For Ricardo and other classical economists, and for neoclassical economists since, comparative advantage has been grounded in differences across countries that are taken to be both *contingent*, owing to distinct national features and historical trajectories, and *natural*. For instance, countries might and indeed do differ with respect to their physical and human endowments (as captured in the "Hecksher–Ohlin" model of trade and assumed by the Stolper–Samuelson theorem). One country might enjoy fertile soil and a propitious climate, while another, lacking these, might enjoy a highly skilled workforce. The first might therefore be expected to have a comparative advantage in agriculture, while the second might instead have an advantage in manufacturing. Alternatively, two countries might have similar endowments but different technological capacities that yield different relative efficiencies across industries. Finally, the inhabitants of the two countries might exhibit distinct patterns of preferences. Workers in one country might prefer agricultural employment but resist the confines and regimentation of factory work, while preferences in another country might run in the opposite direction. In this latter case, the labor supply curves and the pattern of wages in the two countries will differ, yielding different technological choices and relative costs of production across industries.

In keeping with the reductionist logic of neoclassical theory all of these differences can be traced directly to the originating essences of the theory. A country's endowments are determined by the relative scarcities established by nature; its technology derives from the exercise of rationality, as economic actors undertake to discover new and better means to produce; and its inhabitants' preferences are simply what they are, exogenously formed in keeping with the essence of human rationality. All of these are treated as natural and given. On this account, and as a consequence, they are also taken to be entirely legitimate determinants of comparative advantage. As we might by now expect, there is no basis in neoclassical theory for asking whether any of these differences should or should not shape a country's market outcomes (including its price structure, product mix, technological choices, income distribution, etc.), or its resulting comparative advantage. To ask, is it right that a country has a comparative advantage in agriculture by virtue of its fertile soil is, to say the least, a nonsensical question. The sources of comparative advantage are not right or wrong, they just *are*.[112]

As I mentioned above (and will examine in greater detail below), the fair trade critics of free trade today demand that countries adopt ethically defensible labor and environmental practices as a precondition for trade. Most of these critics do not reject the concept of comparative advantage *per se*, nor the logic of the argument in favor of trade predicated upon it. Instead, they argue that differences across nations in *policy regimes* may obstruct the mutual benefits usually associated with free trade (Dorman 1988). Differences in environmental or labor standards, for example, are likely to distort the trade and financial flows that would otherwise obtain by giving many firms in those countries with lower social standards a competitive advantage in global markets. Based on this reasoning, many advocates for labor and human rights and environmental quality argue that free trade jeopardizes their political projects.

This new attack on free trade has led orthodox economic theorists to undertake a subtle and yet profound elaboration of the concept of comparative advantage. In this revised account, the domain of natural heterogeneity that conditions comparative advantage and that consequently gives rise to mutual benefits from trade has been implicitly expanded to include national policy choice. A poor country might adopt policies that reflect a willingness to "exploit" its natural resources or large supply of child labor, for example. Were it forced to implement environmental or labor standards already adopted by wealthy countries, it would sacrifice this legitimate source of comparative advantage. Turning the heterodox argument on its head, neoclassicals claim that the imposition of uniform labor or environmental standards across countries would distort natural trade patterns, to the detriment of global economic efficiency and welfare in the North and the South (cf. Krueger 1990). The controversy over comparative advantage treated here is summarized in Table 6.1.

This argument has been advanced mainly in policy debates intended for a general audience, and has yet to be assimilated into the canon of orthodox thought.[113] But it has been advanced by many of the most prominent of neoclassical trade theorists, not least the respected economist Jagdish Bhagwati who has been particularly outspoken on this matter. The argument is also entirely faithful to the underlying structure of neoclassical theory. It therefore warrants close scrutiny.[114]

This theoretical elaboration retains and extends the naturalist

Table 6.1 Sources of comparative advantage

	Legitimate sources	Distortions
Fair trade perspective	Differences in preferences, endowments and technology	Differences in standards
Free trade perspective	Differences in preferences, endowment, technology and standards	Harmonization of standards

presumption of comparative advantage. Policy differences are now taken to be the direct result of differences in preferences, endowments and technology, and the differences in income levels to which these give rise (Dorman, 1992).[115] Like other natural differences between countries, then, they provide an unambiguous source of efficiency and welfare gains from trade.

This way of thinking infuses most recent neoclassical writing against harmonization of labor and environmental standards. For instance, Bhagwati and Srinivasan reveal this commitment in a carefully crafted and extended critique of environmental policy harmonization.[116] In their words:

> We will argue, in section 4.2, that environmental diversity is ... perfectly legitimate, that it can arise not merely because the environment is differently valued between countries in the sense that the *utility function* defined on income and pollution is not identical and homothetic, but also because of differences in *endowments* and *technology* across countries.
>
> (Bhagwati and Srinivasan 1996, 163, emphasis added)

Later they argue:

> It is best to take, as a general policy, the option of *mutual recognition* of standards, recognizing the fact that diversity of [environmental] standards is basically a natural and appropriate phenomenon, consistent with free trade and the consequent gains from trade for all.
>
> (Bhagwati and Srinivasan 1996, 175)

In the same vein the editors of *The Brookings Project on Integrating National Economies* make the case simply in their preface to each of the books in this series:

> Arguments for creating a level playing field are troublesome at best. International trade occurs precisely because of differences among nation – in resource endowments, labor skills, and consumer tastes ... When David Ricardo first developed the theory of comparative advantage, he focused on differences among nations owing to climate or technology. But

Ricardo could as easily have ascribed the productive differences to differing "social climates" as to physical or technological climates. Taking all "climatic" differences as given, the theory of comparative advantage argues that free trade among nations will maximize global welfare.

(Aaron *et al.* 1994, xx)

Policy choice, comparative advantage and cultural relativism

The claim that policy difference is a natural and therefore legitimate source of comparative advantage originates in the interpersonal relativism that we have discovered lying at the heart of neoclassical theory, and in its strict reductionist logic. Let us pursue these two causal factors in this order. As we have seen, neoclassical theory is studiously silent with respect to the content of preference orderings. The presumption of rationality suggests nothing about what an individual will *or should* prefer. Instead, it suggests that preference is a fully private matter that does not submit to normative evaluation by reference to any independent standard. Each rational actor is deemed a sovereign entity, determining for himself what it is he should (and does) desire. That he values something more or less singly determines its value for the economist. In this sense, the economist serves merely as a keeper of the accounts, recording faithfully and without judgements the values that are reported to her.

As we have also seen, the neoclassical notion of preference is extensive, reaching far beyond one's consumption predilections to the full array of one's judgements. These include not insignificantly one's views on matters of public policy, such as whether and to what degree the environment ought to be protected. Indeed, neoclassicals typically refer to such judgements by the term "ethical preferences"; notably, the seemingly laden qualifier does not in any way affect the manner in which such preferences are handled in computations of social welfare. Just as there is no warrant to interrogate one's preferences in the private domain of commodities, so is there no warrant to interrogate one's preferences in the public domain of ethical judgements. You choose a blue car, I choose red; you choose habitat preservation, I choose its development; you have your private reasons, and I have mine. For the economist, that much information is enough.

Having traveled this far, we can readily understand the basis of the inclusion of national policy differences among the natural and inherently legitimate determinants of comparative advantage. For the reductionist logic of the theory assures us that a nation's policy regime is in principle reducible to the essences of the theory – to its endowments, technology, and the preferences of its citizens. Since this is so, there is no basis for us to interrogate its legitimacy. Country A enacts strong environmental protections, in keeping with its endowments, technology and preferences; country B chooses to do otherwise, in keeping with its own distinct "fundamentals". As the difference between their respective fundamentals is natural, so must be the resulting difference in policy choice. Just as we have no basis for interrogating their respective sets of preferences, so do we have no basis for interrogating the respective policy choices that these preferences induce.

This refusal to judge preferences demands that we take an agnostic view of the policy sources of comparative advantage. In an extended defense of free trade, noted trade theorist Anne Krueger can therefore note in passing:

> The comparative advantage case for free trade *is independent of why there might be cost differences* [between countries]. It simply asserts that, if foreigners can produce something relatively more cheaply than it can be made at home, it pays to produce something else and trade it for the item in question.
>
> (Krueger 1990, 70, emphasis added)

This is a critically important and disarming stratagem in defense of free trade. If one were to investigate why there might be cost differences between two countries with an eye toward assessing the propriety of national policy regimes, the simplicity of the defense of free trade would quickly evaporate. Far more elegant to assume that a policy regime captures a constituency's aggregated preferences, which are valid merely by virtue of the fact that they exist.

What we find in this re-conceptualization of comparative advantage, then, is an apparent commitment to a rather strong form of cultural relativism – one that springs naturally from the opening essences of neoclassical theory.[117] Distinct domestic policy regimes are not right or wrong, better or worse – they are merely different. Inhabitants of countries with strong standards might prefer that other countries enact the same standards – that is their right. But it is not their right to demand that other countries conform to their own standards as a precondition for trade. Absent a universal, objective moral base for adjudicating such matters, they ought instead to respect the equal legitimacy of the policy regimes existent elsewhere, and the alternative ethical preferences that sustain them. As with Walzer's "outsiders", they lack the moral authority to use the instrument of the power of their own state to force international policy convergence around their own preferred practices.

The neoclassical antipathy to harmonization under the auspices of fair trade draws relatedly on the concept of national sovereignty. In the neoclassical view, nations are seen to be characterized by different but equally valid sets of preferences and endowments, and so should be allowed to choose domestic policies free of constraints imposed by other nations. In the words of Aaron *et al.* (1994, xxxi), "The core of the idea of political sovereignty is to permit national residents to order their lives and property in accord with their own preferences". From this perspective, only those choices that have unambiguously harmful (by which is meant efficiency-reducing) cross-

border effects (such as externalities) should become the basis for international concern. While international accords should be constructed to resolve
such problems – such as voluntary agreements which compensate those
countries that suffer external costs imposed by their neighbors, and so forth
– these accords must not impose a uniform code of conduct on reluctant
countries, as such an imposition would violate their national sovereignty.

Having wedded cultural relativism to national sovereignty, neoclassical
advocates reject the call for global harmonization of standards as an unwarranted crusade to impose a particular normative code *as a universal*. Since
there is no single universal ethical framework for critiquing national policies
or for challenging the sanctity of national borders, the default position must
be to take alternative doctrines as valid *in their own domains*. In the words of
one critic, then, the harmonization project amounts to an illicit attempt to
impose "social correctness" on countries with alternative preferences (Steil
1994).

In making these arguments, neoclassicals are joined by some progressive
activists of the South. Martin Khor, editor of *Third World Economics*, argues
that even when harmonization is promoted by right-minded labor, feminist
and other activists of the North, it reflects a deep-seated imperialist impulse
that holds Western liberal democratic ideals to be universal norms for social
organization. As such, harmonization poses a threat to indigenous ethical
systems that differ from the Western ideal in fundamental ways (Khor 1994a;
1994b; Raghavan 1993; Cavanagh 1993).

The argument for cultural autonomy is often combined uneasily in the
same accounts with a very different argument that anticipates policy convergence associated with "modernization". This is the claim that while the
values advanced by the fair traders are indeed universal, they require rapid
economic growth as a precondition for their implementation in poorer
countries. In neoclassical terms, we can think of this as a case in which countries exhibit the same preferences but face different budget constraints
owing to their different levels of national income. In this view, then, weak
standards in low-income countries reflect "regrettable necessity" rather than
distinct sets of values. The solution in this case is growth: growth will induce
rising incomes and an eventual increase in the desire for (and the ability to
achieve) the higher standards that already exist in wealthy countries. The
regrettable necessity argument is usually offered by those who defend the
use of child labor by poorer countries (cf. Basu 1994). In contrast, those who
oppose the imposition of gender equality in societies that do not afford
women equal protections typically invoke cultural relativist claims. Arguments against the harmonization of environmental standards take both
forms, as evidenced by the contribution of Bhagwati and Srinivasan examined above (see Table 6.2).[118]

In short, we find in the neoclassical vision a deep antipathy toward
imposed harmonization of labor and environmental standards, an antipathy
that is grounded in inter-cultural respect and national sovereignty on the

Table 6.2 Origins of differences in standards in Neoclassical accounts

	Regrettable necessity	*Cultural differences*
Child labor standards	X	
Gender relations		X
Environmental standards	X	X

one hand, and basic economic principles on the other. Just as the natural international differences in endowments, technology and preferences provide a natural basis for mutual gains from trade, so do international differences in policy regimes. And just as the former factors are entirely legitimate sources of comparative advantage, so are the latter. We have no warrant to cancel these differences as a precondition for trade, *nor should we want to.* We gain most, after all, when we trade with countries that are most unlike our own. Fair trade initiatives are, therefore, both unfair and unwise.

ASSESSING FREE TRADE

As with its stance on national competitiveness, the neoclassical position on trade is laudable in several important respects. First and foremost, the defense of free trade is internationalist. Trade is advocated on the grounds that it is mutually advantageous. Taking countries' respective endowments, technologies, preferences and resulting levels of incomes as simply given, the neoclassical vision undertakes to demonstrate that all stand to benefit from a regime shift toward free trade. This is indeed the essence of the concept of comparative advantage – even a country that is technologically inefficient in each and every industry stands to gain from trade with more advanced countries. We find in the defense of free trade further signs of the deep neoclassical commitment to impartiality. The gains available under free trade to one's own country count for no more than the gains available to others in computing the effect of trade on global social welfare. This impartiality separates the free traders from the progressive nationalists, who as we have seen, endorse competitiveness strategies and strategic trade.

The neoclassical objections to harmonization reflect another sort of impartiality as well. The neoclassical vision denies the validity of treating one's own values as more legitimate than those of others. As we investigated in Chapter 4, this is the chief virtue of cultural relativism. Its refusal to judge values that appear in other cultures and the practices to which these values give rise seems to induce a healthy degree of inter-cultural respect. This, at least, is what neoclassical visionaries claim.

But matters in this regard are not quite as simple as this discussion would suggest. This is because, in the hands of neoclassical visionaries, the adherence to cultural relativism paradoxically serves a most extreme universalist project. *This is the neoliberal project to establish one specific kind of economic system across all people in all communities, regardless of whatever differences in culture or values they might exhibit.* The neoliberal project is, after all, a global one – one that will not be complete until the market ideal has been spread to and fully absorbed in each and every economy across the face of the earth.

The roots of this paradox, in which cultural relativism is placed in service of this unbending, uncompromising and hegemonic political project, lie in the originating essences of neoclassical theory. We find here a commitment to the ontological presuppositions of moral objectivism. The assumptions of rationality and scarcity are taken to be universal propositions, as we have seen. As such, the market ideal to which these assumptions give rise is taken to be the ideal form of economic integration for all people for all time, regardless of whatever particular values they may hold dear. Those nations that have chosen alternative economic systems are seen to have deprived themselves unwittingly of the gains in wealth and social welfare that the unencumbered neoliberal market economy is uniquely capable of promoting. Even worse, they have failed to implement the one kind of economy that uniquely accords with human nature. They have denied their inhabitants the kind of economic freedom to which they are by nature entitled. Hence, those countries that have embraced neoliberalism are licensed to encourage those that have not to undertake the most thoroughgoing economic reform – using even the coercive powers of the IMF and World Bank – when they do not choose of their own accord to help themselves in this way. All told, neoclassical visionaries manage to exploit the normative position of relativism to achieve precisely the kind of universal conformance that this was designed to resist. As a result they manage to commit the sins associated with both moral objectivism and cultural relativism – they seek to impose one kind of economic system on all communities, while providing little basis for interrogating and resisting even rather egregious oppressions, as long as these oppressions are seen to accord with a community's "ethical preferences".

Policies, preferences and politics

A further important objection must be raised against the neoclassical extension of the concept of comparative advantage to include policy differences. In this account, the policies that emerge in a society are taken to reflect the preferences of its citizens. This maneuver requires a simplistic view of politics and policy formation, one that effaces enduring divisions of class, race, gender, etc. At worst, this model of governance is predicated upon a conception of the nation as a unified actor with consistent preferences, so that all citizens are seen to value and benefit equally from a particular policy choice. Though extraordinarily naïve, this device appears frequently in the trade literature. By analogizing the state as a unified economic actor, theorists are spared consideration of the deep conflicts over values and interests that permeate all societies. Hence a nation's policies can be taken as simply reflecting the national will.[119] At best, this is predicated upon a pluralist conception in which a neutral state responds to competing and equally mobilized constituencies that have relatively equal access to the levers of power. Such a model treats national policy choice as compromises between these equally empowered constituencies. The view of nation as unified actor obscures the tensions, struggles and cleavages that mark all societies, while the pluralist view obscures the manner in which these are expressed in policy making, institution building and market outcomes. But once we take account of the existence of such enduring divisions, we recognize that different groups in society may face very different opportunities to participate meaningfully in the political life of the community and nation. In this case, of course, a nation's policy choices will reflect the values and interests of those with the greatest political capabilities.

From the capabilities perspective, we recognize that "nations" do not "choose" social policies in any transparent or meaningful sense of the term. Policy outcomes result from struggle among differently positioned social actors and reflect the inequalities of political capabilities that are embedded in economic and political structures, culture, and the other facets of society. Weak labor and environmental standards (for example) arise as a complex outcome of these diverse factors and forces. Indeed, the absence of strong worker protections is often associated with a general absence of basic personal and political freedoms (Dorman 1988). Consequently, it is rather unseemly to attribute weak protections to the expression of aggregated preferences through political channels.

In the paper discussed earlier, Bhagwati and Srinivasan do try to respond to this concern. They acknowledge that unresponsive authoritarian governments sometimes impose policy regimes on the people they govern that comprise weaker protections than those citizens' preferences would otherwise dictate. They then investigate whether the demands of fair traders – that the resulting weak standards be strengthened as a precondition of trade – are warranted in this specific case.

Their answer is again in keeping with the tenets of neoclassical theory, and is on that account instructive. They argue that *all* governments – democratic and non-democratic alike – are subject to "political failure", for the reasons we considered in Chapter 2. Hence there is no reason to presume that the policies adopted even in democratic societies are correct indicators of citizens' preferences. Indeed, they argue, it might very well be the case that labor and environmental standards in such societies are *too strong*, given the disproportionate influence of small groups of well-organized activists who often shade policy toward their own preferences. In this case, there is no good reason to take the difference in policy regime between the authoritarian and democratic state as evidence that the former is too weak; we might just as well conclude that the latter is too strong. Given the impossibility of ever knowing how closely a policy regime matches society's preferences, Bhagwati and Srinivasan conclude that we must treat each policy regime as appropriate in the national context within which it occurs.

This clever argument largely misses the point. Fair traders do not take existing policy in high-standard countries as true reflections of national preferences, because the concept of national preferences makes no sense. As we have just seen, nations are ensembles of diverse groups whose values, interests and aspirations are generally distinct and often conflicting. Under these circumstances, there is no sensible way to theorize the aggregation of preferences in pursuit of some true national preferences – such as some consensus that best accords with what a nation's inhabitants prefer. The policy regime that exists at any particular moment may be better thought of as a temporary outcome of continuing struggles among these distinct groups – one that will change as the respective interests, values and influence of these groups evolve.

The fair trade position does not depend on treating any one nation's policy regime as the one true standard against which all others are to be judged (although, as we will see, some of the specific policy proposals that have been advanced by fair traders do implicitly make this implausible presumption). Instead, it recognizes that all sites of policy formation, from the local to the national to the international, are sites of contest over values and interests. It also recognizes the interdependence of these different sites: the outcome of policy deliberations at any of these levels will affect the goals that can be achieved at all others. A trade agreement that affects the international flow of goods and services will necessarily affect the ability of a community to protect its economic security through local policy initiatives. Hence, trade agreements are critical sites whereat to militate for rules and institutions that will promote global justice.

When we interrogate free trade from the perspective of egalitarianism, things are equally complicated. On the one hand, free trade is promoted partly on the grounds that it will (ideally) induce equal compensation for those who provide the same factor of production internationally, as predicted by the FPE theorem. Even where the restrictive conditions for the FPE theorem do not hold, Stolper–Samuelson predicts that free trade is likely to induce rising compensation for unskilled labor in poorer countries. In the world we inhabit, where gross international inequality in rewards for those performing similar services is rampant, and where the unskilled in poorer countries earn meager wages, this is not a trivial result. If trade can indeed promote the incomes of those with least incomes, it ought to be given high marks by those committed to international equality.[120]

This is not the end of the matter, however. In the neoclassical view, free trade is not apt to bring about an egalitarian distribution of income or substantive freedoms. Rather, it is likely to engender increasing income inequality between the low-paid unskilled workers and other economic actors in wealthier societies. Recall that Stolper–Samuelson predicts that free trade will reduce the incomes of the low-skilled in capital-rich nations, while increasing the incomes of high-skilled workers and the owners of capital. But the latter already enjoyed higher incomes prior to free trade. The welfarist standard does require that the losers be fully compensated for their losses, of course. With the winners enjoying a net benefit following compensation, income inequality increases following a shift to free trade. On this basis, neoclassicals endorse free trade regardless of the degree of inequality existing prior to its enactment, or the degree of inequality that it induces. After all, some are now better off, while none are worse off.

A commitment to capabilities equality leads us to evaluate this situation very differently. In this broader view of what constitutes valuable states or conditions for humans to achieve, we should recall, inequality in one functioning (such as access to income) induces substantial inequalities and even absolute failures in other functionings. The relatively poor, for example, are likely to find it difficult to achieve sufficient education and training; the unemployed, self-respect. If we acknowledge that these failures are likely to be exacerbated by increases in income inequality, then what neoclassicals call "full compensation" for those who lose under the shift to free trade will not suffice to prevent a loss in quality of life. The minimum that full compensation would require is a level of payment that prevents an increase in income inequality. In the case of those displaced due to trade, it would also require sufficient training and assistance to find comparable employment opportunities.

As many economists have noted, full compensation for those actually harmed by trade liberalization never occurs (cf. Rodrik 1997). Hence, in the world in which we live, instances of trade liberalization actually fail the test laid down by welfarist normative principles. From a capabilities perspective, this anomaly is easily resolvable. Those harmed by policy shifts, the so-called losers, generally possess less political capabilities than those who win under the shift; if they did not, they presumably would have had the political wherewithal to prevent the harmful policy shift in the first place. This also means that they generally lack the political capabilities to secure full compensation. Moreover, we might hypothesize plausibly that the greater the inequality prior to the regime shift, the less politically efficacious will be those harmed by the shift, and the less adequate will be the level of compensation that they are able to secure.[121] For all of these reasons, a regime shift that increases inequality is less defensible the greater is the previous level of inequality. The greater the level of inequality prior to a regime shift, the greater will be the capabilities failures that it induces, and the less adequate will be the level of compensation for the losers that is actually forthcoming.

FAIR TRADE

These criticisms point us toward the internationalist egalitarian perspective in the trade debate. The internationalist principle of capabilities equality –

harmonization of capabilities at a level that is sufficient, universally attainable and sustainable – generates an alternative approach to trade, one that breaks with both strategic and free trade. This approach is commonly referred to as "fair trade".

The import of capabilities equality in the trade debate is to provide a compelling basis for rejecting neoclassical theory's strict agnosticism regarding the sources of comparative advantage. The principle encourages us to interrogate the strategies that nations (and indeed, communities and firms) adopt in pursuit of their economic interests, and to adjudicate what should and what should not serve as sources of comparative advantage. The test follows directly from the principle advanced here. It is a simple one to write down, although by no means trivial to apply: *nations should be allowed (and indeed encouraged) to adopt strategies that promote capabilities equality, and should be barred from undertaking those strategies that interfere with this end.* From the capabilities perspective, then, we are likely to conclude that gender discrimination in employment or weak worker health and safety standards do not qualify as legitimate policies. Global policy regimes should therefore disallow (or counter the effects of) such strategies in the formation of comparative advantage.[122]

From the capabilities perspective, there is nothing sacrosanct about comparative advantage. As we have seen, this perspective refuses the neoclassical presumptions about both the naturalism and legitimacy of the determinants of market price. It therefore grants no particular normative weight to market outcomes (even absent market imperfections). In this view, a market outcome is not right simply by virtue of the fact that it exists. It is right instead to the degree to which it accords with the overarching normative principle of capabilities equality. This is equally true of outcomes in domestic and in international markets. Whenever market outcomes are found to conflict in substantive ways with capabilities equality, we have reason to indict them as unjust.

For neoclassical visionaries, fair trade amounts to the forfeiture of economic efficiency and growth, and as a consequence, social welfare. This is, to say the least, a high price to pay for one's ethical preferences. But a normative commitment to capabilities equality undermines this argument, for, once we jettison the welfarism of the neoclassical vision, we come to see that there is no good reason to presume that efficiency and growth are unequivocally virtuous. When efficiency and growth are predicated upon or produce inequality in substantive freedoms across society's members, we have good reason to indict rather than celebrate them. It might indeed be the case that a society (or more accurately, a substantial segment of it) is best served by what neoclassicals would call "inefficiencies" of all sorts – such as when protective legislation channels technological innovation in ways that reduce the rate of economic growth, but that also reduce the extent and depth of social dislocation that technological change often induces (Polanyi 1944). In such a case, the sacrifice of growth and efficiency may be no sacrifice at all.

There may of course be situations in which the expansion of capabilities for the capabilities-impoverished does depend on economic growth. In such cases, the capabilities perspective would seek means to promote this end. Even in this case, advocates of this perspective would be unlikely to endorse the neoclassical view that the liberalized market is the single appropriate avenue to achieve growth, or that the immediate goal in such cases must be *maximum* growth. Instead, having rejected the reductionism of neoclassical theory, egalitarians would promote those approaches to growth that are consistent with the promotion of equality of substantive freedoms – even when this entails the achievement of a rate of growth that is less than could otherwise be achieved. This is because while neoclassicals reduce the quality of life to one indicator – the flow of psychic satisfaction that follows from one's choices – the vantage point of capabilities reveals the multiple sources of substantive freedoms, and the interdependence among them.

Growth also factors so highly into the neoclassical vision because of its steadfast refusal to consider redistribution as a means to enhance social welfare. Hence the only legitimate way to raise the welfare of those worst off is to promote economic growth. But of course, egalitarians by definition promote redistribution whenever inequality of substantive freedoms is seen to have reached egregious levels.

For all of these reasons, efficiency and growth are demoted in the egalitarian view. The effects of efficiency and growth on peoples' substantive freedoms must be investigated on a case-by-case basis. Where growth does seem to be warranted, egalitarians are nevertheless skeptical of claims for the virtues of growth at all costs, and search instead for means of achieving growth that do not systematically undermine capabilities equality. Hence, and to conclude this discussion, policy measures that cancel those determinants of comparative advantage which run counter to capabilities equality have no reason to be embarrassed on account of the fact that they reduce global economic efficiency, growth or social welfare.[123]

FAIR TRADE PROPOSALS

Over the past decade or so, several fair trade proposals have been debated extensively. Each in its own way seeks to ensure that comparative advantage derives from appropriate government and corporate behavior. Nevertheless, each of these individually is inadequate when considered against the standard of capabilities equality. In the remainder of this chapter, I will examine briefly the chief attributes of several fair trade proposals.

The social charter approach

One approach to the goal of achieving fair trade (and fair FDI flows) that has received substantial support is the social charter. A social charter mandates that nations recognize and protect some minimum set of social rights as a condition for participating in a common market. Established through multi-lateral negotiations among the affected nations, these rights might be taken to reflect what are deemed by member states to be valued functionings. The charter may therefore be interpreted as establishing a capabilities floor across the common market. In the view of its proponents, a sufficiently strong charter prevents nations from undertaking unethical practices in pur-suit of comparative advantage.

Recent interest in a social charter originated in Europe. The negotiations over European integration in 1992 (the Maastricht Treaty) included provi-sions for a Social Charter. Included in the Charter are fundamental rights ranging from employment protections to the protection of children, elderly and disabled persons (Kraw 1990). Though the ultimate Charter approved by the parties fell far short of the aspirations of its supporters, it does harmo-nize certain (limited) social and labor standards throughout Europe (Silvia 1991).

Inspired by the European initiative, many fair traders in North America argued unsuccessfully for the inclusion of a social charter in NAFTA (Rothstein 1993; Castañeda and Heredia 1992; Brown *et al.* 1992; Shrybman 1991–2). The proposed charter includes provisions for harmonization of minimum environmental and labor standards, greater community and worker participation in their enforcement, and a strengthened social safety net (Brown *et al.* 1992). In the event, the Clinton administration attempted to pacify the fair traders in Congress by negotiating two side agreements to NAFTA on labor rights and environmental protection. Notably, while the side agreements compel each of the three signatories to enforce their own respective labor and environmental laws, they do not harmonize these laws across the continent (Hufbauer and Schott, 1993).

While there is much to commend the approach of a social charter, it is marred by a number of significant weaknesses. First, as the outcome of nego-tiations between countries with differing levels of standards, the social char-ter is apt to establish a minimum floor rather than a unified code of conduct comparable to the standards in place in the high-standard countries, as the European example demonstrates (Lange 1993). A member country that chooses to make unilateral improvements in its domestic protections above those required by the charter – or that promotes capabilities in other ways – might find that its firms suffer from a competitive disadvantage *vis-à-vis* firms located in other member nations with lower social standards. The threat of a loss of competitiveness due to higher standards may only be apparent, of course. Nevertheless, progressive groups seeking stronger domestic stan-dards may now face the daunting burden of proving that stronger standards will not harm the domestic economy.

Second, the approach is a sluggish vehicle for advancing rights and protections over time because improvements require consensus across coun-tries marked by profound differences in cultural heritages, economic means, etc. These differences present problems for the social charter approach even across Europe; they would be substantially exacerbated in the context of a charter that would link countries marked by larger income differences than those that obtain there (such as a North American social charter). Hence, the social charter approach provides no mechanism for improvements in social standards above the specified minima, and it leaves the relatively high-standard countries vulnerable to competition from firms operating in low-standard countries. As a result, a social charter is not apt to empower progressive groups in their pursuit of increased social protections. In short, the approach is "sticky upward": it lacks sufficient force to generate a dynamic of improving standards (and capabilities) over time.

Third and finally, the social charter approach primarily addresses formal rights and freedoms – such as the right to secure vocational training, and the freedom of movement and occupational choice (Watson 1991). While these are important functionings that a capabilities approach should recognize, they are by themselves incomplete determinants of the actual substantive freedoms that people may enjoy. The guarantee of these freedoms alone may not translate into the equal ability to achieve secure incomes or to be politically efficacious, which the capabilities approach recognizes also as fundamental. Even more troublesome, capabilities equality may at times conflict with equality of formal rights: it may be, for example, that a society that has invested resources in the training of health care professionals is justified in denying absolute freedom of movement to its doctors (see Chapter 7). In short, while the social charter might be a necessary means to promote upward harmonization of capabilities, it is by itself insufficient.

The social tariff approach

A second approach entails the imposition of "social tariffs" on goods produced in countries with relatively weak labor rights and environmental protections. The goal of this approach is to protect the gains in labor and environmental protections achieved in high-standard countries and to encourage the adoption of higher standards in low-standard countries. It seeks these results by canceling the competitive advantage enjoyed by firms operating where standards are weak (see Dorman 1992; Lebowitz 1988; Chapman 1991; Ramstad 1987; Rothstein 1993).

Peter Dorman (1992) considers the optimal structure of a social tariff designed to insulate the worker rights enjoyed by US labor. In his view, a properly structured tariff would be leveled unilaterally by the high-standard country, due to the unlikelihood that low-standard countries would agree to multilateral accords that include a social tariff. The tariff would be calibrated commodity by commodity (rather than apply equally to all exports from an offending country) to cancel the precise competitive advantage gained on the basis of inferior standards. Under this approach, a nation's own standards would be taken as the relevant benchmark for instituting tariffs. Workers and/or firms who believe they had been harmed by unfair competition from foreign firms that exploited lower standards would seek redress in the form of a tariff through a petition to an authority established for this purpose. After hearing evidence by both parties, the authority would dispose of the petition on its merits.[124]

The social tariff approach seeks to remove environmental degradation and the denial of worker rights as sources of competitive advantage, but there are significant weaknesses in this approach as well. First, the proposal entails a unilateral response to forces that should and can only be addressed effectively by international co-operation. Unilateral policy initiatives are prone to exploitation in service of nationalist agendas at odds with their explicit intent. This risk is greatest in the case of the most powerful countries, of course. In this regard, the track record of the US is particularly troubling. During the 1980s Congress passed various pieces of trade (and other) legislation which restricted preferential access to US markets to those countries that enforced, or were taking steps to enforce, internationally recognized labor rights (see Chapter 5). At the time of passage, these initiatives were hailed by labor and civil rights activists as potent new levers by which to advance the campaign for global justice. In practice, this legislation was used by the US government to punish political enemies, such as Nicaragua's Sandinista regime, while political allies with egregious labor rights records, such as Guatemala, were rewarded with uninterrupted access to US markets (Cavanagh *et al.*, 1988). Though there are no guarantees against misuse of policy instruments, these risks might be reduced through participatory, co-operative multilateral approaches that establish new global policy regimes.

In the absence of such co-operation, we should expect countries that are harmed by the imposition of a unilateral social tariff to retaliate, if they are capable of doing so. As the number of countries affected by the social tariff grows, retaliation may not only cancel the benefits that the social tariff was designed to create, but might substantially interfere with beneficial world trade. Moreover, given the unequal ability of countries to retaliate, the approach is likely in practice to punish the weakest and poorest nations.

For all of these reasons, the unilateral social tariff approach is unlikely to forge international co-operation among workers seeking to respond to the pressures associated with global neoliberalism. Indeed, many labor activists from developing countries have opposed US efforts to tie trade preferences to labor standards, because they see such measures as protectionist, nationalist and paternalistic (Cavanagh 1993). These objections are not unwarranted. After all, under the procedures advanced to implement social tariffs, there is no space for participation by those workers whom the tariffs are designed to assist in their quest for greater rights. In this sense, the approach treats these workers merely as passive victims of oppression, rather than as partners in a campaign for global justice. While there may indeed be times when such workers cannot participate meaningfully in endeavors designed to advance their substantive freedoms (for reasons I examined in the critique of Walzer), it is shortsighted and paternalistic for progressives in the North to design policy initiatives that do not consider the agency and vital contributions of workers in the South.

Finally, many proponents of this approach exclude differences in wage levels as a legitimate basis for the imposition of a social tariff (cf. Dorman 1992). The rationale is rather orthodox: by allowing capital to flow freely to those countries with lowest wages, the benefits of development will spread where it is most efficient and equitable to do so. Gradually, the expansion of modern industries in such regions will induce higher wages and improving standards of living. The imposition of a social tariff in a high-wage country to counter the advantage enjoyed by the low-wage country would therefore violate the principles of economic efficiency and social equity. Dorman therefore concedes that the social tariff approach will not suffice to induce an upward harmonization of wages. In his words, if "the policy imperative is that international equity be attained by raising wages in the Third World rather than depressing them [in the North], additional measures must be taken" (1992, 218).

While it would be unreasonable and counter-productive to demand an immediate harmonization of wages across national borders, it is reasonable to demand that wages be set at achievable levels which provide for a decent and improving quality of life in the South. Once we reject the reductionist model of wage determination of the neoclassical vision, we are led to examine policy tools that promote fairness in wage levels in the South, and in the North. Hence, if social tariffs are to be used at all, the proposals on offer must be adjusted to incorporate such mechanisms.

The Sullivan Principles approach

Under an alternative approach, high-standard countries would require domestic corporations that invest in low-standard countries to respect certain worker and social rights and environmental protections. This policy was proposed by Bhagwati (1993b) in the case of North American integration and is reminiscent of the "Sullivan Principles" which required US corporations that invested in South Africa during the apartheid era to comply with US laws against discrimination. As a resolute free trader, Bhagwati proposed this approach only as a second-best alternative to the free trade that he preferred, in hopes of defusing the anti-NAFTA sentiments that almost succeeded in derailing the agreement. But despite its parentage and the intent of its architect, we can safely treat this proposal as reflecting the principles of fair trade.

The Sullivan Principles approach is designed to prevent corporations in high-standard countries from relocating to developing countries simply to secure cost savings owing to the lower standards that generally exist in the South (a practice that critics have termed "social dumping"). Bhagwati and other advocates argue that this approach removes the possibility of social dumping, but does so in a manner that respects the policy autonomy of the host country. As we have seen, Bhagwati opposes a requirement that developing countries adopt the same standards as developed countries on the grounds that it would infringe upon their sovereignty and reduce their level of economic welfare. For example, the demand that Mexico harmonize its environmental standards and practices with those of the US, expressed by some opponents of NAFTA, is unacceptable to Bhagwati:

> [Surely] the manner in which Mexico divides its overall effort to meet environmental objectives among different industries and regions must reflect its own priorities just as ours reflect our own interests. Demands on Mexico to do exactly what we would do are therefore not sensible. Since we would properly not submit to them if made by others, they are also unreasonable.
>
> (Bhagwati 1993a, 13).

Bhagwati is correct to argue that one country must not be required to follow the path of another's development priorities. But the principle of sovereignty must be balanced against the competing principle adopted here, the equality of freedoms to pursue goals that people have reason to value. The task is to devise policies which will promote this result without mandating that individual countries achieve it in identical ways.

The Sullivan Principles approach fails on this front. One weakness of this approach is that it lacks mechanisms to ensure a universalization of the higher standards in the low-standard country receiving the FDI. While it retards FDI, it provides no proactive incentive (such as financial assistance) for indigenous advancement of standards. Its principal effect is to improve the living standards of the relatively few workers in developing countries who find employment in foreign-based firms. As Bhagwati argues, it might also provide a "demonstration effect", encouraging non-governmental organizations and others to advocate for nationwide adoption of the higher standards that are introduced by the foreign corporations. But it is unlikely that this demonstration effect will suffice to induce universal improvements in rights and living standards in the absence of other measures, given the relative absence of right of association and political expression that obtains in many low-standard countries.

Finally, like the social tariff approach, the Sullivan Principles approach is unilateral. While Bhagwati cites this as a virtue, unilateralism is prone to exploitation for nationalist purposes unrelated to the intent of the measure, as we have seen. It is noteworthy that in the one instance in which this approach was implemented, to bring pressure to bear on South Africa, it was opposed by the African National Congress (ANC). The ANC argued that it served the interests of multinational corporations (by providing them with a profitable alternative to full economic isolation of South Africa, which the

ANC preferred) rather than those of South African Blacks. But there may be a way to integrate the Sullivan Principles approach into a multilateral framework, as we will examine in the next chapter.

CONCLUSION

We have found three distinct positions in contemporary trade debates. Strategic trade entails the use of state power to secure an advantage over one's rivals in global markets. We found this position to be ethically deficient. Not only does it privilege the interests of one's own nation over others, it also expresses little concern for domestic equality. In contrast, the free trade perspective of the neoclassical vision is internationalist in the sense of being adamantly impartial. Domestic interests count for no more than do foreign interests in the welfarist normative principle it uses to assess economic outcomes. It defends free trade predicated upon comparative advantage on the grounds that it is mutually beneficial. It takes cross-national differences in preferences, endowments and policy regimes as entirely natural and therefore legitimate determinants of comparative advantage and trade flows. It rejects all demands for the harmonization of labor and environmental standards as imperialist interference in others' equally valid ways of life, and as impediments to global economic efficiency. Harmonization is therefore both unfair, and unwise. In contrast, internationalist egalitarians promote fair trade. Their normative commitments provide them with a basis for assessing just which policy strategies are legitimate determinants of comparative advantage. As a precondition to liberalized trade, in this view, those policies which enhance capabilities equality should be promoted, while those which undermine this end should be prohibited.

The policy challenges facing internationalist egalitarians turn out to be rather difficult, as the foregoing discussion indicates. Unlike the neoclassical vision, whose reductionist logic generates extraordinarily elegant policy recommendations, the anti-reductionist social analysis generated by institutionalist theory generates less precise prescriptions, and recognizes that all prescriptions are apt to lead to unintended (and even contradictory) consequences. But if we risk paying the price of inelegance, we just might discover new policy avenues that do indeed further the objective of capabilities equality.

But this needs to be demonstrated, not just claimed. This is the goal of the next chapter. There we will explore just how these fair trade proposals can be amended and combined in pursuit of global justice.

Part 3

Rethinking global policy regimes

"A global policy regime is just to the degree that it promotes the harmonization of capabilities to achieve functionings at a level that is sufficient, universally attainable and sustainable." There is a very demanding principle, indeed. It calls for nothing less than a thoroughgoing transformation of the way in which societies create and distribute substantive freedoms. And it also calls for new international policy regimes that equalize capabilities across the North and South.

We might fairly ask whether this principle demands far too much of us. If that is the case, then perhaps the principle is actually counterproductive. Placing the bar far too high for us to leap, it leaves us hopeless and immobilized. That we would be self-righteous (even pious) in our incapacity should provide us small comfort.

We must therefore brace ourselves for the difficult task of considering what practical value, if any, the principle might have. Chapter 7 concludes the book with an examination of this matter. First, it presents a range of global policies that are consonant with the principle. These are framed as proposals for the year 2025. Then it turns to an examination of the kinds of politics that are in keeping with the principle, but that also might suffice to secure the policies presented here.

7 Global economic policies for the year 2025

INTRODUCTION

We must now consider the practical virtue of the internationalist principle of capabilities equality. While this principle could be applied within virtually any domain of social policy, we will focus here on some of those areas at the heart of the contest over global neoliberalism. We will look explicitly at trade, corporate practices (including foreign direct investment, or FDI), and labor mobility. As we will see, these issues all relate to the matter of labor rights and interests, while the first two also relate to the matter of competitiveness and the environment. By focusing on these three policy areas, then, we will have something to say about matters that have deeply troubled the critics of global neoliberalism.

Though it will be obvious from what follows, it needs to be emphasized that this discussion is exploratory, provisional and at best suggestive. I do not attempt to be comprehensive, as it is not the purpose of this chapter to present a fully adequate policy alternative to global neoliberalism. An endeavor of that sort would require a level of hubris that I have not yet been able to cultivate. The purpose instead is to test the usefulness of the normative principle of capabilities equality when we turn to the task of envisioning new policy regimes that might provide for better economic outcomes.

To anticipate a reasonable concern, let me reiterate a caveat expressed at the outset. The policy proposals that follow are to be taken *seriously but not literally*. The proposals follow from a consideration of just what capabilities equality might require of us in the way of institutional reform in the world we currently inhabit. The feature of that world that bears most upon this project is the egregious and historically unprecedented degree of global inequality – in income and wealth, and life chances broadly construed. Though inequality between the North and the South is particularly extreme, there are stark (and rapidly deepening) inequalities within each of these regions as well. The principle of capabilities equality demands of us that we do far better in the next century than we have up until now, and so we should not be surprised to find that it leads us to policy measures which differ rather dramatically from those in force today. It is my hope that those who share a commitment to equality of substantive freedoms will find these proposals worthy of serious consideration.

This brings us to the caveat that they are not to be taken literally. As first approaches to policy from the perspective of capabilities equality, they are no doubt flawed – perhaps even fatally. They are offered as a place to begin a conversation about policy, not as a pronouncement about where that conversation should conclude. Moreover, as we will consider below, new proposals that seek genuine equality must not ultimately come from the pen of a solitary academic, but from negotiation and co-operation among advocates for justice in the North and the South. Those conversations are multiplying and deepening today thanks to new political and civic spaces opening up, partly as a consequence of the global reach of new communications technologies.

The proposals offered here could not realistically be imposed tomorrow, absent other substantial changes in many other policy areas, and in domestic and international politics. They are not offered as quick fixes, but as medium-range targets to which we might aspire as we remake global policy regimes in pursuit of economic justice. Fortunately, as we will also consider below, they are also not rigid, take-it-or-leave-it prescriptions which preclude smaller, more manageable reforms. While capabilities equality demands a lot from us, it also grants us tremendous latitude for pursuing practical political projects.

TRADE REFORM: THE SOCIAL-INDEX TARIFF STRUCTURE

A global trading regime that is consonant with the principle of capabilities equality should achieve several interrelated objectives. First, it should incorporate incentives for countries to take steps to promote capabilities equality domestically. But given the extreme gap between the North and the South, it should also provide the means necessary for impoverished countries to expand the capabilities of their inhabitants in the aggregate. Second, and *contra* neoliberal trade agreements that are silent on the matter of the policy sources of comparative advantage, this regime should penalize countries for pursuing strategies to enhance export performance that are capabilities-reducing for those with relatively meager capabilities sets. As a corollary, it should prevent corporate or government competitiveness strategies that exploit or that deepen capabilities inequality. The regime should also preclude domestic policies which induce international capabilities inequality, such as those that benefit a wealthy country at the expense of a poorer trading partner. Finally, the regime should assist activists to secure policy reform that deepens capabilities equality, and should provide a basis for new forms of international co-operation among them.

In our consideration of the policy proposals offered by the fair traders, we found that each has particular merits, but that each also fails to accord with the principle of capabilities equality in some way or other. I raised the prospect in Chapter 6 that there might be ways to build on these proposals in a manner that retains their strengths, while overcoming some of their weaknesses. Let us now explore one possible means for achieving this goal – what Stephen Cullenberg and I (1994 and 1995) have elsewhere called the "social-index tariff structure", or SITS.

A SITS regime would remove critical aspects of social life from the sway of competition, in keeping with the tenets of internationalist egalitarianism examined in Chapter 5, while simultaneously rewarding countries for pursuing benevolent means for pursuing successful trade performance. It does this through the implementation of a global system of social tariffs. Unlike the unilateral social tariff approach examined above, this approach would arise out of multilateral negotiations that would determine the criterion for establishing social tariffs and establish a new institution for imposing and policing them (see below). Under a SITS regime, each country would be assigned an index number reflecting both the average level of the capabilities of its citizens relative to its means, and the degree to which these capabilities are distributed equally. This index number provides a basis for assessing and ranking countries' respective capabilities performance. Countries with relatively similar levels of performance would then be grouped together for trade purposes. These groupings would determine the application of social tariffs: tariffs would be applied when one country exports products to another with a significantly higher index number (which places it in a higher performance group).

Let us consider how a SITS regime might be constructed, and how it would function. First, we need some measure of each country's level of capabilities. The Human Development Index (HDI) generated by the United Nations Development Programme and reported yearly in the *Human Development Report* (*HDR*) represents an explicit first approximation of a measure of capabilities. Indeed, Sen was a consultant for this project, and participated in the drafting of the first annual report (Crocker 1992). The *HDR* insists on a broad definition of human development that, in its words, "makes it possible to capture better the complexity of human life – the many concerns people have and the many cultural, economic, social and political differences in people's lives throughout the world" (UNDP 1990, 11). The HDI is therefore a composite measure based on three indicators: welfare, life expectancy and educational attainment. On the basis of this index, countries are ranked according to levels of "human development". Based on the 1994 data used to construct the 1997 index, Canada is ranked first, the US fourth, and Sierra Leone last (UNDP 1997).

Each of these three indicators is taken to be important in its own right, and to serve as a proxy for other indicators of capabilities that are harder to measure. The indicator of *welfare* is derived from per capita national income, and reveals a good bit about people's access to vital commodities and other amenities, while correlating with many important freedoms (such as the freedom of mobility). But in calculating the welfare indicator, increments of per capita income above a threshold (set at the world average, which was $5,835 in 1994) are progressively devalued at higher levels of income, reflecting the view that each successive increment above the threshold is less valuable in enhancing well-being.[125] Hence, though France has a per capita income that is four times that of Poland, its welfare indicator is only 1.2 times that of Poland.

Life expectancy provides insight into the ability of people to avoid preventable mortality, of course, but also reflects their ability to get access to health care, and to be properly nourished and sheltered. It might also provide some indirect information about relative equality, for if income and other opportunities are distributed very unequally, a country might exhibit a life expectancy index number that is very low relative to its per capita income. For example, though Brazil enjoyed a per capita income substantially above Bulgaria in 1994, its life expectancy index value of 0.69 fell far below Bulgaria's 0.77. In part, this difference in life expectancy reflected the much greater degree of income inequality in Brazil (see below).

The *educational attainment* indicator is generated by combining a country's adult literacy rate with educational enrolment data. This indicator reveals something about the ability of people to make sense of and respond to the events and forces shaping their lives, to use new (information and other) technologies, etc. These may be vital to (but are by no means sufficient for) their political efficacy.

There are limits to the information provided by any one component of the HDI – and even to all three components taken together. Certainly there are important functionings that the HDI misses – such as the ability to achieve self-respect, or to voice one's opinion on pressing political matters free of the fear of reprisals.[126] While we should exercise some caution in interpreting HDI data, then, we can fairly treat the index as a source of useful information on at least certain basic vital functioningsthat are no less vital or consequential for that.

Wealthier countries are far more likely to achieve a high HDI ranking relative to poorer countries. This is because per capita income appears in the welfare component of the index, but also because wealthy countries can better afford health care and educational services. What we want to know is how well a country is performing in promoting capabilities levels and equality *relative to its means*. Hence we need to adjust performance by accounting for differences in per capita income.

For the sake of simplicity, let us correct for the difference in means by dividing all countries into per capita income deciles. Within each of these ten income groups, we can then compare countries to see how each is performing relative to other countries with relatively similar levels of income. Let us take the mean HDI for the countries in a particular income group to be a measure of the "expected" level of human development for countries in that group. We can then compute the ratio of the actual HDI for each country in an income group to the average HDI for the group. Good performers in the group will earn a ratio value greater than one; poor performers will earn a value less than one. Once we perform this calculation for all countries in all groups, we have a basis for comparing countries across income brackets. This approach precludes a bias in favor of rich countries. Let us call the number yielded in this way the *"means-adjusted HDI."* [127]

As an aggregate measure, the HDI provides no direct information about the degree of capabilities inequality in a country (though it does provide some indirect information, as discussed above). Unfortunately, aggregate statistics obscure inequality levels: two countries with the same level of per capita income might exhibit very different patterns of distribution of that income. If the goal is to devise an index that is sensitive to both the level and degree of equality of capabilities, then we need to incorporate other information.

In recent years the *HDR* has begun to provide modified HDIs that incorporate measurement of some forms of equality. Not least, the *HDR* now presents what it calls a "gender-related development index", or GDI. This measure "adjusts the average achievement of each country in life expectancy, educational attainment and income in accordance with the disparity in achievement between women and men" (UNDP 1997, 123). When this adjustment is undertaken, we find that Ireland falls twelve places and Saudi Arabia thirty-three places from their respective rankings in the HDI, while the Czech Republic jumps twelve places and Poland, thirteen.

Systematic inequality in a country takes many other forms, tied as it often is to differences in class, ethnic origin, race and so forth. Under the principle of capabilities equality, these are all illegitimate. Our measure of a country's performance must also account for them. In the absence of good cross-national information on these matters, and insofar as all of them may be expected to contribute to national income inequality, we might take the latter as an imperfect but relevant proxy for these diverse forms of inequality. One way to proceed, then, is to weight each country's HDI by some measure of its relative income equality. A commonly used measure of relative equality is the ratio of the income share of the poorest 40 per cent of the population to the income share of the richest 20 per cent. The greater this ratio, which I will call here the "income equality coefficient" (IEC), the greater the degree of income equality.

Weighting the means-adjusted HDI by the gender coefficient and the income equality coefficient gives us what I will call the *"equality-means adjusted HDI"* (EMAHDI). The formula for the EMAHDI is given by:

$$P_i = \left(\frac{H_i}{A_j} \right) (G_i)(IEC_i) \qquad \text{(Equation 1)}$$

where P_i = performance, country i; H_i = the actual HDI, country i; A_j = the average HDI for countries in income decile j; G_i = the gender equality coefficient, country i; and IEC_i = the income equality coefficient, country I.[128]

There are many ways to measure income inequality other than the IEC presented here. One alternative is to focus on the share of income flowing to labor (wages), capital (profit), landowners (rent), and lenders (interest). The incorporation into SITS of information on this "functional" distribution of income might serve the purpose of discouraging firms from exploiting the international differences in wage levels which result from differences in labor standards. The idea here is to discourage governments from suppressing wages to attract FDI or to achieve good export performance, and to discourage firms from pitting workers across the globe against each other for employment and incomes. But we need to be mindful in this regard that different countries have achieved different levels of productivity. Wages that are low due to low productivity do not threaten higher wages elsewhere; nor are they normatively objectionable. What is objectionable is the case in which wages are suppressed through corporate power or government policy, to the benefit of firms that could afford to pay higher wages.

One way to penalize wage suppression is to incorporate into our index a measure of labor's share of national income. In order to make this adjustment, we might multiply each country's means-adjusted GDI by the ratio of "earnings to value added for its manufacturing sector", as reported annually by the World Bank. According to the Bank, earnings as a percentage of value added shows "labor's share in income generated in the manufacturing sector" (1992, 290). It must be emphasized that this weighting does not penalize poor countries for being poor, because it does not target low wages *per se*, but only those that are low relative to established productivity levels.

The formula for what I will call the "class–means adjusted GDI" or CMAGDI is given by:

$$P_i = \left(\frac{H_i}{A_j}\right)(G_i)(C_i) \qquad \text{(Equation 2)}$$

where C_i = earnings/value added in manufacturing, country i.[129]

A new trade regime

With this new index we can develop a multilateral tariff structure that rewards or penalizes countries based on their capabilities performance relative to their means. The social tariff between any two countries is determined by their relative index values: if Sweden earns a significantly higher index number (P) than Germany, Germany would face a social tariff in its exports to Sweden. If, at the same time, German performance exceeds that of the US, it would win tariff protection on US imports.

Let us use the first performance measure provided above in Equation 1 to devise a hypothetical global SITS regime. At present there are 82 countries for which the data necessary to calculate the EMAHDI are available.[130] The P values derived here approximate a normal distribution, and I have standardized these values by transforming them into standard deviations about the mean. This provides a simple (albeit by no means unique) basis for grouping countries into five social tariff bands (see Table 7.1).

Under this regime, a social tariff would be levied on the exports of a country when it exports to another country in a higher band. For example, a country that exports to countries in higher bands might face an *ad valorem* tariff (one based on the value of the product) of 5 per cent per band. Exports to countries in the same or a lower band would face no social tariff. For the purposes of establishing the SITS regime, the computation of P values might be based on a moving average of data over some multiyear period (say, five years) to smooth out the adjustments in trading patterns that result from movements between tariff bands. This would minimize the effect of short-term fluctuations in a country's performance, so that placement in SITS bands would be determined more by secular trends in performance rather than by short-term cycles.

The logic of the SITS regime is straightforward: *countries would be rewarded in global markets for making improvements in the conditions of social life measured and codified in the index.* This result is fundamental. Unlike under the emerging global neoliberal regime, in which a country can expect to be penalized with diminished competitiveness and capital flight for expanding worker rights (so as to improve income equality), or for policies that promote equal gender rights, it would instead win improved access in foreign markets for its exports. In addition, the SITS regime serves the defensive purpose of protecting workers and their communities from the pressures they face under global neoliberalism to accept lower income and protective standards in order to secure and/or retain employment. In short, the SITS regime turns the incentive structure of global neoliberalism on its head by rewarding those strategies that promote capabilities equality, and by punishing those that undermine it.

Table 7.1 SITS performance and tariff bands

Country	Performance	SITS tariff band	Country	Performance	SITS tariff band
			Moldova, Republic of	1.430	2
			Hungary	1.357	
Slovakia	2.785	1	Czech Republic	1.337	
Belarus	2.403		Slovenia	1.121	
Romania	1.736	2	Spain	1.120	
Ukraine	1.659		Sri Lanka	1.113	
Viet Nam	1.622		Sweden	1.074	
Latvia	1.574		Belgium	1.069	
Poland	1.553		Bangladesh	1.061	

Table 7.1 SITS performance and tariff bands (cont.)

Japan	1.019	2	Algeria	−0.427	4
Netherlands	0.982	3	Tunisia	−0.450	
Bulgaria	0.856		Morocco	−0.540	
Norway	0.764		Singapore	−0.562	
Kazakstan	0.726		Cote d'Ivoire	−0.591	
Lithuania	0.697		Peru	−0.596	
Finland	0.671		Nicaragua	−0.657	
Lao People's Democratic Republic	0.614		Uganda	−0.667	
			Thailand	−0.698	
			Costa Rica	−0.744	
India	0.490		Mauritania	−0.782	
Indonesia	0.447		Zambia	−0.796	
Germany	0.344		Niger	−0.812	
Denmark	0.342		Ecuador	−0.818	
Israel	0.337		Russian Federation	−0.869	
Canada	0.317				
Ghana	0.261		Nigeria	−0.869	
Italy	0.250		Honduras	−0.956	
Pakistan	0.193		Malaysia	−0.965	
France	0.172		Dominican Republic	−1.016	5
Egypt	0.098				
Estonia	0.092		Mexico	−1.052	
China	0.065		Lesotho	−1.052	
Tanzania, United Republic of	0.021		Colombia	−1.071	
			Kenya	−1.164	
Nepal	0.003		Venezuela	−1.186	
			Zimbabwe	−1.209	
USA	−0.048	4	Guinea	−1.250	
New Zealand	−0.108		Chile	−1.323	
Australia	−0.113		South Africa	−1.365	
Switzerland	−0.147		Panama	−1.405	
Bolivia	−0.177		Senegal	−1.411	
Jamaica	−0.226		Guinea–Bissau	−1.499	
Philippines	−0.244		Brazil	−1.588	
United Kingdom	−0.361		Guatemala	−1.593	
Hong Kong	−0.371				

Virtually every aspect of the SITS regime, from the calculation of index numbers, to the determination of tariff band groupings and the size of the tariffs, is flexible. Constructing a SITS regime necessarily reflects political and normative as well as economic factors and judgements. For example, in the SITS calculations undertaken above, the adjustment for equality was taken *after* the adjustment for means. This reflects the view that while a country's levels of welfare and educational attainment and rate of mortality are directly related to its level of income, its degrees of gender and income equality are not. Countries at any given income level can and do differ dramatically with respect to their degree of equality. But if we were to reach the alternative judgement that equality, too, is income-dependent (i.e., that it is substantially easier for a wealthy country to promote income equality), then the equality adjustments could be taken prior to the means adjustment. In this case, countries would be compared on the basis of their average capabilities *and* their degree of equality only against other countries of similar income levels. The formula for performance would then appear as:

$$P_i = \frac{[(H_i)(G_i)(IEC)_i]}{A_j} \qquad \text{(Equation 3)}$$

where A_j = average $[(H)(G)(IEC)]$ for countries in income decile j. In comparison with Equation 1, this approach on balance would boost the standing of countries with greater inequality in the final SITS rankings. Whether this adjustment is warranted on theoretical, political or normative grounds would likely be the site of some substantial dispute. Which (if either) of these approaches ought to be implemented, then – along with all other features of the SITS regime – must therefore be negotiated in a new and fully representative trading organization (see UNDP 1992).[131]

If we take the principle of inter-cultural respect seriously, then we should recognize that one key virtue of the SITS regime is its flexibility with respect to the manner in which a country increases its performance (thereby improving its social tariff position). A country can enhance its position by improving its national income, educational attainment, longevity, or gender or income equality. A composite index of this sort grants maximum latitude for progressives in each society to define for themselves the content of their political campaigns. Progressives in one country might push for stronger worker protections, while their counterparts abroad might concentrate on securing greater rights and freedoms for women (though these are by no means mutually exclusive). Their efforts in pursuit of objectives that reflect their own economic circumstances and social priorities would be rewarded in terms of the trading relationships facing their respective countries.

Critically, such a trading regime would begin to shift the burden in domestic political struggles. Labor rights activists would be able to seek new regulations without facing the objection that such measures would necessarily imperil the competitive survival of domestic firms or induce capital flight. At a minimum, a well-structured social index tariff would mitigate the effects of the increasing costs attending the new protections.

The EMAHDI presented here is but a first approach to an appropriate index. The basic idea behind the SITS approach can be broadened to include indices of environmental protection, political freedom, and so forth. These elaborations would be reflected in simple extensions of P. As with the gender and equality terms, additional indices further weight the means-adjusted HDI. The greater the number of terms, the less weight that each would have in establishing P, but the greater would be the flexibility granted to each participating nation in seeking to advance its relative position.[132] In a fully elaborated SITS regime, an increase in per capita income should have a lesser effect than other terms on a country's ranking, given that the purpose of the SITS regime is not to reward high income *per se* but to reward improvements in and equality of human capabilities. Indeed, we might extend the UNDP's approach of progressively discounting per capita income, and conclude that above some threshold additional increments should be given no credit whatsoever in computing P. This is especially true if it could be shown that such increases in per capita income and consumption in wealthy countries exacerbate overall global capabilities inequality. The SITS approach is not anti-growth, but neither is it indifferent with respect to the effects of rising incomes for the wealthy on the capabilities of the relatively impoverished. Nor is it indifferent to the means by which growth is pursued: capabilities-impoverishing strategies (such as labor suppression) would be penalized in global markets.

To be effective, the tariffs associated with a SITS regime must be substantial enough to penalize countries that perform poorly in terms of capabilities. To the degree that these are poorer countries, this is not a desirable consequence of the SITS, since its purpose is to encourage human development especially among those who face the most impoverished capabilities. But the SITS revenues could serve as a substantial new source of development funds that could be collected by an international agency and used for human and social development projects in those countries with low performance that are engaged in efforts to promote human development. In this way, the burden of the tariff would not fall disproportionately on developing countries. Indeed, for SITS to be ethically viable, the net flow of tariff-generated resources to the South must be positive and significant. One way to achieve this is to restrict the flow of these funds to countries with per capita national income below some threshold (such as some multiple of the world average), so that poorer countries would compete exclusively among themselves for funds based on their efforts to promote the capabilities of their inhabitants. Like the SITS penalties, these rewards would reverse the incentive structure many countries now face in the emerging global neoliberal regime.

The SITS rankings provided in Table 7.1 are no doubt objectionable on multiple grounds. Some countries that we have good reason to consider good performers do not do so well; in contrast, some countries fare

surprisingly well under the SITS ranking. On the one hand, we might properly infer from this that the SITS regime by itself is an inadequate means to
promote capabilities equality; indeed, we will investigate below just how the
SITS might be combined with (and complemented by) other policy tools.
On the other hand, we should recognize that the dynamic introduced by the
SITS is ultimately more important than the initial rankings. The SITS regime
provides the means and incentives for all countries – especially those that lag
behind – to improve their performance over time. As countries improve,
both the number of the tariff bands and the magnitude of the tariffs could be
reduced in order to lessen the regime's penalties and its impact on trade
flows. Finally, we should take note that a shift from global neoliberalism to a
SITS regime could and should be undertaken in phases. The first phase
would entail negotiation of the details of the SITS regime, including the formula to be used in calculating performance, the number of tariff bands, the
size of the tariffs, the means for distributing the tariff revenues, etc. A second
phase might entail an adjustment period in which countries would have time
to take steps to improve their performance. A third phase, perhaps beginning five to ten years after the completion of negotiations, would entail a
gradual introduction of the SITS tariffs. Moreover, the initial SITS performance calculations might include a term that rewards countries for their
improvements during the adjustment period. Countries that perform well
during this period might also be guaranteed a greater share of SITS-
generated revenues.

A SITS-augmented social charter

A SITS regime should be instituted alongside a strong social charter that
spells out the minimum labor, environmental and social standards that all
countries must adopt in order to be able to join a trading system. Indeed, a
SITS-augmented social charter rectifies the deficiencies of the social charter
approach. Under a SITS-augmented social charter, countries would be
required to meet the minimum protections detailed in the charter, as before.
Now, however, those countries wishing to strengthen these social protections
beyond these minima – or to promote and equalize capabilities in other ways
– would gain trade protection against other countries that did not take these
steps. Countries would therefore be rewarded for making improvements
(relative to their means) in the protections detailed in the charter. Moreover,
as the lagging countries improved their own standards over time in order to
close the gap with their trading partners – helped by the development funds
automatically generated by SITS – the terms of the charter could be more
easily negotiated to raise the relevant standards. Indeed, the charter could
contain the provision that as the lagging country improved above the charter's minima, the minima would rise automatically in step with its improvements. Taken together, the inducements to advance for leading and lagging

countries imply that the SITS-augmented social charter would generate dynamic improvements in social protections and capabilities over time.

The dynamic imparted to the social charter by a SITS regime has other important virtues. First, insofar as the SITS provides a measure of protection for higher standards countries, it might ease the negotiation of the social charter by allowing for less stringent initial minima. Second, in the event that the lagging country reached a threshold with respect to a standard that the trading partners deem sufficient – such as achieving a substantial degree of equality between men and women in incomes and educational attainment – the standard would be removed from the SITS regime as a source of tariff protections, to be replaced by a now-strengthened provision in the charter. *Ideally, over an extended period we might hope that the SITS regime would become obsolete, as countries converged on a level of capabilities that is sufficient, universally attainable and sustainable.* By then, after all, it would have achieved its purpose.

REGULATING CORPORATE BEHAVIOR

A second set of policy regimes would specify just what kinds of corporate behavior are legitimate in the pursuit of profit and competitive advantage. We will consider two regimes here: one that would establish a global corporate code of conduct, and one that would introduce a global, harmonized MNC income tax. Like the SITS regime, these would also remove certain deleterious practices from competition, so as to ensure that corporate behavior serves higher social purposes. Also like SITS, this regime would be multilateral, and would generate revenues to promote capabilities where they are most impoverished.

A global corporate code of conduct

We considered above Bhagwati's proposal for the unilateral adoption by the US of a Sullivan Principles approach that would require US firms that invest in countries with lower labor and/or environmental standards to follow US standards. We found that one of the chief weaknesses of this proposal is its unilateralism. This weakness could be corrected by the negotiation of a new multilateral agreement that would establish a *Global Corporate Code of Conduct* (GCCC). Under this regime, a corporation undertaking FDI – or establishing inter-corporate linkages (such as subcontracting relationships) with firms abroad – would be required to follow the terms of the code of conduct, and to ensure that its corporate partners did so as well. This code would therefore apply equally to all MNCs, regardless of their nation of origin. Any exceptions to this requirement, that might make allowances for firms based in poorer countries, would also be spelled out in the agreement (see below). The GCCC would ensure that firms undertook FDI for legitimate reasons rather than to exploit differences in employment and environmental standards; and it would reduce the incentive for nations to weaken their standards to attract or retain investment.[133] Moreover, if a firm finds it advantageous to relocate, it makes sense on efficiency and equity grounds that it should bear the lion's share of the adjustment costs imposed on the abandoned workers and their communities. The GCCC would ensure that it did so.

Advocates of the neoclassical vision oppose the imposition of global corporate codes of conduct for many reasons, some of which we reviewed in previous chapters. Another objection should also be addressed here. In the neoclassical view, if consumers place a high value on firms' behavior – that is, if their "ethical preferences" include views on how firms should behave – then firms will find it profitable to introduce codes of conduct *voluntarily* as a means of winning market share. In this view, sovereign consumers impose their values on firms by casting their dollar ballots in favor of responsible corporate practices.

This view is objectionable on multiple grounds. It presumes that consumers possess sufficient information to make responsible purchasing decisions. Given the complexity of inter-corporate linkages due to global outsourcing, this is a rather implausible assumption. It also presumes that each consumer, acting independently, will feel that her own purchasing practices will be sufficient to make a difference. But neoclassical theory itself provides reasons why this assumption is apt to be false. In the absence of enforceable sanctions, each consumer may rightly be unwilling to shoulder the higher costs of responsibly produced products because she knows that others may undermine her action by buying cheaper goods. Acting alone, her efforts will be in vain. Finally, many products do not reach consumer markets directly, and in these cases it is extremely difficult for consumers to affect corporate behavior via their purchasing decisions.

The notion of consumer sovereignty carries forward the agnosticism of neoclassical theory with respect to consumer preferences. In this account, corporate strategies are objectionable only if and to the degree that they arouse consumer revulsion. If they do incite widespread consumer antipathy, then an imposed code of conduct is *unnecessary* because firms will voluntarily reform their behavior. If they do not incite consumer antipathy, then a code is *unwarranted* because it does not accord with consumers' preferences. But just as we do not rely on consumer sovereignty to determine if slavery ought to be permitted in the production of goods, so should we not rely on it to determine whether firms act in a manner that systematically undermines human capabilities in other ways. Just which corporate behaviors are deemed legitimate has nothing at all to do with consumers' private preferences. It has to do instead with citizens' public values. These should not find expression only in market choices, but should inform public policy debate and, ultimately, legislation.

The deficiencies in the consumer sovereignty argument point to the need for a binding GCCC. The GCCC should spell out what is and what is not a permissible strategy for pursuing competitiveness, export performance and profits. Citizens groups, NGOs and firms must be empowered to file complaints against violators (nations and/or firms) before international tribunals that have the authority to levy substantial fines and impose other meaningful sanctions on offending parties.

A multilateral regime of this sort must address the question of the differential position of wealthier and poorer countries in the global economy. Not all restrictions that make sense in the US are appropriate in sub-Saharan Africa, or even in Latin America. In particular, small MNCs with home bases in poor countries often do not have the same means as wealthy MNCs to meet expensive restrictions. This hardly means that citizens in developing countries are best served by the neoliberal ethos of *laissez-faire*, however. The task of distinguishing those regulations and restrictions that are universally appropriate from those that are context-dependent (e.g. to which the claim of "regrettable necessity" rightly applies) is a difficult and contentious one, to be sure. Hence such decisions must rightfully be made multilaterally, with participation from broad sectors of the affected societies (including labor, human rights and environmental advocates, among others). Following the lead of the International Labour Organization (1998), we can safely conclude that there is never any justification, regardless of the level of national income, for forced or compulsory labor, the exploitation of child labor, infringements of the right to form independent unions and to bargain collectively, and employment discrimination. The regulatory regime must require these basic rights and protections as a condition of a country's full participation in international trade and investment agreements. Last but not least, the regime must also provide the means for poorer countries to improve their standards. We must therefore consider new sources of funds for this endeavor.

Corporate taxation and subsidies

Our GCCC must be supplemented by a new multilateral agreement that comprises a harmonized, global MNC income tax and rules regulating publicly funded corporate subsidies and other incentives.[134] Both neoclassical and heterodox economists understand that a mobile factor of production can often escape taxation, thereby shifting the tax burden on to relatively immobile factors. Under present global conditions, this means that capital has been able to shift a substantial portion of its tax burden on to labor (Rodrik 1997). Paradoxically, this shift in the tax burden from capital to labor has occurred at the same time that labor has become more susceptible to economic turmoil stemming from global economic integration, and therefore more reliant on state services. Hence, labor today is forced to pay an increasing share of the taxes that are required to fund the adjustment costs imposed on it by the processes of globalization. Moreover, local and national governments routinely compete amongst themselves for investment by providing firms incentive packages that reward them for relocating (or for staying put). It is noteworthy that the extremely orthodox Federal Reserve Bank of Minneapolis found it necessary to issue a report condemning the mutually destructive competition that has broken out among the fifty US states. The report's authors argue that this "war among the states" over investment must be stopped through national legislation that imposes controls over tax subsidies and other incentives (Burstein and Rolnick 1994). A global MNC income tax, combined with a global code restricting public enticements to firms, would prevent this kind of mutually destructive competition among nations, while shifting the burden of taxation back on to capital.

As with the SITS revenues, the proceeds of the global MNC income tax should be distributed on the basis of negotiated criteria that promote the advancement of capabilities where these are most meager. The tax revenues should also assure adequate compensation (in the form of income, training and relocation) to those workers who are displaced as a consequence of technological and economic change. Just as individual workers are affected by economic dislocation, so too are communities, regions and even nations. These revenues should therefore also be used to promote alternative community and regional economic development initiatives that are likely to promote capabilities equality, and to insulate these initiatives from the pressures of market competition.

LABOR MOBILITY

The law and practice of international labor mobility today could hardly be more inconsistent with the principle of capabilities equality. Today, those who are most capabilities-enriched in other ways are also endowed with the greatest formal and substantive freedom of domestic and international mobility. Indeed, mobility provides a particularly clear example of the interdependence among functionings, and of the manner in which inequality in one set of functionings induces inequality in others. If one is wealthy, one is fairly free to live and work where one likes, and to relocate at will in pursuit of greater income or wealth, or merely better cuisine or climate. If one is poor, one possesses neither the formal right nor the substantive freedom to relocate in search of greater income or wealth, health care or well-being. Instead, the greater is one's privation, the more one is constrained to the region one inhabits by accident of birth. Where the need for mobility is most dire, the barriers precluding it and the costs attending it are greatest. In short, we have managed to produce a set of arrangements that provides the resource of mobility most freely to those who need it least.

New international agreements do vary in this regard. The European Union has moved toward the full mobility of labor among its members (though it certainly does not extend this right to laborers seeking entry from beyond its external borders). In contrast, NAFTA represents the more general trend. NAFTA provides continental citizenship rights for the owners of capital. Corporate managers and investors can relocate their resources across national borders without restriction. Investors and those professionals deemed vital to corporate operations may also relocate relatively freely across national borders. But NAFTA is virtually silent on the matter of the mobility rights of "unskilled" labor, such as Mexican laborers who might desire to move north in search of employment. Indeed, in the case of the US, the passage of NAFTA was defended on the grounds that it would *reduce* the flow of Mexicans into the US. It is associated with greater efforts by the US Naturalization and Immigration Service to police the border separating the two countries. The proposed Multilateral Agreement on Investment also provides mobility rights to the owners of capital and key corporate personnel, but makes no mention of the mobility of labor.

What should be the alternative? The answer implicit in the neoclassical vision is certainly worthy of consideration. We have taken note above that one strong impulse of the vision is to divest national borders of their economic significance. Just as capital should be free to roam the globe seeking highest returns, so should labor. Economic efficiency, it bears repeating, requires that every factor be allowed to migrate to that location and function where its marginal product and reward are highest. While the neoclassical vision undertakes to show that capital mobility and free trade can serve as a second-best means to bring about efficiency in a world in which labor is not mobile, the first-best means to achieve efficiency would be for labor and capital to enjoy equal freedom of movement. With labor and capital both free to relocate, the neoclassical vision predicts a much quicker movement toward global equalization of marginal productivity for each factor, and a faster consequent global equalization of factor prices.[135]

When we approach this matter from the perspective of capabilities equality, we come to see that this formulation improves substantially upon current arrangements, but is nevertheless incomplete. First, equal formal freedom to relocate is not the same thing as equal substantive freedom to do so. Absent legal restrictions on international migration, we would still find it far easier for those with greater income and other resources to relocate in search of better opportunities. Those with least, who are most in need of relocation, must be provided various forms of assistance to make the right to relocate an effective option. Nevertheless, the elimination of legal restrictions on labor migration would certainly represent a consequential step toward the promotion of the capabilities of those who are presently worst off. Working toward full labor mobility for those most in need stands as an entirely worthy goal for those seeking global equality of substantive freedoms. That this objective cannot be achieved overnight is indisputable; but this fact does not provide license for us to discard it as a long-term goal. Instead, we ought to seek manageable steps that reduce political barriers to migration when possible, and that prepare the way for more dramatic reform in the future.

A second shortcoming of the neoclassical vision concerns its stand on the migration of those with greatest human capital and income. We need to ask whether the unqualified right of mobility of these people also serves the purpose of capabilities equality. There are good reasons to believe that it does not. Those with the greatest knowledge in sciences and technology, engineering, medicine, education, social policy and so forth may stand to make the greatest contribution to capabilities precisely where the financial reward for their services is least. In a world of perfectly functioning markets, in which the factor–price equalization theorem held sway, this would not be so. But we do not live in that world, as even the most ardent neoclassicals recognize. In the world we do inhabit, those with greatest human capital have both the ability and financial incentive to relocate away from those nations and regions where their skills are least concentrated. As they relocate, they may undermine the ability of those communities where capabilities are most meager to make substantial improvements.

Though it might be unpalatable today to say it out loud, we might therefore recognize that a global mobility regime that is consistent with the principle of global capabilities equality might afford greater mobility rights to those with least capabilities, while restricting the mobility of those with greatest human capital. We need to consider both how such a regime might work, and separately, whether such a regime is normatively defensible. We will consider these factors in turn.

Many countries do now or have in the past placed restrictions on the mobility of those with greatest human capital. Some countries have assigned experts to particular communities within their borders; others, in the name of stemming the "brain drain", have allowed experts to live where they will within the country, but have barred their emigration. Some countries also provide financial assistance for candidates seeking advanced training, with the proviso that the candidate work off this debt through service to a needy community. Virtually all countries have taken these steps (and more) during periods of wartime, when the national interest is taken to supersede the formal rights of the individual. These measures provide both precedent and some guidance for the formation of a global regime that is consonant with the capabilities principle.

One such regime might take the form of a *Global Convention on International Mobility* (GCIM). The GCIM would emphasize as a general principle the salience of the right of mobility as a vital component of an individual's substantive freedoms. The GCIM would nevertheless recognize explicitly that there might be trade-offs between the absolute right of mobility for the individual and the principle of capabilities equality, and that on these grounds the former must be compromised. These compromises should be temporary – that is, individuals with important skills may be assigned to live and work in a region where their skills are badly needed for some specified period of time following the completion of their studies, perhaps something in the order of five to ten years. After completion of this service, they would acquire the same level of freedom of mobility that is enjoyed by all others. The assignment of candidates could be undertaken by a clearing house that matches candidates (as far as possible) with targeted locations based on expressed preferences. Such a procedure is used in the US to place medical interns with the hospitals where they will complete their training.

Unlike most other initiatives of this sort, this regime would apply equally in wealthy and poor countries, and to those living in capabilities-rich and capabilities-poor regions and communities. It is not enough to limit the mobility of professionals in poor societies – to stem the brain drain – while leaving professionals in the North free to live and work where they please. The capabilities principle requires a global mobilization of physical and human resources to promote genuine global equality. On balance, we would expect a regime of this sort to lead to a substantial net outflow of professionals from the North to the South, but we would also expect a net flow within each of these two regions from wealthy to poorer regions.

Are the restrictions incorporated into the GCIM normatively defensible? Advocates of the neoclassical vision (particularly but not only libertarians) bristle at draconian measures of this sort. What right do we possibly have to limit individual freedoms (even if only temporarily) in such ways? The normative defense of this proposal has two components. The first is that if we determine that the principle of capabilities equality is indeed an (if not the only) appropriate normative foundation for assessing economic policy and outcomes, then we are warranted in devising social policy that places some restrictions on individual rights when these can be shown to promote this objective. This is just another way of saying that we have chosen equality of substantive freedoms over formal equality as our guiding normative principle. The second component might prove to be more palatable to neoclassical visionaries, as it identifies an implicit voluntary bargain at the heart of this regime. Against those who posit the isolated individual as foundational – as arriving on the scene with an autonomous set of preferences and capacities upon which he should be allowed to act without "unnatural" political constraints – I have argued above that the individual is shaped in powerful ways by the community he inhabits. The community not only shapes the individual's preferences, but (more importantly) also shapes his endowments and delimits the range of human capital available to him. As institutionalist economists remind us, the output of a factory and the productivity of an individual worker are fully social products – the results of the community's endeavors present and past which devised the norms, languages, concepts, technologies and know-how without which production could not take place. In this account, the individual is largely the embodiment of the community's investment rather than an autonomous entity who confronts society as an instrumental construction designed to protect his individual rights.

This notion of the individual as a social product is an abstract one, to be sure. But in the case of the training of professionals of the sort we have described, it appears quite concretely in the form of massive public subsidy. All countries with even meager means do now and have for some time promoted advanced training by shouldering all or at least a major share of the expense. Nowhere do students in higher education pay all the costs of their education. On paper, the US appears as an outlier in this regard, given the predominance of private universities to which students pay large sums in the form of tuition. Virtually all of these institutions are, however, quasi-public: their viability depends heavily on government subsidies in the form of research grants and numerous other forms of assistance. Even the most profitable of these institutions are designated "private non-profits", a legal fiction that exempts them from income and property taxation. Consequently, they receive vital and costly government services for which they do not pay. In all countries (including the US), then, each degree holder represents a substantial social investment that takes the form of her expertise and knowledge. As such, the community is well within its rights to require reimbursement for this expenditure – reimbursement in the form of the application of the resulting expertise to pressing social problems where these are most pervasive. Under the GCIM, a student in Boston or Bangalore considering career options would be apprised that certain choices will require reimbursement in the form of so many years of service in a targeted location as a quid pro quo for the community's support. Those who are unwilling to make this payment in labor service will be entirely free to choose another career path – or perhaps even to buy themselves out of this service via some substantial monetary reimbursement that fairly compensates the community for its investment and perhaps subsidizes the training of others.

The demand for global mobility rights for the majority of workers should not be interpreted to mean that migration is a panacea – far from it. While one can relocate financial investments without much disruption to one's personal life, relocating one's labor often entails breaking away physically from family, community and culture. Migrants often find themselves in a new locale lacking the necessary social networks and knowledge of local institutions, customs and language to live a full life. These problems can arise even when the migrants are officially welcomed; they are particularly acute when local law, custom or sentiment is biased against them. Moreover, their departure may cause significant disruptions in the family and other institutions of the community left behind. For these reasons, the GCIM must not be taken as an alternative to other policy regimes that would encourage the promotion of capabilities across all communities, especially those most impoverished. Instead, the promotion of migration rights is to be seen as but one of myriad substantive rights that must be ensured in a just, global regime.

Creating new global institutions

It hardly needs saying that these institutions could not be achieved today. Neoclassical visionaries are not apt to be persuaded by the arguments of this book. In addition, those advocating for even modest breaks with the neoliberal agenda may seem marginal, fragmented and powerless. And some organizations that oppose global neoliberalism seem to be in decline. Not least among these are labor unions, which find themselves today waging defensive battles in the North and in the South in the face of globalizing capital.

That these reforms are not immediately possible tells us little about their feasibility in the near future. Most major reform efforts in the past did not announce their own imminent arrival. Reform often breaks out when it is unexpected, disrupting institutions and other ways of being that had up until that moment seemed entirely secure. It is far beyond the scope of this book to explore just why this happens. Suffice it to say that the conditions which prove fertile to efficacious reform efforts are quite varied, ranging from periods of severe economic, social and/or political crisis, to seemingly tranquil moments in which rising expectations take hold. At any given moment, both of these extremes exist somewhere across the globe. Reform movements have also often proven to be extraordinarily contagious. This was true in the early nineteenth century, when communication of events abroad required the physical movement of people who could spread the news; it was true in 1968, when the press reported social protests across Europe as they occurred; and it is likely to be far more so today, when those militating for reform across the globe can and do communicate with each other directly and instantaneously (and even co-ordinate their actions) through the new communications technologies that have recently become widely available and are promoting economic globalization.

Achieving the kinds of policy reform proposed here would certainly require new forms of solidarity and co-operation among advocates of justice across the globe. Non-governmental organizations and activist networks would have to take the lead in constructing a set of proposals for alternative global regimes that might address the diverse needs of their constituents in the North and the South. They would then have to militate for the enactment of these alternatives in new multilateral agreements that would bind the world's national economies. They would also have to be represented at the table in multilateral talks that gave definition to these new agreements. This last requirement seems the most unobtainable today. But it would be a grave historical error to dismiss the possibility of it in even the very near future.

THE POLITICS OF CAPABILITIES EQUALITY

A Global Social Charter augmented with a Social Index Tariff Structure, a Global Corporate Code of Conduct, a Global MNC Income Tax and Subsidies Regime, and a Global Convention on International Mobility – these are offered as policy initiatives that better accord with the internationalist principle of global capabilities equality. Even were they to work as planned, they would no doubt be insufficient by themselves. But if we take the principle of capabilities equality seriously, then we must recognize that there may be no way of avoiding the difficult and radical kinds of change that they embody.

All well and good. But is this all that the principle of capabilities equality gives us – just one more utopian scheme for human emancipation that, though perhaps appealing in principle, is entirely implausible in practice? And in this case, ought we not recognize that the principle actually does little for us, as we endeavor to participate in the concrete political campaigns of the here and now?

The link between politics and policies is often sidestepped by those who propose radical policy reform on the one hand, and those who propose new forms of politics on the other. The former often give scant attention to just how the policies they propose might be achieved; the latter sometimes proceed as if appropriate policy regimes will come into view once we have installed an appropriate form of political activism and mobilization. There is nothing wrong with this division of labor, of course. But we need to keep in mind that the policies we can achieve tomorrow are largely the consequence of the kinds of politics we pursue today. Hence, if we are unable to specify a link between our long-term policy aspirations and our present-day political circumstances and capacities, then we have little reason to place much value in those aspirations. We can speak usefully of *policies* for the year 2025, but only if we can relate them plausibly to the *politics* of today.

I have advanced two normative commitments throughout this discussion – to anti-essentialist social analysis, and to the principle of capabilities equality – and I have pursued the matter of the policy implications of these commitments. It remains now to conclude the argument by indicating just what value these commitments might hold in the domain of politics. I cannot do justice to this difficult matter in the space that remains. In consequence, my arguments here will be even more tentative and illustrative than those offered so far. I nevertheless hope to show that these commitments do indeed provide a viable foundation for the kinds of politics that might be necessary to achieve the radical policy reform that the principle of capabilities equality requires. I will consider just two issues here: the manner in which these commitments help us to resolve the tension between "revolution" and "reform" that has plagued many radical political projects; and the contribution that these commitments can make to global solidarity among those seeking global justice.

Revolution versus reform

Political discourses that offer radical critiques of existing society typically distinguish between two types of political change – those that uproot and eradicate entirely the source of oppression, and those that merely ameliorate its effects. The orthodox Marxist tradition in particular has tended to distinguish on this basis between revolution and reform (Luxemburg 1973). In this account, only those political campaigns that seek nothing less than the total elimination of capitalism (and other forms of class oppression) achieve the status of revolution; and only these have a hope of emancipating working people and the poor from their bondage. Campaigns that seek something less than the overthrow of capitalism may indeed lessen the burdens for some who are oppressed, but they necessarily have the effect of solidifying the oppressive system that induces these burdens. They also necessarily shift these burdens on to others less able to defend themselves. On this basis, for instance, prominent Marxian theorist James O'Connor (1988) criticizes the environmental movement in the North for seeking domestic reforms that have the effect of displacing the burdens of environmental degradation on to the South. Without a complete overthrow of capitalism on a global scale, O'Connor contends, all environmental reform must lead to deepening eco-logical and social crisis.

The argument of this book has been advanced on the foundation of anti-essentialist social analysis. We have spent a good bit of time considering and rejecting the reductionism of neoclassical thought, in particular. But we can now turn anti-essentialism against those radical traditions that embrace the revolution–reform dichotomy. For this dichotomy too depends on a reductionism in which human history is interpreted as the consequence of some founding essence. In the case of orthodox Marxism, this essence is the deep contradiction inherent in class antagonisms, in which those who pro-duce the social surplus are exploited by those able to appropriate it (see Chapter 3). Orthodox Marxists are not alone in theorizing in this way. Other radical traditions posit alternative essential contradictions. For some reductionist feminists, it is gender oppression; for some reductionist envi-ronmentalists, it is humanity's anthropocentrism that induces us to treat non-human nature as an object laying ready to hand for our domination. In contrast to all of these modes of social analysis, the anti-essentialist view encourages us instead to investigate the overlapping effects of these diverse forms of oppression, without privileging any single one as the fundamental determinant from which all others are derived.

This anti-essentialism encourages us to reject the revolution–reform dichotomy on the grounds that insofar as there is no essential source of all oppression, there is no basis for privileging any one kind of political cam-paign as necessarily fundamental, true, or deeply efficacious – in a word, as revolutionary. Hence, there are also no grounds for demoting other kinds of political campaigns as epiphenomenal, false, or merely ameliorative – in a word, as reformative. Rather than undertake exhaustive battles over which contradiction is the irreducible source of all oppressions, activists can instead seek space for co-operation in broad campaigns for justice.

This reorientation in thinking has important political consequences. Reductionist theoretical formulations often have the unintended conse-quence of leaving their adherents overburdened and defeated by the appar-ently Herculean task of making revolution. As Katherine Gibson and Julie Graham (Gibson–Graham 1996) demonstrate, orthodox Marxism in n particular teaches those seeking the elimination of class oppression (in their view, an entirely worthy goal) that merely human efforts to resist capitalism must ultimately fail. Theorized as internally unified, all-powerful, all-determining and all-encompassing, capitalism cannot be effectively challenged except by a unified, equally powerful and global political movement that, armed with the uniquely correct social and revolutionary theory, unflinchingly seeks this explicit agenda. Those populating this movement must be eternally dedicated and courageous, uniformly right-minded, uncompromising and tireless. They must, indeed, be entirely virtuous and endowed with capacities we encounter only in fiction. Such a movement seems most unlikely to emerge – today or ever. Contrary to its explicit purpose of teaching us that capitalism can and must be eliminated, then, its overriding implicit message is that capitalism (and all its associated oppressions) is here to stay!

The anti-essentialist perspective produces a more manageable politics – one better suited to the impaired, mortal, decidedly non-heroic actors who populate movements for social change. It suggests that we can make consequential improvements in the world we inhabit at every site in which humans coexist – from the family, to the local community (and all its institutions) to the arena of global policymaking. At each of these levels, we can identify sources of inequality and oppression, and take meaningful steps to challenge them. In contrast to orthodox Marxian theory, whether what we produce as a consequence still qualifies as "capitalism", "socialism" or something else entirely is at best a secondary matter. The anti-essentialist presumes no endpoint to social experimentation, and so never ceases to explore alternative arrangements that might better promote the objective of capabilities equality.

Approached in the light of these anti-essentialist commitments, capabilities equality serves a dual purpose of holding out an ideal vision of how the world should be while providing direction for the real-world politics of compromise, give and take, and piecemeal policy initiatives. For those determined to retain the distinction between revolution and reform, we might then say that it demands revolutionary changes from our current institutions and practices, while allowing for rather mundane reforms all along the way. We recognize that any particular reform might enhance capabilities equality in some domain, while undermining it in some other – and that, as a consequence, compromises and trade-offs will be necessary. We recognize that this principle refuses to provide any neat formulas for deciding these trade-offs. Some might therefore disparage capabilities equality as a hopelessly imprecise guide to politics; I would offer instead that its open-endedness and flexibility better accord with the project of discovering new avenues toward human emancipation and equality.

Promoting global solidarity

The kinds of policy proposal that might be necessary to bring about substantial improvements in capabilities equality would certainly meet tremendous opposition from those who benefit most from contemporary inequality – and from those, like the neoclassical visionaries, who view global neoliberalism as the ideal form of economic and political organization. At present, advocates of neoliberalism dominate the most powerful governments and multilateral agencies across the globe. An effective challenge to global neoliberalism would certainly require deepening global solidarity and co-operation, especially among activists in the North and in the South. Absent such solidarity, it is difficult to see how the trend toward global neoliberalism might be reversed.

To date, co-operation between activists in the North and in the South has been hampered by often largely unexpressed normative conflict. For example, workers and their advocates in the South welcome the employment and income created by capital flight from the North. They argue, correctly, that workers in the South have the right to exploit these new opportunities, and that justice dictates a closing of the gap between living standards in the North and in the South. Labor advocates in the North resist the insecurity and loss of income that capital flight induces. In a world in which they have little control over the global or even the domestic distribution of income, corporate investment decisions, market outcomes and, consequently, their economic fates, they are right to oppose capital flight that devastates their communities. While activists in the North tend to promote harmonized labor standards as a condition of trade, many activists in the South resist these on the grounds that they are merely protectionist measures that deepen global inequality.

The principle of capabilities equality would seem to provide a basis for meaningful dialogue among people facing dramatically different sets of life chances. It embraces the notion that the gap between the North and the South is normatively indefensible; it therefore demands of activists in the North a steadfast commitment to the promotion of international equality and sensitivity to the particular needs of those who populate the poorest societies. It requires of them a response to capital flight, for instance, that extends beyond mere opposition that protects Northern workers. It demands that they couple a defense of the interests of workers in the North with strategies that simultaneously improve the lot of those far worse off. But it also demands of labor advocates of the South that they place the contest for jobs and income in a broader social, political and economic context, recognizing that capital flight undermines the substantive freedoms of those in the North who already possess least capabilities, and thereby exacerbates inequality there. They might therefore recognize that those harmed by capital flight have a normatively defensible stake in resisting the disruptions that flight induces. Together, these advocates might begin to explore new initiatives that promote global harmonization of capabilities. These would entail net transfers of investment, income and wealth from the North to the South, to be sure. But they would also entail increasing political and economic equality within each of these regions. In short, sharing a commitment to capabilities equality, they might find that workers in both regions could secure enhanced substantive freedoms via new co-operative campaigns that seek to construct new global policy regimes of the sort examined above. They might seek policy regimes that simultaneously shift wealth to the South while enhancing rather than diminishing economic security for workers in the North.

Endorsement of capabilities equality does not end political controversy. There is no reason to believe that all disputes among activists in the North and the South would evaporate were they simply to commit to this or any other principle. As we have by now seen, the principle raises as many new questions as it answers. But the principle might provide a framework within which productive conversation between activists from the North and the South can take place. Influenced by the principle, these conversations just might generate new strategies that extend beyond a zero-sum competition for the spoils associated with corporate investment. In the context of SITS, for example, activists would negotiate among themselves to decide just which terms ought to be incorporated into the SITS index, how SITS revenues ought to be distributed, and other key matters as a prelude to an aggressive international, co-operative campaign to secure and implement the new regime. Fortunately, dialogue and negotiation of this sort have flourished in recent years. Hundreds of activist groups and countless thousands of individuals across the globe have debated amongst themselves alternatives to NAFTA, the WTO and the MAI that would better serve the goal of global justice.[136] To the degree that the principle does induce such deepening international co-operation and solidarity, it will have helped to create the political terrain upon which the radical policy reforms it demands can in fact be realized.

Advancing a dialogical politics

We have seen that the principle of global capabilities equality is compatible with an anti-essentialist view of society and culture, and of human nature, rights and obligations. It attempts to incorporate moral objectivism's opposition to oppression with cultural relativism's respect for cultural difference. I have argued that this tension cannot in fact be solved. Rather, capabilities equality is offered as a means to manage the tension in a way that is politically and normatively defensible. I would now submit that this aspect of the capabilities principle also commends it as a basis for international solidarity. On the one hand, the principle demands that all people be provided equal substantive opportunity to live valued lives. It therefore refuses systematic inequalities based on race, ethnic origin, gender, class or caste, regardless of the cultural mores within which these kinds of inequality are inscribed. On the other hand, the principle does not deign to tell individuals or communities just what exactly a valued life entails. The principle itself allows for multiple specifications of what are to be valued functionings, and how these are to be ranked. Conflict will necessarily arise among those with distinct rankings, and in practice these disputes will need to be addressed. There is no reason, however, for every society to resolve them in the same way. From the anti-essentialist perspective, there simply is no meta-ranking against which all actual rankings are to be judged.

Capabilities equality provides us with a means to assess social practices in our own and others' societies. Without this it could not bear the weight of rooting out oppressions at home and abroad. It therefore provides us with the right to evaluate and criticize. But it conveys this right not just to *us*, whoever we might be, nor to *any of us*. It grants this right equally to *all of us*. And this implies that it demands of all of us a willingness to be judged by others who may carry distinct conceptions of what it means to live a valued life. This may be uncomfortable, especially for those of us in the North who have become accustomed to our status as the world's ethical police. We may learn that the pursuit of utility, wealth or power in our society is undermining the life chances of others in their pursuit of substantive freedoms. We may learn that our manner of transporting ourselves using energy-inefficient vehicles, domiciling ourselves in spacious homes or protecting our property rights (intellectual and otherwise) at home and abroad is deeply deficient when assessed against the principle of capabilities equality. Consequently, we may find legitimate demands placed upon us to alter our institutions and practices so as to further the campaign for global justice. If we are willing to embrace this aspect of the capabilities principle, then we are also apt to promote the basis for a genuine global solidarity of the kind that has proven up till now so difficult to build and sustain.

Finally, the anti-essentialist presumptions underlying this principle should induce a healthy degree of humility in crafting our political projects. This does not mean that these projects should be timid. It does mean that we need to be humble about the claims we make for them, and about our own political significance. Regarding the first, we need to recognize that policy reforms are apt to generate all manner of unanticipated and unintended consequences, and that the most appealing initiatives on paper may have to be jettisoned so as to minimize the harm they cause in practice. Policy enactment is therefore to be seen as a perpetual series of experiments rather than the unfolding of some grand plan. Regarding the latter, anti-essentialist premises would seem to call forth a transformation in the way political visionaries have tended to think of their relationship with those on whose behalf they advocate. Armed with the uniquely correct word or analysis, visionaries have often campaigned on the premise that "*you need us*" – that we can help you if only you would abandon your false consciousness and listen and conform to our teachings. This is the approach of neoclassical visionaries, to be sure. But it is also the approach of many advocates for economic and social justice, especially but not only in the North. Anti-essentialist premises lead to a very different view of this relationship, offering the respectful proposition that "*we need you*". We who seek a world of genuine equality – equality in peoples' substantive freedoms – need the help of countless others who may be doing just fine without us. We need to articulate the kind of world we hope to build, and ask for their consent and assistance. In the ensuing dialogue, we need to investigate just how our vision of a better world might articulate with their own, so that we might build a campaign that speaks to our respective conceptions of the good.

One last related point remains to be made. To adopt capabilities equality as a general normative principle for assessing economic outcomes does not preclude a simultaneous commitment to other normative principles. Indeed, no single normative principle can and should dominate over all others in adjudicating every policy matter. Moreover, we should expect that reasonable people concerned about distributive justice will maintain deep attachments to other normative principles, some of which require compromise with distributive justice (however defined). Surely, the principle of equal political capabilities – which ensures that people have the ability to devise the principles by which they will live – implies their right to revise, combine and modify normative principles. Rather than seek normative formulas that seem to end controversy, the anti-essentialist remains ever alert to new avenues of exploration and insights about how to theorize and construct more just societies.

All of this is foreign to the worldview and practice of the contemporary partisans of the neoclassical vision. For them, what is good and right is given once and for all by the interaction between our ineradicable human nature (our rationality) and the condition of the physical world we inhabit (its scarcity). For them, what constitutes a good economic outcome, and how this outcome is to be achieved, are equally decided. Economic science now provides the irrefutable blueprint for devising economic affairs. If only we would all learn its lessons and submit to its prescriptions – if only we would remove the final remaining obstacles preventing the ultimate and final perfection of global neoliberalism – we would achieve the end of economic history.

I have now argued at length that the neoclassical vision is normatively deficient. I have offered the principle of capabilities equality as a compelling basis for assessing economic outcomes and for devising new policy regimes. I have argued that alternative economic regimes are both necessary and available, and that the principle of capabilities equality might also help to sustain new productive conversations among advocates for justice in the North and in the South. These are ambitious claims, and I worry that by making them I have created a standard for judging capabilities equality that it cannot possibly meet. But I would hope that those advocates of global justice who would depose it as somehow inappropriate or deficient are prompted by this account to risk an alternative normative principle that can better answer the question, *"what makes for a good economic outcome?"*, and that can better serve the campaign for global justice. If my errors serve as stepping-stones for others to tread, then let there be many of them.

Notes

1　The phrase is adapted from Walzer (1994) who speaks of the "last philosopher".
2　In the essay by this title, published during the period of radical reform in the Soviet Union, Fukuyama (1989) argues that the Western liberal idea (comprising political freedom, democracy and a market economy) had triumphed over the contending ideologies of fascism and communism. Their demise signals the bankruptcy of non-liberal forms of state and economy, and hence represents a giant step toward the inevitable convergence of all nations upon economic and political liberalism.
3　Panitch (1994) argues correctly that the emergence of global neoliberalism does not represent an erosion of state authority or involvement in the economy, insofar as states have been the principal "authors" of this regime, but marks instead a shift in the nature of state mediation of economic outcomes. See also Polanyi (1944). We might therefore say that the present era is marked by the state-directed shift toward market mediation, in which the state continues to play the central role of shaping just what form "the market" will take and the character of market outcomes. We will return to this matter in this and subsequent chapters (particularly Chapters 2 and 5).
4　Polanyi (1944, 143) identifies the same response to economic crisis among economic liberals of the late nineteenth and early twentieth centuries. Polanyi contends that when confronted with an apparent crisis in the free market system, the liberal economist simply argues that the source of the difficulty is the "incomplete application" of liberal principles rather than any inherent imperfections in these principles. Insofar as no actually existing economy ever can realize the pure neoliberal ideal, this rhetorical strategy is and always will be available to its defenders.
5　The IMF in particular has advanced the crony capitalism thesis. See the *IMF Surveys* through 1997 and 1998 for its arguments. Some leading heterodox economists have taken issue with this explanation of the crisis, contending instead that it was the shift toward economic liberalization (including financial deregulation) that promoted the opportunities for investors to engage in risky and ultimately destabilizing activities. Chang (1999) makes this case forcefully.
6　These critics do not object to trade *per se*, but they do find trade under neoliberal rules to be harmful, particularly to workers with low skills. We will examine this matter systematically in Chapter 6.
7　Indeed, they argue that the degree of concentration of FDI is even higher than these figures indicate, since it is unevenly distributed *within* recipient countries (especially China).
8　For a discussion that examines the effect of global neoliberalism on policy autonomy, sovereignty and state capacity, see DeMartino (1999a). Here I argue for the importance of distinguishing among these three concepts when investigating the effects of global economic integration on the effectiveness of the state.
9　Though it is not the focus of this book, I should add that the alternative developed here also breaks in important respects from orthodox Marxism. Like neoclassical theory,

orthodox Marxism generates a "reductionist" account of the economy (to be examined in the Introduction to Part 1), and of the relationship between the economy and other aspects of society. For an elucidation of these matters, see Resnick and Wolff (1987a). Nevertheless, the normative position that is developed and applied throughout is very much in keeping with the normative commitments of Marxian theory. This will be examined in Chapter 3.

10   Actually, the matter of assessing a policy's impact is more problematic still; the discussion in the text presumes the legitimacy of a kind of cause–effect model of explanation that is predominant in the natural sciences. Different critics have made various arguments against the use of this model in social science. One is that the social world does not represent a "closed system" – both the social environment in which a policy unfolds and the agents who are its target change as a consequence of the policy, so that the *ceteris paribus* assumption is not so much a simplification as it is a distortion (Sayer 1984). A second, anti-modernist claim is that the theorist participates in the construction of the social and natural world through the process of theorization. Theory cannot then simply reflect or correspond to the object of analysis; it actually participates in its construction. It is not my goal to adjudicate this matter here. Rather, the goal is to note how fraught with difficulties is policy assessment (both *ex ante* and *ex post*), even if we take a more conventional view of social science.

11   It should be added here that all of these apparently empirical questions (questions of fact) are also theoretical questions. What, after all, is "unemployment", "meritocracy", and even "growth"? All of these are concepts whose meanings are neither obvious nor universal. Different theoretical narratives will yield distinct definitions of these concepts, if they recognize them at all. We will return to this matter below.

12   Summers made this argument in an internal memo for World Bank staff, which was then leaked to and published by *The Economist* (2/8/92). Summers concludes this thought with the following statement: "I think the economic logic of dumping a load of toxic waste in the lowest-wage country is impeccable and we should face up to that".

13   An extensive literature in the field of the philosophy of science now exists that addresses the matter of theory choice (and the related matters raised here). At one end of the spectrum are those who hold an objective view of theory choice and progress – relying most often on the notion of sensory data (the facts) as dependable arbiters. These include the logical positivists and empiricists. At the other end are those who view theory choice as a thoroughly socially-embedded process that is subject to all manner of contingencies and vicissitudes that are anything but objective. This camp includes some postmodernists, feminists, Marxists and others (see Resnick and Wolff 1987a; and Gibson-Graham 1996). In between stand those who recognize that theory choice is not an objective endeavor, but who hope to devise dependable rules that will allow us to discriminate between better and worse theories. For a compact presentation of a broad range of such perspectives, see the collections of essays edited by Latsis (1976) and by Lakatos and Musgrave (1970); see Caldwell (1982) for an assessment of the role of positivism in neoclassical economics; and Amariglio (1987) for a postmodern intervention into this debate.

14   Fuss (1989) provides a detailed and nuanced discussion of the debate over reductionism and essentialism.

15   I will use the terms "reductionism" and "essentialism" interchangeably when referring to the kinds of theory that comprise them. Though it is possible in principle for a theory to embrace essentialisms but not reductionism, and vice versa, in practice the two generally appear together. Reductionist theories are almost always founded upon some set of privileged essences. In contrast, anti-reductionist theory generally eschews essences.

16   Milton Friedman's essay "The Methodology of Positive Economics" (1953) is widely taken to have sufficiently established the separation of fact from value, thereby licensing the pursuit of objective economic science free of normative contamination.

17   Perhaps the most prevalent contemporary example is the way in which modernists and postmodernists dismiss the views of their opponents.

18 Despite their pragmatism, these economists are indeed neoclassical in important respects. By virtue of their training, they approach economic problems in a particular way. They recognize and employ the concepts and logic provided by neoclassical theory, rather than those of Marxism or institutionalism. Hence, their ultimate policy prescriptions are deeply constrained by neoclassical thought.

19 This treatment of neoclassical theory, and indeed much else in this book, is heavily indebted to the work of Stephen Resnick and Richard Wolff. Their account of neoclassical theory (Resnick and Wolff 1987b) stands as one of the most insightful discussions presently on offer, and I borrow from it liberally in what follows.

20 Indeed, the question is generally not even broached in microeconomic textbooks, from which the student is to infer that it is self-evidently not a legitimate question for economic theory. Here, as in other cases, we learn a good bit about a theory by exploring just what questions it does not ask. A theory's silences are not neutral – they often perform important rhetorical service by implicitly discounting those matters not addressed.

21 We will examine Marxian theory in Chapter 3.

22 In Bentham's words, "it is the greatest happiness of the greatest number that is the measure of right and wrong" (1776, cited in Harrison 1987, 226). This approach is entirely "consequentialist", in that it assesses social practices by exclusive reference to their consequences – neglecting the question of whether the practices are intrinsically right or correct.

23 Other objections to utilitarianism have been put forward by critics. One important objection concerns its "neglect of a person's *autonomy*" and its "lack of interest in a person's integrity" (Sen and Williams 1982, 5). Together, these omissions yield startling results. For instance, a strict utilitarian computation might validate the public torture of a person for sport because the utility that would thereby flow to sadists might more than offset the disutility to the hapless victim. Critics argue that the generation of such ethically perverse conclusions certainly invalidates utilitarianism as a *bona fide* normative framework. See Williams' contribution to Smart and Williams (1973), the contributions to Sen and Williams (1982), and Sen (1987) for a fuller discussion of these and related matters.

24 A substantial literature exists on the difficulties associated with assessing social states and outcomes in the absence of interpersonal utility comparisons, when preferences vary across individuals. Kenneth Arrow's "impossibility theorem" sketches out a series of reasonable conditions that a social choice mechanism should meet, and then demonstrates that no such mechanism exists. (Arrow (1987) provides a succinct discussion of the issues surrounding this matter, and the theorem itself.

25 The *potential* compensation test entails theoretical difficulties that are beyond the scope of this discussion. For example, Scitovsky demonstrates that the criterion could lead to inconsistencies, in which it is possible for each party to fully compensate the other (while retaining net benefit) under the policy option that it prefers (see Little 1957, 96–100).

26 Once we consider alternative normative criteria (in Chapter 3), we will have grounds for taking issue even with actual compensation (as neoclassicals define it).

27 There might be efficiency grounds for this redistribution, however. The inoculations might yield a healthier workforce that then generates increasing aggregate output. With greater total output, the winners might be able to fully compensate the loser (the billionaire) and still retain a net benefit. Alternatively, the inoculations might prevent negative externalities (discussed below), and so enhance economic efficiency. For instance, the inoculations might prevent epidemics that would reduce social welfare. Absent these findings, however, welfarism provides no basis for the redistribution. The implication follows that a neoclassically trained economist who seeks greater equality must concentrate on exposing the *inefficiency* (not the inequity) of existing inequality.

28 Note the universalist claims contained in the assertions provided in the question and the explanation of the answer. Making best use of scarce resources is the most important task of "all" societies; economic wants are limitless in "any" society. This universalism follows

from the reductionism of neoclassical theory, which critics find deeply objectionable. We will explore this matter in Chapter 2.

29   Neoclassical visionaries would contend that at least some of these cases, such as the infirmed, should be addressed through private insurance schemes. Knowing that (temporary or permanent) infirmity is a possibility, the rational agent will take steps to insulate himself from the resulting financial hardship through an insurance policy. Whether and the degree to which the agent invests in insurance will depend upon his risk tolerance, which is embedded in his own unique preference ordering. Hence, government programs that impose a defined insurance benefit in cases of infirmity will represent an inefficient allocation of society's resources. Moreover, publicly funded protections might induce "moral hazard"; that is, provide rational agents with an incentive to undertake socially harmful practices so as to qualify for these payments.

30   A market does not require money. In a barter economy goods are exchanged directly for other goods. For simplicity, I focus throughout on a monetized economy only, in keeping with the typical presentation of the market provided by introductory economic textbooks.

31   This discussion abstracts from a thorny problem in neoclassical thought – namely, how do prices change in a perfectly competitive market if all agents take prices as given and therefore cannot change them. Neoclassical theory attempts to resolve this problem by specifying the existence of a fictitious economywide "auctioneer" who announces hypothetical sets of prices, checks the quantity that would be supplied and demanded at that set of prices, and then determines whether that set of prices should be established. Only when a set of prices is discovered where supply equals demand in each and every market is trading actually allowed to occur. Hence, in this model, there never would be a price at which supply is greater or less than demand.

The reliance of the neoclassical model on this fictitious auctioneer to secure a fundamental conclusion of the theory (that markets will equilibrate costlessly and instantaneously) strains credulity, and substantially undermines the proof of the virtues of the market. Rather than prove that the market economy is well behaved and always finds the correct prices, this demonstration establishes quite the opposite. It shows, after all, that without some central (government or other non-market) authority to determine just when and at what prices market trading can go forward, the market economy will be prone to all sorts of disequilibria and instability. See Leijonhufvud (1968) for a Keynesian critique that builds upon these insights.

32   This is a simplification employed for the sake of exposition only. Technically, given that utility is measured on an ordinal scale, we cannot associate a particular level of utility with a particular magnitude. We can say, however, that a person will receive greater satisfaction from a good for which he is prepared to pay more than from a good for which he is prepared to pay less.

33   The same caveat applies here.

34   We ignore for the moment the existence of externalities. We will consider these below.

35   See question seven of the Minneapolis Federal Reserve Bank's (1998) "Economic Literacy Survey".

36   The remaining steps of the proof need not concern us here, but they can be found in any introductory microeconomics textbook, such as Baumol and Blinder (1988).

37   Though it is largely ignored in the neoclassical tradition, Musgrave has advanced the concept of "merit goods" as a class of goods to which alternative criteria of distribution should apply, rather than contribution. Neoclassical theory *per se* has nothing to say about which goods should qualify as merit goods, or which distributive criteria ought to apply to them. Answering these questions would require explicit value judgements that the neoclassical tradition refuses to make. For a concise discussion of merit goods, see Musgrave (1987).

38   For simplicity, I ignore here the possibility of a backward-bending labor supply curve (see Ehrenberg and Smith 1991).

39   Many conceptual problems that are beyond the scope of this discussion arise in this

context. Critics charge that production often entails complicated sorts of teamwork, for instance, and in this case it is not useful to think of the individual worker as having a certain level of productivity. As we will see in Chapter 3, institutionalists go one step further and claim that the entire community (not just those actually engaged in production) is responsible for the firm's output. In view of this claim, they reject the idea of individual productivity and, as a consequence, the idea that it should govern distribution.

40   This argument assumes that firms can gain a competitive advantage over their competitors – which contradicts the assumption of perfect information associated with perfect competition. This is not always made explicit by those making this argument (see the World Bank argument, quoted below). It is, however, explicit in what is called "new" or "endogenous" growth which assumes that firms have market power and so can increase profit through technological advance (see Romer 1994).

41   Hayek is a chief architect of the "Austrian" school of economic thought. This school rejects certain central neoclassical propositions, not least its assumption of perfect information. Austrian theory nevertheless generates a strong defense of neoliberalism. Hayek's work has been particularly influential among neoclassical and other critics of competitiveness policy (to be examined in Chapter 5).

42   Indeed, not every neoclassical theorist would make such claims. Following Milton Friedman (1953), some might argue that these entry-point concepts are merely productive propositions with which to commence theorizing. In this "instrumental" view, the choice of initial assumptions simply reflects a pragmatic decision, not a deep epistemological claim. The true instrumentalist happily replaces initial assumptions whenever a new set produces better empirical results. The manner in which neoclassical theorists have responded to critiques emanating from other theoretical paradigms, however, indicates that this instrumental view is not sustained in practice. Rather than consider alternative assumptions, neoclassicals tend to reassert the essences of neoclassical theory with particular vigor whenever neoclassical predictions seem to be disconfirmed. See DeMartino (1993) for an examination of this matter in macroeconomic theory; see Grabel (1999b) for evidence of this strategy in developing country policy debates.

43   Stigler and Becker (1977) provide a neoclassical rejoinder to the notion that marketing changes consumers' preferences, emphasizing instead the information (and other services) that marketing provides.

44   Beyond merely shaping preferences over commodities, critics allege that the market system actually encourages the kind of egoistic, self-oriented behavior that neoclassicals specify as a universal attribute of human nature. We will return to this issue shortly.

45   This is not to say that in the heterodox view preferences are irrelevant in evaluating economic outcomes, only that other factors should be accorded substantial (and indeed, far greater) weight (see Chapter 3).

46   Not all critics accept this distinction between absolute needs and relative wants. As many have argued, needs are always socially mediated. Even the necessity of food is interpreted differently in different cultural and historical contexts; hence any attempt to divide goods into the categories of needs and wants will run foul of intercultural disagreement. This view is persuasive. Yet, one need not endorse Daly's need/want distinction to grant the point that we can (and indeed, all societies do) distinguish among objects of desire in terms of the significance and importance that attaches to them in that social context. To say that an intense need is socially constructed (and variable) is not to say that it is not intense, and/or that deprivation of the badly needed object does not cause substantial harm simply because the need is social rather than "natural".

Having said all this (and putting semantics aside), Daly's way of distinguishing absolute needs from relative wants does provide one useful way of ranking desires in any given context, and it may be a normatively appropriate way of doing so where what we deem to be absolute needs are not being adequately met across all of society's members. We will return to this difficult matter of ranking needs in our discussion of Sen's work, below.

47   Sen has written widely on this matter. See the discussion in Crocker (1992), which brings together many of his arguments.

48   It is perhaps more accurate to say that some institutional*ists* (rather than all of institutional*ism*) reject reductionism. Like other intellectual traditions, institutionalism is internally heterogeneous, and comprises many distinct perspectives on central matters of this sort. Nevertheless, and speaking broadly, one of the features that distinguishes this tradition from neoclassical thought is its suspicion of essences and methodological reductionism.

49   I will refer to the alternative perspective here and throughout as institutionalist, and will not take the time necessary to identify and distinguish among the other related approaches that share its anti-essentialism. One deserves particular mention, however. The "anti-essentialist" Marxism that has evolved out of the combined intellectual labors of several faculty members at the Department of Economics of the University of Massachusetts and their many students has pursued the methodological challenges of anti-reductionist theory with particular vigor and clarity. Building on the pioneering work of Louis Althusser (1977), Stephen Resnick and Richard Wolff (1987a) established the concept of overdetermination as foundational to the critique of reductionist theory. In so doing, they broke with both neoclassical theory and with traditional approaches to Marxian theory. Today the journal *Rethinking Marxism* provides a forum for discussion of and debate over the virtues and pitfalls of anti-reductionist theory. A bibliography of the work produced by members of the Association for Social and Economic Analysis (AESA), the organization that publishes this journal, may be found at http://www.nd.edu/ ~remarx/Aesa/aesa.html. Having myself been trained in this tradition, I have come to be struck by the methodological affinities between it and "radical" institutionalist theory. Leading figures in the latter tradition include Veblen (1899, 1904) and Polanyi (1944), among many others. These matters are addressed explicitly in a symposium in the institutionalist *Journal of Economic Issues*; see DeMartino (1999b), also Dugger and Sherman (1994). The essays in Dugger (1989) provide a comprehensive introduction to radical institutionalism.

50   It is noteworthy that various studies of the attitudes and behavior of economics students have found that exposure to neoclassical theory makes students less co-operative and more self-interested (Frank *et al.* 1993). This result is not surprising, given that neoclassical theory teaches the naturalness and ultimate virtues of self-interested behavior. The related institutionalist point is that immersion in a market economy is likely to have the same effect.

51   They might also differ with respect to the kinds of "class processes" that produce the goods that are exchanged within them (see Chapter 3 for a discussion of this Marxian concept).

52   The reader may notice that this line of argument follows Rawls' recent *Political Liberalism* rather than the earlier *A Theory of Justice*. The latter presupposed a commitment by society's diverse members to a comprehensive doctrine predicated on justice as fairness, which Rawls was later to reject as inconsistent with the precepts of democratic society. In the later work, Rawls re-establishes the legitimacy of justice as fairness in the more realistic case where we have no reason to presume consensus around a comprehensive doctrine that incorporates justice so defined (1996, xlii).

53   The presumption of the commitment of these actors to democratic citizenship raises the question of the applicability of Rawlsian justice to non-democratic societies. We return to this matter in Chapter 4.

54   This emphasis on substantive as opposed to formal rights and freedom runs through all of the heterodox positions, as we will see.

55   Principles *a* and *b* require a standard of interpersonal comparison and hence the use of a cardinal scale. This return to interpersonal comparisons based on cardinal measure follows from Rawls' rejection of utility as the appropriate desideratum for assessing social states.

56   Radical institutionalists (such as Dugger) do tend toward strict equality, however.

57 This discussion is largely taken from Ramstad (1987), who provides a more nuanced and detailed treatment than is possible here. See Commons (1924).

58 The confusion about the concept of class for non-Marxists derives in large measure from the fact that it is contested within the Marxian tradition. Different Marxists offer distinct definitions of class, and deploy this concept in many different ways. The discussion of class in the text should be taken, then, as one particular view of this concept, most clearly articulated by Resnick and Wolff (1987a).

59 Much more detailed and precise Marxian treatments of feudalism and the transition from feudalism to capitalism can be found in Resnick and Wolff (1979) and the essays in Hilton (1976).

60 This idea is also contested within the Marxian tradition. For example, following Ellerman (1992), Burczak (1996–7) argues that exploitation occurs whenever workers do not appropriate the full social product that their labor creates (rather than simply the surplus). See the exchange on this matter in *Rethinking Marxism* (8/2/1998).

61 "The Roman slave was held by chains; the wage-labourer is bound to his owner by invisible threads ... In reality, the worker belongs to capital before he has sold himself to the capitalist. His economic bondage is at once mediated through, and concealed by, the periodic renewal of the act by which he sells himself, his change of masters, and the oscillations in the market-price of his labour" (Marx 1977, 719, 723–4).

62 The concept of justice has been widely debated in the Marxian tradition. Geras (1992) argues that the confusion can be laid directly at the feet of Marx, who both associated capitalist exploitation with theft, and argued that the wage relation was not "unjust". Geras argues that Marx simply contradicts himself in this regard. For present purposes we should note Geras' demonstration that Marx's attack on exploitation was deeply normative, and derived from a rather straightforward notion of justice. But, as Geras also demonstrates, Marx himself failed to generate more than a sketch of a full account of distributive justice.

63 Resnick and Wolff (1988) examine some of these issues in their examination of the nature of surplus appropriation and distribution in communist society.

64 Of course, these kinds of society generally redistribute some income from the wealthy (including those who appropriate the surplus) to the poor, through various public programs. In the Marxian view, these represent a return of a portion of the social surplus to those from whom it was illicitly taken in the first place. These redistributive measures may be essential to ensure social stability, especially when the level of inequality reached in a society is seen to surpass conventional views about what is right or just. But these limits are extraordinarily elastic, as is demonstrated by the relative absence of social protest against the spiraling global inequality of the past several decades.

65 It might be argued that the second of these contradicts or, minimally, renders unimportant, the first. After all, if social output is to be distributed according to need (ultimately), then why would it matter to whom the surplus flows in the first instance? Indeed, it is sometimes held that Marx treated these two normative principles as historically separable. Non-exploitation was to mark the advance to socialism, a way station between (exploitative) capitalism and (egalitarian) communism in which the principle of ability/need governs. I would argue that it is better (politically and theoretically) to investigate just what justice entails simultaneously in each of these three class sites. One of the virtues of Marxian theory is that it allows us to distinguish between these various economic activities. We would do well to avoid re-conflating them in a simplistic account of justice, especially one that treats one aspect of class as the epiphenomenon of one or more of the others. Each of the three aspects of class may be taken to be consequential in the lives of those affected by it, and in conditioning other aspects of society.

66 Sen has published numerous articles and volumes that explore the matters discussed here. The following discussion draws most extensively on his *Inequality Re-examined* (1992) because it is a fairly recent text, and because it draws upon and brings together his earlier writings on equality. This text provides both a good introduction to Sen's contributions,

and a thorough elucidation of the concept of capabilities equality. Except where otherwise indicated, all arguments reproduced here are taken from this work.

67   As Sen notes, we may think of a person's capabilities in a manner that is analogous to the way in which economists think about her command over commodities. Just as a person's "budget set" comprises the range of commodity bundles that she can attain, so does her capabilities comprise the full set of functionings that she can achieve (given her allocation of primary goods and other circumstances). Absent from the capabilities approach, however, is any presumption that a person will maximize her utility – or anything else. She may choose to starve herself (fasting for a cause) despite her ability to be well nourished.

68   Whether and to what degree this approach countenances instrumental inequality – like Rawls' difference principle – is a question we will explore momentarily.

69   This appealing proposition does introduce a temporal complication, one that is common to all needs-based accounts of justice. One's decisions today influence one's needs in the future. For example, one who chooses to smoke may eventually require greater medical care. Is the smoker's greater claim to health care ethically warranted? Should the smoker be insulated from the deleterious consequences of his own choices? Or, alternatively, is it legitimate for society to discount those needs that arise from "bad" choices? These questions must be addressed concretely in all needs-based systems of social provisioning. In practice, adjudicating this matter will depend upon judgements about the degree of volition involved, the extent of the demands on society's resources that result from bad decisions, etc., rather than on application of some fixed ethical standard.

70   Easier said than done, of course. Policy decisions are not always (easily) reversible. Moreover, insofar as people commit to courses of action based on previous policy decisions, reversal is not always fair, either. Hence, the claim to a unilateral right for those harmed by inequality to reverse course would need to be operationalized with some care, keeping in mind that it would not always be possible or appropriate. At a minimum, the legitimacy and feasibility of possible reversal should be debated at the time a policy that induces inequality is being considered, so that those voting on it can take these features of the policy into account. Notwithstanding this important caveat, the privileging of those who receive less under the difference principle in decisions about when the principle is to be invoked stands as a reasonable (if imperfect) defense against self-serving justifications for inequality.

71   As Sen notes, although this approach is generally taken to be anti-egalitarian, it is itself founded on an egalitarian principle in which what is equalized (its focal variable) is liberty. Libertarians would hardly countenance differential degrees of formal liberty, but rather demand equal liberty for all of society's members.

72   Cullenberg (1994) and Levins and Lewontin (1985) present careful analyses of this overdetermined relationship between society and its members. Both reject what they call "Cartesian" reductionism in which the parts (individuals) are posited as the pre-given ontological entities that then give rise to the whole (society). Cullenberg also explicitly rejects the opposite relation, which he calls "Hegelian" reductionism, which has been advanced by many (though by no means all) Marxist theorists. In this form of analysis, the whole is the privileged entity that determines the attributes of the parts. For instance, individuals are taken to be mere bearers of the roles (such as capitalist or laborer) to which they have been assigned. These roles then determine their interests, goals and behaviors.

73   "Labour is, first of all, a process between man and nature, a process by which man, through his own actions, mediates, regulates and controls the metabolism between himself and nature ... He sets in motion the natural forces which belong to his own body, his arms, legs, head and hands, in order to appropriate the materials of nature in a form adapted to his own needs. Through this movement *he acts upon external nature and changes it, and in this way he simultaneously changes his own nature*" (Marx 1977, 283, emphasis added).

74   It is noteworthy that the expansion of US MNC activity may ultimately place upward pressure on CEO pay globally. For example, the recent merger of Germany's Daimler–Benz with America's Chrysler Corporation has necessitated substantial pay

increases for the German executives to bring them up to par with their new American partners (*New York Times*, 1/17/99).

75   This statement entails a strong normative judgement that might not be shared across distinct social groups – say, by those without a commitment to democratic governance. Whether this statement then "applies" to these groups is the very problem to be taken up in this chapter.

76   Neoclassical theory certainly holds to this form of essentialism, as we have seen. In this account, human nature is taken to entail the ability to choose (and to transform nature) rationally. But unlike the moral objectivism discussed here, in neoclassical hands this essentialism provides the basis for a commitment to interpersonal and cultural relativism. We will explore this matter in Chapter 6, where we examine the trade debate.

77   The phrase is taken from Plato, who aspired to achieve this perspective so as to ascertain the eternal truths of human existence. It is no coincidence that other anti-essentialist theorists often refer to the objectivists pursuing universal truth as suffering from a "god complex".

78   Like Walzer, Rawls also presents his theory of justice as applicable only to liberal democratic society. Those in the original position are presumed to commit to the principles of mutual regard, in which each willingly grants to all others the same rights and obligations that she claims for herself. The resulting conception of justice as fairness applies only to a community in which this liberal conception applies, to a society of citizens who are "free and equal persons" (Rawls 1985).

79   See the essays in Nussbaum and Sen (1989) and in Krausz (1989) for insightful discussions of the mutual constitution of distinct cultures, and other matters related to the debate over relativism and cross-cultural critique.

80   This passage is cited by Crocker (1992, 602). See this article for a concise treatment of Sen's diverse writings on this matter.

81   As some Keynesians have argued, redistribution to the South (and especially the poor in the South) might also redound to the material benefit of the North if it increases global aggregate demand. See Mead (1990) and Greider (1997).

82   Indeed, the ability to live in a community of a particular kind (where institutions reflect one's functionings priorities) and to participate meaningfully in political campaigns to form such a community might be considered one of the central functionings that this approach would recognize. Were the capabilities principle not permissive with respect to institutions and practices, it would deny the vital functioning of self-governance.

83   Many of the policy proposals associated with this project concern trade. I will review these in Chapter 6. I will argue there that, though laudable, the proposals advanced to date fail to achieve capabilities equality. I will propose alternatives that build on the strength of these proposals, while correcting some of their weaknesses.

84   Though this is not true of all those who advocate competitiveness. We will focus here on a subset of competitiveness enhancers. As signaled by the term "progressive", these are those analysts whose support of competitiveness stems from concerns about the well-being of working people in the global neoliberal economy. Excluded from consideration, then, are management theorists and those whose primary concern is for the political and economic prestige, influence and power of the nation in international affairs.

85   These literatures are voluminous. On regulation theory see Aglietta (1979) and Lipietz (1987); on the social structures of accumulation, see Bowles *et al.* (1990) and several of the essays in Marglin and Schor (1990); and on long-wave theory see Mandel (1980). For a variety of such perspectives see the essays in Schor and You (1995).

86   For a detailed discussion of productivity and profitability in OECD countries see Glyn *et al.* (1990) and Armstrong *et al.* (1991).

87   For examples see Magaziner and Reich (1982), Adams and Klein (1983), the President's Commission on Industrial Competitiveness (1985), Lenz (1991) and the Cuomo Commission on Competitiveness (1992). Stokes (1992) surveys the various competitiveness councils formed in the US in the late 1980s and early 1990s.

88   For discussions of industrial policies in OECD countries see Zysman (1983), Curzon Price (1981), Hall (1986) and Amable and Petit (1996). For a discussion of industrial policy in East Asia see Chang (1994), Johnson (1985), Vestal (1993) and Wade (1993).

89   See Chang (1994) and Sawyer (1992) for alternative theoretical justifications for industrial policies.

90   This term is taken from a talk given by Joel Rogers at the University of Denver, December 1995.

91   For example, see Beje *et al.* (1987), Fröhlich (1989), Hirst and Zeitlin (1989), Cowling (1990), Hughes (1993), and the numerous OECD and EC reports cited in Montagnon (1990). Curzon Price's (1981) study of European industrial policy exemplifies this ideological transition.

92   For example, Cousins (a Labour member of parliament and spokesperson for Labour on industry) sums up the British Labour party's view on the revival of the British economy: "Building the basis for competitiveness and social cohesion is a task for the left" (Hughes 1993, 170).

93   See also Best (1990). Note that some critics charge that the advocates of flexible specialization err in their interpretation of the Third Italy – of its origins, desirability and the degree to which it can (and should) be generalized. For instance, Curry (1992) argues that the Third Italy is not at all the worker utopia portrayed by its advocates; that the trend toward flexibility generally occurs within large firms and concerns innovation of style rather than content, and continued use of de-skilled, casualized labor; and that flexible specialization is associated with labor market fragmentation which benefits a minority of workers and consumers at the expense of the increasingly vulnerable majority.

94   This entails giving pride of place to extra-market relationships and institutional arrangements that neoclassicals would identify as rigidities or sources of inefficiency. The essays collected in Matzner and Streeck (1991) make this point especially forcefully.

95   Cf. the arguments advanced by Marshall (1987), Best (1990) *et al.* (1990), Thurow (1992) and Bluestone and Bluestone (1992).

96   While the parallels between the corporate governance approach and the developmental state approach as pursued by Japan and the East Asian NICs are apparent in Lazonick's work, he does not envision a central role for state agencies. Instead, the state is to assume an accommodating role, while the chief impetus for reform is to come from corporate leaders once they come to appreciate the benefits of enlightened self-interest and inter-firm linkages.

Like most of the progressive competitiveness-enhancing literature, Lazonick's contribution appeared prior to the onset of the current Japanese crisis, and the apparent resurgence of US firms in many sectors. By the latter half of the 1990s, many observers were trumpeting the relative decline of Japan and the restoration of US capitalism. For those like Lazonick who had claimed the inherent superiority of the Japanese over the US model of industrial organization, this reversal of fates presents something of a problem. Presumably, they would account for the demise of Japan by reference to macroeconomic and political factors that have derailed the industrial sector. They might also (rightly) contend that many US industrial sectors that have performed particularly well in recent years (particularly high-tech industries) have adopted precisely the kinds of organizational co-ordination that they recommend.

An alternative explanation, one that is encouraged by Lazonick's own analysis, recognizes that *any* successful strategy lays the foundation for its own ultimate difficulties. Those with a stake in the system resist social and organizational (as opposed to strictly technological) innovations that may undermine their own standing or security. Hence, the Japanese model (which Lazonick extols for its flexibility) may have developed rigidities of its own by the late 1980s. In addition, insofar as particular models of industrial organization are institutionally embedded, substantial change may require deep and extensive social re-engineering, which may not be easily forthcoming. If this line of argument is correct, then we should expect changing industrial leadership to be the norm, not the exception. We should therefore be suspicious of those accounts (like that of Lazonick or neoclassical theory) that propose one model (organizational and market co-ordination, respectively) as the universally optimal form of industrial and economic organization.

97 See also Cutcher-Gershenfeld (1991), Magaziner and Reich (1982), Ehrenberg (1990), Freeman (1994) and OECD (1995).

98 For theorists in this camp, a progressive industrial relations system is the key building block for the construction of what is today called a "high performance economy". Appelbaum and Batt (1994) and Bluestone and Bluestone (1992) argue that a commitment of strong unions in co-operation with management provides the most progressive means to achieve restored competitiveness (cf. van Liemt 1992).

99 As we will see, this institutionalist perspective on appropriate market interventions as dynamically instrumental pervades the competition-reducing perspective as well.

100 Paradoxically, the neoclassical vision provides a better potential normative basis for defending competitiveness-enhancing strategies than does progressive nationalism, due to its emphasis on absolute productivity growth as the fount of prosperity. In the neoclassical view, if it can be shown that enlightened corporate governance yields higher productivity growth, then all countries can become better off by pursuing it.

101 There can be exceptions to this rule, such as when changing relative productivities harm a country's "terms of trade" (or the ratio of export to import prices). But these exceptions are taken to be sufficiently rare in practice (especially for large countries) as to allow us to ignore them in policymaking. As Krugman (1994a) and others have argued, the general rule is that an economy's purchasing power (its "command GNP") is tied to its own level of productivity.

102 Of course, investors make investment decisions in the light of existing information, which may be incomplete or misleading. Hence a potentially viable firm might fail to secure sufficient finance. But in the neoclassical vision, recognition of this possibility does not validate state intervention, because there is no good reason to expect that the state will have better information than market participants. Indeed, owing to the problems of government failure discussed above, we might expect the state to direct resources to the firms with the greatest political influence rather than the greatest market potential.

103 This insight provides the analytical foundation for the human capital approach, as we have seen.

104 The fate of the MAI changed repeatedly over the course of 1998 and early 1999. At present (May 1999) progress on the agreement is stalled, due to the decision of the new French government to pull out of negotiations. The MAI has been opposed by a diverse set of critics, including those who promote the rights of the state to pursue indigenous development strategies (especially but not only in the South); small farmers who protest its property right provisions; nationalists who see it as a threat to national sovereignty; and egalitarians (and others) who reject the rights and power that it conveys to investors. It now seems that the proponents of the MAI attempted to achieve too much too quickly, in a high-profile venue that was easy for opponents to expose and indict. It is a fair guess that the investor rights enshrined in the draft will continue to find their way to the bargaining table whenever new trade agreements are under consideration. But the vibrant activist networks that have arisen (especially in the wake of the expansion of the Internet) also foreshadow increased opposition to any further deepening of the neoliberal regime.

105 It is instructive that neoclassical theory does not present a strictly delimited set of conditions that must be in competition in order for it to yield innovation. Neoclassicals would not routinely condone the purchase of votes or human beings, or the purchase of the execution of the CEO of a rival firm, even though these practices might indeed induce greater efficiency. By removing these from competition, beneficial innovation is enhanced, not retarded (see below).

106 An example would be an immediate ban on the use of child labor in the formal sector in developing countries. *In the absence of other substantive measures*, a ban of this sort might be

expected to push children into the informal sector, where conditions of work and remuneration are arguably worse. This is not to say that child labor should be taken as a necessary stage of economic development that will pass automatically as a society grows more prosperous, as neoclassical visionaries are apt to claim. Rather, it is to argue that the state must implement institutional reform (in the areas of social welfare provisioning, public education, and so forth) so as to allow for the successful introduction and enforcement of a ban on child labor.

107 Unfortunately, the term "fair trade" has been appropriated both by international egalitarians who seek ethical trading patterns and outcomes, and by those who merely seek a "level playing field" in which firms from different countries enjoy the same level of government protections, subsidies, etc. For the sake of consistency, I will use the term "fair trade" to refer only to the former.

108 Indeed, prominent neoclassical theorists first advanced the rationale for strategic trade in the early 1980s. Since then, however, many of its earliest defenders (such as Krugman) have distanced themselves from its policy implications.

109 This is not to say that distributional concerns are entirely absent from these accounts. How the gains are distributed may depend in part on whether a coalition with sufficient political influence forms in pursuit of any particular strategic trade initiative (Olson 1965). But this concern has little to do with the normative matters with which we are concerned.

110 The exceptions to this rule are treated in all standard trade textbooks, and need not concern us here.

111 There is some debate over whether this compensation must actually be forthcoming in order for one social state to be deemed Pareto superior to another. As we saw in Chapter 1, Kaldor and Hicks emphasized potential rather than actual compensation in assessing alternative social states. Bhagwati laments the fact that following this lead, many economists today hold that potential compensation is indeed a sufficient criterion. Bhagwati disagrees, and argues that compensation must actually be paid (see Bhagwati 1994).

112 To say that the sources of comparative advantage are natural and given is not to say that they are fixed. The discovery of a new technology, for instance, might alter a country's comparative advantage directly – by increasing the relative efficiency of the industry in which the new technology is applied – and indirectly, by altering the input requirements of production. This insight has led some economists to conclude that the most important determinants of comparative advantage are established through human practice. But it has also touched off a heated debate over whether the state can and should override market signals through direct intervention in markets in order to generate particular comparative advantages. Advocates of industrial policy typically argue that state authority should be directed to this end. Neoclassicals argue instead that the market should be the ultimate driver of technological innovations (and hence, comparative advantage), as we found in Chapter 2. This debate has focused in particular on the East Asian economies which have grown spectacularly over the past several decades. In many of these countries, we find rapid growth alongside active state intervention in the economy. See the World Bank (1993) for a neoclassical interpretation of the Asian experience, and the critical responses to this report that appeared in a special symposium in *World Development* (1994).

113 To date, this debate has not yet been taken account of in orthodox trade texts. Krugman and Obstfeld (1997), Caves *et al.* (1999) and Kreinen (1998) are all largely silent on the question of policy differences and free trade.

114 Dorman (1988 and 1992) investigates systematically the issue of international policy differences in orthodox trade theory. He argues that this issue was initially addressed by US economists following the passage of the National Environmental Policy Act in 1970. The latter precipitated demands that the costs associated with the Act be offset through trade restrictions or other measures.

115 We will take note below of the one major exception to this rule discussed in the literature, which has to do with "political failure", as when an authoritarian regime imposes policy that does not accord with the preferences of a nation's citizens.

116 The essays in Bhagwati and Hudec (1996) provide the most extensive treatment of the matter of fair trade from an orthodox perspective. The other essays by Bhagwati included in the reference list also examine this matter, and make essentially the same claims as those found in his essay with Srinivasan.

117 I say "apparent" for reasons that will become evident below.

118 At recent official international gatherings on the environment, however, regrettable-necessity arguments have more commonly been advanced. For example, this view infused the 1992 UN Conference on the Environment and Development in Rio de Janeiro, and the 1997 UN Conference on Climate Change in Kyoto, Japan.

119 This is an area where free traders take great liberties with the neoclassical theory upon which it is based. Severe methodological difficulties attend the inference of social preference orderings, welfare functions and hence, policy choice from individual preference orderings. As Arrow instructed economists through what have come to be known as his "impossibility" theorems, this inference of social choice from individual choice can be sustained only by making a host of very restrictive and unrealistic assumptions about the nature of individual preference orderings (see Chapter 1). This warning is largely suppressed in the new debates over the role of domestic policy regimes in the construction of comparative advantage. Theorizing the nation as a unified economic actor with well-defined and consistent preferences allows for these problems to be sidestepped. But as we will see momentarily, Bhagwati and Srinivasan do address this matter in passing.

120 Whether this prediction of Stolper–Samuelson (that free trade will necessarily lead to rising wages for the unskilled in poorer countries) will be borne out in practice is a contentious matter. It depends, after all, on the reductionist, mechanical view of market price determination that we examined in Chapter 2. We took note of the criticisms of this reductionism above, and need not reproduce them here.

121 In this case, neoclassicals ought to consider endorsing equality not for its own sake, but because it is conducive to the full compensation that the normative principle of Pareto optimality requires.

122 We will examine one such regime in Chapter 7.

123 It bears repeating that once we reject the severe reductionism of neoclassical theory, we may discover good reasons for believing that a society with relatively more equality can grow as quickly as one with relatively less equality.

124 Chapman's proposals regarding environmental standards and trade are similar. Lebowitz (1988) develops a simple game theoretic analysis to argue the case for a social tariff, although in his view the tariff is a second-best strategy made necessary by the current inability of workers to organize internationally – for him the first-best solution. See also Ramstad (1987) for a discussion of Commons' defense of social tariffs.

125 For the sake of meaningful cross-national comparisons in income, the UNDP figures are given in terms of "purchasing power parity". This adjusts per capita income by taking into account the price of a standard basket of goods in each country.

126 The UNDP has experimented with the construction of a political freedom index, but has found the exercise to be fraught with difficult conceptual and measurement problems (UNDP 1992).

127 In computing this ratio, the two top deciles have been combined due to the fact that the second decile exhibited a mean HDI above that of the highest decile. This reversal is not terribly surprising, as it reflects the fact that a country's relative HDI performance is less dependent on income at higher income levels. This is because additional increments of per capita income above the world average are progressively discounted in computing welfare (as mentioned above), and because beyond a certain threshold additional increments of income are less valuable (relative to other factors, such as government policy) in promoting education and good health.

128 To derive the gender equality coefficient from the UNDP data, I took the ratio of the GDI to the HDI for each country. The greater the degree of gender equality, the higher this

ratio. This allows me to calculate the means-adjusted HDI prior to taking the gender and income equality adjustments. Alternatively, one could take the equality adjustments prior to the means adjustment (see below).

129   One important limitation of this approach is that manufacturing remains a small component of total economic activity in many countries. Hence, the information provided by this ratio is incomplete at best, and its use in SITS may generate counterproductive results, as Amsden (1994) has argued. Though Stephen Cullenberg and I included this adjustment in our earlier presentation of SITS, I am now inclined to think that it is better to replace it with an aggregate measure of inequality, such as the ratio of income shares described above. I include it here to indicate the range of possible ways for taking account of income inequality.

130   The 1997 *HDR* utilizes 1994 data to calculate the HDI and GDI. The income shares data presented here are taken from the World Bank's 1997 *World Development Report*. The Bank draws on national data ranging from 1985 to 1994 to calculate the income shares.

131   All of the performance equations provided here give equal weight to the *level* of capabilities and the *equality* with which these are distributed within a country. This reflects the view that relative inequality today plays a substantial role in depressing the absolute capabilities level of the impoverished, in the North and in the South. But were there to be compelling reasons to do so, the level of capabilities could be either more or less heavily weighted in calculating P. As with all other aspects of the SITS, the relative weighting reflects normative and political considerations rather than a strict economic logic.

132   It should be noted that the greater the elaborations of the P formula, the greater become the difficulties associated with identifying appropriate data and collecting it. These difficulties are not trivial, even when comparing levels of national income; they become more pervasive as we undertake to measure more complex indicators of people's substantive freedoms. Hence we may face trade-offs in determining just what variables should be incorporated into the calculations of P. Recognition of this difficulty also highlights the need for a SITS regime to arise out of multilateral negotiations in which those most affected by its implementation are fully represented, as discussed below.

133   Just what amounts to legitimate reasons for FDI would be spelled out as a consequence of the establishment of the GCCC. As the prevailing theories of FDI indicate (such as Dunning's "eclectic" approach), corporations engage in FDI for a host of reasons that would likely be deemed fully acceptable under such a code – such as proximity to markets, suppliers and critical inputs (see Dicken (1998) for an extended discussion of theories of FDI). The point of the GCCC is not to stifle FDI, but to ensure that it occurs for the right reasons and with the right effects.

134   The tax on MNC income discussed here is distinct from, but certainly compatible with, what has come to be known as the "Tobin tax". The Tobin tax would apply to all foreign exchange transactions (i.e., the purchase and sale of a nation's currency). The idea behind the Tobin tax is to reduce instability in currency markets – and in particular, to punish speculative activity in this market. For an examination of the Tobin tax, see Arestis and Sawyer (1997).

135   Sutcliffe (1998) presents a compelling "rights"-based argument in favor of open borders that is consistent with the arguments advanced here. See also Griffin (1998) for a persuasive discussion of the economic virtues of international labor mobility that emphasizes both efficiency and equity considerations.

136   To take just one example, activists across the globe contributed through Internet discussions to the document "Towards a Citizens' MAI: An alternative approach to developing a global investment treaty based on citizens' rights and democratic control", prepared by the Polaris Institute in Canada (Polaris Institute 1998). The resulting document was then debated and revised by a gathering of activist campaigns and non-governmental organizations from around the world in Paris prior to the OECD meetings of MAI negotiators in October, 1998.

Bibliography

Aaron, H.J. *et al.* (1994) "Preface to the Studies on Integrating National Economies", in R.G. Ehrenberg *Labor Markets and Integrating National Economies*, Washington D.C.: Brookings Institution.

Adams, F.G. and Klein, L.R. (1983) "Economic Evaluation of Industrial Policies for Growth and Competitiveness: Overview", in F.G. Adams and L.R. Klein (eds) *Industrial Policies for Growth and Competitiveness*, Lexington, MA: Lexington.

Aglietta, M. (1979) *A Theory of Capitalist Regulation*, London: New Left Books.

Althusser, L. (1977) *For Marx*, trans. B. Brewster, London: New Left Books.

Amable, B. and Petit, P. (1996) "New Scale and Scope for Industrial Policies in the 1990s", *International Review of Applied Economics* 10 (1): 23–41.

Amariglio, J. (1987) "Marxism Against Economic Science: Althusser's Legacy", *Research in Political Economy* 10: 159–94.

—— (1988) "The Body, Economic Discourse and Power: an Economist's Introduction to Foucault", *History of Political Economy* 20 (4): 583–613.

Amsden, A. (1994) "Macro-sweating Policies and Labour Standards", in W. Sengenberger and D. Campbell (eds) *International Labour Standards and Economic Interdependence*, Geneva: International Institute for Labour Studies (ILO), 185–93.

Anderson, E. (1990) "The Ethical Limitations of the Market", *Economics and Philosophy* 6 (2): 179–205.

Appelbaum, E. and Batt, R. (1994) *The New American Workplace*, Ithaca: ILR.

Arestis, P. and Sawyer, M. (1997) "How Many Cheers for the Tobin Transactions Tax?", *Cambridge Journal of Economics* 21: 753–68.

Armstrong, P., Glyn, A. and Harrison, J. (1991) *Capitalism Since 1945*, Oxford: Basil Blackwell.

Arrow, K. (1987) "Arrow's Theorem", in J. Eatwell, M. Milgate and P. Newman (eds) *The New Palgrave, Volume I*, London: Macmillan Press, 124–6.

Baran, P. and Sweezy, P. (1966) *Monopoly Capital*, New York: Monthly Review Press.

Basu, K. (1994) "The Poor Need Child Labor", *New York Times*, November 29, Section A, 25.

Baumol, W.J. and Blinder, A.S. (1988) *Economics, 4th edn*, San Diego: Harcourt Brace Jovanovich.

Beje, P.R. *et al.* (1987) *A Competitive Future for Europe?*, London: Croom Helm.

Bentham, J. (1977) *A Fragment on Government*, London: Athlone Press (originally published in 1776).

Berlin, I. (1958) *Two Concepts of Liberty*, Oxford: Oxford University Press.

Best, M. (1990) *The New Competition*, Cambridge: Harvard University Press.

Bhagwati, J. (1993a) "American Rules, Mexican Jobs", *New York Times*, March 24, 13.

—— (1993b) "The Case for Free Trade", *Scientific American* 269, November: 42–9.

—— (1994) "Free Trade: Old and New Challenges", *Economic Journal* 104: 231–46.

Bhagwati, J. and Hudec, R.E. (eds) (1996) *Fair Trade and Harmonization*, Cambridge, MA: MIT Press.

Bhagwati, J. and Srinivasan, T.N. (1996) "Trade and the Environment: Does Environmental Diversity Detract from the Case for Free Trade?" in J. Bhagwati and R.E. Hudec (eds) *Fair Trade and Harmonization*, Cambridge, MA: MIT Press.

Bluestone, B. and Bluestone, I. (1992) *Negotiating the Future*, New York: Basic Books.

Bluestone, B. and Harrison, B. (1982) *The Deindustrialization of America*, New York: Basic Books.

Bowles, G. and Gintis, H. (1990) "Contested Exchange: New Microfoundations of the Political Economy of Capitalism", *Politics and Society* 18 (2): 165–222.

Bowles, S., Gordon, D. and Weisskopf, T. (1990) *After the Wasteland*, Armonk, NY: M.E. Sharpe.

Boyer, R. (1995) "Capital–Labor Relations in OECD Countries: from the Fordist Golden Age to Contrasted National Trajectories", in J. Schor and J.I. You (eds) *Capital, the State and Labor*, Aldershot: Edward Elgar, 18–69.

Brecher, J. and Costello, T. (1991) *Global Village vs. Global Pillage*, Washington, D.C.: International Labor Rights Education and Research Fund.

Bronfenbrenner, K. (1996) *Final Report: The Effects of Plant Closing or Threat of Plant Closing on the Right of Workers to Organize*, submitted to the Labor Secretariat of the North American Commission on Labor Co-operation, September 30.

Brown, G. Jr., Goold, J. W. and Cavanagh, J. (1992) "Making Trade Fair", *World Policy Journal* 9 (1): 309–27.

Buchanan, J., Tollison, R. and Tullock, G. (eds) (1980) *Toward a Theory of the Rent-Seeking Society*, College Station, Texas: Texas A & M University Press.

Burczak, T. (1996–7) "Socialism after Hayek", *Rethinking Marxism* 9 (3): 1–18.

Burstein, M. and Rolnick, A. (1994) "Annual Report of the US Federal Reserve Bank of Minneapolis: Congress Should End the Economic War Among the States", *The Region* 9 (1): 2–20.

Business Week (8/19/91) "What Happened to the American Dream?" 80–85.

Caldwell, B. (1982) *Beyond Positivism*, Boston: George Allen and Unwin.

Castañeda, J. and Heredia, C. (1992) "Another NAFTA: What a Good Agreement Should Offer", *World Policy Journal* 9 (3): 673–85.

Cavanagh, J. (1993) "Strategies to Advance Labor and Environmental Standards: A North–South Dialogue", *Capitalism, Nature, Socialism* 4 (3):1–6.

Cavanagh, J. *et al.* (1988) *Trade's Hidden Costs*, Washington D.C.: International Labor Rights Education and Research Fund.

Caves, R.E., Frankel, J.A., and Jones, R.W. (1999) *World Trade and Payments, 8th edn*, Reading, MA: Addison-Wesley.

Chang, H. (1994) *The Political Economy of Industrial Policy*, New York: St. Martin's.

—— (1999) "The Hazard of Moral Hazard", a paper presented at a session of the annual meetings of the American Economics Association, January 3–5.

Chapman, D. (1991) "Environmental Standards and International Trade in Automobiles and Copper: The Case for a Social Tariff", *Natural Resources Journal* 31 (3): 449–61.

Charnovitz, S. (1992) "Environmental and Labor Standards in Trade", *The World Economy* 15 (3): 335–56.

Commons, J.R. (1924) *Legal Foundations of Capitalism*, New York: Macmillan.

Council of Economic Advisors (1997) *Annual Report of the Council of Economic Advisors*, Washington, D.C.: United States Government Printing Office.

Cowling, K. (1990) "A New Industrial Strategy: Preparing Europe for the Turn of the Century", *International Journal of Industrial Organization* 8 (2): 165–83.

Crocker, D.A. (1992) "Functioning and Capability: The Foundations of Sen's and Nussbaum's Development Ethic", *Political Theory* 20 (4): 584–612.

Cullenberg, S. (1994) *The Falling Rate of Profit*, London: Pluto Press.

Cuomo Commission on Competitiveness (1992) *America's Agenda: Rebuilding Economic Strength*, Armonk, NY: M.E. Sharpe.

Curry, J. (1992) "The Flexibility Fetish: a Review Essay on Flexible Specialization", *Capital and Class* 50 (3): 99–126.

Curzon Price, V. (1981) *Industrial Policies in the European Community*, London: St. Martin's Press.

Cutcher-Gershenfeld, J. (1991) "The Impact on Economic Performance of a Transformation in Workplace Relations", *Industrial and Labor Relations Review* 44 (2): 241–60.

Daly, Herman E. (1991) *Steady State Economics*, 2nd edn, Washington, D.C.: Island Press.

DeMartino, G. (1982–3) "Industrial Relations – Britain", *TIE-Europe* 13–14: 8–13.

—— (1993) "Beneath 'First Principles': Controversies Within the New Macroeconomics", *Journal of Economic Issues* 27 (4): 1127–53.

—— (1999a) "Global neoliberalism, Policy Autonomy, and International Competitive Dynamics", *Journal of Economic Issues* 33 (2): 346–9.

—— (1999b, forthcoming) "Anti-Essentialist Marxism and Radical Institutionalism: Introduction to the Debate", *Journal of Economic Issues* 33 (4).

DeMartino, G. and Cullenberg, S. (1994) "Beyond the Competitiveness Debate: An Internationalist Agenda", *Social Text* 41: 11–40.

—— (1995) "Economic Integration in an Uneven World: An Internationalist Perspective", *International Review of Applied Economics* 9 (1): 1–21.

Denver Post (10/4/97) "Unbridled Capitalism Runs Amok in Some Countries", Section A, 21.

Dicken, P. (1992) *Global Shift*, 2nd edn, New York City: Guilford Press.

—— (1998) *Global Shift*, 3rd edn, New York City: Guilford Press.

Dohse, K., Jürgens, U., and Malsch, T. (1985) "From 'Fordism' to 'Toyotism': the Social Organization of the Labor Process in the Japanese Automobile Industry", *Politics and Society* 141 (2): 115–46.

Dorfman, R. (1993) "An Introduction to Benefit–Cost Analysis", in R. Dorfman and N. Dorfman (eds) *Economics of the Environment: Selected Readings*, 3rd edn, New York: W.W. Norton, 297–322.

Dorman, P. (1988) "Worker Rights and International Trade: a Case for Intervention", *Review of Radical Political Economics*, 20, (2 and 3): 241–6.

—— (1992) "The Social Tariff Approach to International Disparities in Environmental and Worker Rights Standards: History, Theory and Some Initial Evidence", in C. Lehman and R. Moore (eds) *Multinational Culture*, Westport, CT: Greenwood Press: 203–23.

Dugger, W. (1989) "Radical Institutionalism: Basic Concepts", in W. Dugger (ed.) *Radical Institutionalism*, New York: Greenwood Press, 1–20.

Dugger, W. and Sherman, H.J. (1994) "Comparison of Marxism and Institutionalism", *Journal of Economic Issues* 28 (1):101–27.

Dunning, J.H. (1979) "Explaining Changing Patterns of International Production: In Defense of the Eclectic Theory", *Oxford Bulletin of Economics and Statistics* 41: 269–96.

Economist (2/8/92) "Let Them Eat Pollution": 66.

Edelman Spero, J. (1990) *The Politics of International Economic Relations, 4th edn*, New York: St. Martin's Press.

Ehrenberg, R.G. (1990) "Introduction: Do Compensation Policies Matter?" *Industrial and Labor Relations Review* 43, February: 3–12.

Ehrenberg, R.G. and Smith, R.S. (1991) *Modern Labor Economics, 4th edn*, New York: HarperCollins.

Ellerman, D. (1992) *Property and Contract in Economics*, Cambridge, MA: Blackwell.

Elster, J. (1982) "Sour Grapes – Utilitarianism and the Genesis of Wants", in A.K. Sen and B. Williams (eds) *Utilitarianism and Beyond*, Cambridge: Cambridge University Press, 219–38.

Federal Reserve Bank of Minneapolis (1998) "Economic Literacy Survey", *The Region*, December.

Fish, S. (1994) *There's No Such Thing as Free Speech ... and it's a Good Thing, Too*, Oxford: Oxford University Press.

Frank, R.H., Gilovich, T. and Regan, D.T. (1993) "Does Studying Economics Inhibit Co-operation?" *Journal of Economic Perspectives* 7 (2): 159–71.

Freeman, R.B. (1994) "How Labor Fares in Advanced Economies", in R.B. Freeman (ed.) *Working Under Different Rules*, New York: Sage Foundation, 1–28.

Freeman, R.B. and Medoff, J.L. (1984) *What Do Unions Do?* New York: Basic Books.

Friedman, M. (1953) "The Methodology of Positive Economics", *Essays in Positive Economics*, Chicago: University of Chicago Press, 3–43.

Friedman, S. (1992) "NAFTA as Social Dumping", *Challenge* 35 (5): 27–32.

Fröhlich, H. (1989) "International Competitiveness: Alternative Macroeconomic Strategies and Changing Perceptions in Recent Years", in A. Francis and P.K.M. Tharakan (eds) *The Competitiveness of European Industry*, London: Routledge, 21–40.

Frost, R.M. (1992) "Losing Economic Hegemony: UK 1850–92, US 1950–90", *Challenge* 35 (4): 30–34.

Fukuyama, F. (1989) "The End of History", *The National Interest* 18, Summer: 3–18.

Fuss, D. (1989) *Essentially Speaking*, London: Routledge.

Garrison, R.W. and Kirzner, M. (1987) "Hayek, Friedrich August von", in J. Eatwell, M. Milgate and P. Newman. (eds), *The New Palgrave, Volume 2*, London: Macmillan Press, 609–14.

Geras, N. (1992) "Bringing Marx to Justice: an Addendum and Rejoinder", *New Left Review* 195, September–October: 37–69.

Gibson–Graham, J.K. (1996) *The End of Capitalism (as we knew it)*, Oxford: Blackwell.

Glyn *et al.* (1990) "The Rise and Fall of the Golden Age", in S. Marglin and J. Schor (eds) *The Golden Age of Capitalism*, Oxford: Clarendon Press, 39–125.

Grabel, I. (1996) "Marketing the Third World: the Contradictions of Portfolio Investment in the Global Economy", *World Development* 24 (11): 1761–76.

—— (1999a) "Rejecting Exceptionalism: Reinterpreting the Asian Financial Crises", in J. Michie and J. Grieve Smith (eds) *Global Instability and World Economic Governance*, London: Routledge.

—— (1999b, forthcoming) "The Political Economy of 'Policy Credibility': the New Classical Macroeconomics and the Remaking of Emerging Economies", *Cambridge Journal of Economics*.

Greenawalt, K. (1995) *Fighting Words*, Princeton, NJ: Princeton University Press.

Greider, W. (1997) *One World, Ready or Not*, New York: Simon and Schuster.

Griffin, K. (1998) "Globalization and the Shape of Things to Come", *Working Paper* 98–05, Riverside, CA: Department of Economics, University of California.

Gunning, I.R. (1992) "Arrogant Perception, World Travelling and Multicultural Feminism: the Case of Female Genital Surgeries", *Columbia Human Rights Law Review* 23 (2): 189.

Hall, G. (1986) *European Industrial Policy*, New York: St. Martin's.

Hampshire, S. (1982) "Morality and convention", in A.K. Sen and B. Williams (eds) *Utilitarianism and Beyond*, Cambridge: Cambridge University Press, 145–57.

Harrison, R. (1987) "Bentham, Jeremy", in J. Eatwell, M. Milgate and P. Newman (eds) *The New Palgrave, Volume I*, London: Macmillan Press, 226–9.

Hayek, F. (1944) *The Road to Serfdom*, Chicago: University of Chicago Press.

—— (1949) *Individualism and Economic Order*, London: Routledge and Kegan Paul.

Helleiner, E. (1995) "Explaining the Globalization of Financial Markets: Bringing States Back In", *Review of International Political Economy* 2 (2): 315–41.

Herrnstein, R.J. and Murray, C. (1994) *The Bell Curve*, New York: Free Press.

Herzenberg, S., Perez-Lopez, J.F. and Tucker, S.K. (1990) "Introduction: Labor Standards and Development in the Global Economy", in S. Herzenberg and J.F. Perez-Lopez (eds) *Labor Standards and Development in the Global Economy*, Washington, D.C.: US Department of Labor, 1–16.

Hicks, J.R. (1939) *Value and Capital*, Oxford: Clarendon Press.

Hilton, R.H. (1976) *The Transition from Feudalism to Capitalism*, London: New Left Books.

Hirst, P. and Thompson, G. (1996) *Globalization in Question*, Cambridge: Policy Press.

Hirst, P. and Zeitlin, J. (1989) "Introduction", in P. Hirst and J. Zeitlin (eds) *Reversing Industrial Decline?*, Oxford: Berg, 1–16.

Hufbauer, G.C. and Schott, J.J. (1993) *NAFTA: An Assessment*, Washington, D.C.: Institute for International Economics.

Hughes, K.S. (1993) "Introduction: Internationalisation, Integration and European Competitiveness", in K.S. Hughes (ed.) *European Competitiveness*, Cambridge: Cambridge University, 1–7.

International Finance Corporation (1997) *Foreign Direct Investment*, Washington, D.C.: International Finance Corporation.

International Labor Organization (1996) *World Employment 1996/97*, Geneva: International Labour Office.

—— (1998) "ILO Declaration on Fundamental Principles and Rights at Work and its Follow-up", adopted by the International Labour Conference 86th Session, Geneva, June 18, 1998, *World of Work* 25, June–July: 14–15.

Johnson, C. (1985) "The Institutional Foundations of Japanese Industrial Policy", *California Management Review* 27 (4): 59–69.

Kaldor, N. (1939) "Welfare Propositions of Economics and Interpersonal Comparisons of Utility", *Economic Journal* 49 (195): 549–52.

Keynes, J.M. (1936) *The General Theory of Employment, Interest and Money*, London: Macmillan Press.

Khor, M. (1994a) "Controversy over Trade and Labor Standards", *Third World Economics* 87, 16–30.

——— (1994b) "Statement to the Second Part of the Fortieth Session of the Trade and Development Board on Agenda Item 3: Developments and Issues in the Uruguay Round of Particular Concern to Developing Countries", posted to the "Third World Network", May 3.

Koechlin, T. and Larudee, M. (1992) "The High Cost of NAFTA", *Challenge* 35 (5): 19–26.

Korpi, W. and Shalev, M. (1979) "Strikes, Industrial Relations and Class Conflict in Capitalist Societies", *British Journal of Sociology* 30 (2): 164–87.

Krausz, M. (ed.) (1989) *Relativism – Interpretation and Confrontation*, Notre Dame, IN: University of Notre Dame Press.

Kraw, G. (1990) "The Community Charter of the Fundamental Social Rights of Workers", *Hastings International and Comparative Law Review* 13, Spring: 471–7.

Kreinen, M.E. (1998) *International Economics, 8th edn*, Fort Worth, TX: Dryden Press.

Krueger, A.O. (1974) "Political Economy of the Rent-Seeking Society", *American Economic Review* 64 (3): 291–303.

——— (1990) "Free Trade is the Best Policy", in R.Z. Lawrence and C.L. Schultze (eds) *An American Trade Strategy: Options for the 1990s*, Washington, D.C.: Brookings Institution, 68–96.

Krugman, P. (1992) *The Age of Diminished Expectations*, Cambridge, MA: MIT Press.

——— (1994a) "Competitiveness: a Dangerous Obsession", *Foreign Affairs* 73 (2): 28–44.

——— (1994b) *Peddling Prosperity*, New York: W.W. Norton.

——— (1997) "In Praise of Cheap Labor", *Slate Magazine*, March 20, http//www.slate.com.

Krugman, P. and Obstfeld, M. (1997) *International Economics, 4th edn*, Reading, MA: Addison-Wesley.

Laclau, E. and Mouffe, C. (1985) *Hegemony and Socialist Strategy*, London: Verso.

Lakatos, I. and Musgrave, A. (eds) (1970) *Criticism and the Growth of Knowledge*, Cambridge: Cambridge University Press.

Lange, P. (1993) "Maastricht and the Social Protocol: Why Did They Do It?" *Politics and Society* 21 (1): 5–36.

Latsis, S.J. (ed.) (1976) *Method and Appraisal in Economics*, Cambridge: Cambridge University Press.

Lazonick, W. (1991) *Business Organization and the Myth of the Market Economy*, Cambridge: Cambridge University Press.

Lebowitz, M. (1988) "Trade and Class: Labor Strategies in a World of Strong Capital", *Studies in Political Economy* 27 (3): 137–48.

Leijonhufvud, A. (1968) *On Keynesian Economics and the Economics of Keynes*, Oxford: Oxford University Press.

Lenz, A.J. (1991) *Beyond Blue Horizons*, New York: Praeger.

Levins, R. and Lewontin, R. (1985) *The Dialectical Biologist*, Cambridge: Harvard University Press.

Lipietz, A. (1987) *Mirages and Miracles*, London: Verso.

Little, I.M.D. (1957) *A Critique of Welfare Economics, 2nd edn*, Oxford: Clarendon Press.

Locke, J. (1690) *Two Treatises on Government, 2nd edn,* P. Laslett (ed.) Cambridge: Cambridge University Press.

Luxemburg, R. (1973) *Reform or Revolution,* New York: Pathfinder.

Lynch, L.M. (1994) "Payoffs to Alternative Training Strategies at Work", in R.B. Freeman (ed.) *Working Under Different Rules,* New York: Sage Foundation, 63–96.

McCloskey, D.N. (1993) "Competitiveness and the Anti-Economics of Decline", in D.N. McCloskey (ed.) *Second Thoughts,* Oxford: Oxford University, 167–73.

McKenzie, R.B. (1981) "The Case for Plant Closures", *Policy Review* 15, Winter: 119–34.

MacKinnon, C.A. (1993) *Only Words,* Cambridge: Cambridge University Press.

McKinnon, R. (1991) *The Order of Economic Liberalization,* Baltimore: John Hopkins University Press.

MacPherson, C.B. (1962) *The Political Theory of Possessive Individualism,* Oxford: Oxford University Press.

Magaziner, I. and Reich, R. (1982) *Minding America's Business,* New York: Harcourt Brace Jovanovich.

Mandel, E. (1980) *Long Waves of Capitalist Development,* Cambridge: Cambridge University Press.

Mansbridge, J. (1990) *Beyond Self-interest,* Chicago: Chicago University Press.

Marglin, S. and Schor, J. (eds) (1990) *The Golden Age of Capitalism,* Oxford: Clarendon.

Marshall, R. (1987) *Unheard Voices,* New York: Basic Books.

Marx, K. (1938) *Critique of the Gotha Program,* New York: International Publishers.

—— (1977) *Capital, Volume I,* New York: Vintage Books.

Matilal, B.K. (1989) "Ethical Relativism and Confrontation of Cultures" in M. Krausz (ed.) *Relativism-Interpretation and Confrontation,* Notre Dame, IN: Notre Dame Press, 339–62.

Matzner, E. and Streeck, W. (eds) (1991) *Beyond Keynesianism,* Aldershot, UK: Edward Elgar.

Mead, W.R. (1990) *The Low Wage Challenge to Global Growth,* Washington, D.C.: Economic Policy Institute.

Milton, D. (1982) *The Politics of US Labor,* New York: Monthly Review Press.

Mishel, L., Bernstein, J. and Schmitt, J. (1999) *The State of Working America, 1998–99,* Ithaca, NY: Cornell University Press.

Mishel, L. and Voos, P. (1992) "Introduction", in L. Mishel and P. Voos (eds) *Unions and Economic Competitiveness,* Armonk, NY: M.E. Sharpe, 1–12.

Montagnon, P. (ed.) (1990) *European Competition Policy,* New York: Council on Foreign Affairs.

Musgrave, R.A (1987) "Merit Goods", in J. Eatwell, M. Milgate and P. Newman (eds), *The New Palgrave, Volume 3,* London: Macmillan Press, 452–3.

Newsweek (7/31/95) "Special Report: The Rise of the Overclass", 32–46.

New York Times (11/17/91) "Trapped in the Impoverished Middle Class", Business Section, 1.

—— (9/20/98) "Experts Question Roving Flow of Global Capital", Section 1, 18.

—— (1/17/99) "American Pay Rattles Foreign Partners", Section 4, 1.

—— (2/7/99) "Pressing the Issue of Pay Inequality", Business Section, 11.

Nussbaum, M. (1992) "Human Functioning and Social Justice: In Defense of Aristotelian Essentialism", *Political Theory* 20 (2): 202–46.

Nussbaum, M. and Sen, A.K. (eds) (1989) *The Quality of Life*, Oxford: Clarendon Press.

Nozick, R. (1974) *Anarchy, State and Utopia*, New York: Basic Books.

O'Connor, J. (1988) "Capitalism, Nature, Socialism: A Theoretical Introduction", *Capitalism, Nature, Socialism* 1 (1): 11–38.

Organization for Economic Co-operation and Development (OECD) (1995) *Employment Outlook*, Paris: OECD.

—— (1996) *Job Creation and Loss*, Paris: OECD.

—— (1997) *Employment Outlook*, Paris: OECD.

Olson, M. (1965) *The Logic of Collective Action*, Cambridge, MA: Harvard University Press.

Panitch, L. (1994) "Globalization and the State", in R. Miliband and L. Panitch (eds) *The Socialist Register*, London: The Merlin Press, 60–93.

Parker, R. (1994) *Flesh Peddlers and Warm Bodies*, New Brunswick, NJ: Rutgers University Press.

Perez-Lopez, J. (1988) "Conditioning Trade on Foreign Labor Law: the U.S. Approach", *Comparative Labor Law Journal* 9 (2): 253–92.

—— (1990) "Worker Rights in the US Omnibus Trade and Competitiveness Act", *Labor Law Journal* 41 (4): 222–34.

Piore, M. (1990) "Labor Standards and Business Strategies" in S. Herzenberg and J.F. Perez-Lopez, (eds) *Labor Standards and Development in the Global Economy*, Washington, D.C.: US Department of Labor, 35–49.

Piore, M. and Sabel, C. (1984) *The Second Industrial Divide*, New York: Basic Books.

Polanyi, K. (1944) *The Great Transformation*, New York: Rinehart and Co.

Polaris Institute (1998) "Towards a Citizens' MAI: an Alternative Approach to Developing a Global Investment Treaty Based on Citizens' Rights and Democratic Control", 502–151 Slater Street, Ottawa, Ontario, K1P 5H3.

Porter, M. (1990) *The Competitive Advantage of Nations*, New York: Free Press.

President's Commission on Industrial Competitiveness (1985) *Global Competition: The New Reality, Volume II*, Washington, D.C.: US Government.

Prowse, M. (1992) "Is America in Decline?" *Harvard Business Review* 70 (4): 34–45.

Raghavan, C. (1993) "Developing Nations Oppose Protectionist Eco-concepts", *Third World Economics* 73: 2–5.

Ramstad, Y. (1987) "Free Trade Versus Fair Trade: Import Barriers as a Problem of Reasonable Value", *Journal of Economic Issues* 21 (1): 5–32.

Rassell, E., Bluestone, B. and Mishel, L. (1997) *The Prosperity Gap*, Washington, D.C.: Economic Policy Institute.

Rawls, J. (1971) *A Theory of Justice*, Cambridge, MA: Harvard University Press.

—— (1985) "Justice as Fairness: Political, not Metaphysical", *Philosophy and Public Affairs* 14 (3): 223–51.

—— (1996) *Political Liberalism*, New York: Columbia University Press.

Reich, R.B. (1990a) "Who is Us?" *Harvard Business Review* 68, January–February: 53–64.

—— (1990b) "We Need a Strategic Trade Policy", *Challenge*, July–August: 38–42.

—— (1991) *The Work of Nations*, New York: Knopf.

Resnick, S. and Wolff, R. (1979) "The Theory of Transitional Conjunctures and the Transition from Feudalism to Capitalism in Western Europe", *Review of Radical Political Economics* 11 (3): 3–22.

—— (1987a) *Knowledge and Class*, Chicago: Chicago University Press.

—— (1987b) *Economics – Marxian Versus Neoclassical*, Baltimore, MD: Johns Hopkins University Press.

—— (1988) "Communism: Between Class and Classless", *Rethinking Marxism* 1 (1): 14–48.

Robbins, L. (1938) "Interpersonal Comparisons of Utility: a Comment", *Economic Journal* 48 (192): 635–41.

Rodrik, D. (1997) *Has Globalization Gone Too Far?*, Washington, D.C.: Institute for International Economics.

Roemer, J.E. (1988) *Free to Lose*, Cambridge: Harvard University Press.

Romer, P.M. (1994) "The Origins of Endogenous Growth Theory", *The Journal of Economic Perspectives* 8, Winter: 3–22.

Rothstein, R. (1993) "Setting the Standard: International Labor Rights and US Trade Policy", *Briefing Paper*, Washington D.C.: Economic Policy Institute.

Sagoff, M. (1988) *The Economy of the Earth*, New York: Cambridge University Press.

Sawyer, M. (1991) "Industrial Policy", in M. Artis and D. Cobhan (eds) *Labour's Economic Policies, 1974–79*, Manchester: Manchester University Press, 158–75.

—— (1992) "Reflections on the Nature and Role of Industrial Policy", *Metroeconomica* 43 (1–2): 51–73.

Sayer, A. (1984) *Method in Social Science*, London: Hutchinson.

Schor, J. and You, J.I. (eds) (1995) *Capital, the State and Labor*, Aldershot: Edward Elgar.

Sen, A.K. (1977) "Rational Fools: a Critique of the Behavioral Foundations of Economic Theory", *Philosophy and Public Affairs* 6 (6): 317–44.

—— (1987) *On Ethics and Economics*, Oxford: Basil Blackwell.

—— (1990) "Gender and Co-operative Conflicts", in I. Tinker (ed.) *Persistent Inequalities*, Oxford: Oxford University Press, 123–49.

—— (1992) *Inequality Re-examined*, Cambridge, MA: Harvard University Press.

Sen, A.K. and Williams, B. (eds) (1982) *Utilitarianism and Beyond*, Cambridge: Cambridge University Press.

Seneca, J.J. and Taussig, M.K. (1984) *Environmental Economics*, 3rd edn, Englewood, NJ: Prentice-Hall.

Shrybman, S. (1991–2) "Trading Away the Environment", *World Policy Journal* 9, Winter: 93–110.

Silvia, S. (1991) "The Social Charter of the European Community: a Defeat for European Labor", *Industrial and Labor Relations Review* 44 (4): 626–41.

Smart, J.J.C. and Williams, B. (1973) *Utilitarianism – For and Against*, Cambridge: Cambridge University Press.

Smith, A. (1982) *The Wealth of Nations*, New York: Penguin Books (originally published in 1776).

Stanfield, J.R. (1996) *John Kenneth Galbraith*, New York: St. Martin's Press.

Steil, B. (1994) "'Social Correctness' is the New Protectionism", *Foreign Affairs* January/February: 14–20.

Stigler, G.J. (1975) "Smith's Travel on the Ship of the State", in A.S. Skinner and T. Wilson (eds) *Essays on Adam Smith*, Oxford: Clarendon Press, 237–46.

—— (1981) "Economics or Ethics?" in S. McMurrin (ed.) *Tanner Lectures on Human Values, Volume II*, Cambridge: Cambridge University Press.

Stigler, G.J. and Becker, G.S. (1977) "De Gustibus non est Disputandum", *American Economic Review* 67, 2, March: 76–90.

Stokes, B. (1992) "Is Industrial Policy Now Mentionable?" *National Journal* 24, 10: 576–7.

Strange, S. (1986) *Casino Capitalism*, Oxford: Basil Blackwell.

Sugden, R. (1993) "Welfare, Resources, and Capabilities: a Review of Inequality Reexamined by Amartya Sen", *Journal of Economic Literature* 31 (4): 1947–62.

Sutcliffe, B. (1998) "Freedom to Move in the Age of Globalization", in D. Baker, G. Epstein and R. Pollin (eds) *Globalization and Progressive Economic Policy*, Cambridge: Cambridge University Press, 325–36.

Thurow, L. (1992) *Head to Head*, New York: William Morrow and Co.

Tilly, Charles. (1995) "Globalization Threatens Labor's Rights", *International Labor and Working-Class History* 47 (1): 1–23.

Tilly, Chris. (1996) *Half a Job*, Philadelphia: Temple University Press.

Todaro, M. (1997) *Economic Development*, 6th edn, Reading, MA: Addison-Wesley.

Tomaney, J. (1990) "The Reality of Workplace Flexibility", *Capital and Class* 40, Spring: 29–60.

Tool, M.R. (1979) *The Discretionary Economy*, Boulder, CO: Westview Press.

Tullock, G. (1976) *The Vote Motive*, Sussex: Institute of Economic Affairs.

Tyson, L.D. (1990) "Managed Trade: Making the Best of the Second Best", in R.W. Dornbusch, A.O. Krueger, and L.D. Tyson (eds) *An American Trade Strategy*, Washington, D.C.: Brookings Institution, 142–85.

United Nations Conference on Trade and Development (UNCTAD) (1994) *World Investment Report 1994*, New York: United Nations.

—— (1998a) *Annual Report 1998*, New York: United Nations.

—— (1998b) *Trade and Development 1998*, New York: United Nations.

United Nations Development Programme (UNDP) (1990) *Human Development Report 1990*, Oxford: Oxford University Press.

—— (1992) *Human Development Report 1992*, Oxford: Oxford University Press.

—— (1997) *Human Development Report 1997*, Oxford: Oxford University Press.

van Liemt, G. (1992) "Economic Globalization: Labor Options and Business Strategies in High Labor Cost Countries", *International Labour Review* 131 (4–5): 453–70.

Veblen, T. (1899) *The Theory of the Leisure Class*, New York: Macmillan.

—— (1904) *The Theory of Business Enterprise*, New York: Charles Scribner's Sons.

Vestal, J. (1993) *Planning for Change*, Oxford: Clarendon.

Wade, R. (1993) "The Visible Hand: the State and East Asia's Economic Growth", *Current History* 92 (578): 431–40.

Wall Street Journal (9/4/98) "Less Cash Flow: Currency Controls Gain a Hearing", Section A, 1.

—— (9/25/98) "Markets Under Siege – Crisis Crusaders", Section A, 1.

Walzer, M. (1973) "In Defense of Equality", *Dissent* 20 (4): 399–408.

—— (1983) *Spheres of Justice*, New York: Basic Books.

—— (1993) "Objectivity and Social Meaning", in M. Nussbaum and A.K. Sen (eds) *The Quality of Life*, Oxford: Clarendon Press, 165–77.

—— (1994) *Thick and Thin*, Notre Dame, IN: University of Notre Dame Press.

Watson, P. (1991) "The Community Social Charter", *Common Market Law Review* 28 (2): 37–68.

Williams, B. (1973) "A Critique of Utilitarianism", in J.J.C. Smart and B. Williams *Utilitarianism – For and Against*, Cambridge: Cambridge University Press, 77–150.

World Bank (1992) *World Development Report 1992*, Oxford: Oxford University Press.

—— (1995) *World Development Report 1995*, Oxford: Oxford University Press.

—— (1997) *Global Development Finance*, Oxford: Oxford University Press.

World Development (1994) "Special Symposium: The East Asian Miracle", 22 (4): 615–61.

Zajac, E.E. (1995) *Political Economy of Fairness*, Cambridge, MA: MIT Press.

Zevin, R. (1992) "Are World Financial Markets More Open? If so, Why and with What Effects?" in T. Banuri and J.B. Schor (eds) *Financial Openness and National Autonomy*, Oxford: Clarendon Press, 43–83.

Zysman, J. (1983) *Governments, Markets and Growth*, Ithaca: Cornell University.

Index